Introduction to
Cultural Ecology

Introduction to Cultural Ecology

Second Edition

MARK Q. SUTTON AND E. N. ANDERSON

ALTAMIRA
PRESS

A division of
ROWMAN & LITTLEFIELD PUBLISHERS, INC.
Lanham • New York • Toronto • Plymouth, UK

Published by AltaMira Press
A division of Rowman & Littlefield Publishers, Inc.
A wholly owned subsidary of The Rowman & Littlefield Publishing Group, Inc.
4501 Forbes Boulevard, Suite 200, Lanham, Maryland 20706
http://www.altamirapress.com

Estover Road, Plymouth PL6 7PY, United Kingdom

British Library Cataloguing in Publication Information Available

Library of Congress Cataloging-in-Publication Data

Sutton, Mark Q.
  Introduction to cultural ecology / Mark Q. Sutton and E. N. Anderson. — 2nd ed.
    p. cm.
  Includes bibliographical references and index.
  ISBN 978-0-7591-1246-9 (cloth : alk. paper) — ISBN 978-0-7591-1247-6 (pbk. : alk. paper)
— ISBN 978-0-7591-1248-3 (electronic)
  1. Human ecology. 2. Social ecology. I. Anderson, Eugene N. (Eugene Newton), 1941– II.
Title.
  GF50.S88 2010
  304.2—dc22
                              2009015117

∞™ The paper used in this publication meets the minimum requirements of American
National Standard for Information Sciences—Permanence of Paper for Printed Library
Materials, ANSI/NISO Z39.48-1992.

Printed in the United States of America

Contents

Figures and Tables

FIGURES

TABLES

Preface

Cultural ecology is one of the two major subdivisions of human ecology, the other being human biological ecology. We felt that the books available for a class in cultural ecology focused either too heavily on general ecology, or too much on human biological ecology, or not enough on cultural ecology. Thus, we faced a "Goldilocks" dilemma: none of the usual text books were "just right" for our introductory classes. So we decided to create a new book. We begin with the assumption that the student has no prior knowledge of anthropology or ecology and try to build an understanding from the ground up.

All peoples and cultures are faced with a number of major environmental issues, problems that can be addressed by anthropology and cultural ecology. How have other people faced and dealt with the same basic problems that face us all today? How can we improve our situation? What can anthropology and cultural ecology contribute to the future?

The key is understanding what the options are, what works, and what does not. This requires a great deal of knowledge that must be obtained through the study of other groups, including the documentation of their environments and adaptations. Next, we must analyze what we have learned to develop alternative responses to environmental situations. We must also understand the consequences of the choices that have been made; we can learn from the successes and mistakes of others rather than having to repeat those same mistakes.

We do not attempt to cover all aspects of the incredibly complex and diverse field of the relationships between humans and the environment. We thought it important to provide a reasonably comprehensive introduction to ecological theory in a simple format, combined with discussions of various human cultures. We spend more time defining the concepts and classifying things typologically than most treatments do. We have concentrated on things we thought would be appropriate for an introductory student, including traditional food production, but have not included more sophisticated materials beyond the introductory level. Many such concepts are important, but it is impossible to do everything in one book. We plead for charity. However, we do spend some time discussing and critiquing evolutionary ecology, primarily because we feel it is so widely used and misunderstood.

We have also had to be highly selective in using and citing the incredibly large literature that now treats even narrow and specialized questions within the field. We can only abjectly apologize to those experts (the vast majority, alas) who find themselves uncited. We have tried, insofar as possible, to confine citations to easily located, basic works or other literature readily accessible to students.

Our main goal was to try to communicate the anthropological side of ecological matters. It is not our intent to cover all the ecological issues or problems of the world, to deal in detail with modern matters of pollution, climate change, environmental degradation, and the like; these issues are now in the center of the world stage (though perhaps not of the U.S. government). Our aim was to explore how traditional cultures operate and adapt to their environments, how they function, and what the Western world can learn from them.

Assuming that the student has no prior knowledge of the subject, we begin with a very basic introduction to anthropology, to scientific inquiry, and end chapter 1 with a brief history of the development of cultural ecological theory. Chapter 2 provides an introduction to the concepts and terms used in general ecology, many of which are heard on the news and read in newspapers and magazines daily, yet are rarely defined in any detail. Human biological ecology (chapter 3) is then discussed as a background to understanding and distinguishing cultural adaptations, which are the subject of chapter 4. We thought it important to clearly distinguish between human biological ecology and cultural ecology, as the two tend to get mixed up in much of the literature, creating a source of confusion for everyone.

The next five chapters (chapters 5–9) deal with discussions of the cultural ecology of the two broad and generalized economic strategies that are the subject of much anthropological study: hunting and gathering and food production, the latter having three basic adaptations, horticulture, pastoralism, and intensive agriculture. This is a rather traditional approach, and we recognize the problems with the pigeonholes in which we place societies. However, we feel that it is a sound approach at the introductory level. Finally, we close (chapter 10) with some discussion of contemporary environmental problems and the role tradi-tional cultures play in them.

The philosophical position of this book is not value-free. One of the primary goals of most cultural ecological work is to use the knowledge in an effort to stem global catastrophe. However, we believe—deeply—that to do this we must study all cultures, past and present, and to learn from each of them. We try to impress on the reader that no one culture has a monopoly on environmental care or on environmental carelessness. Only by combining the best of many plans will the human species save itself.

In this second edition, we have updated our treatment with new references and ideas. We have added a number of small sections dealing with new ideas, tightened the text, and added a new case study on American ranchers (written by our colleague Kimberly Hedrick). We believe that this edition is a significant im-provement over the first.

Acknowledgments

We acknowledge the intellectual contributions of Eugene P. Odum (1975, 1993) in ecology and of John Bennett (1976), Roy Ellen (1982), and Julian Steward and his students, including Sidney Mintz, Andrew Vayda, and Eric Wolf; also Robert M. Netting (1986), Carole Crumley (1994), and Bernard Campbell (1995) in understanding the interrelationships between culture and ecology.

Among those who have helped with information, suggestions, and materials shared with us, it is necessary to single out Paul Buell, Scott Fedick, Alan Fix, Jean Hudson, Michael Kearney, Bonnie McCay, Sidney Mintz, Endre Nyerges, Richard Osborne, Jason Parker, Evelyn Pinkerton, Alexander K. Rogers, Philip Silverman, Maria Cruz Torres, and Andrew P. Vayda. Many others have helped with information and encouragement, and we thank them all.

We appreciate the advice and comments of Barbara Anderson, Jill K. Gardner, Brian E. Hemphill, Becky Orfila, Kristin D. Sobolik, Melinda B. Sutton, Linda Wells, and a number of anonymous reviewers, several of which provided extensive and useful comments. We greatly appreciate the work of Gina Bahr and Janet Gonzales at the CSU, Bakersfield Library, who contributed greatly to this project by their hard work in obtaining the many books and articles we ordered through interlibrary loan.

We also thank Francesca Bray, Ping-ti Ho, Philip Huang, Richard Pearson, Pierre-Etienne Will, and Bin Wong for providing unpublished materials and discussion of their work. Grateful acknowledgment is also made to the many persons who helped ENA in field research, especially to Marja L. Anderson, Chow Hung-fai, and Choi Kwok-tai.

1

Introduction

In the four or five million years since their development, humans have colonized virtually every terrestrial environment of the planet. Humans everywhere are virtually the same biologically (in spite of visible but superficial differences) but have been able to adapt to the enormous environmental diversity of the planet through culture, an incredibly flexible and adaptive mechanism that other animals lack. Thus, humans have been a very successful species. Human activity has a wide range of impacts on the environment, however, from exceedingly minor to catastrophic. Today, human activities are having huge impacts on the very environment on which we depend, ultimately threatening our own existence. Understanding and dealing with these challenges is a daunting but essential task.

Anthropology, including cultural ecology, differs from other fields in that it studies all humans, everywhere, from the earliest times (millions of years ago) to today and from the Arctic to the Antarctic. No group is so small that it is not important, and no period of history or prehistory is without interest. This wide approach has allowed anthropologists to disprove many generalizations based only on modern or Western societies and to demonstrate some other generalizations that were not obvious once, such as the universality of complex kinship systems and dietary rules.

People in Western societies tend to hold the view that humans are separate from the environment, above it in some way. This can be traced back to the Bible. In Genesis 1 the world (the environment) was first created, and then "man"—an entity separate and superior to nature—was created and given the task of subduing nature (Genesis 1:28; also see Wilson 1967:1205). Genesis 2 argues otherwise, for "stewardship," but Western philosophy continues to include the view that it is the goal and mission of people to "conquer" nature. Thus, many people today continue to believe that humans are not participants in the environment but that we must overcome it and bend it to our will. This conviction continues to permeate Western thought and action, as we strive to separate ourselves from our natural surroundings by artificially creating closed environments, including our homes, offices, and cars. Ironically, some (mostly corporate and government people) have conveniently shifted their view on this matter, arguing now that human activity is part of nature and so changes in climate caused by humans (e.g., global warming) is "natural" and thus not of concern.

One could argue that many traditional societies do not hold the view that people are separate from nature, and that they are somehow "ecologists" living in harmony with their environment (e.g., White 1997; but also see Krech 1999; Hames 2007). It is true that the activities of many societies have less impact on the environment than others, and it is also true that some of these groups hold a more ecologically friendly philosophy of life than westerners generally do. It has also been argued, however, that traditional societies often make less of an impact on the environment only because their technology is less complex and their populations smaller. Given the right conditions and incentives, the argument goes, they would do as Westerners do. In support of this argument, one can point to the destruction of the habitat on Easter Island (Diamond 2005; also see Hunt 2007), the deforestation of most of Europe during the Neolithic, and the Norse degradation of the northern islands (McGovern et al. 1988; Diamond 2005), among other examples.

Fortunately, local traditional people can be trusted to take care of their resources—not out of fuzzy-minded love for Mother Earth but out of solid, hardheaded, good sense, often shored up by traditional religion and morality (Anderson 1996; Berkes 1999; Lentz 2000). Biologists are beginning to realize this. Kent Redford, who coined the sarcastic term "the ecologically noble savage" (Redford 1990; see the superb refutation of that article by Lopez [1992]) has since repented and now takes a more balanced position (Redford and Mansour 1996; cf. Sponsel 2001).

We now recognize that humans and their cultures are an integral part of the environment. Human activity affects the environment, which is then altered, in turn affecting human activities. The shape and form of the environment is dependent on its history, a history that includes humans. Yet it is also important to realize that humans are not just another animal. Humans are self-aware, cooperative, technological, and highly social. This unique combination does separate humans from other organisms, making their interactions with the environment more complex and fascinating.

WHAT IS CULTURAL ECOLOGY?

Ecology is the study of the interaction between living things and their environment. Human ecology is the study of the relationships and interactions among humans, their biology, their cultures, and their physical environments. The term provides the title of *Human Ecology*, a leading journal in the field. Human ecology includes ecological anthropology (which includes a great deal of biological anthropology) and environmental anthropology (a more "cultural" or humanistic side of the field).

A number of comprehensive treatments of the field are available. Most impressive is *Human Adaptive Strategies: Ecology, Culture, and Politics* (Bates 2005). The title suggests the grounding in the new knowledge and also the way Bates integrated the field around the concepts of adaptation and strategizing. Patricia Townsend brought out a brief but extremely well-targeted overview, *Environmental Anthropology* (2000), that covered basically the same ground from a very similar point of view, but at an entry level. In addition, Bates and Susan Lees, longtime editors of *Human Ecology*, have produced a collection of articles from that journal, *Case Studies in Human Ecology* (1996a). Among several other readers, particularly noteworthy are *Environmental Anthropology: A Historical Reader*, edited by Michael Dove and Carol Carpenter (2008), and *The Environment in Anthropology*, edited by Nora Haenn and Richard Wilk (2006). The former includes important articles from the entire history of cultural ecology and environmental anthropology; the latter focuses more on the newer work. We support using one of these readers in connection with the present book.

Human ecologists study many aspects of culture and environment, including how and why cultures do what they do to solve their subsistence problems, how groups of people understand their environment, and how they share their knowledge of the environment. The broad field of human ecology includes two major subdivisions (see figure 1.1). Human biological ecology is the study of the biological aspect of the human/environment relationship, and cultural ecology

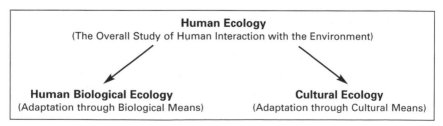

Human Ecology
(The Overall Study of Human Interaction with the Environment)

Human Biological Ecology
(Adaptation through Biological Means)

Cultural Ecology
(Adaptation through Cultural Means)

FIGURE 1.1
The general relationship of the major subdivisions within human ecology.

is the study of the ways in which culture is used by people to adapt to their environment.

The primary focus of this book is cultural ecology, which encompasses everything from pet dogs to the fall of Rome—an ecological catastrophe caused in part
by misuse of resources (e.g., Ponting 1991). This book examines, among other
things, salmon ceremonies among Northwest Coast Indians, Maya agriculture
today and in the past, sacred groves in southern China, and the use of various
foods. For example, insects are an abundant and nutritious source of food, yet
many cultures consider them pests. Some of the very cultures that loathe insects
see shrimps and lobsters as delicacies, although all three are very similar biologically. Why is there such a difference?

Consider a food question that is far more serious. Significant deforestation
has resulted from the creation of cattle pasture. As much as Americans may feel
they depend on their hamburgers, beef is really a luxury item, producing relatively little protein at huge expense. To produce it, millions of acres of land that
were once covered in forest and/or farmland growing food for local people have
been converted into pasture (Painter and Durham 1995). The devastation to
wildlife and biological diversity is bad enough; the impoverishment—and frequently the starvation—of local people may be considered even more serious.
Thus, cultural beliefs about food can dramatically affect the world environment.

The study of the relationships between culture and environment is not just academic, it is vital, not simply because it is interesting but because it offers understanding and possible solutions to important contemporary problems. Issues
of deforestation (e.g., Anderson 1990), loss of species (e.g., Blaustein and Wake
1995; BBC News 2008), food scarcity (Brown 1994, 1996; Roberts 2008), and soil
loss (Pimentel et al. 1995) are on the minds of many and are addressed by human ecologists. (For general discussions on human impact on the environment,
see Ehrlich and Ehrlich 1996; Meyer 1996; Redman 1999; Molnar and Molnar
2000; and Diamond 2005, among others.) Some of these issues reflect overexploitation of resources and require conservation measures to correct. Such measures may threaten certain short-term economic activities, such as unrestricted
logging, and many leaders launch verbal, and sometimes even physical, attacks
on conservationists (see Helvarg 1994) to protect their short-term interests.

Cultural ecologists record other traditional and local knowledge that is of
value to the wider world. Thousands of useful drugs used by westerners have
been derived from traditional medicines; more are being tested and developed
almost daily. Ancient crops of the Andes and Tibet, such as potatoes and barley,
respectively, are becoming important worldwide. Long-established land manage-

ment techniques used in Indonesia and Guatemala (for example, multilayered and multicropped orchard gardens) are inspiring new ideas in the greater arena. The accumulated cultural knowledge of billions of people over tens of thousands of years is available and is a tremendous resource for our resource-short world.

ANTHROPOLOGY

Cultural ecology is generally included within the discipline of **anthropology**, the study of human beings. Anthropology includes the study of human biology, language, prehistory, religion, social structure, economics, evolution, and anything else that applies to people. Thus, anthropology is a very broad discipline, holistic in its approach, and comparative, or cross-cultural, in its analyses. Anthropologists generally concentrate their work on small-scale cultures and tend to have considerable personal contact with the people of those cultures.

Culture, *learned* and *shared* behavior, is the fundamental element that sets humans apart from other animals. (Many animals learn some of their behavior socially, but only humans make an enormous project of it.) The vast complexities of human behavior derive from culture, based to be sure on biology. Culture is largely transmitted through language, which, as far as we know, is unique to humans. In addition, every person belongs to **a culture**, a group of people who share the same basic pattern of learned behavior, the same values, views, language, and identity. Each culture's bearers hold an identity unto themselves, such as the Cheyenne, the Germans, or the Yanomamo, and recognize that they are different from other cultures.

On the other hand, cultures interact and learn from one another, and people (especially young ones) easily shift from one to another. The idea of cultures or ethnic groups as steel-walled, separate universes is currently popular in the mass media but is utterly wrong. Cultures may remain separate while learning a great deal from their neighbors, or they may merge totally.

Anthropologists traditionally hold a set of basic beliefs in their study of other cultures. First, it is recognized that all cultures are at least a bit **ethnocentric**— that people believe their culture is superior to others (although many envy the more rich or powerful). Americans tend to view non-Americans as being inferior, less cultured, or backward. Germans have the same view of non-Germans, as do the Chinese of non-Chinese. In fact, every culture seems to include this view; it is a normal part of the self-identification process. Yet ethnocentrism has often been used to rationalize mistreatment of peoples. Virtually all colonial powers exploited native populations on the belief that they were inferior, which was used to justify their enslavement or murder. In North America, the natives were considered "savages" who were "in the way" of "civilization." The Native Americans were thus moved, incarcerated, or killed with government approval. A similar situation currently exists in a number of countries attempting to "develop."

Anthropologists are usually—though far from always—from a culture other than the one being studied. Thus, the researcher views the culture through the lens of his or her own culture, in essence an outsider's view. The other perspective is that of the insider. One's perspective, whatever it is, influences what is observed and ultimately what can be learned. Anthropologists deal with this problem as best they can. Perhaps the best way is to draw on both outsider and insider views, comparing them with each other and (hopefully) respecting both.

A basic conviction in anthropology is cultural relativism, that cultures and cultural practices should not be judged. This term has been misunderstood to imply that anthropologists approve of anything practiced in any culture. More correctly, it means that anthropologists study cultures to understand them without trying to show that one is "better" than another and without trying to impose their culture or standards on other people. This relativity is methodological and not moral. Indeed, anthropologists have traditionally taken a very strong stand against genocide and "culturocide," or forcing people to give up their culture against their will. Anthropologists attempt to avoid being ethnocentric and believe that all people and cultures are valid, that they have the rights to exist, to have their own culture and practices, and to speak their own language, and that individuals have fundamental human rights (Nagengast and Turner 1997; Merry 2003). These are moral positions and conflict with moral relativism.

Anthropology can be divided into many subdisciplines—perhaps dozens, depending on how they are defined and who is defining them. Here, we follow the traditional basic division of the field into four subdisciplines: cultural anthropology, biological (or physical) anthropology, anthropological linguistics, and archaeology.

Cultural Anthropology

Cultural anthropology, including social or sociocultural anthropology, is the study of existing peoples and cultures. Cultural anthropologists conduct two major types of studies: **ethnography**, the study of a particular group at a particular time, and **ethnology**, the comparative study of culture. Cultural anthropologists strive to learn everything they can about a culture, such as kinship systems, marriage rules, economics, language, and politics. Cultural anthropologists generally live for a year or more with the group under study, observe and record their activities and behavior, and ask people questions. They can sometimes even participate in, and so can better record, community activities. As such, cultural anthropologists can get a rich, though still incomplete, record of a group.

Biological Anthropology

Biological anthropology (or physical anthropology) is the study of the biology and evolution of people as well as the study of the biology, evolution, and behavior of nonhuman primates and other animals for clues to understanding humans. While humans are all very similar biologically, some differences between groups do exist. These differences may take a variety of forms, including stature, blood type, and adaptations to cold or high altitude. An understanding of past human biology can help us understand evolution and suggest relationships with other populations, such as intermarriage and/or migration, changes in past environment, and changes in subsistence.

Anthropological Linguistics

Anthropological linguistics (linguistic anthropology) is the study of human language. This includes the historical relationships between languages, common "ancestors" of languages and language groups, syntax, and meaning. Cultural anthropologists are interested in linguistics because a great deal about a particular culture can be learned by looking at its language. Archaeologists are interested in linguistics—especially historical linguistics—because languages (and cultures) can be traced back in time. Cultural ecology includes the study of how people in different cultures talk about plants, animals, and environments; a fair knowledge of linguistics is essential for this.

Archaeology

Archaeology is the study of the human past. Archaeology overlaps cultural anthropology, as archaeologists want to learn the same things about past cultures that cultural anthropologists do about living ones. (In earlier times, cultural anthropology was taken to include archaeology.) Archaeology was defined by Laurence Flanagan (1998:3) as "the story of Man's attempts to keep the wolf from the door by means of better doors and better wolf-traps," and this suits its use in ecological anthropology. Archaeologists often study the present as well, either to find clues for interpreting the past or by using archaeological methods to investigate present-day problems.

The major differences between archaeology and cultural anthropology are in the available data and the methods used to obtain those data. The material remains with which archaeologists work are limited, partly due to excavation techniques, and as a result, archaeologists do not obtain the entire picture of a past culture. Archaeologists, however, are able to detect change over long periods of time, can identify broad trends, and can examine transitions, such as the change of some cultures from hunting and gathering to agriculture. In addition, an archaeologist can detect the traces of behavior that a cultural anthropologist might not usually see. This access to "hidden behavior" is another advantage of archaeology. In addition, understanding the ecology of past peoples is a major goal in archaeology (see Butzer 1982; Dincauze 2000).

THE STUDY OF HUMAN ECOLOGY

Human ecology, and all of anthropology, is an empirical science. It generally adheres to the procedures and rules of modern Western science, including the scientific method. All cultures have some form of science, and other approaches are discussed in chapter 4; human ecologists often draw on other cultures' ways of knowing as well as on modern science.

Science

The goal of any science is to generate new knowledge and to learn new things. Many sciences are empirical and employ data that are as objective as possible, observable, measurable, and reproducible (on this scheme and problems with it, see Kitcher [1993]). Information not meeting the standards of objectivity, measurability, and reproducibility is taken as tentative (at best).

The scientific method is a specific, systematic set of rules on scientific inquiry. Ideally, in this method empirical data are first observed and then recorded. Next, ideas regarding the relationships between data are used to form hypotheses. An experiment is then formulated to test the hypothesis using additional empirical data, and if the hypothesis is not testable, it is immediately dismissed. Based on the results of the test, the hypothesis is either supported or rejected. If the hypothesis is rejected, it may be abandoned or revised and retested. If supported, the hypothesis is tested again with even more data. A set of interrelated hypotheses is called a theory, which is then subjected to yet more testing. Even generally accepted hypotheses and theories get tested over and over, making science self-correcting. If a theory survives considerable and repeated testing, it may then be called a law.

In practice, scientists do not always act so systematically (Kuhn 1962). They have their own personal agendas and even biases. Even the best of them make mistakes—sometimes honest ones, sometimes based on their biases. This is where constant testing, especially by scientists of other theoretical persuasions, is valuable. Thus, science still manages to function (Kitcher 1993).

It is useful, in the case of ecological anthropology, to define science broadly. We do not rule out humanistic and interpretive perspectives. Culture includes such matters as religion, myth, art, song, dance, and poetry—not very amenable to cut-and-dried laboratory analysis. Often these are critical to environmental adaptation, as when religious taboos protect forests or fish. Coming to some conclusions about such matters involves sensitive interpretation and attention to personal experience as well as objective recording and comparison. Scientific and humanistic approaches thus must be combined for a full account.

Some General Theoretical Approaches to Human Ecology

Human ecology, much like the rest of anthropology, is an eclectic science. As scientists, we want to learn, understand, and apply the knowledge about how people interact with their environment. We will utilize any theory or idea that might help us learn about how people adapt and why they might do things in a particular way. As such, many approaches can be employed in the study of human ecology.

For a significant number of human ecologists, including many cultural ecologists, people are seen as animals much like any other animal (Park 1936), concerned solely or mainly with obtaining food and mates by the most efficient means possible. This general approach, embodied in evolutionary ecology (see chapter 3), directs our attention toward serious studies of food getting, among other things, and has produced much useful research. It also directs our attention toward serious consideration of the environment: what resources it offers, how difficult it is to obtain those resources, and any other problems it may present. Most human ecologists find this model inadequate because it predicts neither the wide variety of cultures observed in the world nor the existence of art, music, poetry, and all the other things people have and do that other animals do not.

A second approach regards humans as rational choosers. In this model, humans set various goals, not solely the pursuit of necessities. They then seek, methodically and rationally, to reach those goals. This model directs our attention to individual choice. It assumes that people choose carefully and seriously on the basis of good information. This model has been shown to be very useful in many situations. However, people do not always have good information about their environment. More importantly, human choice is greatly affected by emotion, by social pressures, by cultural traditions, and by plain, ordinary mistakes. Thus, this model alone is also inadequate.

A third approach looks at political processes, from individual negotiation to worldwide political forces. This model directs our attention most especially to power differentials, from the power of village authorities to the far greater power of multinational agencies and corporations. This model has a number of major empirical successes to its credit, but it does not adequately deal with human long-term goals.

Other approaches and models will be discussed throughout this book. We take something of a flexible position toward all these theories. We suggest at the outset that understanding will come only from combining models, both existing and new. People have biological needs, and they have to fulfill them. People choose, and they make the best choices they can—and mistakes cannot be ignored or denied. They have to negotiate with others; they cannot do what they please in a social vacuum. Cooperation and competition are the common lot of social life.

To comprehend ecological practices, we must understand the history of those practices. We must look at the whole chain of specific events, including pure chance, that actually caused the behavior to become established (Vayda 1996). For example, could any rational choice theorist, in the absence of previous knowledge, predict that most Americans would celebrate December 25 by piling gifts around an evergreen tree? December 25 was not the actual birthday of Jesus Christ; the date and tree were originally part of a pagan Yule festival of northern Europe that was taken over by Christianity as it expanded northward. If we want to explain why Americans cut down millions of trees every year for a holiday, we must look at history. The individual choices that brought us to this ecological adjustment may have been rational, but no rational choice theorist could ever have predicted the present situation on the basis of existing theory.

Evolution and Adaptation

Fundamental to any inquiry in human ecology are the concepts of change and adaptation to change. All environments are dynamic, and changes will vary in the scales of both time and space. As environments change, organisms must adapt to those changes, a process that can entail a variety of mechanisms. Humans use both biological and cultural mechanisms.

The concept of **evolution** is widely misunderstood. Quite simply, evolution is change. All things change, and so all things evolve. Biological anthropologists define evolution more specifically as the change in gene frequency in populations from generation to generation. Other disciplines might define evolution in different ways, but in essence, it is simply change.

Many also believe that evolution has direction. It is commonly thought that as something evolves, it advances up some kind of evolutionary ladder, that it somehow advances toward a goal or an ideal of some sort, that it embodies some sort of progress. These notions are false. While it is true that some things become more complex over time, not all things do; complexity itself is not necessarily an advantage. A simple amoeba living today is as "evolved" as any human being—not as complex to be sure, but certainly as evolved. It has a long evolutionary history, and its continued existence reflects biological success. In the same vein, all living human cultures are equally evolved, although to different environments. They are equally far from whatever culture may have existed among prehistoric human ancestors. As there is no direction in evolution, there is no such thing as devolution, there is no more or less advanced, and there is no external scale of progress.

In biological evolution, species adapt to their environment through natural selection, the process by which some traits are selected for—by allowing their bearers to leave more descendants—and retained in the gene pool of the next generation, while deleterious traits are selected against (with some neutral traits going along for the ride). For selection to occur, variation, differing traits to be selected for or against, must exist within the population. With the exception of clones, all individuals vary. (Even identical twins can be surprisingly different, thanks to developmental events.)

Heritable variation is ultimately due to mutation, accidental changes in a gene. Most mutations are deleterious, and most are quickly selected against and deleted from the population. However, some mutations are advantageous in that they allow their bearers to leave more descendants.

An example of human biological evolution is provided by lactose intolerance. By about the age of six, most humans cease producing the enzyme lactase, which allows digestion of lactose, the sugar found in milk. Thereafter, milk upsets their stomachs. By sheer genetic accident, some humans continue producing lactase throughout life. Genes for continued lactase production have been selected for in milk-drinking areas, notably western Europe and eastern Africa. Most people whose ancestors came from these regions can happily drink milk all their lives (Huang 2002). In most of the rest of the world, people must ferment the milk into yogurt, using *Lactobacillus* bacteria to break down the lactose for them.

Human cultures also evolve, and cultural evolution has been an important concept in anthropology. Cultural anthropologists could view cultural evolution as differential persistence of behaviors through time. It is known that this sort of cultural evolution does occur, although it is not known exactly why or how. In some analytical approaches, such as evolutionary ecology, cultures are equated to organisms, and the concepts of biological evolution are applied (see chapter 3). Cultural evolution has gotten a bad name in some quarters because of its former identification with "progress" and thus with pejorative attitudes toward "backward" societies, but we repeat that this is a misunderstanding of evolution. Change over time is not "good" or "bad"; it simply happens.

As environmental conditions change, some sort of response is necessary. That response, or **adaptation**, is an ongoing process, as environmental conditions are always dynamic. The variability within an organism allows for an appropriate response to be selected, and the greater the variation, the more likely it is that an adequate adaptation can be made.

For most organisms, adaptation is purely biological, ultimately regulated by natural selection. However, for humans, adaptation will also be cultural, a mechanism that can act in a much shorter time. Culture is a way in which *groups* of people can adapt to the environment, through collective behavior and/or technology. This concept is discussed in greater detail in chapter 4.

Solutions

If conditions presented by the environment are solved, the organism adapts. For any problem, there may be multiple solutions through the adoption of traits and/or behaviors. In some cases, a solution may be the best available, and the organism adapts well. In other cases, a solution may be bad, perhaps due to poor decision making or other factors, and the organism goes extinct. In many cases, a solution may be adequate, good enough to get by. If the truth were known, probably most solutions would turn out to be just good enough. To win, a football team does not necessarily have to score every time it has the ball; it just has to score more points than the other team.

In some environments, a limited set of solutions is possible. For example, in the climate of the Arctic, the Yuit and Inuit developed cultural solutions to the cold environment, along with some physical adaptations, including the use of animal skins for clothing, building houses with snow, and obtaining food from hunting the animals of the region. Given their technology, the solution was as good as it could be. However, when Euroamericans entered the region, they adapted to the environment using *their* culture and technology (although a few things were borrowed, such as parkas and dogsleds). This included clothing made from artificial materials, housing made from wood and metal, heat and light from imported and processed fuels (gasoline), and foods imported from other areas. Although the two adaptations were quite different, they were both successful.

In other cases, there seems little connection between solutions. When we learn that the ancient Irish and ancient Haida of the Northwest Coast of North America, who lived in a similar environment, both ate salmon, we are not too surprised. When we learn that they both viewed wolves as symbols of power and ferocity, that seems a little less obvious, but still hardly surprising. But when we find that they both regarded the tiny winter wren as a powerful supernatural being, we are astonished. There was no way to predict that. Only intimate knowledge of both cultures and of the winter wren solves the mystery: both the Irish and Haida value song greatly, and the tiny, delicate winter wren fills the whole forest with loud and triumphant song during the most violent winter storms. The belief in the supernatural power of this bird makes sense because the ancient Irish and Haida both believed that power over song was part of a wider power over all things.

A HISTORY OF THOUGHT ON CULTURE AND ENVIRONMENT

Scientists and laypersons alike have long been interested in how people lived in and utilized the natural environment. Throughout history, a variety of theories on the interaction of culture and environment has been proposed, accepted as fact, disproved, resurrected, and codified in mythology. We still live with, and must respond to, many of these old prejudicial, ethnocentric, and downright wrong ideas.

Ecological anthropology in the twentieth century has proposed, or drawn on, several useful and innovative theories. All of these theories were valuable contributions; their limitations are those expected of theories in a developing field. Science grows through translating new facts into more comprehensive theories. The value of a theory often lies in the stimulus it provides for further research and thought. Sometimes, the best theory is thus the first to be superseded.

It has been proposed (Kormondy 1996:383–385; also see White 1967) that the development of the field of human ecology be divided into three historical traditions: imperialist, arcadian, and scientific. The imperialist tradition holds that humans are superior to, and hold dominion over, nature (see White 1967:1205). This tradition is long-standing but gained great power after the Industrial Revolution and the expansion of Western culture across the globe at the expense of the environment and traditional cultures (much like the Borg of Star Trek fame). Many still adhere to this tradition, and ecological imperialism by governments and corporations is still very widespread.

The arcadian tradition advocates that people should live in satisfaction, harmony, and idyllic contentment with nature. The ancient Greeks idealized in this way the Vale of Arcady, actually a poor and hardscrabble region. The tradition has taken on new life in the past couple of centuries with the rise of industrial society (Kormondy 1996:384).

The scientific tradition is a long-standing approach, one that dominates the field of human ecology today. The first scientific theories regarding culture and environment date from thousands of years ago. By about the fourth century BC, the Greeks developed an explanatory view of culture and environment in which people and their potential were classified based on climate. The view was that cold climates made for "stupid" people, warm climates made for "perfect" people, and hot climates made people listless and lazy. It was no coincidence that Greece was located in a warm climate. The Greeks also saw that human society had moved from hunting and gathering to agriculture to urban life, though they wrongly thought that herding came before agriculture.

At about this same time, the Chinese philosopher Mencius (see Mencius 1979:164–165) pleaded for conservation, recounting how a certain mountain was deforested by woodcutters and the new brush eaten away by livestock. The mountain then eroded and seemed as if it had always been bare. Mencius drew a parallel with people who were bad; they, too, were once good, but poor management had corrupted them. Mencius, as well as many other early Chinese writers, provided a great deal of information on environmental management, showing that it was already a highly evolved science in China at that time. Chinese environmental science continued to develop, with increasing influences from western Asia and Europe.

By the seventeenth century, western Europe took a commanding lead in the study of natural science with the development of universities, learned societies, open publishing, open debate, and rewards and grants for science. These innovations led to an explosive increase in scientific activity (Gaukroger 2006). A series of ideas on the relationship between culture and environment was proposed, including a notion of geographic determinism quite similar to the early Greek view (Montesquieu 1949) and a concept of cultural evolution, also close to the Greek, with stages progressing from "savagery" (hunting and gathering) to herding to agriculture to states and commerce (Smith 1920). This idea was widely accepted throughout the nineteenth century. Smith, along with Thomas Malthus, developed the ideas of competition in nature and in human affairs that later fed into contemporary ecological theories.

These and other thinkers of the Enlightenment era were the real founders of all social science. Immanuel Kant was the first to foreground the word *anthropology* for the new field, though his anthropology included a good deal of what we would now call psychology (Kant 1978, 2007). The main contribution of this period was the basic concept of systematic, comparative studies of human society. Studies became more objective, more systematic, classificatory, and a bit more tolerant of non-European practices.

Environmental Determinism

The first major theory regarding the interaction between culture and environment, one that has been in circulation since the time of classical Greece, is **environmental determinism**, or environmentalism. This idea basically states that environment mechanically "dictates" how a culture adapts. In the twentieth century, the idea was championed by Huntington (1945), who added detail about the importance of rainfall and drought. Many still believe that the environment does dictate cultures, at least those that are viewed as somehow being more closely tied to "nature."

Environmental determinism is attractive due to its simplicity, but there are obvious problems with the approach. The first is the belief that the environment and the life within it is fixed and unchanging, a view held for thousands of years. This premise is now known to be false, as environments are constantly changing. The second major problem is the depreciation of the role of culture and in the compulsory role of environment. While this second premise seems to have merit in some environments with very few options, most environments contain a variety of alternatives, resulting in a much greater set of possible choices. If the environment dictates responses, then responses should be the same for different cultures in the same environment, and the same response should not be present in different environments.

For example, following environmental determinism, the Inuit must hunt seals and live in snow houses because they live in the Arctic. The Polynesians must fish and live in grass huts because they live on tropical islands. Anyone who has been to the Arctic or Polynesia knows that some people do live as described above, but others live very differently in that same region. The difference is culture (including technology), not just environment, and this is where environmental determinism fails. As Georg Hegel wrote (speaking of western Turkey): "Where the Greeks once lived, the Turks now live, and there's an end on it" (quoted in Geertz [1963:6]).

A different position, emphasizing human agency, was best expressed by George Perkins Marsh in his great work *Man and Nature* (2003). Marsh showed at length how people had profoundly changed the face of the earth—sometimes for better, sometimes for worse (by his standards). This book was profoundly influential, and Marsh's view prevailed. We now see people changing the environment as they adapt to it, rather than passively reacting to it.

The Culture Area Concept

Somewhat related to environmental determinism is the idea of **culture areas**, large-scale geographic regions where environment and culture were similar to each other, particularly in economics. Culture areas were recognized in the

1890s, first in North and South America (Mason 1894) and then in other regions of the world. For example, a number of culture areas have been defined for North America, and various schemes have been proposed and argued; the current consensus recognizes ten culture areas (eleven if you separate the Prairies area from the Plains area) in North America (see figure 1.2).

FIGURE 1.2
Culture areas of North America (presented as a guide rather than a representation of actual territories). Adapted from *Handbook of North American Indians*, vol. 4, *History of Indian-White Relations*, W. E. Washburn, ed., p. ix; copyright © 1988 by the Smithsonian Institution. Used by permission of the publisher.

The use of the culture area concept gives anthropologists the opportunity to broadly compare cultures within generally similar environments and to determine the extent of influence from cultures outside the culture area, such as diffusion or migration. Nevertheless, the concept has many weaknesses, including the definition of a single area that contains considerable environmental and cultural diversity, the use of somewhat arbitrary defining criteria, the assumption of a static cultural situation, and the tendency to equate environment with cause (see Forde 1934:467; Kroeber 1939). However, the concept continues to be useful as a unit of comparison or reference and most anthropologists use it, even if informally, to refer to geographic regions and general culture traits.

A good example of the concept is the Plains of North America. Geographically, the Plains is a relatively flat grassland extending north from the Gulf of Mexico to southern Canada and west from the Mississippi River to the Rocky Mountains. Relatively few trees and little water are present on the Plains, except in the rivers that cross the region from west to east. The dominant animal on the Plains was the bison (*Bison bison bison*), often called the buffalo. Prior to the acquisition of the horse in historical times, the human population on the Plains was relatively small, and bison were hunted on foot. With the arrival of horses, new groups entered the Plains, some of whom gave up farming to do so, and quickly developed a general culture based on bison hunting on horseback. The pre- and post-horse cultural patterns were similar to each other, particularly the subsistence (bison-hunting) system. Even though technology had dramatically changed, the basic Plains economic pattern remained the same.

Cultural Evolution

It had long been recognized that cultures changed over time, although it was not understood how or why. Not until after the new theory of biological evolution (Darwin 1859) had been proposed did a comprehensive theory of cultural evolution develop.

Unilinear Cultural Evolution

The first major theory in anthropology was the concept that cultures evolved upwards along a single line. This idea was developed by Lewis H. Morgan (largely from Adam Smith's work; see above) and amplified by Edward B. Tylor and others, and later known as **unilinear cultural evolution** (UCE). It was proposed that cultures evolved progressively through three basic stages: from "savagery" (hunting and gathering), to "barbarism" (pastoralism, later agriculture), and then up to "civilization" (see esp. Morgan 1851, 1871, 1877, 1882). This view encompassed the nineteenth-century notion of progress. Morgan saw human life as a search for "livelihood," that is, subsistence—food, clothing, and shelter. He was aware that humans need social life and a sense of control over their world but thought of these as constant, while ways of obtaining food, and therefore technology, varied according to local creativity and local environment. Morgan held that certain inventions, such as the bow and arrow, pottery, and agriculture, were keystones in cultural evolution. Each one led to a new, "higher" phase of society.

At about the same time, Marx and Engels (see Engels 1942) proposed a six-stage theory of unilinear cultural evolution, but with politics and economics, rather than technology, being the most important factors. It was proposed that societies would ultimately evolve to advanced communism, the pinnacle of development.

From the point of view of contemporary human ecology, perhaps the most important contribution of the evolutionary ideas of Marx and Engels was the assertion of the creativity and resourcefulness of human beings. Earlier thinkers (e.g., Montesquieu) gave nature pride of place and claimed that nature determined culture. Marx and Engels gave human creativity pride of place over nature, and this is a point that has come to lie behind much contemporary human ecological work.

The theory of UCE was accepted throughout the social sciences in the nineteenth century, only to be disproved in the early twentieth century (see Boas 1927, 1940), partly due to the understanding that technology alone does not dominate cultures and partly due to the realization that historical process was an important factor. However, it is still recognized that technological innovations have played a major role in cultural change and that certain innovations are more important than others. The use of UCE's tripartite division of "hunting-gathering, pastoralism, and agriculture" has also survived and is still widely employed by anthropologists, but now only as a classificatory scheme (as in this book), not as a description of evolutionary progress.

Whatever their details, cultural evolutionary theory proposed relationships between culture and environment, including natural, political, social, and technological environments. Even today, the details of how cultures evolve remain unresolved, but it is clear that there is a relationship between environment and cultural change.

Multilinear Cultural Evolution

By the early twentieth century, the unilinear cultural evolutionary model was in trouble. Key postulates, such as the idea that herding preceded agriculture, were not standing up under investigation. Worse, the simple scheme of progress as proceeding through neat, regular stages was inadequate to deal with the accumulating ethnographic data. It was also realized that food was not the only thing people got from the environment. Early theories (like contemporary ones such as optimal foraging theory) dealt almost exclusively with food. But, in fact, other activities, such as art and religion, also draw on resources.

It soon became obvious that evolution was not always unidirectional. Many groups have abandoned agriculture to become herders or hunter-gatherers (e.g., on the plains of North America). Some broad ethnic categories include elements of each of the supposedly distinct evolutionary stages: hunter-gatherers, agriculturalists, and "advanced" townsfolk—all of which were trading with one another and giving every appearance of being economically specialized subgroups of one broad social formation, rather than mixtures of ancestors and evolved descendants. Arthur Herman (2001) pointed out that Adam Smith could observe all his stages—foraging, herding, farming, and commerce—in the Scotland of his time, without having to leave home. Some hunter-gatherers, such as those of the Pacific Coast of North America, had exceedingly complex social and technological systems—much more complex than those of many farmers. It was realized that if cultural evolution were to survive as a theory, it would have to be viewed as following many lines. Thus, Julian Steward (1955) proposed "**multilinear evolution.**"

Neoevolution

Despite the rejection of cultural evolutionary models in the early 1900s, by the middle of the twentieth century many anthropologists began to accept the reality that cultural evolution had occurred, even if in a multilinear way. Leslie White, one of the founders of the ecological tradition in anthropology, made an attempt to revive unilinear cultural evolution by framing it in a new way (**neoevolution**). White (1949) argued that cultures evolved as they increased their control of energy sources: from fire to animal power, to coal, to oil, to electricity, to thermonuclear power. At every stage, we become more adept at using greater and greater amounts of energy. Contemporary theorists would add that we increase in ability to use energy more efficiently and to control it better. White expressed this in summary form, $C = E \times T$, where C is culture, E is energy, and T is technology. It was not intended to be taken as literal mathematics; White did not argue that the United States is twice as advanced as Sweden because it used twice as much energy per capita. But White was arguing—rightly or wrongly— that energy, and the means of harnessing it, are basic to a culture, in a way that art styles or dynastic genealogies are not. White also held that symbols were the basis of culture, and humans were symbolizing animals. However, he saw this as equally typical of all humans and thus not causing change or evolution per se.

Steward (1955; also see Harding et al. 1960; Service 1962; Johnson and Earle 2000) introduced an evolutionary scheme based on increasing sociocultural complexity. The least complex was the **band**, consisting of small, relatively mobile hunting and gathering groups with informal leaders. Next was the **tribe**, consisting of larger, more or less settled groups of hunter-gatherers or incipient agriculturalists (horticulturalists or pastoralists) with several settlements and relatively formal decision-making authority but still no centralized authority. Third was the **chiefdom**, which had large, sedentary populations (usually of agriculturalists), elites, some social stratification, and leaders with the authority to impose their will. Last was the **state** (sometimes called "civilization," a highly loaded term), a large and complex system based on grain agriculture with larger and more dense populations, complex social and political structures, elaborate record keeping, urban centers or cities, central authority, monumental architecture, and specialization. While there has been much criticism of this scheme, it is still widely utilized by anthropologists to describe political entities and ecological adaptations.

There now seems to be a growing acceptance of some sort of scheme of increasing complexity, or at least complication. This would have band-level hunter-gatherers as the original societies, with some evolving to tribes in the sense of local independent settlements or groups of about five hundred to one thousand persons. With the incorporation of agriculture or sophisticated hunting-gathering as the economic base, some tribes grew into chiefdoms. Some tribes and chiefdoms, under certain circumstances, developed into states. While there is ample archaeological and other evidence of this general trend, there is no reason to believe such evolution has been unidirectional, still less good or bad.

Possibilism

As anthropologists began to accumulate more general knowledge of culture and detailed knowledge of specific cultures, it became apparent that culture was highly adaptive, that most environments had been modified by humans, that there was a variety of responses possible to most environmental situations, and that cultures were considerably influenced by other cultures. There was no illusion that environment did not influence culture, but it became clear that it did not dictate it. In **possibilism**, the environment is seen as a limiting or enabling factor rather than a determining factor. To be sure, the environment may deny certain possibilities, such as the use of snow houses in Arabia, but will open a variety of other possibilities, such as houses of wood, grass, mud, cloth, stone, or skins, all of which occur in Arabia. The culture makes the choice of which of the possibilities to employ.

The culture also has limiting factors, including technology, belief systems, and extracultural relations. In our housing example above, metal houses are a possibility offered by the environment (e.g., iron ore exists), but if a culture does not possess the technology to mine, process, and fabricate metal, it is not really a choice. However, if that culture has access to metal through trade, perhaps it could be a choice. Possibilism is really an interactive process between culture and the environment. The choices available in the environment may be limited by the capabilities of the culture, or vice versa, and as culture and the environment evolve (change), the interplay also changes.

While the culture area concept related similarities between cultures and environment, it was recognized (Wissler 1926; Kroeber 1953; also see Meggers 1954) that the same environment (or culture area) might include cultures with quite different ecological adaptations. For example, the Southwest culture area contained Pueblo agriculturalists, hunting-and-gathering Apaches, and the sheep-herding Navajo. These groups coexisted by filling complementary niches. Thus, culture shaped environmental response. The environment did not control behavior; it merely made some behaviors more reasonable than others. Another classic study along these lines was the work of Birdsell (1953) on the relationship between rainfall and population density in aboriginal Australia.

Some would view possibilism as the opposite of determinism. In fact, however, possibilism is deterministic from the standpoint that some options are excluded, and the solutions are limited to a subset of all possibilities—a determination of which are possible and which are not. Possibilism seems much more realistic than strict determinism, because the role of culture is considered to some extent. Human culture has a penchant for changing the conditions and rules; as human cultural institutions and technology become more complex, the environment seems to play less and less of a role in limiting or determining human responses and adaptation. Thus, possibilism has been frequently criticized (e.g., Smith 1991) as not being a theory at all, as it predicts nothing specific. It is difficult to refute this charge.

THE RISE OF CULTURAL ECOLOGY

While always embedded in general anthropological theory (e.g., Adams 1935; Park 1936), cultural ecology did not come into its own until after the late 1930s, primarily through the work of Julian Steward. He began his career working with the Paiute and Shoshone people of the Great Basin in western North America but later worked in South America and eventually in Puerto Rico, a colonial-type society in the contemporary world. He was one of the first anthropologists to look at complex societies and their place in the even more complex world of today. Steward also drew on the concept of possibilism. Societies could adapt in any of a number of possible directions, rather than being subject to environmental determinism.

Steward's Ecology

Steward was the first to combine four approaches in studying the interaction between culture and environment: (1) an explanation of culture in terms of the environment where it existed, rather than just a geographic association with economy; (2) the relationship between culture and environment as a process (not just a correlation); (3) a consideration of small-scale environment, rather than culture-area-sized regions; and (4) the connection of ecology and multilinear cultural evolution.

Steward's landmark ecological work, *Basin-Plateau Aboriginal Sociopolitical Groups* (1938; also see Steward 1936), dealt with native peoples of the Great Basin. In that work, Steward first described the general environment, listed important resources, and then discussed how those resources were utilized. He then discussed the sociopolitical patterns and how they related to technology, the environment, and the distribution of resources. His approach was groundbreaking. Steward's (1955) primary arguments were that (1) cultures in similar environments may have similar adaptations; (2) all adaptations are short lived and are constantly adjusting to changing environments; and (3) changes in culture can elaborate existing culture or result in entirely new ones. Steward (1955:5, 30) coined the term *cultural ecology* to describe his approach and is frequently referred to as the father of ecological studies in anthropology.

Steward (1955:31) recognized that the ecology of humans had both distinct biological and distinct cultural aspects, though they were intertwined. He argued that the cultural aspect was associated with technology, which set humans and their cultures above and separate from the rest of the environment. While Steward was correct in recognizing the difference between the biological and cultural aspects of human ecology, he was wrong to view humans as separate from the rest of the environment.

The "New Ecology"

While Steward tied culture into the environment, a new approach, called the "new ecology," tied culture into the emerging science of systems ecology (e.g., Vayda and Rappaport 1968). It was argued that human cultures were not unique but formed only one of the population units interacting "to form food webs, biotic communities, and ecosystems" (Vayda and Rappaport 1968:494). This approach placed humans within a unified science of ecology so that what was learned about human behavior would have greater applicability.

This approach has had the effect of moving the analysis of human behavior from strictly qualitative ethnography to quantitative science, leading to a whole new way to look at humans. One weakness of this approach is that analysis is based on data that describe situations at a single point in time. While variables can be measured and compared to each other and relationships between variables can be described and modeled, it is difficult to model cultural change and evolution using such data. This problem is also an issue with much of the more recent work, such as the use of optimization models (see chapter 3). Another weakness is that systems in ecology have proved to be more difficult to analyze than they seemed in the 1960s and are often chaotic and weakly bounded (Botkin 1990). Vayda has thus moved toward what he calls "event ecology," analyzing particular events and their complex causes, rather than systems.

Cultural Materialism

Cultural materialism is a practical, rather straightforward, functionalist approach to anthropology with a focus on the specific hows and whys of culture. It is based on the idea that "human social life is a response to the practical problems of earthly existence" (Harris 1979:ix) and that these issues can be studied in a practical way. Cultural materialism emphasizes very empirical phenomena, such as technology, economy (e.g., food), environment, and population, takes an evolutionary perspective, and has an unwavering commitment to the rules of Western science.

Marvin Harris (1966, 1968) espoused a concept of "techno-environmental materialism" that initially held that all cultural institutions could be explained by direct material payoff. Harris did not claim that this always provided a total explanation; he saw it as a research strategy. One starts by looking for a direct material payoff—typically in food calories—for a cultural institution. If that is inadequate, look for a payoff in protein or in shelter. Only when all material payoffs have been eliminated should one investigate psychological and sociological factors. This has proved an exceedingly useful research approach (e.g., see Smith 1991), but only if one remembers to carry out the whole agenda, looking to psychology and society when necessary (as Harris did in his later works).

Materialists tend to look at specifics rather than trends and at distinctive traits rather than general ones. The task was to explain the trait and why it is done in that particular way. Detractors would consider this approach to be biased away from nonmaterial aspects of culture, often overlooking important, if not critical, information. Proponents would argue that the overlooked information is not empirical and so not science. Nonetheless, cultural materialism has formed the basis for much anthropological research since the 1960s.

An excellent example of the functionalist/materialist approach is the analysis of the role of sacred cows in India (Harris 1966, 1974). To Hindus, cows are sacred and cannot be eaten. Hindu religion includes a belief in reincarnation, and so it is possible that a relative may have been reincarnated as a cow, and eating the cow would be the equivalent of cannibalism. To many Westerners who eat beef on an almost daily basis, it seemed silly to have starving people refusing to eat their cows.

However, an analysis of the function in Indian society of cows revealed that they were simply too important to eat. First, cows provided labor for plowing; few farmers could afford a tractor, and there was no infrastructure for the support of such machines. Next, cow dung was used as fertilizer and fuel; no substitutes were available, and the fields had to have some fertilizer to maintain productivity. Cows did not have to be fed; they survived by foraging trash and weeds, helping to keep the area clean. In addition, they provided milk, a renewable resource.

Thus, slaughtering the cows for food would provide a wonderful few weeks of steak and ribs but would also result in no labor to pull plows, no fertilizer, no fuel, no milk, no weed or trash disposal, the rapid collapse of the entire agricultural system, and the death of millions by famine. As it turns out, the cows are eventually eaten. When cows die naturally, members of the "untouchables," the lowest caste in Indian society, butcher them, eat the meat, and manufacture useful products from their skins and other parts. It is a system that functions well under the circumstances. However, it does not necessarily explain the origin of the practice (e.g., Simoons 1979).

A Note on Function and Origin

To many cultural materialists, explanation centers on the question of function and origin. If something serves a specific function, the rationale goes, it must have originated or been designed to fulfill that function. Many human ecologists focus their research on functional aspects, such as food procurement or technology. However, it is a mistake to assume that function must be equated with origin. Some, if not most, things have multiple functions. Choosing one and then determining the origin will likely result in error. Also, some things may have multiple origins and may have been recombined to serve different functions. Technology and culture are constantly being modified, changed, and adjusted to fit new conditions. It may be that the origin of a particular practice is lost in all the changes.

The reverse investigative approach also is true; knowing an origin does not necessarily mean the function is known. The function of things may change over time, so their origin may have little to do with their current use. Sleeve buttons once used to attach gloves are now mere decoration, and old engine parts are now paperweights.

Rational Choice Theory

Currently, one paradigm in environmental social science is some form of **rational choice theory** (Elster 1987; also see Frank 1988; Green and Shapiro 1994). This theory, popular in economics and political science as well as in some fields of anthropology, asserts that people decide how to achieve their goals on the basis of deliberate, individual consideration of all available information, that they seek out better information as required, and that they are good calculators of their chances; that they know where to hunt deer, which crops will grow, and how to trade off the potential yields of hunting deer versus cultivating crops. Some would consider rational choice theory to be related to evolutionary ecology because poor choices would be subjected to negative selective pressure. Thus, people have evolved to make better choices.

It is true that much conventional behavior is rationally chosen. Some behavior is not rational, however, even if there is a seemingly reasonable argument made for such conduct. In practice, people rationalize irrational behavior (Green and Shapiro 1994; Taylor 2006). It seems obvious that cultures vary in their approaches to adaptation and that if rational choice were always correct, much less variation would be expected. However, each culture has different goals, different technologies, and different concepts of what is rational, so the rational choice of group A will likely be different from that of group B, even in the same environment.

In addition, people have many of their choices made for them before they are old enough to choose for themselves. People take on many traits, such as language and diet, long before they are old enough to make rational choices. Also, people do not have time to decide everything in detail. They have to take shortcuts, which usually means going with habit or imitating others. When we are forced to change, we are forced to make more or less rational decisions. The rest of the time we tend to find that the most rational course is to minimize the effort of making decisions; we go with our habits or with quick approximations.

It has been argued that the whole Western attitude toward nature is cultural and irrational. Westerners tend to regard nature as something separate from humans, ours to exploit and ruin at will. This belief is neither scientifically sensible nor conducive to maximizing any of the many resources we get from the nonhuman world. A rational chooser would choose to believe something quite different.

Rational choice is an indispensable tool of human ecological analysis, but it leaves a good deal for us to explain. In fact, it leaves almost all the content of culture for us to explain. We might freely grant that *all* cultural practices were adopted because they seemed, at one time, the most rational things to do under the existing circumstances. Like cultural materialism, rational choice makes a good starting place for an analysis; it is not usually the final resting place.

Political Ecology

A recent development in human ecology is the rapid spread of **political ecology**. The term was coined by Steward's student Eric Wolf in 1972 (Wolf 1972, 1982). It was popularized in the mid-1980s and became particularly popular in geography (Blaikie and Brookfield 1987; see Greenberg and Park 1994; Kottak 1999; Robbins 2004). Political ecology is concerned with power relations and specifically with the day-to-day conflicts, alliances, and negotiations that ultimately result in some sort of definitive behavior. It directs our attention to immediate processes and conflicts. It also is notably concerned with scale, analyzing conflicts from the household level to the local to the global. It has therefore meaningfully supplemented the other branches of human ecology that tend to look at the long term but that have often ignored the wide scale. Where cultural ecology tends to focus on a particular small ethnic group over a long time, political ecology tends to focus on larger forces impinging on a community at one point in time. Steward had done both, but his students had often narrowed their focus until Wolf (with his fellow Stewardian and close friend Sidney Mintz; see Mintz [1985]) restored a balance.

The field of political ecology rose rapidly in the late 1980s and the 1990s, heavily influenced by contemporary economic and political theories (Bennett 1976, 1992; Robbins 2004). Perhaps most important of these influences was environmental politics. Worldwide battles between exploiters and conservationists have always had a serious impact on indigenous communities (see Bodley 1999). For example, by the 1990s, even remote native groups in rainforests found themselves used as pawns in power struggles between national governments, multinational companies, and international conservation organizations. Such struggles are not limited to native groups, as African American communities in the southern United States suddenly find themselves targeted as sites for toxic waste disposal (Bullard 1990). As a result, gender, ethnicity, and identity—all concepts that are notorious political battlegrounds as well as traditional subjects for anthropologists to examine—emerged as important topics of ecological-anthropological research.

Most political ecology falls into two broad categories. First is the work on resource management in complex contemporary societies (e.g., McCay and Acheson 1987; Pinkerton and Weinstein 1995). Much of this work involves management of resources owned by the community or not owned at all, and studies of common property water resources have been important (Ostrom 1990). Second was research on the fate of small-scale, indigenous societies caught in the midst of "modernization" (e.g., Netting 1974, 1986; Gladwin and Truman 1989; Sheridan 1988; Wilk 1991; Stonich 1993; Anderson 1994).

At first, many studies naively demonized globalization and multinationalism, discrediting local people, labeling them as "mere victims." This sort of abuse of the term led to a sharp critique of the whole field by Andrew Vayda and Bradley Walters (1999). They argued the term itself should be dropped and that we should return to a holistic, event-centered ecology. Their critique, however, touches only the highly oversimplified literature, leaving unscathed the works cited above. Thus, in spite of problems with the naive literature, the term *political ecology* seems here to stay (Paulson and Gezon 2005).

Partly in consequence of critiques, political ecology has broadened its view. The *Journal of Political Ecology* and new collections such as *Political Ecology* (Stott and Sullivan 2001) go far beyond politics. Biology and culture have been brought back into the fold. Political and cultural ecology continue to blend into each other.

In recent years, cultural/political ecology has been increasingly influenced by world systems theory. This theory was developed largely by Immanuel Wallerstein (1976). He began to look seriously at the interconnections of societies around the world—going beyond the simple "rich-poor" and "developed-less developed" contrasts to see how the rise of one society might lead to, or be linked with, the fall of others. He separated the world into "cores" (the rich nations: Europe, North America, and Japan today; China and the Near East a thousand years ago); "peripheries" (poor and isolated societies); and "semiperipheries." These last are the countries in between, fairly well off but with much poverty and displaying a contrast of highly developed and much less developed sectors. Mexico, Turkey, and China provide current examples; in the world of a thousand years ago, southernmost Europe qualified (the rest was "periphery"), and so did much of southeast Asia. Long cycles of empire and dominance occur, reflected in economic swings and geographic shifts of power.

Wallerstein's theory has been used to evaluate the rise and fall of cultures and the problems of smaller, more remote societies in today's world (Bodley 1999, 2001) and in their own earlier worlds, where they could create small, local "world" systems (Chase-Dunn and Mann 1998). In general, world systems are unfair, and today's globalization—which is no new phenomenon—is perhaps the least fair of all. No one seems to have figured out a way to deal with an economy of goods and information that is inevitably global—in this age of container shipping, jet planes, and the Internet—but is dominated by a few warlike or predatory nation-states.

Still more recently has come a veritable explosion of major, pathbreaking works that increase the range and depth of political-ecological analysis. Research has ranged over such topics as forest management (Agrawal 2005; Tsing 2005), ranching (Sheridan 1998; Hedrick 2007), mining (Kirsch 2006), indigenous agriculture (Gonzalez 2001), and fisheries (McCay 1998). An emerging focus has been the problems faced by local people impacted by parks and other conservation activities (West 2006; West et al. 2006). Politicial ecologists have even looked at ecology itself (Latour 2004).

Unlike cultural ecology, which nests in anthropology, political ecology now involves geographers, political scientists, environmental scientists, and others, as well as anthropologists. In spite of some polemic (see Robbins's [2004] basic introduction), the fields are at least complementary, and we view them more as two aspects of the same thing. Both are solidly derivative of the Stewardian agenda.

Historical Ecology

Recently, the number of terms in the human-ecological field has been increased by the addition of *historical ecology* (Balée 1998a, 2006; Crumley 1994; Winthrop 2001). The term has been around at least since the 1970s, when Edward Deevey directed a historical ecology project at the University of Florida (Crumley 1998:xii). This field is close to environmental history (Cronon 1983), landscape history, and similar historical subfields, as well as to cultural geography. In practice, it has been something of a blend of these fields—anthropology with more historical detail than usual, or history with more holistic cultural and environmental data than usual (e.g., Ehrlich 2000).

A specific theory for this subfield was proposed by Balée (1998b, 2006), who emphasized interactions ("dialectical" in his usage) between people and environments, with the two being active players rather than as humans merely adapting to the environment. Balée (1998b:14) argued that: (1) human activity has affected virtually all environments; (2) human activity does not necessarily degrade or improve environments; (3) different cultural systems have different impacts on their environments; and (4) human interaction with the environment can be understood as a total phenomenon. This directs attention to *individual action* as opposed to such things as evolutionary dynamics, cultural ideologies, or social systems. These latter are abstractions that do not really interact per se.

Historical ecologists, like other human ecologists in recent years, have paid much attention to the influence of small-scale societies on their environments. Such people were once dismissed as "primitives" and "savages" who had minimal effect on their surroundings—who were, according to earlier formulations, part of "nature" rather than "culture." In North America, we still find Native American exhibits in museums of natural history rather than in museums of history or art. From such unthinking prejudice, contemporary ecological anthropology—including historical ecology—can deliver us.

In short, historical ecology focuses much more on *change, contingency*, and *human agency* than did some of the other traditions within cultural ecology. In this, it continues a long-standing agenda in the field (e.g., Anderson 1972, 1988; Bennett 1976; Netting 1986). The counteragendas include evolutionary ones, whether Darwinian or cultural, and highly determinative "adaptation" theories that view human action as more or less a reflex of the environment.

Historical ecology, along with recent archaeological theory (Ashmore 2004) and cultural ecology in general (Feld and Basso 1996), has revivified the old cultural-geography concept of "landscape." The concept stems from the work of Carl Sauer (beginning with Sauer [1925]). Since Sauer, geographers have used *landscape* to refer to the face of the earth as modified, created, or perceived by people. A particularly stunning example is the recent encyclopedic trilogy by Sauer students on the cultivated landscapes of Native America (Doolittle 2000; Denevan 2001; Whitmore and Turner 2001). By contrast, *environment* is far wider, including everything from cosmic rays to bacteria. People may know very little about their environment, but, by definition, the landscape is what they see, know, and interact with.

The effect of humans on landscape may be seen today as "good" or "bad"; it is, perhaps, hard to avoid judging. (In the above trilogy, Denevan emphasized the success of native cultivators; Whitmore and Turner, their failures; while Doolittle maintained a careful balance.) Balée (1998b) emphasized the need to look at actual influences, without prejudging, in order to understand. This is doubly true if we wish to maintain or revive traditional land management techniques (such as controlled burning). Impartial analysis and understanding must preempt the field from the sort of naive, condemnatory judgment that we critique elsewhere in this book.

Sauer was far ahead of his time, and only recently has his concept of landscape broadened its scope and exploded into widespread use. This has followed on the realization noted above: even the "simplest" peoples not only know an incredible amount about their environments, but also profoundly modify them.

The landscape concept also has the benefit (again, emphasized by Sauer) of uniting science and humanities (cf. Balée 1998b, 1998c). Not only archaeologists, ecologists, and historians, but also students of traditional art and myth, to say nothing of phenomenological philosophers and poets, all talk about landscape (Ashmore 2004) and can find here a common ground in a thoroughly literal sense. Human ecology profits considerably from such meetings of the minds. (It does not, however, profit from the endless multiplication of terms; one truly wonders whether we need *historical ecology*, *political ecology*, *event ecology*, *social ecology*, and the rest for what are, after all, merely aspects of one discipline.)

Postmodernism

A fairly new paradigm in contemporary social thought is **postmodernism**. The postmodernists were critical of all modern things and argued that science itself was flawed. Extreme postmodernism took a very subjective and antiscientific stance in opposition to the objectivism of the modern world. This view holds that science is subjective; thus, our interpretations of cultures are also subjective (see Clifford and Marcus 1986). Postmodernists argue that there is no objective reality and that fact lists have no place in anthropology.

This approach is not science but has evolved within studies of literature, religion, and expressive behavior. Insofar as it directs our attention to interpreting and understanding cultural practice, it is a valuable contribution. However, it has not spread far into human ecological studies because ecologists find that humans do have to consider some blunt truths: the need for food, the need to avoid extreme cold and heat, the brutal facts of disease, broken bones, grizzly bear attacks, and the like. Humans confront these details of life in a multitude of ways, and cultural interpretation plays a vital role in our understanding of those ways. However, we cannot ignore the life-and-death matters that force humans to adjust.

Postmodernism is a philosophical position that runs counter to science. In a succession of articles, Vayda (1993, 1995, 1996) argued against the anti-science view of postmodernism and maintained that ecological anthropology should be carefully establishing cause-and-effect links (when possible). He also argued against certain views that have been broadly labeled as functionalist and that often lead to the construction of models rather than cause-and-effect explanations.

On the other hand, a "softer" form of postmodernism directs our attention back to texts, discourse, and expressive culture, basic to early ethnography but rather ignored in much of ecological anthropology. It also has the salutary effect of displacing narrow focus on Western ideas, subjecting them to the same analysis that anthropologists give to traditional people (e.g., Latour 2004), while giving local people credit for having their own very good ideas. Some of the best recent work thus combines solid biology and exquisite attention to local people's words, concepts, and contributions (e.g., Tsing 2005; Kirsch 2006; West 2006). Again, this is not really new; Steward and many other early workers published extensive texts. But the new work makes much more use of local ideas in actual analysis and theory building.

THUS . . .

As noted earlier, anthropology and human ecology are eclectic sciences. Human ecology does not have its own theory; it uses ideas taken from other disciplines, modified as needed and then applied to problems. Any approach that can be used to learn about how people and cultures interact with the environments will serve. If something does not inform us, it will be abandoned and another procedure used. This flexibility in research approaches is a strength and helps us to better understand humans, their cultures, and their relationship with the environment.

A Note on Methods

Ecological anthropology uses methods from biology and biological conservation (see Borgerhoff et al. 2005), but more especially from cultural anthropology. The standard work for that methodology is H. Russell Bernard, *Research Methods in Anthropology* (2006). To this general work, cultural ecologists interested in traditional knowledge need to add knowledge of how to elicit local traditional knowledge such as classification systems (Frake 1980), how to study decision making (Gladwin 1989), how to do at least preliminary assessments of nutritional and other payoffs (Winterhalder and Smith 1981), and other specialized techniques according to subfield; archaeology, historical ecology, and the other subfields noted above all have their own techniques, most of which are covered in the references cited herein.

Ethics have become an increasing concern in anthropology. The American Anthropological Association and the International Society of Ethnobiology have excellent and comprehensive ethics codes for research, available on their websites (most easily accessed by computer searching the organizational names). A new book by Linda Whiteford and Robert Trotter (2008) provides a thorough and straightforward introduction to ethical practice for cultural anthropologists.

CHAPTER SUMMARY

People occupy most of the diverse environments of the planet, and cultural ecology is the story of how they do that. Some do it well, others less so. In any case, humans are the key species in most environments, and whatever their practices, we can learn from them.

The study of humans' interaction with their environment is called human ecology, with human biological ecology emphasizing the biological aspect of the adaptation (including evolution) and cultural ecology emphasizing the cultural aspect. Human ecology generally falls within anthropology, the study of humans (through time and space).

Human ecology has a long history, with many ideas and concepts being proposed. The ideas of environment dictating culture (environmental determinism), of cultures evolving through stages, and of cultures operating within environmental parameters (possibilism) have been proposed, rejected, refined, argued, and reconsidered. However, modern human ecology, including cultural ecology, was founded by Julian Steward, who argued that human adaptation was an interplay among environment, biology, and culture.

Today, most human ecologists utilize the principles of empirical science in their investigations and approach it in a number of ways. These include a "humans as animals" procedure that relies heavily on biological principles. Some view humans as rational choosers and use a functional and materialist approach. Others emphasize political processes and the interaction between power, modernization, and globalization.

KEY TERMS

adaptation
anthropology
band
chiefdom
cultural ecology
cultural materialism

cultural relativism
culture
a [specific] culture
culture area
ecology
empirical science
environmental determinism
ethnocentrism
ethnography
ethnology
evolution
human biological ecology
human ecology
multilinear cultural evolution
neoevolution
the new ecology
political ecology
possibilism
postmodernism
rational choice theory
state
tribe
unilinear cultural evolution

Fundamentals of Ecology

Ecology is the study of the relationships between organisms and their environment, the "economics" (or livelihood) of the earth and its totality of life forms. The term *ecology* comes from the Greek words *oikos* ("house" or habitat) and *logos* ("word," here in the sense of "academic discipline"). It was given its contemporary usage by Ernst Haeckel in 1866 (see Goodland 1975). Most of the concepts used in human ecology have been borrowed from biology, so an understanding of the basic notions of biological ecology is essential (Richerson 1977). For more detailed treatment of ecological concepts, see Odum (1975, 1993), Kormondy (1996), or Molles (1999). Emilio Moran (2006, 2008) is perhaps especially useful to study because he focuses on humans.

THE ENVIRONMENT

The **environment** consists of the surroundings within which an organism interacts, a pretty broad definition. One of the problems in defining the environment is this breadth; it can be viewed as different things in different places and at different geographic or spatial levels or scales—a pond, a valley, a continent, the earth, the solar system, or even the universe. Perhaps the concept of the operating environment, that area in which the population under consideration operates, is more useful. On the other hand, today, global forces such as global warming influence all communities, so working at different scales is essential (Tsing 2005).

The environment can be divided into two primary components, **abiotic** and **biotic** (see Kormondy 1996:6). The abiotic component consists of the inorganic materials present in the environment, including elements such as oxygen, nitrogen, sodium, carbon, and compounds such as water and carbon dioxide. The abiotic component also includes physical factors, such as weather, climate, geological materials, geography, time, solar radiation (the source of most energy), and even the cosmos.

The biotic component consists of all of the materials that are biological in origin: plants, animals, and microbes, either living or dead. Thus, a living tree is part of the biotic environment, as is a dead, fallen, and decomposing tree. Eventually, the tree will be broken down into its inorganic constituents, and those materials will again enter the abiotic environment.

Classifying Environments

As we noted, environments can be defined based on any number of criteria, and operational definitions differ depending on the situation. Here we define two basic divisions of the biotic environment, biomes and ecozones, differentiated based on scale.

Biomes

A **biome** is a large-scale, broad region of similar temperature, rainfall, and biology. The biome concept is frequently used by ecologists, biologists, and anthropologists as a general descriptive category and as a starting point for classification and analysis. Culture areas, discussed in chapter 1, are essentially biomes with an added layer of culture, and each has a human carrying capacity and trends of economy.

While it is possible to define any number of biomes (figure 2.1), some of the basic terrestrial biomes (see Campbell [1995:Fig. 1.1]; Molnar and Molnar [2000:Figs. 2-1a and 2-1b]; Kormondy [1996:338–379]) illustrate the diversity of environments across the globe. They are briefly described in table 2.1, although these biomes contain considerable diversity within them. These regions begin at the north and south poles and generally extend toward the equator and from higher to lower in elevation.

In addition to the terrestrial environments, all of which are inhabited by humans, several aquatic environments have been, and continue to be, heavily utilized although not generally inhabited by humans. Aquatic environments are divided into marine (ocean) and freshwater components (see figure 2.2 and table 2.2). Until recently, most human utilization of marine environments was largely confined to shores and shallow waters.

Environmental Zones

An **environmental zone**, or **ecozone**, is a geographic area defined by fairly specific biotic communities (a plant association dominated by a certain species) within biomes. Thus, a river running through a savanna would contain a riverine

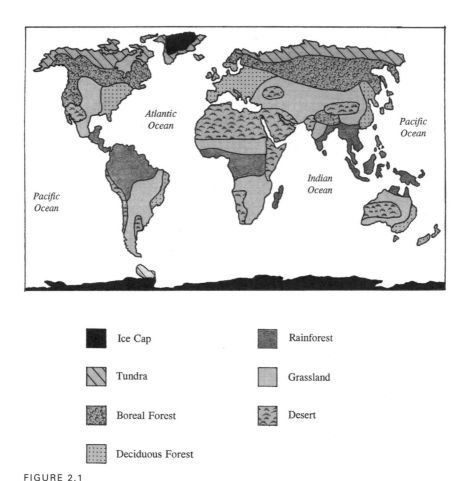

FIGURE 2.1

The general terrestrial biomes around the world (adapted from Campbell 1995:Fig. 1.1). Reprinted with permission by Bernard Campbell. Human Ecology, 2nd edition. (New York: Aldine de Gruyter). Copyright © 1983, 1995 by Bernard Campbell.

ecozone within the savanna biome. The definition of any particular ecozone is based on judgmental criteria, depending on the goals of the researcher. Ecozones are most commonly defined based on dominant plant communities because they are easy to recognize and map (animals are harder). The "pinyon-juniper" forest, the "pine belt," and the "aspen zone" are typical examples of ecozones.

Ecotones

An **ecotone** is the geographic intersection of—as well as the transition between—ecozones (see figure 2.3). Since ecozone boundaries may also be biome boundaries, ecotones exist between biomes as well. Examples of ecotones

Table 2.1. The Major Terrestrial Biomes

Biome	General Location	Primary Vegetation	Temperature and Precipitation	Comments
Tundra	Near the poles	Lichens, mosses, some grass	Very cold, often frozen, generally low precipitation, but little evaporation	Very low biodiversity
Boreal forest	Just south of the tundra in the Northern Hemisphere	Evergreen coniferous trees (e.g., pines)	Long, cold winters and variable precipitation	Generally low biodiversity, poor soils, and short growing season, not well suited to agriculture
Deciduous forest	Mid-latitudes	Deciduous trees (that drop their leaves in the winter, e.g., maples, willows)	Moderate temperatures but cold winters, considerable rainfall	Considerable biodiversity, fertile soils, and long growing season, well suited to agriculture
Tropical rainforest	Equatorial zones	Evergreen (not conifers) trees and shrubs	Warm with abundant (often daily) rainfall, general lack of "seasons"	Enormous biodiversity, generally poor soils but suited to some types of agriculture
Grassland (a.k.a. plains, savanna, pampas steppe)	Large, flat regions	Grasses, a few trees	Warm summers and cold winters, wet and dry seasons	Moderate biodiversity, large herd animals common, suited to some forms of agriculture
Desert	Regions of low precipitation	Generally sparse	Often very warm, but some deserts are cold; generally low precipitation	Low biodiversity, not well suited to agriculture except in regions with rivers

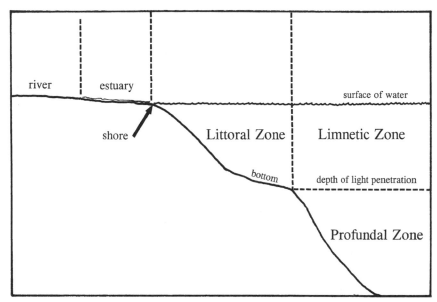

FIGURE 2.2
A general diagram of the aquatic biomes.

include estuaries (places where freshwater meets saltwater, such as where a river empties into the ocean), shorelines, and areas where forests and grasslands meet. An ecotone is usually a more productive place than either of the individual eco-zones because species of both zones intermingle within it. Even in cases where there is less diversity, an ecotone is a good place for an organism to be located as access to both ecozones is easier.

This same concept could be applied directly to cultural systems, where the border between two cultures would form a cultural ecotone. This might create a more "culturally productive" place, where ideas and goods could intermingle. Examples of such places would be trading centers, ports, and centers of learning.

Refugia

Most biomes and ecozones are defined based on the current distribution of plants and animals. Researchers studying past environments also use the ecozone concept but define an ecozone based on past biotic distributions. Occasionally, a remnant of a past biome or ecozone will survive into the present as sort of a living fossil. These areas, and the life within them, are called **refugia** and can be quite valuable in the study of past environments.

For example, a number of desert regions once contained different vegetation. If a small pine forest were found on top of a mountain now within a

Table 2.2.   The Major Aquatic Environments

	Location	General Characteristics	Comments
	Marine Environments		
Estuary	Where rivers and streams enter the ocean	Sea water mixes with freshwater, forming an ecotone with tidal marshes and mudflats	Diverse and productive areas, heavily utilized by people
Littoral zone	From the beach into coastal waters to the depth of light penetration	Rocky and sandy beaches and bottoms	Diverse and productive areas, heavily utilized by people
Limnetic zone	Open water to the depth of light penetration (above about three hudred feet)	Open water away from coastlines	Moderate diversity, some utilization by humans with large watercraft
Profundal zone	Open water below the depth of light penetration (below about three hundred feet)	Dark, not inhabited by plants	Unknown diversity but not often utilized by humans
	Freshwater Environments		
Still water	Lakes, ponds, and marshes	Shallow to deep waters, some with profundal zones	Considerable diversity, heavily used by humans
Moving water	Rivers and streams	Generally shallow, some very muddy, some treacherous	Less diversity than still water, but some resources (c.g., salmon) heavily used by people
Riparian	Along shorelines	Ecotone between land and water	High diversity, heavily used by people

desert, the forest may be a surviving remnant of a larger forest that once covered the area. This refugium could provide clues to the past plant and animal life within the region and provide a starting point for the reconstruction of the ecozone at that time.

Ecosystems

An **ecosystem** is a geographically bounded system within which a defined group of organisms interact with both the abiotic and biotic components of the environment. Ecosystems are active and dynamic places and may be contained within or overlap with biomes and ecozones (see figure 2.4). The size and scale of ecosystems can vary, depending on how and why they are defined. The largest

FIGURE 2.3
An example of an ecotone between two ecozones.

ecosystem currently defined is called the **biosphere** and is the global environment and all of its interacting ecosystems.

The concept of the ecosystem was formalized by Odum (1953), and a history of the idea was provided by Golley (1993). Ecosystems are conceptual entities, often being defined by a researcher based on the goals of the research, but the phenomena are real. For example, a person studying a pond could define it as an ecosystem and would find it inhabited by a variety of species. These species would form a community linked to one another in an overall symbiotic relationship. One could study the various species, how they related to one another, their population cycles, and so on. However, to fully understand the pond, one would have to realize that it was linked to other things, that it was part of a larger

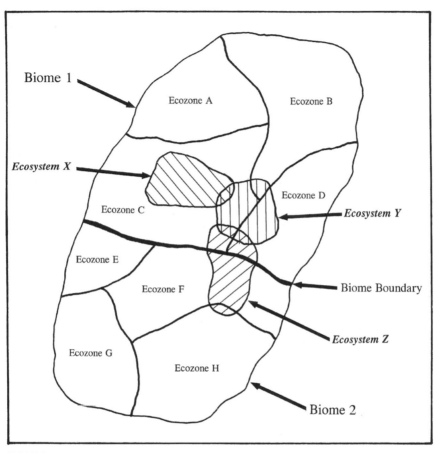

FIGURE 2.4
The general relationship among biomes, ecozones, and ecosystems (note that an ecosystem can cross biome and ecozone boundaries), no scale.

system. One would have to account for the source of the water and the inorganic nutrients that are critical to the system, so the watershed would have to be considered. As sunlight powers the plants, which in turn support all other life, the sun would have to be included, and so on. If a predator, such as an eagle, visited the pond and ate fish from it, the eagle would then become part of the ecosystem of the pond. That same eagle might interact with other ponds that share nothing else in common and thereby link the two systems. And over time, the pond will fill in or otherwise transform.

Thus, while ecosystems can be defined at a variety of scales for different purposes, all are ultimately linked to one another, making the separation of ecosystems somewhat arbitrary and a matter of convenience. Some ecosystems, such as islands, may be "more separate" than others and therefore provide better laboratories for the analysis of ecological interaction.

Measuring and Analyzing Ecosystems and Ecozones

At least two measures of an ecosystem can be made, that of productivity and/or that of complexity. The productivity of an ecosystem is commonly assessed by measuring its **biomass**, the quantity (mass) of living matter within a specified area at a specific time (e.g., a standing crop). The amount of time it takes to replace the biomass through natural processes is called turnover and is a measure of biological activity. Another such measure is the quantity of chlorophyll per square meter. Biomass "productivity" is an important aspect of the human use of ecosystems.

The complexity of an ecosystem is measured by its **biodiversity**, the number and distribution of species present in an ecosystem. Biodiversity is an index, a combination of the gross number of species (variety) and the dominance of species (evenness). The greater the variety and the lower the dominance, the greater the biodiversity, although this is often difficult to measure because many species are unknown to Western science. High diversity provides resilience in any ecosystem, as genetic diversity does in biological evolution. If an ecosystem contained only ten species, one could say it was not very diverse. If that same system contained one hundred species (greater variety), it would have much greater diversity. If five species dominated the other ninety-five, the system would be less diverse than if no species were dominant (greater evenness). Recently, biocomplexity has also entered the conceptual field. This implies not only biodiversity, but complex interactions among the biota. Analysis of biocomplexity involves highly sophisticated models that are only beginning to be used in human ecology.

Highly diverse ecosystems have sometimes been called generalized, while ecosystems with low diversity are called specialized. The Arctic and some desert ecosystems could be characterized as specialized. An agricultural ecosystem is almost always more specialized than the ecosystem it replaced, as diversity is lowered artificially with the clearing of land and of many species to plant a single crop. Specialized ecosystems are always more unstable and unpredictable than generalized, more complex ecosystems.

It is necessary to consider how species are distributed within an ecosystem, a very important distinction in optimization models (see chapter 3). Species can be distributed more or less evenly or clustered in patches. These two conditions form ends of a continuum, with most ecosystems being more patchy than even.

Humans almost always lessen the diversity of the ecosystems they inhabit. Farmers specialize in a few species, modifying ecosystems to focus on those species and so decreasing diversity through a reduction in variety and an increase in dominance. For example, a parcel of rainforest may contain a large number of species with none really dominant. Once that forest is cleared and planted with corn (or any other crop), only a few species will be present, all dominated by corn.

Succession Stages

In the early twentieth century, Clements and Shelford (1939; also see Tobey 1981) defined the concept of climax vegetation: a stable, self-reproducing, interrelated plant community that will arise naturally on a site. After a forest burns, the vegetation goes through stages of **succession** (figure 2.5): grass and herbs, then shrubs and vines, then weedy trees that require a large amount of sun, and finally the "climax forest" that grows up under the weedy trees. The climax vegetation then reproduces itself until the next fire. However, it was quickly realized that this was an overly simplistic, static model. Environmental change is constant (sometimes sudden and drastic), and a place that has been stable for long enough

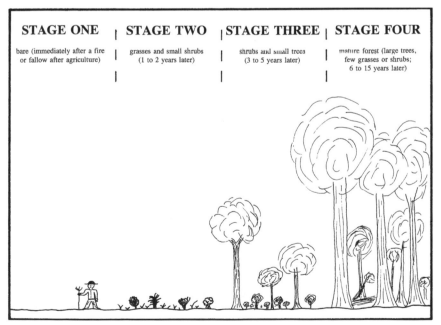

FIGURE 2.5
A hypothetical series of forest succession stages.

to develop a full, mature, self-reproducing forest is rare. Even redwoods and Sierra sequoias proved to be "weeds," sun-loving, disturbance-following plants that cannot reproduce in old-growth forests. Yet their lifespans are long enough to stretch across major climatic fluctuations. Studies of contemporary forests have demonstrated that many (if not most) of them have not stabilized due to the massive climatic changes at the end of the last Ice Age. Moreover, it turns out that virtually all land areas have been significantly affected by humans. Climax communities are almost nonexistent because systems are in constant flux.

However, the concept of succession is useful. As a community evolves, it often follows an orderly and predictable pattern through developmental stages and ultimately to maturity, each with varying degrees of productivity and diversity. Succession stages relate to the classification system of a particular group and its use of the environment. For example, some groups of contemporary Maya recognize six stages of forest regrowth after the land is cleared for agriculture. Understanding this succession and its associated agricultural implications is critical to the timing of reuse of the land for agriculture. In some cases, succession can be very rapid, as some tropical and Mediterranean trees often grow six feet per year, and a fifteen-year-old forest in southern Mexico is a most impressive forest indeed.

Studying Ecosystems

Ecosystems are very complex things. To study them, measurements are made and models of how they are thought to work are constructed. Many of these models are highly sophisticated and deal with the flow of nutrients and energy within lakes, watersheds, islands, and other fairly well-bounded systems. The goal of such models is to understand the effects of each component of an ecosystem on the other components. Models provide ways to describe and measure this flow within systems and to understand the relationship between organisms and the physical environment.

However, change is so universal and rapid that it is very difficult to construct a model that is accurate for very long. If a model were constructed for a particular lake, the model would probably not be applicable to the next lake. If a watershed were modeled, the model would have to change as soon as weeds from the next watershed invaded or a flood swept through the area. Fires occur frequently, and a fire during a wet spring will have a totally different effect from a fire in a dry summer. The first will merely char things, while the second could be catastrophic.

Trying to utilize ecosystem models to deal with humans has proved even more problematic. Culture is constantly changing, and people's reactions, desires, and wants also change. Even societies that are viewed as changeless and ageless, such as China, have gone through profound ecological changes at frequent intervals (see Anderson 1988). Stable, predictable systems are rare.

NICHE AND HABITAT

Each species occupies a niche, the role it plays within its environment, community, or ecosystem. A niche is defined by what the species eats, how it reproduces, and what it does. For example, some species eat just a few things while others, such as humans, will eat most anything. Some organisms (e.g., fish) have large numbers of offspring but provide no care, but the number of offspring is so large that at least some survive. Others will have far fewer offspring but give them a great deal of care, such as humans. Niche can also be defined by what a species does, such as humans hunting bison, gathering shellfish, or farming mixed crops in a rainforest. Like ecosystems, niches are loosely bounded and rather arbitrarily defined.

The geographic location where a species lives and operates is called its **habitat**. Niche and habitat are interrelated and somewhat dependent on each other as the type of habitat will influence the possible niches present. For example, some species of primates eat only fruit, others only leaves, while others will eat just about anything. All three species of primate could coexist in the same habitat because they occupied three different niches. In a forest, different species may live in the canopy while others live on the ground. In this case, one could have different habitats (high and low) on the same tree.

Ecosystems will contain innumerable niches. If a beetle lives in the bark of a tree and eats wood, and is then eaten by a bird, the bird and the beetle have quite different niches but share a portion of the same tree habitat. While a niche is specific and can be occupied by only one organism in the same geographic place—although several may be competing to occupy a niche—the same geographic space may serve as habitat to a large number of species in different niches. In different geographically isolated habitats, the "same" niche may be occupied by different organisms. For example, the medium-sized terrestrial carnivores in North America are placental mammals: wolves, coyotes, and dogs. In Australia, that same niche was filled by marsupial mammals until they were replaced by dogs after the arrival of humans.

As systems change, niches come into and go out of existence. The niche of a high-canopy leaf eater does not exist in a young forest, so that forest would not serve as habitat to such an animal. As the forest matures, that habitat comes into being, and the niche then exists. A high-canopy leaf eater may migrate and settle into the niche in the new habitat, or the niche may remain unoccupied. Alternatively, an existing species may evolve an adaptation to the niche, as behavioral changes or random mutations that result in the ability to utilize new resources become more advantageous and are selected for.

Humans have come to occupy and dominate most terrestrial habitats and through the use of technology will modify a habitat to suit their needs and will even create artificial habitats, such as cities. Adding to human adaptability is the capability of humans to rapidly alter their practices and to eat many different fungi, plants, and animals.

Humans occupy a very broad niche, eating about everything except cellulose. However, using a slightly different meaning of niche than that used by biologists, humans could be seen as occupying different niches based on general subsistence systems, such as hunter-gatherer, herder, or farmer (Barth 1956:1088; also see Hardesty 1975, 1977) as some of the resources they use are different resources and they live in different habitats. Indeed, it could be argued that contemporary human culture has created a new "urban-industrial" niche (Molnar and Molnar 2000:xiii).

RESOURCES

A **resource** is something that is actually used by an organism. If some material exists but is not used, it is not a resource, although it may be a potential resource if conditions were to change. Something may be a resource to one entity (organism or culture) but not to another, even at the same place and time. Some resources, such as water, are universal, while others change over time as technology and/or customs change. For example, many traditional cultures consider insects to be food resources (e.g., Bodenheimer 1951; Sutton 1988), while most industrialized societies consider them pests. The food value of these animals does not change, only the opinion and use of them.

Natural resources are those that are not manufactured by humans, including land, water, air, and time. Renewable natural resources are those of unlimited quantity, that is, they can be used and replaced within a relatively short period of time. These include solar radiation, water, firewood, and food. Nonrenewable natural resources are those of limited quantity and that can only be replaced over a considerable period of time, such as fossil fuels, minerals, and metals.

Resources generally have two dimensions: time and space. Most resources are available only at certain times, for example, when the seeds or nuts of specific plants ripen or when certain animals migrate through an area. Other resources, such as stone, may not have time limitations. The other dimension is space, where resources are located in the landscape. No resource is randomly distributed (air might be pretty close—but not air pollution), and so the organism has to know where resources are.

All species are limited in population size by resource availability and distribution, most notably water. The distribution of many species is limited by the availability of water; in other words, they are **tethered** to water. While frogs can leave the water, they cannot be out too long or they will die. Their tether is the distance they can travel (round trip) from water without drying out and dying. Humans are also tethered to water, although they have overcome many of the resulting limitations through technology, such as aqueducts, water containers, and wells. Other resources, such as certain kinds of food, may also create tethers.

Carrying Capacity

Carrying capacity can be defined in a number of ways (see Brush 1975; Glassow 1978; Dewar 1984) but is commonly viewed as a measure of the maximum number of individuals of a species that can be supported within a specific ecosystem for a specific period of time. Some define time as indefinitely large (e.g., Ellen 1982:41; also see Baumhoff 1981), but as all systems are dynamic, carrying capacity will fluctuate.

Carrying capacity applies to all organisms. It is possible, for example, to determine the carrying capacity of trout in a lake using an analysis of oxygen content of the water, number and density of prey species, water temperature, and other factors. If these conditions change, however, the carrying capacity also will change. Thus, the measure of carrying capacity is dynamic and dependent on conditions as well as the definition of the geographic boundaries of the ecosystem.

In human carrying capacity, the variables of culture must also be factored into the determination. The human carrying capacity of a specific area may be one hundred people with a hunting and gathering economy but may be one thousand people if their subsistence system was agriculture. However, if rainfall were low, the carrying capacity might be greater for hunter-gatherers than farmers; it all depends on environmental conditions, technology, and cultural practice. In addition, a single human group usually occupies more than one ecosystem, and so carrying capacity would be variable depending on conditions in each ecosystem; thus, an average would be calculated to describe the total carrying capacity. Moreover, people learn fast. A local inventor, or a strategic borrowing from the neighbors, can introduce an invention—perhaps a new maize variety, a new fertilizer, or a new irrigation device—that increases the local carrying capacity by an astonishing amount in a very short time.

Liebig's Law of the Minimum

The carrying capacity of a region can only be as high as its most limiting resource will permit. This principle of a limiting resource is known as **Liebig's Law of the Minimum** (or the "Convoy Principle," as the speed of the slowest ship determines the speed of the convoy). The limiting factor can be anything, such as food, water, temperature, or space. For example, if there is enough food to support fifty individuals, enough land for seventy-five individuals, but enough water for only thirty individuals, the carrying capacity is thirty, despite the abundance of food and land. In this case, water is the limiting or minimum factor; if the amount of water were increased, the carrying capacity would be correspondingly increased up to the level of the next minimum resource, that is, if water were increased to support eighty, the carrying capacity would rise to fifty, limited by the amount of food.

Whether it is resources or environmental and cultural conditions, all ecosystems are dynamic, so the minimum is often changing. In addition, human societies can be very innovative in seeking solutions to minimums. In fact, whole theories of economics are based on the inveterate tendency of humans to do this (Hayami and Ruttan 1985).

Boom and Bust Cycles

As noted above, carrying capacity is the measure of the maximum number of individuals that can be supported in a particular system for a specific amount of time. Carrying capacity will vary seasonally, annually, and over longer periods. Some species, such as many plants and some rodents, will enter boom cycles when resources are abundant, substantially increasing their populations. If the resources are short lived and the carrying capacity falls, the population will be too large and a bust cycle will result, with individuals starving until the population falls below the new carrying capacity (figure 2.6). As carrying capacity always fluctuates, these **boom and bust cycles** can be very common.

Human populations do not often go through such cycles, although they do happen for a variety of reasons, including wars and embargoes. Humans tend to stay below the carrying capacity of an area for several reasons. People can manipulate the environment and thus "control" their carrying capacity to some extent. Human culture provides a variety of solutions for resource shortages, including storage, trade, kinship assistance, and warfare. Humans almost never eat everything that is possible to consume in any particular environment, so they have the capability to expand their diet if the need arises.

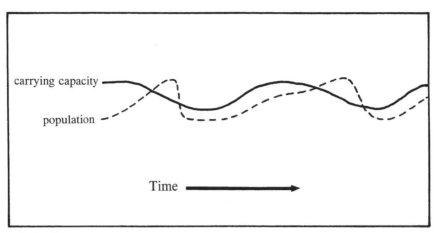

FIGURE 2.6
A model of boom and bust cycles.

ENERGY

All systems depend on energy. The first law of thermodynamics states that energy can be transformed but not created or destroyed, although it can move around within or between systems, such as plants converting light energy to chemical bond energy. The second law of thermodynamics holds that some energy always escapes in the conversion process from one level to another, that conversion is never 100 percent efficient. This energy is usually lost as heat, such as the heat generated within the body by muscles that do not completely convert their fuels. Thus, energy flow in the system is one way.

The vast majority of the energy used in natural systems is derived from the sun, although there are a few natural systems that are not solar powered, such as those fueled by heat from thermal vents in the ocean. Plants combine solar radiation with nutrients and water to manufacture matter, some of which is then consumed by animals, with both the plants and animals in turn eventually being consumed by decomposers. The nutrients are recycled in the system. Thus, energy and matter are converted in a series of trophic levels (see below).

Humans consume plants and/or other animals for food, converting that material into the energy required by the individual. This metabolic energy is used both for body maintenance and as fuel for any work performed, or it is converted into stored energy, such as fat (see Giampietro et al. 1993:242).

Energy in human systems is usually measured as "food energy," or the number of calories consumed. This number would be far less than the total available energy in a system because humans cannot consume all possible foods. While

calories are the items generally measured, others (e.g., protein) are also important factors in human systems. One must distinguish between subsistence energy
expenditure and total energy expenditure.

Humans also utilize supplemental energy, that derived from biological materials such as firewood, oil, and gas (see Giampietro et al. 1993:242). For most of
human history, such energy was derived from plants and animals used by people
to accomplish various tasks. For example, in 1850, about 91 percent of the energy
used in the United States came from burning wood and other biological materials (Pimentel et al. 1994:207). In about 2002, most of the supplemental energy
used by humans originated from fossil fuels such as gas, coal, and oil used to
power machinery, and fossil-fuel energy comprised some 81 percent of the energy
used in the United States. Thus, Americans now operate using a fuel-subsidized
system with manufactured fuels being used for various energy needs, such as
gasoline for plows. Efforts are being made to develop alternative energy sources
to replace fossil fuels, as they pollute the environment and are nonrenewable.
However, some (e.g., Price 1995) are very pessimistic about our ability to find
an appropriate alternative and predict the demise of industrialized culture as a
result.

The Trophic Pyramid

The **trophic pyramid** (figure 2.7) describes the levels of relationship among
producers, heterotrophs, and decomposers: what is eaten and how many conversions from solar energy have taken place. Humans utilize food resources from
several trophic levels, generally recognize the differences in energy, and usually
use those differences to their advantage.

Producers are species that can synthesize their own food, green plants being
the most common examples. Green plants take energy directly from the sun and
combine it with water, gases, and minerals to manufacture food in a process
called photosynthesis. Ultimately, we all depend on green plants to capture solar
energy and convert it into compounds that humans can consume or utilize. Producers are the initial level of the trophic pyramid and have the best energy conversion rate. Interestingly, a nonsolar energy source, hydrothermal vents in the
ocean floor, has recently been discovered that may support nonphotosynthesiz-
ing producers, such as vent worms. Studies currently are underway to determine
the role of these vents as energy sources separate from the sun.

Heterotrophs are species that consume other species as food, such as cows eating plants or people eating cows. Heterotrophs cannot directly utilize energy
from the sun and are able to obtain energy only by consuming producers or

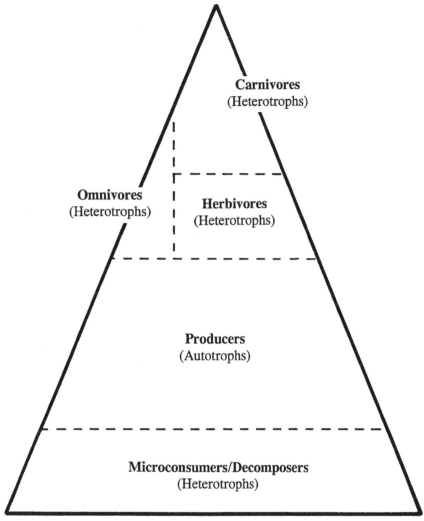

FIGURE 2.7
A generalized trophic pyramid.

other heterotrophs. The decomposers (technically heterotrophs) are small species, such as bacteria, that feed on dead organisms. They break down organic materials and allow the nutrients to be recycled to producers.

As one moves up the trophic pyramid, the number of species and individuals decreases; for example, there are fewer animals than plants and fewer carnivores than herbivores. The ratio between energy consumed and that converted to body mass is called the conversion ratio and is based on the second law of thermodynamics. For example, plants convert about 1 percent of the energy they receive from the sun to actual matter (a 100:1 ratio). Cows generally have a 10:1 conversion ratio (i.e., it takes one hundred calories of grass to make ten calories of cow), pigs have a 5:1 ratio, commercially grown chickens have about a 2:1 ratio (they do not move around much), and catfish that are fed on smaller fish rank an efficient 1.3:1 ratio. So if a person eats one calorie of beef, it would have taken one thousand calories of solar energy to produce it (i.e., one thousand solar calories to make ten calories of grass, to make the one calorie of cow).

It is obvious that humans need to stay as low as possible in the trophic pyramid to make the most efficient use of the environment. The prudent human diet should consist mostly of plant foods, which is precisely what anthropologists currently find in surveying diets around the world (e.g., Eaton and Eaton 1999). Exceptions occur in areas where almost all the plant material is tied up in cellulose (indigestible by humans), such as in the Canadian forests and parts of the Chaco of Paraguay, or where little plant material grows, such as in the Arctic. In such cases, people must live primarily on game or fish unless they can farm—still impossible in the Arctic and in many deserts.

The members of the different trophic levels form a **food chain**: a hierarchy of organisms that consume other organisms. For example, humans eat sharks that eat tuna that eat mackerel that eat squid that eat minnows that eat zooplankton that eat phytoplankton that capture solar energy. A *food web* is a series of food chains linked together by common threads. Food webs can be exceedingly complex. Disruptions of any one link of the food chain can result in disruptions in other links, ultimately affecting people.

In living systems, nutrients, energy, and information circulate through the food chain (figure 2.8) and are ultimately returned to the environment as the living entity dies and decomposes. Unlike energy, nutrients are recycled in circular paths and can be used over and over. Nutrients required by the human body are discussed in chapter 3.

Nutrients and other resources needed and/or used by human groups are unevenly distributed in the landscape and must be obtained, transported, and traded. Thus, human social structure and economics influence the paths of materials and are integral parts of material circulation.

Diet

Within the broad category of macroconsumers (animals) are several more detailed distinctions based on diet. A **herbivore** is an animal, such as a cow, that consumes mostly plants. Herbivores may have either generalized or specialized

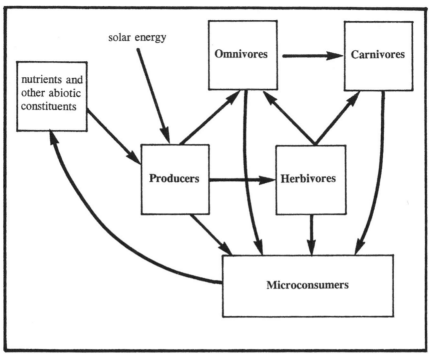

FIGURE 2.8
A generalized food chain showing trophic levels and circulation of nutrients.

diets, and some species may be very specialized, such as fruit eaters (frugivores), depending on conditions (niche). An omnivore is an animal, such as a human, that eats both plants and other animals. As such, omnivores can have quite a broad diet, although there are specialized omnivores. A **carnivore** is an animal, such as a shark, that primarily eats other animals, although carnivores may occasionally consume plant materials. Because carnivores often eat entire animals, they consume sufficient nutrients to ensure a balanced diet. This is not true for those who primarily eat muscle tissue.

Humans are omnivores; in general, our current diet averages between 80 percent and 90 percent plant foods and between 10 percent and 20 percent animal foods. This ratio makes perfect sense from a trophic and conversion perspective; there is much more plant material available to us. However, people cannot digest long-chain polysaccharides—cellulose and lignin, for example—and thus cannot consume the vast majority of plant material. We might be better off to eat ten pounds of hay, but we cannot; we have to cycle the hay through a cow to get any value from it at all. The vast amount of plant tissue that is taken up in wood is not edible by humans, but termites can eat it (thanks to symbiotic gut protozoa that digest cellulose), and termites are a major delicacy in parts of Africa. While it is possible to be a vegetarian, it is difficult to do so without extensive knowledge or dietary supplements.

Species Interactions

Species interact in a variety of ways, and humans will adopt one or all, depending on the situation. Some species directly compete for resources, with the loser suffering some negative consequence, such as extinction. A predator/prey relationship exists between many species, where the predator kills and consumes the prey. While this is of obvious benefit to the predator, it may also be of benefit to the prey, such as in keeping populations down or removing unfit members from the breeding pool of the prey. Such a relationship may be **symbiotic.**

These relationships are quite different from parasitism, where one organism (the parasite) exploits another (the host) to the benefit of the parasite and the detriment of the host. For example, many disease organisms are parasites, infecting and reproducing within the host and using the host to spread themselves and so ensure their survival. However, it is to the advantage of the parasite not to kill the host, at least not too quickly, so that it can successfully propagate. If the host dies too quickly, the disease will not spread, and the parasite will not be as successful. In essence, then, parasites have a tenuous relationship with their host, and they tend to coevolve, with the parasites becoming less detrimental and the host developing resistance.

In some cases, species will develop a relationship that is mutually beneficial. An example of this **mutualism** is the general relationship between dogs and humans. People provide dogs with food and habitat, and dogs provide people with companionship, labor, and other services.

CHAPTER SUMMARY

Ecology is the study of the interaction of organisms with their environment, defined as the surroundings in which the organism interacts, commonly called an ecosystem. Environments have both abiotic and biotic components in which all organisms interact. Biomes and ecozones, geographic regions defined by particular biotic communities, plus the ecotone between ecozones, are measured by productivity and diversity and commonly form the basis for initial analysis of ecological questions. Understanding change in ecozones is also important for analysis.

All organisms occupy a niche and live in a habitat, with humans having a very broad niche and occupying most habitats. However, one could view humans as occupying different niches, such as hunter-gatherer, herder, or farmer. Resources, things actually used by organisms, are important factors in defining and understanding niches and habitats.

The number of organisms an environment can support is called its carrying capacity and is dependent on the availability of necessary resources, with population limited by the least available resource. With humans, culture is also a key element, and cultural practices can significantly alter carrying capacity.

Energy is utilized and converted from one form to another, always with some loss. Materials move through the trophic pyramid, with plants converting solar energy into biomass, herbivores eating plants and converting it into tissue, carnivores eating herbivores and converting that tissue into new tissue, decomposers eventually eating everything, and that material being used by plants to make new biomass. All of these species exist in some relationship with each other, be it mutually beneficial, as predators or prey, or as parasites. Humans exist as all of these, depending on circumstance.

KEY TERMS
abiotic
biodiversity
biomass
biome
biosphere
biotic
boom and bust cycles
carnivore
carrying capacity
ecosystem
ecotone
ecozone
environment
environmental zone
food chain
habitat
herbivore
Liebig's Law of the Minimum

mutualism
niche
refugia
resource
succession
symbiotic
tether
trophic pyramid

3

Human Biological Ecology

Human biological ecology (HBE) is the study of the biological requirements of humans for survival, reproduction, and genetic success. Because culture plays a central role in fulfilling the biological aspects of human existence, there is considerable overlap between HBE and cultural ecology. As the focus of this book is on cultural adaptations, this chapter presents only a brief outline of the strict biological components of human existence, including nutrition, physical adaptations, and biological models of genetic success. An extensive discussion of HBE was presented by Kormondy and Brown (1998). An important application of HBE theory to conservation is provided by Borgerhoff Mulder and Coppolillo in their excellent book *Conservation* (2005).

HUMANS AS ANIMALS

Biologically, all humans are almost identical. Cultures vary enormously, and sometimes the anthropologist almost despairs of finding any common threads among them. Yet humans are all one biological group, the genus and species *Homo sapiens*, and are very closely related genetically. Indeed, living humans all belong to one subspecies, *H. sapiens sapiens*.

It is important to consider human needs in the context of human biology. Different human populations do vary in a few important ways. Some groups of people need less food than others because of smaller body size. Some groups can resist a particular disease better than others. On the whole, however, humans are remarkably uniform creatures. No differences in intellectual or behavioral abilities and tendencies have been conclusively demonstrated among human populations. (Actually, homogeneity is true of most species. Domesticated species, such as horses and dogs, are interesting exceptions, as humans have purposefully bred physical and behavioral differences into the various types of domesticates.)

Like all animals, humans are subject to stress, conditions that require a response, either short or long term. We have biological requirements and tolerances and must operate within certain environmental parameters. We require adequate temperature, oxygen, health, nutrition, and a few other things that must fall within a range of tolerance with certain minimums and maximums (the Law of Tolerance). The body needs to maintain itself at about 98 degrees and has a rather narrow range of tolerance, between about 85 degrees and 105 degrees. Outside this range, the brain will not operate properly and the individual will die. Humans must also operate within a certain range of oxygen concentration. As we cool ourselves by sweating, we have to have relatively more water than most other animals. Finally, we must maintain some level of health and nutrition in order to function and reproduce.

BIOLOGICAL ADAPTATIONS

Like all other life forms, humans adapt biologically to changing environmental conditions. These responses fall into two broad categories, **physiological adaptations** and **anatomical adaptations**, and species will manifest aspects of both types of adaptation to changing conditions (table 3.1). However, with the advent of culture and the increasing complexity of technology, cultural adaptations are becoming increasingly important.

Physiological Adaptations

Physiological adaptations are relatively short-term changes in the body in response to rapid changes in environment. Genetics and selection determine the presence of these mechanisms, but environmental conditions determine whether they are used. For example, the presence of sweat glands in the skin is genetic, but they do not produce sweat unless the body is warm. If the environment becomes hotter and the body is constantly warm, there may be selective pressure for a greater number of sweat glands in the skin of subsequent generations. Thus, there is an interplay between physiological and anatomical adaptations.

Some of the most common stressors that require physiological adaptations include excesses in sunlight, altitude, cold, heat, malnutrition, and disease (see Kormondy and Brown 1998:162–226). Two basic physiological responses are defined here: primary and secondary. Primary responses, often called acclimatization, are immediate, occurring within minutes or days. These may include alterations in

Table 3.1. Biological Adaptations to Some Stressors

Stressor	Primary Physiological Adaptations	Secondary Physiological Adaptations	Anatomical Adaptations
Sunlight	Production of melanin in the skin, resulting in a tan	Continued and increasing melanin production, deepening of tan	Genetic selection for darker skin
Altitude	Increased respiration, blood pressure, and heart rate	Increase in red blood cell production, increase in number of mitochrondria, expansion of vascular system	Enlargement of lung and chest size, increase in size and thickness of placenta
Heat	Sweating, increased respiration, blood pressure, and heart rate	General peripheral vasodilation (GPVD)	Elongation of body and extremities, increase in number of sweat glands
Cold	Shivering, cold-induced vasoconstriction (CIVC)	Systemic, whole-body physiological responses	"Rounding" of body, shortening of extremities, addition of fat layer
Malnutrition	Reduction in stomach tension, mobilization of stored sugars, then fats, then proteins	Decrease in ability to work, decrease in muscle and body mass, reduction in metabolic rate, growth arrestment and resorption of vital nutrients from body tissues	Genetic changes in rates of metabolism, propensity to develop problems such as diabetes, reduction of body size to adjust to fewer nutrients
Disease	Autoimmune response, macrophagic activity	Decrease in ability to work, reduction in metabolic rate	Changes in genotype to reflect the development of genetic resistance through selection

metabolism, respiration, blood distribution, sweating, and many other responses. Secondary responses may take months or even years and can include changes in fertility, work abilities, and even population distributions.

An example of people moving from a low to a high altitude will illustrate both adaptations. Upon their arrival at the high-elevation place, people will experience oxygen deprivation (hypoxia) due to lower atmospheric pressure by which oxygen passes through the membranes of the lung. The primary physiological response will be increased respiration, blood pressure, and heart rate, as well as the dilation of blood vessels. These measures suffice until secondary responses can be initiated. Secondary responses take longer and include an increase in the production of red blood cells, an increase in mitochondria in the cells (which transform oxygen and sugars to energy at the cellular level), and an expansion of the vascular network.

A series of cultural adaptations may also be taken. The ability of people to work will be lower, and adjustments to work schedules may be needed. Lower oxygen pressures may also cause increases in miscarriages, and in some cases, females are temporarily moved to lower altitudes to give birth. Interestingly, European females generally have difficulty reproducing at high altitudes; therefore, during the period of European colonization in the Andes, few European settlements were established there. An additional cultural adaptation to high altitude in the Andes is the use of drugs (e.g., coca leaves) to mitigate the effects of lower oxygen availability.

Physiological adjustments to cold climates include the variation of blood flow to exposed skin surfaces such that heat loss is reduced and tissues are kept alive. Another adaptation is an increase in metabolic rate, which burns energy at a higher rate, a condition that requires a greater daily caloric intake. Cultural adaptations to cold include the use of fire and clothing (skins or other materials). In addition, alcohol is used in some cultures as a means to keep warm for short periods, as it increases blood flow to the extremities.

Anatomical Adaptations

Anatomical adaptations are long-term genetic changes in genotype (and so phenotype) due to selective pressures. Unlike physiological adaptations, anatomical adaptations reflect changes that are passed to subsequent generations. If the people discussed above in the example of physiological adaptations to high altitude stayed there long enough, those with larger lung capacities would be more successful, have more children with larger lung capacities, and eventually outcompete those with smaller, less efficient, lung capacities. In time, increased lung capacity and a resultant enlargement of the chest cavity would be selected for and become the dominant phenotype. Indeed, people adapted to high altitudes, such as in the Andes of South America, have larger torsos and lung capacities than people at lower altitudes.

Humans will also adapt anatomically through alteration of basic body structure. To help regulate temperature, the shape of the body will evolve to have either more or less surface area, known as Bergmann's Rule. For example, in cold environments, a shorter, rounder, more compact body is more efficient to preserve heat. The rounder the body, the less surface area there is through which heat can escape; thus, being short and round is adaptive in cold environments. In warmer climates, a tall, lean body is more efficient for temperature regulation.

Other examples of anatomical adaptation to cold include the reduction of extremities, such as short noses and ears to prevent frostbite (Allen's Rule), and the addition of a fat layer, both for insulation and energy reserves.

HUMAN POPULATION REGULATION

All species face the problem of maintaining their populations within the carrying capacity of the environment. Human populations grew slowly (at an annual rate of under 0.001 percent) for millions of years, reaching perhaps about ten million at the end of the Pleistocene (the last Ice Age; see Hassan 1980; Kormondy and Brown 1998; Molnar and Molnar 2000). With the advent of agriculture some ten thousand years ago, human population skyrocketed to the six billion of today, with an annual growth rate of about 2 percent. A variety of factors influences population growth and size, primarily the natural aspects of infant mortality, predators, disease, food supply, and habitat size. Humans, of course, add the dimension of culture (see Cowgill 1975; Campbell and Wood 1994; Molnar and Molnar 2000).

Life expectancy is closely related to population growth and is high and rising in most nations, mostly due to declining infant mortality. In prehistoric and early historic times, life expectancy was around thirty years. Today, thanks to better diet and medical care, people are living well into their seventies in all developed countries, and to over eighty in Japan and Iceland. Only the poorest nations have life expectancies below sixty.

Life expectancy is not actually a measure of how long you can expect to live. It is the average age at death of all the people who died in a particular year (as it is measured in the United States). If two people are born at the same time, and one dies at one day of age and the other lives to be seventy, the average life expectancy is thirty-five $(0 + 70 \sqrt 2 = 35)$. Such a figure can be misleading and may actually reflect a high infant mortality rate rather than how old most people are when they die. In most cultures, if a person survives past four or five years of age, he or she can usually expect to live a fairly long life.

Natural Mechanisms

Predators

Predators are a major problem with most species, but not with humans. No animal habitually hunts humans as a major portion of its diet. Parasites, perhaps a form of predator, do impact human populations. They rarely cause death but are vectors of disease.

Disease

~~Human populations have most typically been regulated by disease~~—apparently a rather rare (but far from unknown) regulator of population size among other species. Infectious diseases have been prevalent throughout most of history, but since the conquest of most of them in the past two centuries, the noninfectious killers—heart disease, cancer, diabetes, and so on—have expanded to fill the gap (see Kormondy and Brown 1998:227–252; Molnar and Molnar 2000:210–247). Tobacco and alcohol—both voluntary choices—have become the biggest killers in the developed world. Environmental pollution is becoming a serious factor and can only worsen. Meanwhile, starvation and infectious diseases remain pervasive in poor nations.

Cultural Mechanisms

The natural aspects of predation, disease, food supply, and habitat size control the population of most species, but humans employ culture (including technology) in an attempt to bypass these factors. Nevertheless, humans are still faced with population control issues. Thomas Malthus (1960) presented an argument that people, like mice, would automatically breed up to and beyond the food supply (carrying capacity), causing food shortages and thus population crashes (boom and bust). Malthus argued that the Four Horsemen of the Apocalypse, traditionally identified as War, Famine, Plague, and Death, set the human population limit. However, human population growth is not automatic but is regulated by conscious and unconscious human factors. Humans manipulate the environment and food supply and employ a variety of cultural rules designed to prevent a too-rapid increase.

Medical intervention is a cultural mechanism and has had a great effect on population growth. Both population size and life expectancy are related to declining infant mortality rates, a direct result of improving medical services. More effective and more available medicine also influences the distribution and impact of disease and malnutrition on the population. For example, the major effort to eliminate polio through inoculation was successful until everyone thought the disease was eradicated. The inoculations were discontinued and the disease returned, and inoculations had to be resumed. Medical science has also given us effective birth-control techniques, allowing people to limit their population growth to roughly replacement levels wherever the new birth-control technologies and other health-care facilities are easily available.

Traditional coping methods are less pleasant and more disruptive. The ecology of migration, displacement, and conflict in the modern world has been treated by Bender and Winer (2001).

Food Supply

Unlike other animals, humans manipulate and manage their food supplies, can improve and/or intensify existing food supplies (commonly referred to as the Green Revolution), expand their habitat (e.g., creating new agricultural lands), and even expand their niche by exploiting new foods. In contrast to the Malthus model, Boserup (1965) and Cohen (1977) argued that population growth had the effect of forcing people to intensify their food production to meet the challenge. This does happen sometimes, but, on the other hand, groups faced with population problems are prone to engage in warfare, to emigrate, or to break up into smaller groups rather than intensify food production. Intensification occurs when other means of coping with the situation are unavailable or undesirable. Peasant cultivators need labor on their farms, so high birthrates are encouraged. Often they are prevented by their governments from emigrating or fighting. Thus, peasants have often intensified.

Famine is a leading cause of moderate or severe malnutrition and is typically associated with agricultural groups. The causes of famine are varied. They are sometimes natural, such as floods destroying crops and extended drought, but are generally due to cultural factors, such as war or embargo. In some instances, the "natural" cause (e.g., flooding) is actually cultural in origin (e.g., deforestation). Amartya Sen (e.g., 1999) has pointed out that no natural famines have occurred since the Great Depression. Famines since are all political; there has always been plenty of available food or capacity to produce it, but leadership or security has been wanting.

Malnutrition affects much of the population of the world—at least a billion people—and is perhaps the largest single cause of death in undeveloped or underdeveloped countries. Malnutrition occurs in several levels of severity. Many populations exist in a slightly malnourished state, a condition in which they can work and reproduce, but not optimally. Moderate malnutrition involves the disruption of the functional abilities of the individual or population, and severe malnutrition is a life-threatening situation, often leading to death.

Birth Control

Every group of people on earth employs techniques to control the number and timing of births. This type of control includes planning, sexual abstinence, and the use of birth-control devices or drugs. Abortion, often a result of poor planning, is also employed by some cultures as a birth-control measure.

Some groups breast-feed for fairly extended periods, up to four years. The fertility of a lactating female is reduced by at least 50 percent. So, other things being equal, the longer a woman lactates, the less likely she is to become pregnant.

Thus, long-term breast-feeding is one technique to space births and is purposefully employed by some groups, including many hunter-gatherers, to help control population (see Lee 1982; Kelly 1995).

The Western medical system has been introduced in much of the world. For religious and ideological reasons, which all too often are no more than that same desire to keep women repressed, birth control has not been introduced as aggressively as other public health measures have. Controlling the death rate without controlling the birthrate simply leads to more and more misery in most of the world. Where birth-control information and technology has been provided, it has led to a reduction in birthrates and, often, to much higher levels of rural health and security. Introducing the full range of birth-control techniques can also reduce abortion and infanticide.

Infanticide

Once born, infants may be killed for various reasons. Infanticide rates of 30 percent or even 50 percent (Smith 1977; Hrdy 1999) have been documented for extremely densely populated regions. Cultures that frown on outright infanticide may allow selective neglect, a virtually certain sentence of death in disease-ridden, food-short areas. Infanticide in dense agricultural communities usually targets females and thus is particularly effective at controlling population (Divale and Harris 1976) and at generating enough males to labor in the fields. In spite of the availability of birth-control technology, female infanticide is still common in many areas of the world.

For example, among the Inuit, life was difficult and hunting was very dangerous, resulting in a high adult male mortality rate and a constant shortage of males. In times of severe and chronic food shortages, a family may not be able to support a newborn without endangering the entire group. In such cases, infanticide might be practiced, but it was always a traumatic decision. Due to the shortage of males, they were more valued and more likely to be kept as infants, leading to a higher incidence of female infanticide. Infanticide was not considered to be murder since a baby was not a person until named and would later be reincarnated in more favorable times (see Condon et al. 1996). One of us (ENA) has studied the same general matter in China. Contrary to some reports, Chinese parents agonize and suffer over the decision to sacrifice or abandon a child, but economic necessity intervenes. Lack of naming and hopes of reincarnation again soothe feelings somewhat.

Geronticide

Geronticide, the killing of old people, is rare. Such people are no longer of reproductive age, and their loss has little direct impact on population numbers.

However, they do consume resources that might be better allocated to younger people during times of stress, and some groups place a high social value on old people committing suicide during famines. On the other hand, the retention of the knowledge of the older people could be a distinct adaptive advantage. Respect for elders is thus universal in human societies, but gerontocide is known from a few, all in areas of extreme food insecurity such as the Arctic and the cold deserts of Nevada.

Warfare

Warfare is commonly seen as a major factor in population regulation. In reality, the death rate of males in small-scale warfare is usually low, and such losses have virtually no influence on population size. There are, however, some notable exceptions, such as the Pawnees in North America (Wishart 1979) and the Waorani and several other groups in South America (Robarchek and Robarchek 1998). Warfare is common in most societies (LeBlanc and Register 2002) and does sometimes reduce population drastically; the Mongol and Turkic conquests of central Asia may be recalled. Even today, conventional warfare, in spite of large numbers of deaths, is still only a relatively minor factor in population regulation. Nuclear war, however, would probably have a profound effect on population size and growth due to the massive number of deaths, especially in regions like southern Asia (e.g., India and Pakistan).

Divale and Harris (1976; also see Ember [1982] and Harris [1984]) looked at the issue of small-scale warfare from a different angle. They argued that in small-scale societies, warfare functioned to control population not through combat deaths of males, but through the presence of a "male supremacist complex" where the males instituted a female infanticide program to favor males (warriors) and thus reduced the growth rate of the population. This has not been confirmed and seems unlikely.

The Future of the Human Population

The human carrying capacity of the earth is unknown, but estimates have ranged from one billion to one trillion (Postel 1994; Cohen 1995; Molnar and Molnar 2000; Smil 2000). From the 6.5 billion people of 2008, it is estimated that with current agricultural technology, the population of the earth will be more than ten billion people in 2050. We doubt that the world can support many more than that. However, new and unexpected innovations in agriculture, storage technology, and transport could substantially increase this figure. On the other hand, pollution and the continued loss of topsoil, forests, safe water, and other vital resources could substantially reduce it. In addition, administrative problems beset application of the best agricultural technology. The question is how much of the leveling off will be due to the demographic transition from high birthrates to lower ones (as in many industrialized countries) and how much to Malthus's Four Horsemen. Current population increase rates do not inspire much hope, although some experts are optimistic (Smil 2000).

All industrial countries today have low birthrates and low death rates, and many are at "zero population growth," with just over two children per woman. By contrast, women in frontier agrarian societies, where labor is especially valued, often have fifteen or even more children.

NUTRITION

Nutrition is a measure of the ability of the diet to maintain the body. It is the raw materials, consumed in the form of "food," needed by the body to function properly (see Johnston [1987] and Anderson [2005a] for anthropological perspectives or Shils et al. [2006] for the whole formidable story in 2,146 pages). These raw materials include protein, carbohydrates, fats, vitamins, and minerals (plus fiber). As body conditions change, such as illness, seasonal variations in food availability, or pregnancy, so do nutritional requirements. These changes in requirements are poorly known (Leslie et al. 1984) and are generally estimated from studies of the general average daily nutritional requirements for people currently living in the United States.

Such recommended daily allowance (RDA) figures probably are not directly applicable to non-Western populations. Requirements needed for growth, reproduction, and physical activity will vary depending on conditions (e.g., Froment 2001; Jenike 2001). For example, individuals in the tropics existing in a chronic state of malnutrition and disease would have very different minimal requirements from those of an individual Inuit living in low temperatures. The daily caloric intake of extant hunter-gatherers in different regions is known to vary, from between 1,600 and 3,827 calories (Jenike 2001:Table 8.2), but seasonal changes in need or food availability can drastically alter these numbers (Jenike 2001:Table 8.3).

However, the RDA figures are still worth considering as a baseline estimate. For example, young persons (eleven to twenty-two years old) require more calories than older ones, but protein requirements typically increase with age and size. Also noteworthy is that pregnant and lactating females require more nutrition, especially minerals and B vitamins (see Thomson et al. 1970; Nerlove 1974; Garber 1987:353, 357 and references therein). Thomson and colleagues (1970:571; also see MacLean 1984) estimated that during lactation, the energy requirements of the human mother increase by about six hundred calories, while Duhring (1984:Table 1) estimated an increase of about five hundred calories. Women normally store brown fat (a special form of easily mobilized fat) in their shoulders and elsewhere during pregnancy and draw it down to produce milk. Human milk is higher in almost all nutrients than cows' milk and needs the extra energy input.

No one food can supply all of the necessary nutrients for optimal human health. Even mother's milk, ideal for infants, has too little iron and vitamin C for toddlers. Many important foods have ingredients that are dangerous in high quantities; for example, acorns must be processed to remove tannic acid. Meat and animal fat contain long-chain saturated fats that can lead to an excessive cholesterol buildup. Thus, every culture must contain rules and guidelines for a varied, nutrient-rich, adequate, and safe diet. Simply assuring that enough calories and protein are consumed is not sufficient.

Garber (1987:353, 357) noted that most mammalian species, including primates, do not generally store fat prior to conception but often will change their feeding habits during pregnancy to "accommodate the nutritional costs of lactation [by increasing] their feeding time and/or exploit[ing] higher-quality food resources." Chimpanzees, on the other hand, are believed to practice such preconception nutritional preparation (see McGrew 1981:41) as they expand their diets during estrus. Humans (and other animals) experience "cravings" to eat certain foods at various times. This may be explained as the body "telling" the individual that it needs certain nutrients, but it may sometimes simply be a bad habit. The diets of people in most cultures are sufficiently broad to provide these various nutrients. In Western societies, with narrow diets and highly processed foods, supplements are frequently consumed, such as daily vitamins, protein supplements, enriched bread, vitamin D–enriched milk, and iodized salt (exactly how much supplementation is actually needed is not clear). While it is true that most traditional societies did not know about specific nutrients or quantify their intake as do Western cultures, they certainly were aware of the consequences of not having enough of certain foods.

Calories often are used as the measurement or currency of "proper" nutrition (see below). However, those using calories as the prime currency ignore the requirements of other nutrients and assume that the subjects are in good health and have no special needs. However, when caloric (and other needs) are not met on a consistent basis, people will die.

A response to inadequate food supplies is to exist and survive in a malnourished condition. In such circumstances, people are not "healthy" by Western standards; some are undersized, are unable to work, have a lower reproduction rate, suffer more sickness, die younger, or have improper development. Yet as a biological population, they survive. This last point is worth noting: Western societies believe that perfect health is normal and that it is abnormal to be in less than perfect health. The opposite is more likely true, as most people throughout history have had a rough time when it comes to diet.

Calories

Calories are units of energy; one "small" calorie is calculated as the energy needed to raise the temperature of one gram of water one degree centigrade. Human nutrition, however, is reckoned in "large" calories, equal to one thousand small calories. Some 70 percent of calories consumed by humans are utilized to maintain body temperature at about ninety-eight degrees, the temperature at which the brain and other metabolic functions work best.

Caloric requirements have been calculated only generally and only for people in industrialized societies (table 3.2), and the caloric needs of humans living in non-Western societies or in the past are not known. However, the data do provide a general estimate of human needs, recognizing that the requirements vary by condition, as noted above for pregnant or lactating females.

Carbohydrates

Carbohydrates are a class of compounds that include starches, sugars, and cellulose. Simple sugars, such as glucose and fructose, are produced in plants and can be combined and stored as starches or double sugars, such as sucrose or lactose. When these substances are consumed, they are again broken down into simple sugars, which provide energy for the animals that ate them. Cellulose is not digestible by humans, but it is an important source of fiber. Glucose is a very important sugar, as it is the only energy supply for the brain. Humans can break down double sugars to release glucose.

Table 3.2.   General Daily Caloric Needs

Age	Children (both sexes)	Males	Females
1–3	1,300	—	—
4–6	1,800	—	—
7–10	2,000	—	—
11–14	—	2,500	2,200
15–18	—	3,000	2,200
19–24	—	2,900	2,200
25–50	—	2,900	2,200
51+	—	2,300	1,900

Note: Adapted from Whitney and Rolfes (1996:Table G-3).

Most cultures obtain the majority of their calories from starch, such as rice or potatoes. A few societies consume large quantities of sugar, such as the Rotinese in eastern Indonesia, who eat a great deal of palm sap (Fox 1977). In this case, the various products of the palm (sap and leaves, the latter of which is made into a bewildering array of products from houses to fishing lines) form the basis of the entire economy and have resulted in a stable economic system that operates without much environmental damage. In nearby regions where palms are not so abundant, people employ a swidden, or shifting cultivation, system.

Protein and Fat

Proteins are complex combinations of amino acids. The protein is broken down, "liberating" the amino acids, which are then used as building blocks for proteins in the consumer or converted into fuel. Twenty-two amino acids are necessary in human nutrition. Some of these can be manufactured by the body in adequate quantities, others can be manufactured but only slowly, and a number cannot be manufactured by the body at all and must be obtained from foods. The last group are called essential amino acids (lysine, leucine, isoleucine, methionine, phenylalanine, threonine, tryptophan, and valine) and must be included in the diet. Proteins contain different amounts of the various amino acids. A deficiency in the intake of new protein will result in the body reusing some of its old protein, that is, proteins from the body will be broken down to provide amino acids for new protein synthesis. This will cause the body to waste away as it digests itself, beginning with muscle tissues. At the extreme, if the body must digest the heart muscle, death ensues. Protein is expensive for plants to produce and so is rarely found in high concentrations; it is found in higher concentrations in animals that eat plants.

Protein containing all of the essential amino acids can be found in various plants, and it is possible for a person to achieve optimal health by consuming only plants. However, being a strict vegetarian requires an extensive knowledge about which combinations of plants must be eaten, in what sequence, and with what frequency to maintain proper nutrition. In any case, it is necessary to have vitamin B12 in the diet, and that must be obtained either from animal or fungal sources or from artificial supplements. Being a strict vegetarian is very difficult, and most people lack the requisite knowledge. Most simply consume some animal flesh, or at least milk and eggs, to meet their overall protein needs.

One example of how cultures may deal with protein deficiencies is that of the bean/corn (maize) complex of Mesoamerica. Beans are generally high in protein but low in lysine, while corn contains little protein but more lysine. Eating beans and corn (squash may also contribute) in combination provides a more balanced protein source. A recent problem is that the new hybrid corn varieties are often low in lysine, and nutritional problems appear where hybrid varieties have replaced native varieties.

Some cultures, such as the Inuit, have a diet high in animal protein. In diets high in meat, it is necessary to ensure that sufficient fat and/or carbohydrates are included. This is due to the fact that lean meat is low in calories and also produces nitrogenous waste products whose elimination stresses the liver and kidneys. In addition, the lack of fat makes it difficult to utilize the fat-soluble vitamins, forcing the body to used stored fat for that purpose. Thus, in a diet high in lean meat, it may actually be that it costs more calories to digest the food than its caloric value, resulting in a state of malnutrition (Speth and Spielmann 1983).

Fat (lipids) occurs in several forms in the body, the most abundant being storage fat. Storage fat contains about double the energy content of carbohydrates and serves as a reserve source of energy. In general, fats contain about twice as many calories per gram as either protein or carbohydrates. In addition to being important as an energy source, fats also are necessary to activate fat-soluble vitamins. Of fats, the omega-6 and omega-3 fatty acids are necessary for survival and should be in balance (roughly equal amounts in the diet) for optimal health. Modern urbanites generally get too much omega-6 and too little omega-3, a problem that is now well aired in the media.

Vitamins and Minerals

Vitamins are organic compounds needed to maintain certain body functions. Most cannot be manufactured in the body and so must be obtained in the diet. The body requires a variety of vitamins, some in fairly large quantities and some in very small amounts. Some vitamins are fat soluble and can be stored in the body for long periods. Others are water soluble and are easily lost in the process of cooking and by the body during urination. The major vitamins include A, the B complex, C, D, E, and K, although many others also are required (see table 3.3). An example of fast-breaking news in nutrition is the rise of folic acid, unknown until the mid-twentieth century and shown in the 1990s to be necessary in large amounts for pregnancy. A very large percentage of birth defects is due to poor folic acid nutrition. In the 2000s, yet further research showed that substantial amounts of folic acid improve immune system performance and decrease risks of many degenerative conditions.

Minerals are inorganic substances (elements or compounds), and many are needed by the body for a number of functions, including bone formation. While

Table 3.3. Vitamins Important for Proper Nutrition

Vitamin	Solubility	Sources	Required For
Retinol (A)	Fat	Liver, milk, carotene in plants	Vision, maintenance of skin, respiratory tissues, bone growth
Thiamin (B1)	Water	Meats, grains, vegetables	Maintenance of nervous and cardiovascular systems
Riboflavin (B2)	Water	Milk, green vegetables, grains	Vision, energy metabolism, and skin maintenance
Niacin	Water	Meats, cereals, eggs	Metabolism of energy, synthesis of fatty acids
Pyridoxine (B6)	Water	Meats, vegetables, grains	Metabolism of amino acids
Cobalamin (B12)	Water	Many animal foods	Synthesis of fat
Ascorbic acid (C)	Water	Fresh fruits and vegetables	Many metabolic functions
Dehydroxy vitamin D	Fat	Milk, fish oil (or exposure to) sunlight	Absorption of calcium and phosphorus in the intestines
Tocopherol (E)	Fat	Vegetable oils	Protects vitamin A and some fatty acids
K	Fat	Vegetables, milk	Variety of functions, including blood clotting

the overall content of minerals in the body is small, such elements are vital (e.g., iron is absolutely necessary for the blood) and are integral parts of many organic compounds. Sodium (salt), potassium, iodine, and manganese are some of the most essential minerals (see table 3.4).

EVOLUTIONARY ECOLOGY

A relatively new way to investigate human behavior is evolutionary ecology, an approach that applies natural selection theory to the choices made by people (see Smith and Winterhalder 1992; Winterhalder and Smith 1992; Boyd and Richerson 2005; Richerson and Boyd 2005). It is related to human behavioral ecology (discussed in chapter 1). Originally developed by biologists (e.g., Fox et al. 2001), evolutionary ecology can be used to apply general biological principles to humans, primarily in modeling resource use. An advantage in using such models is in their testability and reliance on quantitative methods (e.g., statistics), thus allowing a more objective and comparable analysis. Archaeologists also employ evolutionary ecology in the study of past groups (see the Special Issue of *World Archaeology*, vol. 34, no. 1, 2002).

Evolutionary ecology begins with the general premise that specific human behaviors are the functional equivalent of biological traits. Thus, different behaviors are seen as trait variation subjected to selective pressure. Selection

Table 3.4. Minerals Important for Proper Nutrition

Mineral	Sources	Required For
Calcium	Dairy foods, leafy vegetables	Bones and teeth, blood clotting, movement of ions
Chloride	Many foods	Stomach acid
Magnesium	Nuts, legumes, cereals, seafood	Protein synthesis
Potassium	Fruits, potatoes	Nerve transmission, muscle contraction
Phosphorus	Animal protein	Bones and teeth, cell membranes
Sodium	Many foods, flavoring	Nerve transmission, muscle contraction
Sulfur	Many foods, meats	Proteins, B vitamins
Copper	Cereals, legumes, shellfish, fruits, vegetables	Hemoglobin, cell respiration
Iodine	Seafood	Thyroid hormone
Iron	Organ meats, nuts, leafy vegetables	Blood, enzymes
Manganese	Cereals, legumes	Bone development
Zinc	Whole grains, fish, milk, eggs	Enzymes, insulin, wound healing, DNA synthesis

then acts on these traits, with the outcome depending on the particular situation (Richerson and Boyd 1992; Fog 1999; also see Dunbar et al. 1999; Moran 2006, 2008).

If people are doing things that do not work well in a given environment, or if they fail to change their practices as conditions change, they will suffer consequences. They may have to move, be incorporated into another culture, or, in the extreme, die. If other people enter an area with different cultural ways, the two may compete if they occupy the same niche, with the best adapted replacing or absorbing the other. This is analogous to biological evolution, where one group of organisms competes with another for space and resources. Remember that flexibility, the ability to change with changing conditions, is itself an important and highly adaptive trait.

Optimization Models

The primary approach used in evolutionary ecology is the study of **optimization,** through the application of **optimization models.** Optimization models are used to explain some aspects of behavior related to the utilization of resources (Jochim 1983:157), usually on a least-cost basis. Originally developed by economists, optimization models were borrowed by biologists to model and predict the behavior of animals in relation to their diet and feeding strategy. They were then borrowed from biology by anthropologists and applied to humans (see Winterhalder 1981; Smith 1983). The central theoretical tenet of these models in anthropology is that humans will adopt "optimal" behaviors to maximize their reproductive success. The optimal behaviors are generally limited to diet based on the premise that, in the long run, one must make more than one spends to survive, a cost-benefit formula that is obviously true. In essence then, resources are ranked relatively to one another based on net return, and a model is constructed that predicts which resources will be used in the diet.

All optimization models operate with a number of working assumptions. The most basic of these assumptions is that humans will behave as do other life forms, that behavior is designed solely to maximize evolutionary (reproductive) success. In making this initial assumption, the models rigidly adhere to rules of cost and benefit, mostly ignoring cultural factors that may override such behaviors. Further, following rational choice theory, optimization models assume that people are rational choosers, a big assumption (as discussed in chapter 1). Importantly, optimization models do not assume that people/cultures make perfect decisions. In fact, optimization models function as ideals against which actual behavior can be compared.

Optimization models are now widely applied by human ecologists, being attractive due to their relative simplicity and their ability to generate empirical data and testable models (e.g., Thomas 1986:254). Optimization models describe small-scale events and detail conditions and behavior over a limited period of time and space. The sum of these behaviors can then be used to explore large scale trends in adaptation (e.g., Pyke et al. 1977:140). Archaeologists find optimization models very useful as a first estimation in the attempt to reconstruct past societies (Winterhalder and Smith 1981; Jochim 1983:158). It has been said that optimization models are a "60 percent solution" to human behavior (a quote attributed to the late Glynn Isaac) because the models account only for biological, and not cultural, behavior. However, newer models are beginning to take culture into account (Goldschmidt 2004; Boyd and Richerson 2005; Richerson and Boyd 2005).

All optimization models have four basic components (Gardner 1992:18). Each requires (1) an actor to choose among the different alternatives, (2) a currency by which the payoff of the decisions can be measured, (3) some range of resources available to the actor, and (4) a set of constraints, factors that limit the alternatives and payoffs. In the study of human systems, the actors in optimization models are the people of the culture being studied.

Currency

All optimization models use a currency, some measure of cost and benefit that can be quantified. Possible currencies (see Jochim 1998:20) include energy, nutrients, information, goals of the actor(s), constraints in the environment, risk, options or choices (Smith 1983:626), or even material items such as hides (e.g., Keene 1979:390). Energy, measured in calories, is the most preferred currency (Pyke et al. 1977:138; O'Connell and Hawkes 1984:530) as they are easily quantified and measurable in foods and as calories expended in work. Other currencies are more difficult to measure and calculate, and some are so intertwined in culture and difficult to deal with that they are often "factored out of the analysis or reduced to residual behavior" (Keene 1983:141).

Net return is often quantified in calories per hour. However, the use of energy alone may result in a poor estimation of the potential of any given area, because it may be that other nutrients, such as vitamins (Reidhead 1979:558), fat (Speth and Spielmann 1983:18–19), or protein (see Jochim 1998:20) are more important. These problems are understood but are generally ignored because, at least for now, optimization models have to be simple in order to even begin to gain a general understanding of complex human behavior (e.g., Hawkes and O'Connell 1985:401; Jochim 1998:21).

The Resource Universe

To build any optimization model, it is necessary to know the resource universe, those resources that were available and utilized by the group under study. Resource universes are constructed by first using contemporary and/or paleobiological data to determine the presence and distribution of resources. Next, ethnographic data are employed to determine which resources were used. In archaeological studies, ethnographic data are used as an analogy to model the behavior of the prehistoric group.

In optimization models, resources are ranked relative to one another, generally by their overall return rate. If the resource universe is incomplete, that is, if resources are missing from the list, there will be an error of unknown magnitude in modeling the diet. Considerable further complication could result if the data on resource distribution are faulty and/or if the ethnographic data on the known resources are incomplete or erroneous. Last, some dietary elements are poorly preserved in the archaeological record, and if not recovered, an error in interpretation could occur.

Constraints

A number of other factors influence the construction, analysis, and interpretation of optimization models, including an incomplete understanding of human nutritional requirements, an uncertainty of the various costs associated with resource exploitation, and a working assumption of complete information. In addition, human culture tends to interfere with the simple cost-benefit formula of optimization models in that social obligations, preferences, and the use of storage can greatly influence actual behavior.

Nutritional Needs. The application of optimization models requires some understanding of the nutritional needs of the people under study. However, as noted elsewhere in this chapter, few such data have been compiled, and only a general estimate of the nutritional needs of people in contemporary Western culture has been made. Thus, the nutritional needs of traditional or past peoples are usually just estimated based on those data.

It is also important that the nutritional content of the various resources be determined. Fortunately, this is a now rather simple process conducted by sending some of the material to a food laboratory and having a machine determine the numbers. However, for the people under study to have made decisions regarding which resources to use, they also would have had to be aware of the nutritional content of the resources. Although lacking machines to provide numbers of calories per gram, most researchers agree that such information was generally available to traditional peoples as a result of thousands of years of experimentation and practical knowledge.

Exploitation Costs. The most difficult aspect of building an optimization model is the computation of the costs involved in resource exploitation. To determine procurement cost, one must calculate a whole series of figures based on the calories expended to complete each of the tasks associated with finding resources and getting them ready to eat. The major factors in this regard are: (1) prey selection, the cost of deciding which resource to obtain, dependent on ranking, reliability, and location; (2) search time, the cost of locating and encountering the resource; (3) transport costs, the cost of moving the resource from where it was obtained to where it will be used; (4) processing, the cost of preparing the resource for consumption (e.g., butchering an animal or grinding seeds); and (5) storage, the cost of storing a resource. Some of these activities require the use of some technology and the cost of obtaining raw materials for tool construction, so the costs of making the tools and then maintaining them also have to be computed (see Ugan et al. 2003). Special costs, like the costs of feed for one's draft animals, also must usually be factored in. All of these costs are then combined to figure the total cost, which is then subtracted from the value of the resource, with the net return being used to rank the resources. An example of how this is done is presented in table 3.5.

Obtaining accurate information on all these costs is difficult, and lacking specific information, general estimates are often used. However, some experimental work has been done to generate real numbers for some resources in the Great

Table 3.5. Hypothetical Resource Modeling for Culture X

Resource (per 100 grams)	Deer	Ducks	Grasshoppers	Acorns	Grass Seeds
Gross calories	600	400	2,000	1,000	350
Calories expended searching for resource	75	25	50	25	25
Calories expended obtaining resource	25	50	50	50	25
Calories expended in processing resource	25	10	75	100	75
Calories expended in storing resource	5	5	5	15	10
Calories needed to make equipment to obtain, process, and store resource	25	50	50	50	25
Net caloric return	445	260	1,770	760	190
Rank in total diet	3	4	1	2	5

Basin (e.g., Simms 1984; Madsen 1986; Metcalfe and Barlow 1992). Although these data are the best available, and much better than just estimates, they are still somewhat problematic because the studies were carried out by relatively unskilled workers (anthropologists are not skilled native people) with replicated technology, leading to an unknown and perhaps variable error. However, the data are useful and could be interpreted to reflect minimum return rates and so might be adequate to rank resources on a relative basis.

Associated with accurately figuring costs and ranking is gaining an understanding of the behavior of the species under consideration, including its reliability, abundance, and seasonal availability. Most resources are more abundant during the spring and summer than during the winter, and in many environments, food is harder to find in the winter. Some resources, such as trees, are stationary, but others, such as some animals, migrate. If animal X is hunted but migrates out of an area for a portion of the year, the people in that area will not be able to hunt it at that time. To mitigate this changing availability, other mechanisms to ensure the availability of food must be developed, including an expansion of the diet to include lower-ranked resources, moving to other locations, and the use of storage. If the behavior of a particular species is not understood, or if data from the wrong species are used, a serious miscalculation of the model can result.

For example, if one were to model return rates for pinyon in the Great Basin, it would be essential to know its distribution, cropping frequency, predictability, size of seeds, nutritional content of seeds, and a variety of other data. One might be tempted to think that all pinyon species are the same, but in reality, considerable differences exist among species and even among populations of the same species. If the wrong species of pinyon were used in a model, the results could be vastly different (see Sutton 1984).

Information. Optimization models assume that the actor(s) will make optimal decisions regarding resource selection and use and that such decisions will be based on complete information regarding resource distribution, seasonality, and concentration. In reality, however, information is never complete and may not even be correct, interpreted properly, or transmitted accurately. Poor-quality information can dramatically affect the efficiency of resource procurement (e.g., Moore 1981, 1983). The price of getting information is often high, but often worthwhile.

Social Obligations. From the viewpoint of a strict optimal diet, one would expect a group to schedule its activities and movements so as to exploit the highest-ranked resources in its area. Thus, optimization models would predict how certain settlement types were located to follow the distributions of the highest-ranked resources. However, the actual activities and movements of a group are heavily influenced by social needs, such as networking, ritual activities, political obligations, mate exchange, and family maintenance. In some cases, meeting these needs takes precedence over economic needs.

Preference. People rarely utilize all possible resources and so make some selection of which to use and which not to use. Optimization models predict that such selection will be based on the currency used in the model, such as caloric return, and it could be argued that some resources were not used due to their low ranking. However, even highly ranked foods may not be consumed due to cultural preference, a factor not considered in the strict application of optimization models. There are many such preference factors, including religious taboos and the desire to have different (e.g., gourmet) foods to provide variety in the diet. Recent European history documents that people will sometimes go to extraordinary lengths for "exotic" goods, such as spices.

Moreover, humans can rapidly change their preferences. Before World War II, pizza was unknown in the United States outside of Italian neighborhoods. During the early 1950s, pizza and related Italian food became so popular that the consumption of oregano (the favored herb of Italy) in the United States increased some 5,000 percent in just a few years. For better or worse, pizza has changed American food habits appreciably.

Another good example of cultural preference is the avoidance of the flesh of other humans. Most cultures consider cannibalism to be quite unacceptable, even abhorrent. However, from a strict optimization standpoint, why not eat human flesh? It is as nutritious as other meats, does not contain toxins, and is readily available. Thus, it should be a highly ranked resource.

Cannibalism is an emotional issue, with some researchers confirming and examining the practice (e.g., Volhard 1939; Hogg 1966; Sanday 1986; Askenasy 1994), while others deny (e.g., Arens 1979) that cannibalism exists as a cultural institution. It seems clear that the practice does exist. In a cultural context, endocannibalism (the eating of people within one's social group) is almost always prohibited, except for the ritual consumption of ancestors. Exocannibalism, eating people from other social units (strangers and enemies), is more common, and in some cases even expected (Turner and Turner 1999:1).

Three general categories of cannibalism can be defined: culinary, ritual, and emergency. A fourth category, criminal, will not be discussed here (see Askenasy 1994). Culinary cannibalism is the eating of other humans as a normal, if infrequent, part of the diet. Such cannibalism seems to have been very rare, but it has been argued that the Anasazi practiced it (White 1992; Turner and Turner 1999) and that the Mexica (frequently called the Aztec) consumed some of their sacrificial victims (Harner 1977; Ortiz de Montellano 1978; Winkelman 1998; Turner and Turner 1999:415–421). Ritual cannibalism, the eating of small portions of people to honor or gain power from them, is much more common. In these cases, very little nutritional value is gained. An interesting case of such a practice was the ritual eating of a small portion of the brains of deceased relatives (endocannibalism) by certain groups in New Guinea. It was discovered that some of the brains contained a virus that causes kuru, a disease that results in madness (somewhat similar to "mad cow" disease). When the brain was eaten, the virus was transmitted to the consumer, who contracted the disease. In the 1960s, the government stepped in to stop ritual cannibalism in order to stop the spread of the disease (Zigas 1990).

The last type of cannibalism, emergency, is the type most commonly known to westerners. People on the verge of starving to death will sometimes resort to eating the dead in order to stay alive until they can be rescued or find other food. Examples of such practices and events include the Inuit (e.g., Saladin d'Anglure 1984), the Donner party (Hardesty 1997), and the soccer team whose airplane crashed in the Andes in 1973 (Read 1974; in 1993, a feature film, *Alive*, was made about that incident). Unlike ritual forms, emergency cannibalism is practiced to obtain nutrition, but only for a limited time. One could argue that emergency cannibalism is a practice retained in the dietary inventory of many groups, held in reserve for extraordinary circumstances and thus an expansion of diet breadth.

So why not regularly eat other people? It almost seems wasteful to discard such a large package of nutrition. Emotional attachment to the deceased seems to be a major factor, but probably more important is the fear that the same could happen to you. Routine cannibalism would lead to rapid social meltdown as people hunted one another.

Power and Access to Foods.   Optimization models do not distinguish which people or groups of people in a culture are consuming resources. However, there is considerable variation in food consumption based on age and sex. In most cultures, children consume at least some different foods than do adults. Males and females may also consume different foods, and in a number of cultures (but not all), males have a greater access to meats derived from the procurement of most animals.

For example, among the Yanomami of northwestern Brazil, Lizot (1977:Table 6) reported that males consumed about 93 percent of all of the protein derived from animal sources, with only about 7 percent being consumed by females. A similar pattern of differential access to protein among the Tukanoan Indians in the northwest Amazon was reported by Dufour (1987). Males generally consumed "high-status" resources (e.g., hunted mammals), while females derived most of their protein from less prestigious sources, such as insects.

Model Refinement.   Finally, it is important to consider the fact that as these models are employed, they are continually refined. We learn new things, recalculate costs, expand the resource universe, determine new rankings, correct mistakes, and improve theory. As a result, it is necessary to revisit earlier results and reexamine past conclusions. This process is integral to scientific inquiry.

The following example will illustrate. Excavations at Lakeside Cave, Utah, resulted in the recovery of a few fragmentary grasshopper parts in the site deposit (Madsen and Kirkman 1988). When a smaller mesh screen was used on some other site soils, more grasshopper parts were found, leading the researchers to consider the possibility that grasshoppers were a resource used at the site. The use of still finer mesh resulted in the recovery of a large number of grasshopper parts, forcing a reconsideration of the role of those animals in the overall subsistence system. It was discovered that grasshoppers could be obtained from the shore of the Great Salt Lake, very near to the cave, where they had been washed up on the shore, dried, and salted. The return rate in collecting the grasshoppers was determined to be about 270,000 calories per hour, a rate that would result in grasshoppers being by far the highest-ranked resource in the region. (Admittedly, this would not be an everyday occurrence, but its frequency is not known.) This would require that the diet models for the region be reevaluated.

In sum, we do not know the ranking of grasshoppers in the Great Basin. They appear to have ranked very high, at least where they could be collected in abundance (e.g., Madsen and Schmitt 1998). A determination of whether the animals were processed prior to transport, whether they were stored, and other factors must be made before the return rate, or rates depending on conditions, can be figured. In the meantime, the ranking of all of the other resources used in that region remains suspect, pending the outcome of the grasshopper case.

Four Optimization Models

A number of optimization models have been employed. The two most commonly used models, diet breadth and patch choice, are derived from optimal foraging theory (OFT), which emphasizes net efficiency and minimization of risk as its guiding principles (Jochim 1976, 1998:14–20; Pyke et al. 1977; Durham 1981; Pulliam 1981; Thomas 1986:251–258; Winterhalder 1986). The two other most commonly used models, central place foraging and linear programming, employ similar criteria.

The Diet Breadth Model

The diet breadth (or optimal diet) model is the oldest and most widely used (see Simms [1984] for a detailed discussion) in optimization studies. In addition to the basic assumptions of any optimization model, the diet breadth model further assumes that resources have a fine-grained distribution, that they are evenly or randomly distributed throughout the environment. This assumption takes a very complex actual situation and simplifies it for analysis. In reality, resources are never randomly distributed in an environment.

In the diet breadth model, resources are ranked by their return rate, with the highest-ranked resource predicted to form the primary basis of the diet. If the highest-ranked resource does not contribute enough calories to the diet, the second-highest-ranked resource would be added to the diet. If the diet is still lacking, the third-highest-ranked resource would be added. The breadth of the diet would increase until the caloric requirement was met. Thus, the model predicts "*the order* in which resources will be added to or deleted from the diet" (Simms 1984:33, emphasis in original).

The composition of the diet will fluctuate, depending on environmental conditions. As all environments are dynamic, the breadth of the diet will always be expanding or contracting. In times of dietary stress, defined as fluctuations in the availability of higher-ranked resources, lower-ranked resources would be added to the diet to make up any caloric shortfalls.

The Patch Choice Model

The patch choice model is similar to the diet breadth model in that resources are ranked based on return rates. However, instead of resources being ranked individually, patches or suites of geographically associated resources are ranked, and decisions regarding diet are based on the average return rate of patches, not of specific resources. The optimal strategy is "to locate oneself in the patch with the highest rate of return and remain there until conditions change" (Smith 1983:631). The central key to the patch choice model is that patches of resources are ranked as a unit and the patch with the highest return rate is selected first, with lower-ranked patches being added to the system in the order of their ranking, which has to include travel time between patches. Once a patch is occupied, the people should remain there until the return rate falls below that of the next-best patch. If the return rate does not decrease until the resources are literally exhausted, this strategy could result in local extinctions (Smith 1983:632).

The ranking of patches, rather than of individual resources, requires making four basic decisions: (1) which patch to visit; (2) how long to stay and when to leave; (3) which resources in the patch to use; and (4) foraging path, or which patch to visit next (Pyke et al. 1977:140). In human societies, the first and fourth of these decisions are largely tied to information systems, as a decision cannot be made prior to the patch being encountered (Pyke et al. 1977:144), as well as to seasonality and cultural considerations. The second decision is related to the total resource potential of the patch and the third to the rank of resources within the patch.

The cost-benefit criterion in the diet breadth model is the return rate of individual resources. However, with the patch choice model, the criterion is the average return of a suite of resources within a patch, the patches being ranked on their total resource return rate. Patch A, containing a lower quantity of a high-ranked resource, may be chosen over patch B with a higher quantity of that resource if patch A contained more of a resource of lower rank. Thus, even the best pinyon stand may be bypassed in favor of a less productive one where deer are also present.

Factors in patch selection include the amount of time that can be spent in a patch before the group must move to another patch and the labor available with which to exploit a patch. If a group is too small or time, including travel, is too limited to exploit a patch, a less productive one may be chosen. Once a patch is chosen and a group has located itself within that patch, the application of diet breadth principles within the patch should be useful because diet breadth does not make any predictions about abundance, only the order in which resources will be used.

The patch choice model has some of the same shortcomings as the diet breadth model in that it makes assumptions that do not always hold true for human groups. Cultural aspects are usually factored out of the model, and like diet breadth, a single currency (energy) usually is used. Costs are computed in the same manner as with diet breadth, except that the additional costs of traveling between patches and the gathering and analyzing of the information necessary to determine the rank of patches must be added.

Central Place Foraging

Central place foraging employs the same basic tenets as diet breadth and patch choice but assumes that the group stays in one central place, with specialized task teams traveling to the resources, obtaining them, and returning to the central place (Orians and Pearson 1979; also see Bettinger 1991:93–97). The central place model analysis is based on the energy expended in travel time (the round trip from the central place to the patch) and time spent in the patch, versus the return rate of the resources.

The major problems for the people to solve using central place foraging are (1) where to locate the central place (e.g., base camp) in relation to nearby resource patches; and (2) once in a central place, which prey to seek, which patch to use, and the load size, how much of the resource can be taken back to the central place (see Orians and Pearson 1979:156). Each of these problems is influenced by patch quality, risk, and competition, and considerable information is required to make good decisions on these issues (Orians and Pearson 1979:156).

In sum, the central place forager should seek larger prey, up to what can be carried back to the central place, as travel distance increases. As the patch moves farther from the central place, the time spent with a patch should increase, and the size of the prey should also increase (Bettinger 1991:94). As prey abundance increases, the requisite quantity of resource is obtained, and the time spent in the patch should decrease.

Linear Programming

Linear programming (Reidhead 1979; Keene 1981, 1985a, 1985b; Shapiro 1984; Belovsky 1987, 1988) is "a mathematical technique of calculating the optimal allocation of resources towards a defined goal in the face of multiple constraints" (Gardner 1992:1). Unlike other optimization models, linear programming can use multiple currencies, which can be an advantage over the single currency of other optimization models. Linear programming is more complex than other models in that it requires calculation of return rates in each of the currencies used in the analysis.

Linear programming models have three components (Shapiro 1984:13–15; Gardner 1992:25): (1) the goal to which resources are allocated; (2) the set of variables; and (3) constraints, factors that limit what can be done. Each of the variables (currencies) is linear, that is, they must be related to one another in a linear manner. A change in one variable must produce a proportional change in the other variables. A sequence of events, that is, the allocation of resources, is specified and programmed (Gardner 1992:24).

A graphic example will illustrate the method (condensed from Gardner 1992:25–28, Fig. 2.1). Say that a family needs 8,000 calories and 180 grams of protein per day and wishes to minimize its time spent getting food (the goal). Available food resources consist of nuts and fish. It takes one hour to get one pound of nuts, and they return 1,600 calories and 20 grams of protein per pound. It takes one and one-half hours to get one pound of fish, with a return of 800 calories and 60 grams of protein. The resources are limited in the environment, and the family cannot obtain more than six pounds of nuts or five pounds of fish per day. Four constrains to the solution are present: (1) the requirement of calories, (2) the requirement of protein, (3) the availability of nuts, and (4) the availability of fish.

To obtain the requisite number of calories, the family could eat five pounds of nuts, ten pounds of fish, or any combination that falls along the calorie line shown in figure 3.1. To satisfy the protein requirement, the family could eat nine pounds of nuts, or three pounds of fish, or any combination that falls along the protein line (figure 3.1). The intersection of the calorie and protein lines is the optimal solution: 4.2 pounds of nuts and 1.6 pounds of fish, a resource mix that requires 6.6 hours of time.

In the above example, the optimal diet solution fell within the region of the chart where the availability of the two resources (nuts and fish) was not a factor, and so those constraints are considered slack. Calories and protein are the only factors that are relevant, and so those constraints are considered binding. If the binding constraints changed or if the slack constraints changed enough so that they became binding, the solution to the problem would also change.

Among the benefits of the linear programming model is the ability to employ multiple currencies in the analysis. In addition, the researcher can alter the various constraints to see changes in the solution, including gaining an understanding of the range of acceptable solutions and the scale of change necessary in the various constraints to alter the system in a fundamental way. The weaknesses of

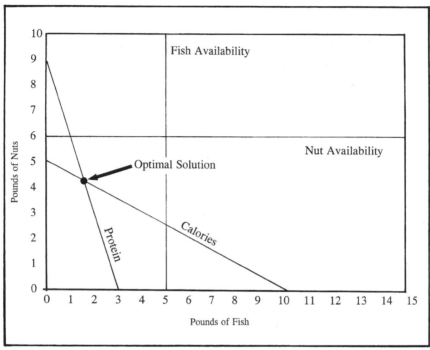

FIGURE 3.1
The graphic solution to diet using a linear programming model under the parameters detailed in the text (adapted from Gardner 1992:Fig. 2.1).

the model are similar to those of the other models, including the assumption of perfect information, the assumption of rationality, a complete understanding of the resource universe, and an accurate modeling of return rates.

Discussion

Optimal foraging models attempt to explain aspects of *human biological ecology*; by themselves, they cannot explain *cultural ecology*, as cultural factors alter and sometimes override decisions that would be optimal from a dietary perspective. This is not to say that OFT models are not useful. In fact, what makes them most interesting is when they *fail* to predict human behavior; when that happens, we can look for cultural explanations.

Of interest is the primary use of hunter-gatherers as the subjects of researchers using optimization models. This is because it is often assumed (even if implicitly) that hunter-gatherers are somehow closer to nature than agriculturalists and that their activities are somehow more amenable to analysis. Hunter-gatherers are supposed to behave like other animals, foraging for their food and wandering about the landscape (Ingold 1987:11). On the other hand, agriculturalists are food-producing land holders who are viewed as somehow set apart from nature, making optimization models difficult to apply (but see Gregg 1988).

In addition to this bias, three major problems with the current application of OFT are apparent. First, and most fundamental to the application of any model, is the working (and implicit) premise that we understand the full range of available and utilized resources—an assumption that is invalid. In this situation, conclusions drawn from any of these models likely are invalid as well. This is not to say that such studies cannot be valuable. In fact, they are critical in order to test and fine-tune any model of adaptation.

Second is the use of the diet breadth model. While this model is a useful tool in gaining some understanding of resource utilization, its assumptions of a fine-grained environment makes its power to predict settlement and subsistence patterns weak in many environments. However, its application within a patch and in the ranking of patches can be quite useful.

Finally, simple optimal foraging models adopted directly from biology cannot account for the diversity of cultural behavior and factors influencing economic decision making (see Jochim 1998:23–26). While admittedly difficult to quantify, analyses of multiple currencies derived from a variety of social factors could provide a more realistic view of economic systems. The lack of food (calories, vitamins, etc.) is a stressor that requires some response, many of which are cultural. Such nutritional adaptations (Stinson 1992) can be central to an overall adaptation.

However, for a given small group at a given time and place, OFT can be very useful (Winterhalder and Smith 1981; Smith 1983). The study of the Aché of Paraguay (Hawkes et al. 1982; also see Hill and Hawkes [1983]; Hurtado et al. [1985]; and Hill and Hurtado [1996]) has been particularly valuable in clarifying this point. Hawkes et al. (1982) found that the Aché do indeed forage more or less optimally except for a clear preference for fat meat. Other important studies of hunting and gathering groups have been carried out in places as diverse as the Australian coast, the Kalahari Desert, and the Arctic. These studies show that people are indeed highly sophisticated at making a living from the environment, but that they make their decisions on the basis of cultural preference and social choice as well as on considerations of simple protein and calorie return. Archaeologists find OFT reconstruction extremely useful as a first pass at reconstructing past societies (Winterhalder and Smith 1981). It is now an important area of study for human ecologists.

Fairly recently, the term *human behavioral ecology* has been applied to the component of human ecology that seeks to explore "the link between ecological factors and adaptive behavior" (Smith 2000:29) through the application of strict empirical and testable biological evolutionary models for humans, such as studies of optimal foraging, population regulation, and evolutionary ecology (Cronk 1991, 1999; Cronk et al. 2000). Such biological models tend to be simplified abstractions of economic models developed for human society, and for that reason their application is limited. The problem in employing such a model for biological use is that it eliminates consideration of conscious choice. While this is useful in dealing with most animals, it is an unfortunate limit to impose on humans. Nevertheless, a great deal of new knowledge about the evolution of human behavior has been generated (Ehrlich 2000; Irons and Cronk 2000:21; also see Ehrlich and Feldman 2003; Bird and O'Connell 2006), and human behavioral ecology is a useful approach.

Use of Darwinian evolutionary concepts has moved forward to reduce the above limitations. Human behavior is seen as having evolved to make certain kinds of learning, including language and facial recognition, particularly easy (cf. Boyd and Richerson 2005, Richerson and Boyd 2005). Even morality is seen as having a strong "hardwired" component, thanks to evolution for family life and social interaction (Henrich et al. 2004). Human ability to find, remember, and direct others to good foraging sites and other ecological resources is also extremely impressive, and this includes ability to rapidly estimate the quality of the resources. We are brilliant approximators, which is more useful in a hunting-gathering context than being perfectionist calculators. Continued Darwinian speculation has also provided alternative explanations of many aspects of foraging. For instance, hunting big game may often have the useful function of impressing the opposite sex and thus helping to acquire mates and descendants. This seems to explain certain cases in which hunters focus on big game when smaller game would pay off better in terms of calories and protein.

Let us conclude with this thought: people and cultures must make a "profit" to survive. No hard-and-fast rules exist on how much of a profit, on whether an adaptation is actually optimal, or on whether the decisions made are the best possible ones. The adaptation must only be good enough. If one culture is competing with another, its adaptation must be better than the other one to survive; there is no rule that it must be exceptional, just better than the competition. In general, we believe that most humans make enough of a caloric profit on the biological side of human ecology that they can afford to do whatever they want on the cultural side.

CHAPTER SUMMARY

Humans are animals and can be studied using biological and ecological models. This approach within human ecology is called human biological ecology and emphasizes how humans adapt biologically. This is done in two general ways, by short-term physiological responses and by long-term anatomical changes.

The overall human population is growing rapidly, and individuals are living longer lives. The carrying capacity of the planet is unknown. Human population is regulated in a number of ways, including disease, food supply, birth control, infanticide, and to some extent, warfare.

Individuals require daily nutrition to function properly. These materials are obtained in foods, and the nutritional requirements vary by age, sex, and physical condition. Calories are a commonly used measure of diet. However, adequate quantities of specific nutrients, including carbohydrates, proteins, fats, vitamins, and minerals, are required for proper nutrition.

A relatively new approach in the study of human adaptation is the use of evolutionary ecological models, those that apply the concepts of selection to human behavior. Such models generally study optimization, primarily as related to diet. Using available information, researchers develop a quantitative model of optimal diet, what people should be eating if they were behaving optimally (generally using calories as the measure), and test that model against what people actually did. In this way, one can determine how actual behavior deviates from the biologically predicted behaviors to gain an understanding of cultural systems. The most common optimization models are diet breadth, patch choice, central place foraging, and linear programming. The successful application of these models requires an understanding of resource distribution, resource value, acquisition and processing costs, and information flow. While very useful, evolutionary ecology addresses issues only in human biological ecology, other issues are addressed by cultural ecology, and culture has traditionally been the central and pivotal concern of anthropology.

KEY TERMS

anatomical adaptations
Bergmann's Rule
calorie
carbohydrates
central place foraging
currency
diet breadth model

evolutionary ecology
fat
life expectancy
linear programming
minerals
nutrition
optimization
optimization models
patch choice model
physiological adaptations
protein
resource universe
stress
vitamins

4

Cultural Ecology

Biological evolution and natural selection are the forces that shape organisms. Beginning at some point in time in the distant past, culture began to influence human development, changing the relationship of humans to their environment from one of strict biology to a mixture of biology and culture. Over the millennia, culture has become more complex and influential in human affairs, and the role of biology has diminished.

To be sure, humans still require a certain level of nutrition, have physical limits to their physiological adaptations, and are still subject to the rules of biological evolution. Today, however, biology plays only a minor role in human adaptation, and now most of the problems posed by the environment have to be solved through the mechanism of culture.

Much of the ecological work relating to humans has centered on diet and subsistence. **Subsistence** is not simply a list of foods but a complex system that includes resources, technology, social and political organizations, settlement patterns, and all of the other aspects of making a living. Subsistence is one of the vast complexities of human behavior largely related to culture. By focusing on food, much of the behavior of people has been excluded from many ecological studies (Jochim 1981:ix). Once we get past the emphasis on food, however, we can begin to look at the influence that other behaviors have on the adaptations of human cultures (e.g., Goodman et al. 2000). The field of cultural ecology focuses on discovering cultural adaptations.

HUMAN CAPABILITIES

The development of humans and cultures capable of building cities and creating art is tied to the development of the human brain. The increases in brain size and complexity through time are the most visible indicators of increasing capabilities, but the important outcomes of these developments are the ability of humans to act thoughtfully, rather than by instinct, and the increases in human sociability and intelligence.

Instinct and Learned Behavior

All animal behavior is guided to some degree by instinct, and there is a considerable debate in anthropology and biology about the extent to which it guides human behavior. The old tabula rasa view (see Locke 1975) held that humans learned most from their culture. Locke is often mistakenly quoted as saying that humans learn everything—that their minds, at birth, are literally blank tablets waiting to be inscribed. On the contrary, he recognized that humans had certain inborn capacities. Individuals differ in learning ability, for instance. Locke proposed that within limits set by innate capacities, people could learn a potentially infinite range of customs. However, later thinkers have not always been so cautious, and a genuine blank-slate view was widely held in the twentieth century (Pinker 2003).

This view does not stand up to investigation. Humans do have instincts, ranging from minor ones like yawning and blinking to broader ones like self-preservation (but also some tendency to sacrifice themselves for relatives and immediate social groups). Most other things, however, are clearly learned. Humans have evolved the capability to learn certain things easily; others are more difficult.

Language is obviously learned. The human vocal apparatus is structurally capable of making a wide range of sounds, but English, for example, uses only some of the possibilities. Newborns can be raised to learn any language, but it is not clear how much of the capacity for language is hardwired (much clearly is; Pinker [1994]) and how much is learned. These issues are currently under investigation (see Barkow et al. 1992).

Similar questions arise about aggression. Clearly, we share with all vertebrates a tendency to fight back when attacked—to deal with perceived threats by using violence. Yet there are people, even entire groups, in which violence is essentially unknown. This eliminates simple theories that postulate universal, uncontrollable aggression as a human trait (Robarchek 1989a, 1989b; Robarchek and Robarchek 2000).

Even art has been given biological treatment (Dissanayake 1992). Humans like regularities, such as rhythm in music, regularity in geometric design, and prosody in poetry. Much of this tendency is undoubtedly inborn; the human love of rhythm has something to do with heartbeat, breathing, and other rhythmic bodily functions. However, much of it is certainly learned; Chinese and Europeans generally do not identify with each other's music. A simple biological explanation fails to account for the complex interaction of learning and genetic programming, although it provides a beginning hypothesis.

Human use of the environment has innate components as well, ranging from our love of sweets to our ability to calculate—roughly but quickly—the payoffs of alternate foraging strategies (Smith 1991). But it also has learned components. Only by studying the ways in which genes influence the cognitive ability of humans can we find ultimate understanding of human biological ecology (Barkow et al. 1992). This understanding will not come easily. The considerable differences among cultures and the total ease with which adopted children can learn any culture if they are raised into it early enough in life are but two examples that demonstrate a far greater capacity for learning and plasticity than many currently allow.

Sociability

No animal on earth, with the possible exception of some insects such as ants and termites, is more social than humans. Human babies cannot survive without years of care, and children must learn a phenomenal amount of cultural knowledge before they can even begin to fend for themselves. Instinct does not guide us adequately in the food quest. Human adults can live alone but very rarely choose to do so, and still more rarely thrive as hermits. Psychological health, even more than physical, depends on sociability. Experiments with monkey and ape infants suggest—and observations of neglected children confirm—that young humans will simply die if they are not involved in warm, close social relationships, even if all their physical needs are met.

On the other hand, humans differ from ants and termites in that they value autonomy. We have a psychological need to feel in control of our lives, and this feeling can be so strong that we may deteriorate and die if we feel hopeless and directionless (Schulz 1976; Langer 1983; see also Jilek 1982). Thus, we are caught in something of a paradox. The existential human dilemma is that we need autonomy yet cannot get along without sociability. This basic tension lies behind many tragedies. It is well to ask how we got this way. Why are humans such strange animals? Why do we have such exaggerated brains, such a curiosity, such a need for both society and freedom? Surely, designing a better world must begin with the knowledge of just who and what we are. The study of human evolution is providing some of the answers. The broad outlines of human evolution are now well known, although there are countless unresolved questions about the details.

Intelligence

Humans are, on the average, intelligent animals. Intelligence has some obvious benefits, but it also has huge costs. The brain and nervous system make up only 3 percent of the weight of an average adult human but use about 15 percent of the body's total energy budget, enough to fuel a good-sized dog.

Moreover, the brain is spared when starvation occurs. During starvation, the body begins to digest itself to provide the basal metabolic energy it needs. First, fat is converted to energy, and then muscle tissue is utilized, until finally the heart and digestive muscles are reduced to the point that death ensues. The brain is sheltered from this process. Chronic malnutrition in utero and in the first few years of life can stunt brain growth and intelligence, but long famines do not appear to have the same effect on adults. Studies of the Dutch who were subjected to starvation during the Nazi occupation, and of people during the Korean War, showed no intellectual deficiencies attributable to starvation.

Given the world history of famines and malnutrition, it is obvious that the brain must provide a huge advantage in survival. While the advantages inherent in human intelligence are obvious today, what about early hominids? How did intelligence evolve? What were early hominids doing that made increases in intelligence so valuable to them? At least part of the answer is, broadly speaking, that early humans were almost certainly social omnivores who shared food (Isaac 1978a, 1978b). They probably foraged on anything they could find and operated in sizable social groups. Everyone would have looked for food, and when it was discovered, alerted others who shared in the benefits. Food would have probably been brought back to the children and to the adults who were tending them.

This sort of foraging pattern is typical of several other social animals quite unrelated to us, such as crows and coyotes. These animals all exhibit a similar pattern of brain development, one larger than that of their less social relatives. Indeed, the brains of crows seem as highly developed beyond solitary birds as human brains are beyond solitary primates (see Marzluff and Angel 2005).

Intelligence evolved for two reasons. First, as omnivores, humans could never rely on specific instincts or simple rules of thumb to obtain food. Even now, one sometimes reads about the "hunting instinct" that people have because of our "hunting past." This seems highly unlikely. Only a few small groups of humans with a highly specialized and highly developed technology have lived solely by hunting—usually in areas where there are few edible plants. All other known human groups live mostly on plants and/or fish and shellfish. Today, the main source of calories, and the favorite food of most peoples worldwide, are seeds. Roots and tubers, fruits and their sugar sources, oily nuts, and tender young leaves are also consumed in large quantities. However, this situation postdates the development of agriculture (ten thousand years ago). Before that time, the case is not as clear.

The evidence supporting a long history of omnivory lies in anatomy and physiology. We have small, unspecialized teeth—no fangs like a carnivore or large grinding teeth like an herbivore. We lack claws, pouncing muscles, and other carnivore equipment. We also have an unspecialized digestive system. We need high levels of vitamin C and other nutrients that are scarce in meat, as well as vitamin B12, which does not occur in plants.

The second reason for the evolution of intelligence is that as social creatures, we had to manage the incredible complexities of social life. This involved, among other things, the development of sophisticated communication. It is sometimes said that language was "invented," and rather recently at that. This may be true of language as we know it—long sentences, complex questions, embedded clauses, subtle puns, and slick lies. However, some sort of complex communication must have existed long ago. Once again, the evidence lies in anatomy. Language centers exist in the brain, usually in the left temporal lobe. Lip, tongue, glottis, and vocal cord anatomy in humans is exceedingly complex and fine-tuned—incomparably more so than in a chimpanzee, who cannot manage human vocal sounds and have to learn sign language when we attempt to teach them to "talk." The evolution of such vocal structures must have been long and gradual, as such a fine-tuned accommodation by hundreds of muscles and cords could not have evolved rapidly or suddenly.

Along with language, facial expressions, and gestures in human societies are also forms of communication. The whole human face is very expressive, and we can display Mona Lisa smiles, broad grins, evil smirks, and false warmth. One hypothesis is that language evolved to communicate about tools. However, this is difficult to accomplish with language alone, as it requires experience to learn to use tools. We are adept, however, at fine-tuning social situations with speech.

This brings up an important point: humans, while intelligent, do not excel at everything. A dog lives in a world of smells that we cannot even imagine. Some fish locate prey via electric fields. Birds find their way during migration by means of magnetic sensor cell systems in their brains. What we call human intelligence is a quite specific bundle of abilities (Barkow et al. 1992), and social skills are by far the best developed. The second-most-developed skill is the ability to know most everything about the environment we live in—every weed, every rock, every trickle of water—and to describe it to others. We have a phenomenal ability to learn about such things. Furthermore, we learn for the purpose of social rewards. Approval and prestige are the greatest of reinforcers.

Basic Human Needs

Cultures exist to satisfy human wants and needs, but how a culture does this is highly variable. Certain needs are inescapable. First, we all must eat and drink, that is, we must ingest water, calories, and certain nutrients, and so some sort of an economic organization is required. Second, we must stay healthy enough to function, so we need some sort of medical system. Third, for a culture to survive, people have to reproduce. Reproduction involves not only bearing live and healthy children but includes all the behaviors associated with ensuring that the children live long enough to reproduce—such as feeding, protecting, and educating them. Fourth, people usually need some kind of protection from the elements. In areas like the tropics, this protection can be minimal, but in areas such as the Arctic, protection from the elements is critical.

Fifth, people need some stimulation and variation. We need to experience arousal, excitement, boredom, calm, wild enthusiasm, active interest, and sleep. Without variation, people may become lethargic and unproductive. Sixth, people need a social life, as people can actually die from negligence and/or boredom, such as neglected children and older people in nursing homes. Seventh, people have to have some sort of control over their lives. As with neglect, stress and helplessness can cause death (Peterson et al. 1993). Humans must also deal with emotion effectively. People tend to make major decisions on the basis of emotion, without considering the environmental consequences. The most extreme case is outright warfare, but any political conflict is apt to lead to environmental costs.

This highly complex social world requires two other critical elements: methods of communication and decision making. Communication invariably goes well beyond language. Gestures, facial expressions, art, music, dance, clothing, and verbal performance are highly developed in all cultures. In small groups, decision making may be undertaken by all the people getting together and discussing issues. In larger groups, there must be some sort of leadership and management organization, such as a council of elders. At the other end of the scale are the huge, convoluted, powerful bureaucracies of the contemporary state. Regardless of the size of the group, however, decisions have to be made.

Being generalists in a very wide niche, humans have a vast range of choices about how to meet their biological needs. In this regard, a diversity of valid solutions to these needs is available to humans, and it is *culture* that determines which set of solutions will be utilized. In addition to the biological needs, culture imposes additional needs on it members, such as religious rites or taboos, needs that also must be met for the culture to be successful. The subdivision of cultural ecology is about learning *how* and explaining *why* people or cultures choose one response over another.

CULTURE AS AN ADAPTIVE MECHANISM

Today, the primary mechanism by which humans adapt to their environment is culture, probably "the most potent method of adaptation" available to humans (Dobzhansky 1972:422; also see Cohen 1974; Kirch 1980). Cultural responses include technology and organization, such as the structure of economic, political, and social systems. Compared to biology, culture is an extremely flexible and rapid adaptive mechanism because "behavioral responses to external environmental forces can be acquired, transmitted, and modified within the lifetimes of individuals" (Henry 1995:1).

All people belong to a specific culture, a group of people who share the same basic but unique pattern of learned behavior. As such, each culture has a distinct ecological adaptation. One might view a culture as a "population" in that it occupies a distinct geographic area, has a defined way of making a living, and occupies a specific niche. Cultures interact with both the natural and cultural environment. A culture must first meet the biological needs of its members. Then the cultural needs of its members must be met, accomplished through religion, social regulation, and other mechanisms. The combination of the biological- and cultural-ecological interplay is quite complex.

Individuals in cultures are born into a system operating within a given environment (Dobzhansky 1972:427). In traditional societies, the cultural system one is born into tends to be more influenced by the natural environment. In industrialized cultures, the environment tends to be much more socioeconomic, with class and income (access to resources) being the major environmental difference between individuals (Dobzhansky 1972:427). Thus, in industrialized cultures, selection processes operate more on socioeconomic factors, influencing the genetic makeup of populations.

As the environment (abiotic, biotic, and cultural) changes, humans adapt both biologically and culturally. As all environments are dynamic (even if the changes are small ones), a culture must make constant adjustments just to maintain some sort of equilibrium, and there is a constant interplay between cultural practices and biological adaptations. For instance, a people can be anatomically cold adapted but still wear coats.

A variety of cultural practices can mitigate the impact of environmental change and so level environmental differences. Such differences might be seasonal, such as differences in food availability between the spring and winter, or longer term, such as climatic fluctuations. Culture chooses from a variety of solutions to various problems, and as some solutions become unavailable, others present themselves. Technological change also will alter the equation, likely increasing the potential set of options available to a culture.

Each culture must somehow solve the problems faced by the culture and its individual members. To do this, each culture has institutions—rules, principles, laws, social contracts—and organizations to keep things working and to maintain a perspective among the various needs. The specific solutions to problems must mesh with the institutions and organizations. If the solutions are valid (adequate), the culture survives. Of importance is the fact that there may be multiple sets of valid solutions, with a particular culture choosing one. A different culture may have chosen a different, but also valid, solution.

Organization

Culture is a system that is organized into a variety of components, including economic, political, religious, and social. Each of these components also has an organization. Such organizations can be relatively simple (e.g., family level) to very complex (e.g., the U.S. government). Different aspects of culture have different organizations. A political system may have a hierarchy, with its members having power and responsibility at assorted levels. The religious system may or may not be interrelated but will also have a hierarchy. The completion of a simple economic task may require a fairly complex organization, including divisions of labor based on sex and/or age, political or social requirements for access to resources, and/or religious involvement. The better we understand the organizations behind such aspects, the better we can understand the aspects themselves.

Those interested in general human ecology, particularly archaeologists, concentrate on the economic part of culture in order to determine how people make a living and thus infer their interaction with the environment. While anthropologists tend to deal with these components separately, they all are interrelated. For instance, religion is intertwined with economics and thus could be considered part of the environmental adaptation.

For example, if a group obtains its food through agriculture, certain environmental variables are important for its success. One such variable is rainfall. If the rains do not come, the crops will fail, the people will starve, and the culture may even die. Rainfall patterns (as part of climate) are part of the abiotic environment but are related to the biotic environment (plants need water) and therefore tied to the cultural adaptation (agriculture). To guarantee success of the entire process, the group may choose to influence both the amount and/or timing of rainfall. To accomplish this, they may institute certain religious practices to ensure rain, such as the rain ceremonials of the Hopi of the American Southwest. Such customs could be viewed as being directly related to economics, including the effort required to organize the group to conduct these activities.

Westerners might believe that such a practice is unnecessary, arguing that the rain would come anyway and is not influenced by "dances." Several flaws exist in this line of reasoning. First, it is arrogant to assume that the group's practices are automatically irrelevant and have nothing to do with rain; there is too much we do not know (cf. Nadasdy 2004). Second, the real purpose may be more about getting everyone together to deal with the social and psychological problems of drought than about actually producing rain. At any rate, as anthropologists, we are interested in understanding, not criticizing, their practices.

Social Networks

Social responses to environmental stress are varied. One simple technique to alleviate uneven resource distribution at the immediate level is sharing, giving materials to someone else in need. Sharing may carry an expectation of return (reciprocity) and can serve as somewhat of an insurance policy against future shortages. A classic example of this type of behavior is the stereotypic view of band-level hunter-gatherer males sharing meat they obtain with the other members of their group (e.g., Gould 1982). Hawkes (1993) argued that the benefit of sharing resources may not be in calories but in the development of social ties.

A larger scale of social networking may be seen in bilateral kinship systems. Unilineal systems establish membership based on relationships through only one side of the family, either the father's side (patrilineal) or the mother's side (matrilineal). Thus, in a matrilineal system, for example, mother's brother may be an important relative while father's brother may not. There may be a variety of reasons why a unilinear system is preferred, but it limits one's functioning relatives to one-half of those possible.

However, a bilateral kinship system includes both sides of the family and one has twice the number of relatives as in a unilinear system. It has been argued

(Helm 1965) that a bilateral system could develop in areas prone to resource shortages, where people would then have twice as many relatives from which to seek assistance.

Settlement Patterns

Different cultures will use the same space in a different manner, reflecting the organization of the culture, and this use will be reflected in the distribution of their settlements across space and time. People, their activities, residences, work localities, facilities, and sacred places are located across the landscape in a culturally significant way, called the settlement pattern. Part of this system is the way in which a particular group conceptualizes and utilizes its space.

Settlement pattern depends on a variety of factors, beginning with the basic economic system used by a group. For example, a hunter-gatherer group would utilize a valley floor quite differently than would a group of farmers, with very dissimilar components, management practices, residential localities, and support facilities. The basic economic system would also influence the types and scales of facilities and technologies employed and the kinds of resources utilized. In general, hunter-gatherers would not have large iron mines, oil fields, or large reservoirs, facilities utilized by industrialized groups. Technological innovations may have huge effects; farmers in Europe were largely confined to areas of light soils before the invention of the moldboard plow (probably in Roman times), which allowed turning over heavy clay soils and thus opened up millions of acres of fertile land. Some things might remain similar, such as the use of transportation corridors (e.g., freeways tend to follow ancient trade routes).

Technology

Technology, including the ability to make and use tools, is a major factor that separates humans from other animals, although some other animals do make and use simple tools. It is mostly through technology, rather than biology, that humans have adapted to virtually every ecosystem on earth. Technology can be very general (a hammer can be used for many tasks) or designed and used for very specific tasks (a space suit). Through an analysis of technology, one can gain insights into the functions of the tools and the relationship between the user (the culture) and the environment.

For example, suppose that an archaeologist finds a rock that is battered on its edges. The archaeologist concludes that the rock was probably used as a hammer, a simple tool. But to hammer what? If we could answer that question, we would have a better understanding of the users, their culture, and their adaptation. Studies of use-wear allow us to make better and better inferences about this. If the hammer were used in the production of flaked stone tools, a more complex technology would be inferred (evidence of which most likely would have been found with the hammer). If the hammer was used to pound in tent stakes, the use of tents would be inferred. The more we know about technology, the more we can learn about how a culture adapts to its environment. This is a materialist and empirical approach, and is useful, but it does not deal with all aspects of cultural adaptation.

Technological Change

All human cultures have technology. Technology is the result of need, available materials, innovation, and influence from other cultures. If one of these conditions changes, the technology will also change, and the environment and culture will be affected.

A quick look at the development of weapons technology is instructive. When thrusting spears were replaced by throwing spears, the number and type of animals that could be successfully hunted changed, thus altering economic systems as well as both human and animal populations. Another dramatic change occurred with the introduction of the bow and arrow. For example, in western North America, one theory (Grant et al. 1968) held that the bow and arrow were so much more efficient than spears at killing mountain sheep that human population quickly expanded, decimated the sheep population, and then had to move due to the lack of game. Another example is the impact on human and bison populations that the introduction of the horse, and then the gun (not to mention the Euroamericans), had on the plains of North America.

Although native peoples had been cutting trees with stone axes in eastern North America for millennia, the rate of cutting was small enough that the forest could recover. However, metal axes are much more efficient, and their introduction in North America altered the rate at which trees could be felled. As a result, Euroamericans with a larger population and agricultural and land-use systems different from those of the Native Americans, deforested large tracts of North America (a process that is still ongoing but seems to be improving). The same basic thing also happened in Europe (with stone axes) and is now occurring in Amazonia and Africa (with chain saws).

Complex technology had allowed for the colonization of areas that could not previously support human life, such as Antarctica, the ocean floor, and space. Technology provided some cultures an advantage that was used to conquer others (e.g., guns over spears; see Diamond [1997]). In addition, technology now allows us to eliminate other species and to alter the environment on a global scale.

Storage

Storage means taking some resource and saving it for later use. All plants and animals store energy within their bodies in the form of fat and carbohydrates, and some, such as hibernating bears, use stored fat as energy over extended periods. A number of species collect biomass from other species for later use, called practical storage (Ingold 1987:202). An example of this form of storage is a squirrel collecting acorns for the winter. Humans do the same thing, storing acorns, corn, meat, or whatever. Humans can also store living resources, such as domesticated animals, for later use.

Human storage practices usually differ from those of other animals in two major ways: scale and technology. Most human groups, especially agriculturalists, utilize storage on a massive scale. For humans, technology plays an important role in storage as resources will often be processed by grinding (e.g., wheat into flour), drying (e.g., jerky), smoking (e.g., many fish and other meats), and roasting or parching (e.g., many seeds so that they will not sprout during storage). Such treatment can make some resources storable for long periods of time, sometimes years. In addition, humans will also often construct special facilities to store resources, such as granaries, cairns, silos, and warehouses. Another way to store resources is by controlling an area where resources are found and not allowing others access, a social storage (Ingold 1987:207).

Some have suggested (e.g., Testart 1982; Binford 1990) that food-gathering economies can be differentiated by their degree of storage, which is one aspect of cultural complexity. Thus, an economy with relatively little storage would be fairly simple, at least in that regard, while another with large-scale storage would be much more complex. The latter society, therefore, could develop a sedentary lifestyle and higher population density. The environment, specifically the length of growing season and the amount of precipitation, may also play a role in the development of storage behaviors leading to cultural complexity (Binford 1990). The Native peoples of the Northwest Coast of North America, for instance, were confronted with runs of salmon that might last only a couple of weeks but could easily produce enough fish to feed a large group of people for a year. Development of smoking and drying technology thus allowed a huge population increase, which in turn led to cultural elaboration of all sorts, partly to organize the labor needed to process thousands of fish in a short time.

TRADITIONAL KNOWLEDGE SYSTEMS

Throughout time, cultures have obtained and categorized knowledge about their environments. The vast majority of this knowledge was unwritten, passed verbally from generation to generation. The amount of knowledge is staggering. Individuals in traditional cultures usually know a great deal about the environment, as they work in it every day. Many hold specialized knowledge relating to medicine, religion, or other fields. The practical applications of traditional knowledge and wisdom have attracted ecological scientists as well as anthropologists (see Ford and Martinez 2000). However, intellectual property rights remain an issue in regard to this knowledge (Posey 2001; also see the special issue of *Cultural Survival Quarterly*, vol. 24, no. 4, 2001).

All of the information (data) obtained through perception (e.g., vision and hearing) are subject to cognitive interpretation and filtration in the mind of the observer/player. **Cognition**, the way a culture views things, is an integral part of any information system and must be taken into consideration in any analysis. Classification systems are part of the cognitive doctrine of all cultures and are important analytical elements (see below).

Each culture has a system by which knowledge is obtained, that is, a science. As noted in chapter 1, modern science is strictly empirical and requires that a specific method be used in scientific inquiry. All traditional cultures also use empirical science, and all recognize objective realities. Relatively few use the strict formal method of Western science, but considerable experimentation occurs in traditional science, although written records are generally lacking. If one were to de-emphasize methods and concentrate on results, the contribution would be rightly viewed as staggering. A traditional doctor might not be able to explain the specific chemical properties of the substances used but clearly understands the results.

An example of such scientific understanding may be found with the Navajo (see Grady 1993; Schwarz 1995). In 1991, healthy Navajo people in the southwestern United States were dying from a mysterious disease. After considerable scientific effort, the culprit was found to be a hantavirus carried by deer mice (*Peromyscus maniculatus*). The virus was spread to humans through exposure to mouse urine and saliva. An examination of traditional Navajo beliefs, much of which was conducted by Navajo trained in Western medicine, showed that they recognized mice as disease carriers and took special precautions to protect themselves from mouse urine and saliva. This knowledge appears to be centuries old, indicating that Navajo science had identified the vector (mice) and had developed precautions to avoid getting the disease. Navajo elders blamed the recent outbreak on the movement away from traditional beliefs.

Many cultures also include a nonempirical aspect in their science. Nonempirical data are those that are not physical, are not objective, cannot be reproduced, and are not subject to verification by experimentation. Generally, nonempirical knowledge is gained by specific individuals under special circumstances. The use of a hallucinogenic substance is a common method by which to gain such knowledge. In some cultures, such knowledge has an equal, and sometimes privileged, status with empirical knowledge. Much religious behavior and belief is nonempirical, being based on faith. Interestingly, despite the pervasiveness of empirical science in Western society, many westerners include a great deal of nonempirical belief in their lives, with psychic readings and astrology being very popular.

Few traditional cultures adhere to the rigorous requirements of Western science, and many Western scientists consider the scientific practices and knowledge of traditional cultures to be inferior (in much the same way as the other components of their cultures are viewed by Westerners) and so ignore their results. However, much of the traditional knowledge base has been utilized by Western science, and now a serious concern exists regarding the intellectual property rights of the traditional peoples who amassed the knowledge (Brush and Stabinsky 1996). In particular, considerable traditional medical lore has been appropriated by multinational drug companies, without compensation. Worldwide, legal authorities are debating the proper course of action—how to extend something like copyright laws to unwritten traditions. One could argue, and indeed many have, that native knowledge is being stolen without compensation to the holder of the knowledge, a sort of copyright or patent infringement. Many see this as an extension of Western colonial practices and a further exploitation of traditional peoples. Ways to deal with this problem have been suggested (Laird 2002).

As traditional cultures disappear, much of their knowledge is lost. Thus, the recording of traditional knowledge is a critical concern in anthropology (e.g., Nazarea 1998, 1999) and in science in general. Even if traditional knowledge does not fit that of Western science, it is still of great interest to anthropologists trying to understand how a culture operated. As cultural ecologists, we want to know how a culture interacted with its environment, and so it is necessary to understand how a culture knows that environment.

Ethnoscience

In the late nineteenth and early twentieth centuries, ethnographers recorded as much information about native cultures as they could, believing that such cultures were rapidly disappearing. Classifications of plants and animals very different from the Linnaean system were soon recorded. World view, cosmology, astronomic beliefs, hunting theories, agricultural lore, and other ecological knowledge was recorded in wonderful detail. Most cultures code much of their ecological knowledge as part of religion (which may be a major function of religion [Rappaport 1971, 1999]) or at least in religious discourse, and the Bible has proved to be a source of considerable information regarding plants (Moldenke and Moldenke 1952; Zohary 1982) and animals (Hunn 1979) of its time. A new component of cultural ecology had been invented: the study of what local people know about their environment, how they classify that information, and how they use it, an approach called **ethnoscience** and later **ethnoecology** (Gragson and Blount 1999:vii; Nazarea 1999).

The first study of ethnoscience after cultural ecology came into its own was *Native Astronomy in the Central Carolines* (Goodenough 1953; cf. 1964), an island group in Micronesia. These people are famous for the long ocean voyages they undertake, navigating by stars and wave patterns. They are among the most intrepid voyagers the world has ever known—setting out over thousands of miles of open water in small canoes with no compass or other technical aids. Other work followed, including studies of the knowledge of soils, forests, plants, and farming of the Hanunóo people in the Philippines (Conklin 1957) and the religious, medical, and nutritional knowledge of the Subanun people, also in the Philippines (Frake 1962).

These works opened the floodgates, and the prefix *ethno-* was attached to all manner of words, from ethnoichthyology (fish) to ethnoconchology (shells). People had already been writing about ethnobiology and ethnobotany for decades, but those terms are now defined to mean the biological/botanical views of the groups in question, rather than a redefinition of those views in Western terminology. Ethnoecological information is the classification and knowledge of the environment possessed by a culture (Toledo 1992:6).

While the study of ethnoscience is important to understand the relationships of traditional cultures with the environment, we also find it useful to translate the information into Western scientific terms. This makes the information more accessible to agricultural scientists, development workers, and archaeologists (DeWalt 1994; Nazarea 1998). There was need for in-depth botanical and zoological study of the plants and animals in question, and for serious evaluation of their reputed properties (e.g., see Etkin [1988] on ethnomedicine).

However, there are several possible problems in this approach. An obvious problem is taking the knowledge of other people, encoded into their classificatory system, and translating it to our own system. It is thus possible to "lose something in the translation" and so miss the point. Another problem is that some researchers, in an effort to be less ethnocentric or more politically correct, place an overemphasis on the traditional view of the environment. In such cases, any questioning of the native view would be seen as unsympathetic, ethnocentric, or racist, making it difficult to evaluate claims. Thus, we need to take more care in studying traditional knowledge systems. Above all, there is the need to compensate local people for sharing their knowledge and for any use we make of it. At least, we have to make resulting publications available to them. This is now normal and is usually required by research protocols.

One truth that emerges is that the Western world has a great deal to learn from other cultures. The wealth of knowledge encoded in even the most outwardly appearing "simple" culture has proved to be beyond anyone's wildest dreams. Countless new medicines, foods, and industrial crops continue to be developed from traditional plant and animal sources. Agricultural practices are being reformed in many areas due to the special knowledge of local people.

Classification

All cultures construct a system to classify the elements in their environment, including plants, animals, soils, rocks and minerals, climate and weather, earth surfaces, and astronomical phenomena. Each of these various systems is based on a particular starting point. One culture may classify animals based on morphology, whereas another culture might classify them based on habitat. Thus, in the first system, a whale would be classified as being very different from a tuna (mammals and fish), while in the second, the two animals would be seen as similar (living in the ocean).

Any classification is, at least in part, a cultural construction of reality and biased by the particular worldview and experience of the culture. Some anthropologists argue that the resulting view of the world is so far from reality as to be totally arbitrary and idiosyncratic. However, people are constantly testing their beliefs against reality and culturally encoding the right ones. Many individuals may not know that poison hemlock is deadly, but it is safe to say that all cultures that occupy areas infested with that plant have encoded its deadliness in their information banks. Sometimes, though, wrong but plausible knowledge is inferred from observation. Many cultures hold that earthquakes are caused by giant underground animals thrashing about; this is probably the most reasonable explanation anyone could come up with before plate tectonics and continental drift provided a better explanation. Equally widespread and less justifiable is fear that all snakes are poisonous; all primates seem to fear snakes naturally, but humans (including Americans) often greatly exaggerate this. More exotic and local beliefs are commonly found, and anthropologists devote much attention to explaining why they are believed and how they work in society. A notably brilliant recent case is Eduardo Kohn's analysis of the Amazon native belief that dogs can foresee the future in their dreams (Kohn 2007). While this belief leads to clearly wrong predictions (as Kohn noted), it is a logical consequence of the way the people in question organize attitudes and behaviors relating to animals.

Studies of cultural classification systems have dealt with the ways in which people cluster the things in the world, what is included with what, and what is overlooked. People tend to finely split domains that interest them, while splitting less salient domains much less carefully. Hong Kong fishermen who specialize in catching rockfish have names for all the dozens of species there, while fishermen who catch rockfish only incidentally would simply call them all "green," "red," or "spotted."

Early students of classification felt that anthropologists should study knowledge and that the proper task for cultural ecologists was to study traditional systems of ecological knowledge. This led to a debate among cultural ecologists, some of whom held that we should study practice and treat knowledge systems as secondary (Harris 1968). This controversy soon passed as almost everyone came to understand that knowledge and practice cannot be separated; they are interrelated and must be studied together. Today, few anthropologists ignore the constant feedback between knowledge and practice—the way that our endless testing of the world is constantly altering our representations of it.

Knowledge of the Biotic Environment

The study of the classification, use, and knowledge of the biotic environment (past and present) is called **ethnobiology** (see Toledo 1992; also see Medin and Atran 1999). Ethnobiology is a major component of cultural ecology and includes studies on human diet, classificatory systems, ritual, and the knowledge and use of plants and animals. Data on such questions are obtained through a variety of means, including standard ethnographic data, the analysis of oral tradition, research by other specialists (e.g., by a botanist rather than an anthropologist), and archaeology.

Ethnobotany

The study of the native classification and use of plants is called **ethnobotany** (see Ford 1994, 2001; Minnis 2000). Plants are used for a great variety of purposes, including food, building materials, tools, textiles, and decoration, among others. If one is dependent on plants for these purposes, one's knowledge of plants would have to be considerable. A detailed understanding of plant locations, season of availability, general chemistry, durability, and biology is required for successful exploitation. The knowledge that traditional people have about botany is considerable, and many plants currently unknown to Western science (including many that would be very useful) are being used on a routine basis in other cultures (e.g., Balée 1994).

Horticulturalists and agriculturalists require a more detailed knowledge of certain specific (domesticated) plants in order to understand growth cycles, nutritional requirements, pest control, and fertility. Inadequate knowledge could result in poor timing and decisions, resulting in crop failure. In situations where a swidden agricultural system (see chapter 7) is practiced, considerable knowledge of the forest environment would be needed.

Ethnozoology

Ethnozoology is the study of "the knowledge of, use of, and significance of animals in indigenous and folk societies" (Overal 1990:127). Such knowledge includes the biology, seasonality, reproduction, edibility, and utilization of animals. Some species may be used for food, some for skins, some for bone, some for poison, and some for many other things. The more intimate the knowledge one has about different animals, the greater flexibility one has in using them.

When most people think of animals, they generally only think of vertebrates, often mammals. However, most animals actually are invertebrates, primarily insects. While Western folk classifications generally ignore insects, this is not the case with many cultures. For example, the Navajo of the American Southwest have a very sophisticated classification of some seven hundred insects (Wyman and Bailey 1964). The hunter-gatherers of the Kalahari Desert in southern Africa identify numerous invertebrates, including about seventy species of insects (Lee 1984:25).

Ethnomedicine

The study of the traditional knowledge used for medical purposes is called **ethnomedicine**. Some of this knowledge includes the setting of broken bones and the like, but it mostly involves **ethnopharmacology**, the classification and use of plants, animals, and other substances for medical purposes. The field also includes the knowledge and use of substances to alter one's reality (e.g., hallucinogenic drugs). In traditional societies, the people who specialize in medicine are often the same people who specialize in religion, and the two fields are often combined by a single practitioner.

Considerable research into ethnopharmacology has been underway for many years. Hundreds of thousands of years of experience with medicinal uses of plants is available if we look for it. Even modern Anglo American culture has an ethnopharmacology separate from the commercial drug industry. We call this home or folk remedies, and it includes many cures not recognized or confirmed by science.

The production of drugs on a mass scale, as demanded by the consuming public, has had a profound effect on our ecology. Considerable resources are expended in drug production that could be spent on food production, and impacts on the land resulting from drug crop production are enormous. For example, the amount of acreage devoted to cultivating poppies in some countries, such as Afghanistan and Colombia, for the production of cocaine and heroin is truly impressive. In addition, the acreage used to grow tobacco in the United States (not to mention the government subsidies) detracts from food production.

Knowledge of the Abiotic Environment

In addition to the biotic environment, all cultures also obtain and classify information on the abiotic environment, including both terrestrial and nonterrestrial elements. Among the important components of the abiotic environment are geography, soils, meteorology, and astronomy.

All groups occupy and interact within landscapes. Western urbanites tend to view landscapes as Cartesian space, geographic localities and distances, often devoid of real meaning. Other groups view landscapes from an experiential perspective, seeing geography as places where important beings interacted and where important events occurred, rather than just x-y coordinates on a map (see Brück and Goodman 1999:9). Such landscapes may have great ritual significance, such as in aboriginal Australia or even the contemporary Middle East.

Landscapes themselves can contain a variety of elements. Forman and Godron (1986:passim) identified three major landscape elements, patches, corridors, and surrounding matrix (figure 4.1). Patches consist of small, specific ecozones separated from one another. Corridors are strips of territory that separate patches, such as roads, rivers, and trails. The matrix is the remainder of the landscape that surrounds the patches and corridors. Thus, one could have patches of forest in a matrix of grassland connected by trails or patches of farmland in a matrix of forest connected by roads. Culturally, it may be useful to view patches as places where people live and work, towns, farms, and the like; corridors as arteries for transportation; and matrix as outlying areas that may be used, but used less intensely than patches or corridors, such as forests or preserves. The degree of management of these three landscape elements would vary greatly.

All cultures recognize and maintain specific geographic places in the landscape. Physical places exist that were the locations of important events, such as

FIGURE 4.1
The major elements of a landscape; patches such as cities and towns (cross-hatched), farmland (diagonal lines), corridors (double lines), and surrounding matrix (shaded).

Mt. Olympus, where Greeks believed the gods lived; Gettysburg, the location of a major battle in the American Civil War; and Uluru (Ayers Rock) in central Australia, where many of the deities of the Pitjandjara tribe reside. Other important localities include sources of power, sources of materials, such as major stone quarries or fishing grounds, or a combination of the above and others. The study of landscapes as perceived by cultural groups has spread from geography into anthropology in recent years, especially following a pathbreaking book, *Senses of Place*, edited by Steven Feld and Keith Basso (1996).

A knowledge of soils and soil types can be critical, especially for agriculturalists. Yet soil type can indicate the presence of other resources, such as plants, animals, water, or minerals, that can be important to a culture. For those people manufacturing ceramics, the soil (clay) itself may be a resource. The same is true in industrialized societies that use a variety of soils for industrial purposes.

Knowing, predicting, and controlling the weather and climate is important in all societies, though most apparent in agricultural societies (see McIntosh et al. 2000). In deserts (e.g., western Australia, southern Africa, northern Africa) the ability to track rain is essential to knowing where water can be obtained and where animals are likely to be. The proper timing of burns is also tied to weather patterns; if it is too early or too late, problems may ensue.

Agricultural societies (including our own) place an even greater emphasis on weather and its control. The effort expended by the Hopi to make rain is a good example. The Maya apparently conducted even more elaborate ceremonies and sacrificed people with the same goal in mind.

People have always watched the sky. All cultures have some classification and explanation of the changing sky, some quite sophisticated. Astronomical observations by traditional peoples have revealed regular patterns of celestial movement, such as of the sun and moon, and some not-so-regular occurrences, such as comets. Every culture has some explanation for these patterns and occurrences, and many incorporate them into belief systems regulating world renewal, agricultural cycles, and other important cultural phenomena. This is also true of past cultures, and the study of the astronomy of past groups is called **archaeoastronomy**.

Art and Environment

For at least tens of thousands of years, art has been the way in which people have demonstrated how they feel about the environment. Yet cultural ecologists have shown an indifference to art. Art has portrayed not only animals and plants, but also cosmological schemes and symbolized religious philosophies. An ecological theory of art is needed, but so far, the nearest thing we have is the theorizing on myth, music, and (to an extent) art by Claude Lévi-Strauss (1962, 1964–1971).

Consider the art of the northern Northwest Coast Indians, specifically the Haida, Tlingit, and Tsimshian groups (see Jonaitis 1986; Anderson 1996; Wardwell 1996). The vast majority of images in this art are of animals, with most of the rest being of humans or supernatural beings. Animals are important to Northwest Coast peoples not only as food and clothing sources, but also as social and cosmological symbols. The major descent groups are named for particular animals, including bears, wolves, eagles, and whales. Many other animals, as well as a few plants, and even meteorological items like clouds, are used as family crests.

The art of the northern Northwest Coast defines parallels between the realms of humans, animals, and plants. Animals and plants are seen as persons—not human persons, but persons nonetheless. They are talked to, prayed to, and taken as sources of magical and spiritual power. Humans and animals are often seen as reincarnations of one another. Animals can sometimes change into humans or can assume human form when they hide under mountains or seas. Thus, when animals are used to portray social facts, there is no thought of using the animals as metaphors. The animals are actually part of society—other-than-human persons. The art says much about human-animal relations.

Western Uses of Traditional Knowledge

Most people are unaware how many ideas and products from other cultures have been adapted for use in our own culture (see Linden 1991). Some are useful in the short term, such as many current drugs, while others are important for the long term, such as learning to adapt a sustainable agriculture to the rainforest, thereby preserving the forest. The plants, animals, ideas, and technology that westerners have borrowed from Native Americans was discussed by Weatherford (1988, 1991). The range is from maize to parkas and from domesticated turkeys to snowshoes.

Medicine

Cultural ecologists have been part of a larger effort on the part of Western science to find plants and animals that contain useful compounds. This is the most simple, direct, and obvious use of field biology. Medicinal plants are one example (see Lewis and Elvin-Lewis [1977]; Etkin [1994]; and above all the huge compilation by Chivian and Bernstein [2008]). Of the thousands of plants used in treating disease, the vast majority has been used in ethnomedicine, and some 50 percent of the medicines we use today originally came from other cultures. Aspirin, one of the most widely used drugs, came from the willow bark used by a number of traditional groups, such as those in the Northwest Coast of North America, long before it was synthesized and mass-produced for Western society.

Large numbers of plants (and animals) have medicinal value. Moerman (1986) compiled a database of 2,147 plant species used by North American native peoples; a large percentage of these are effective, and several have become sources of important medicines. A very large number of plants and animals are still unknown to Western science and may contain compounds of great value. That these species are being driven to extinction faster than we are able to find and test them (as depicted in the movie *Medicine Man* with Sean Connery) is a serious problem, and major efforts are underway to document and test such species.

Sometimes, a plant that was studied because of its value in ethnomedicine turned out to be useful in quite another way. One famous case is that of the common or Madagascar periwinkle (*Catharanthus roseus*). Its traditional uses did not include treatment for cancer, yet it became the source for vincristine and vinblastine, the drugs that revolutionized therapy for childhood leukemia. Variants of these two chemicals are now widely used and are credited with saving hundreds of thousands of lives.

Traditional peoples discovered most of the common poisonous plants of the world, and in many cases found the antidotes. Thus, they saved Western investigators a great deal of time and danger. In such investigations, the role of the ecological anthropologist is usually limited to recording data on local uses of plants and collecting the plants in question. Specialists in botany and biochemistry must identify them and study their potential for medicine. It seems that much traditional medical understanding evolved as people sought to understand the properties of plants (see Johns 1990).

Food and Fiber

New sources of food, fiber, and other valued goods also appear frequently, though they currently have less media glamour than the medicines. In the United States, about one-third of the calories we ingest come from a single plant—corn (maize). We get corn calories from many sources; corn meal is fed to most of the domestics animals that we eat, corn oil is in many foods, and there is the corn we eat directly. However, corn is a plant that was domesticated in Mesoamerica by Native Americans. We have borrowed it from them and adapted it to our own use. The same is true of many other plants, including potatoes, tomatoes, and tobacco.

At present, the world is dependent for food and fiber on a very few crop species that have come to dominate the world's agricultural systems due to demand, their adaptability, and the relative ease of growing them. Wheat, rice, corn, and potatoes now contribute most of the food calories, and the New World variety of cotton produces most of the natural fiber. Most of the meat consumed comes from only a few animals: cows, pigs, sheep, and chickens. Such a narrow base is an unstable situation; a few virulent plant diseases could create havoc. For example, a potato disease spread through Europe between 1846 and 1848 and hit Ireland, heavily dependent on the potato, particularly hard. A famine ensued; hundreds of thousands of Irish starved to death, and millions left (Salaman 1949). So we need to know as much as possible about alternative crops, foods, and agricultural methods, as well as the myriad of other uses of other plants and animals.

Anthropologists and economic botanists have described local traditional uses for literally thousands of species of plants and animals. These species provide a vast and proven reserve for the future. Not only do we now know what and where many of them are, we now know how to process them and utilize them. With perhaps seven thousand cultural groups in the world, many thousands of useful wild species have been discovered. Even species requiring complicated processing have been brought into the realm. Both Koreans and native Californians prepare acorn meal, leaching out any bothersome tannic acids; in the future, some of the human food supply could well depend on having this technology already perfected. The deserts of the Southwest, at present little used, contain many valuable species of great potential importance (see Nabhan 1985, 1989).

Already, traditional varieties of native plants are especially useful in breeding. The inhabitants of Chiloe Island, Chile, have an incredible variety of cultivated potatoes. Some of these are so disease resistant that the farmers of Chiloe have begun to sell seed stock to international potato-breeding companies. Local Mexican cultivated bean varieties have served as sources for drought- and blight-resistant beans. Teosinte (wild or partly wild corn/maize) is so valuable for its disease-resistant genes that a major biosphere reserve has been established in western Mexico to serve as a center for corn biodiversity.

Agricultural Techniques

Moreover, traditional techniques of agriculture are proving to be valuable, or even necessary, in many areas (Marten 1986; Wilken 1987). Ethnographers and agronomists must work together to document the vast storehouse of knowledge (Atran 1993; Nazarea 1998, 1999). In Bali, traditional water management proved so much more successful than the new innovations that the new techniques had to be abandoned (Lansing 1991). Even hunting and gathering peoples had (and many still have) extremely valuable land management techniques, many of which can still be used. The native peoples of North America, often disparagingly described in older literature as "primitive" and "backward," actually had extremely sophisticated land management skills, now of great interest to contemporary land use planners (cf. M. Anderson 2005; Blackburn and Anderson 1993; Hammett 1997).

Thought and Philosophy

Cultural ecologists come into their own when they study the ways people think about resources. Culturally encoded beliefs about plants, animals, soils, diseases, and even time and space have been studied in various parts of the world. Usually, local people know their resources well and have rich and complex knowledge relating to them. Everyone recognizes that sparrows are closer to finches than to ducks, and closer to ducks than to fish. Everyone recognizes that water is wet and rocks are hard. However, different groups construct very different cultural and psychological environments, and such differences are of great interest. Obviously, each group may know important facts not known to another. More interesting are the different beliefs that appear nonfactual to the outside observer. Why do many North American native peoples believe that plants, animals, and even mountains and rocks are persons—conscious in some sense and often able to communicate with humans and affect human destinies? Why do so many groups around the globe share a belief in a sacred mountain at the center of the world? Why is disease so often ascribed to witchcraft? Why do neighboring peoples often classify plants in quite different ways? The answers to these questions directly and immediately affect us all.

In the process of dealing with these and other questions, anthropologists have greatly informed debates about human psychology and cognition. The first and most obvious conclusion, reached before the end of the nineteenth century, was that "primitive" peoples are not ignorant, nor are their lives dominated by magic; they invariably have a deep, rich, and more or less systematic knowledge of their environments. As time has gone by, we have learned how traditional peoples can maintain a religious view of the world and still combine it with a hardheaded, factual view. By contrast, Western society has developed its characteristically detached and disenchanted view of nature. As a result, many are now saying that the Western world has lost something.

If, indeed, religion functions to maintain knowledge and ecological adjustments in so much of the world, as argued by cultural ecologists such as Roy Rappaport (1984, 1999), does the Western world need something functionally similar? Some students of environmental ethics have argued that it does (Callicott and Ames 1989; Berkes 1999). At present, the degree to which non-Western peoples managed and conserved their resources is highly controversial. Some say they failed and that Western science is our only weapon in the fight to preserve a livable environment (Lewis 1992). If so, we are in trouble, as experience shows that science alone is not always persuasive.

On the other hand, if some traditional people succeeded, to some extent, in "selling" conservation through ethics or moral teachings, then there is more hope for us. We may not find their religions persuasive or their techniques infallible, but we may be able to build on their experiences to devise more powerful ethical teachings. It seems likely that we will survive only through combining Western science with a new ethical, moral, and religious attitude toward the environment (White 1967). Certainly, the beauty and poetry of traditional peoples' views of the environment have proved extremely moving and powerful to many contemporary writers, such as anthropologist-turned-poet Gary Snyder (e.g., Snyder 1969).

Development

Finally, traditional knolwedge is often used by modern development agents in development plans (Bicker et al. 2004; Pottier et al. 2003). Traditional knowledge is usually better adapted to small-scale, capital-short agricultural and craft operations than high technology. It is often recycled, so to speak, from one group to another, or preserved for one group's own use. Thus, simple pottery stoves, used in Greece and China from ancient times, can cook a meal on a handful of grass; they have been propagated worldwide in recent years. Even using traditional knowledge, however, is not always a panacea, and top-down control of development—including traditional knowledge use—has its problems (Dove 2006; Nadasdy 2004). Tanya Murray Li (2007) provided a truly daunting history of attempts at sustainable, resource-sparing development in Sulawesi, Indonesia; lack of constant attention to on-the-ground realities subverted every well-meant attempt.

HUMAN CONTROL OF THE ENVIRONMENT

All cultures employ practices designed to exert at least some level of control over their resources and environment. These activities include management in the form of conservation, exploitation, and manipulation. Management can occur at several scales, from individual plants to entire landscapes, and for a variety of maximizing interests, short term or long term. The access to and exploitation of resources is determined by some factor, such as kinship or wealth, with some being individually owned and others being communally owned (or "not owned" as the case may be).

Domestication and Control

People impact and alter their environment to varying degrees, particularly plant and animal populations (e.g., Preston 1997; Martin and Szuter 1999; Doolittle 2000; Grayson 2001; Kay and Simmons 2002). The scale of this impact depends on the scale of human population and the technology possessed by the group. Most groups feel that they have some control over their environment, perhaps through their ability to influence the supernatural, or their ability to change the course of a river, or perhaps through their air conditioning. In fact, many groups consider their environment to be controlled and so **domesticated** to at least some degree, although few would believe that they are in total control.

The typical definition of domestication is one related to agriculture. In that context, a domesticated species is one in which humans have developed some intentional and detectable genetic control over a species such that the domesticated form is different from anything in the wild. While it is true that genetic alteration is an effective method of control, plants, animals, or ecosystems can also be controlled in other ways (Blackburn and Anderson 1993).

A more expansive definition of domestication could mean control in a more general sense. All cultures have methods to exercise some control over, and so domesticate, their environment (whether these are effective or not is another matter). Environments are controlled by a variety of techniques, including the manipulation of landscapes and management of individual resources. If a culture "controls" its environment, that environment could be considered to be "domesticated."

However, Western groups moving into a region inhabited by traditional peoples generally see much of the land as being "pristine wilderness," landscapes somehow untouched and unaltered by humans (Denevan 1992). This view is almost always wrong. For example, when European farmers colonized the New World, they saw what they thought to be a wild and untamed landscape. In reality, however, the native populations had long been practicing a variety of management techniques and had altered the landscapes by their use (see the major trilogy on this subject: Denevan [2001], Doolittle [2000], Whitmore and Turner [2001]). The landscape was not wild at all, but was a domesticated and highly productive environment. The Europeans interpreted the matrix surrounding the patches and corridors intensively used by the Indians as being unused (and so available for colonization) rather than as being used differently (Forman and Godron 1986; also see Vale 1982).

Humans consciously alter and manipulate their environments, generally to achieve a desired result. Such changes brought about by humans are called **anthropogenic** (*anthro* = human, *genic* = produced). The scale of change depends on a variety of factors, including the goal of the alteration. Technology is also a factor, as someone with a bulldozer can impact the environment to a greater degree than someone with a stone axe. Large-scale alteration of the environment is called environmental manipulation; smaller-scale manipulation of resources is called resource management (see table 4.1). Alterations of the environment

Table 4.1. Some Methods of Environmental Control

Method	General Principle	Scale	Examples
Environmental Manipulation			
Active	Actual hands-on purposeful modification of landscapes to achieve a goal	Large, as in landscapes	–Burning tracts of land to clear brush and encourage new growth –Clearing of large tracts of land for agricultural fields –Alteration of natural water systems for irrigation
Passive	Ritual activities to effect control and change	Large, as in landscapes	–Ceremonies for world renewal –Stewardship of areas to maintain their power
Resource Management			
Active (light to moderate)	Actual hands-on purposeful alteration of a resource to achieve a result	Small, generally individual resources (e.g., a species or a water source)	–Pruning specific plants to enhance production of some product –Limiting access to a spring by members of other groups so as to preserve the water
Active (intensive)	Actual hands-on purposeful alteration of a resource to achieve a result	Small, but intense focus on an individual species, often to the point of genetic control	–Management of reindeer herds –Agricultural domestication of a species, such as corn or cattle, where the movements, reproduction, and lives of the individuals are controlled
Passive	Ritual activities to effect control and change	Small, focus on specific need	–Fertility rituals for specific species –Giving thanks to a species (e.g., deer) for allowing themselves to be hunted and killed

include those that affect both the abiotic and biotic components, that is, both living and nonliving aspects of the environment are altered and manipulated.

Environmental Manipulation

Large-scale changes made to the environment by humans is called **environmental manipulation**, the alteration of entire landscapes. Manipulation can be advantageous, or at least perceived to be advantageous, to humans in the short term or the long term. The clearing of the rainforest in Brazil (and other places) has a very short-term economic benefit to the farmer or rancher but a very negative long-term effect on the environment and human welfare in general. Some alteration of the environment is undirected, but much manipulation is planned and conducted for specific purposes. Manipulation tactics fall into two general categories: active and passive.

Active Environmental Manipulation

Active environmental manipulation is the purposeful, physical alteration of groups of species and of ecosystems on a large scale. This is the active manipulation of landscapes rather than of individual species.

Burning.   Burning may be the most widely employed method of environmental manipulation in human prehistory and history (see M. Anderson 2005; Boyd 1999; Flannery 1995; Lewis 1973, 1982; Pyne 1995, 1998). Fires clear away dry, dead understory and grasses, reduce competition, and eliminate thorns and animals dangerous to humans. The fires are usually timed and managed so that they do minimal damage to forests and other long-lived resources. Most of the world's plant cover has been burned repeatedly by hunter-gatherers and agriculturalists. This is a point to remember in contemporary management schemes; fire control is not always the best thing in areas where humans—to say nothing of lightning—have been causing fires for millennia.

Many plants are well adapted to fire, and some even require burning for seed germination. The ash contributes fertilizer and makes room for new growth. Natural fires periodically consume the fuel on the ground, never permitting it to build up to the point of allowing a catastrophic fire to occur. A recently burned area can be quite productive in its abundance of new growth.

Hunter-gatherers know this and would often set fire to areas with the specific purpose of eliminating dead materials and encouraging new growth. In this way, a good stand of seed plants, after harvesting, would be encouraged to produce another good stand the following year. This was common practice among the California Indians (M. Anderson 2005; Blackburn and Anderson 1993; Lewis 1973, 1982; Timbrook et al. 1982) and was widely employed to produce materials suitable for basketry (Anderson 1999). It would also kill weeds and help preserve the biological purity of the stand.

In addition, the resultant new growth would attract certain animals to eat the new foliage. This often served to augment the numbers of animals available for hunting, thus raising the rate of successful hunting. In optimal foraging terms, encounter rates would be increased, resulting in a lower caloric expenditure for procurement, changing the ranking of that particular animal!

Burning also may be related to religion, such as world renewal activities. Among the Gagadju in north-central Australia (as seen in the documentary film *Twilight of Dreamtime*), the burning of the river plain signals the renewal of an annual cycle of life. Without the ceremonial intervention by "proper" people, as caretakers of the land, this cycle would be broken and life would cease to exist. In fact, Aboriginal burning does indeed renew the land. Controlled burning by Australian Aborigines has been reintroduced at Uluru (Ayers Rock) to save wildlife that was dying out for lack of it (ENA, personal observation of displays, presentations, and actual burning at Uluru, 2005).

Cultivation. Another good example of environmental manipulation is that of cultivation and agriculture. To plant a crop, land (often substantial amounts) must be cleared of its natural ecosystem so that an artificial ecosystem can be installed (planted). This results in the loss of biodiversity through the replacement of the many wild species with a few domesticated ones, an often considerable alteration of the ground surface through mechanisms such as plowing, and a disruption of adjacent ecosystems.

Constructed Landscapes. All cultures strive to regulate their landscapes, part of the abiotic environment, to some degree. Some modify landscapes in a relatively minor way while others actually construct new landscapes to suit their needs. A classic example of this is *feng-shui*, the Chinese science of proper arrangement of elements in a landscape to ensure harmony (Anderson 1996). Groups will also move materials great distances around the landscape for the construction of specific facilities. This was true even in early societies long before cities (let alone machinery), as in the long-distance movement of large stones used in the construction of Stonehenge in England.

The most common example of constructed landscapes are those associated with agriculture, where a whole series of alterations are made to fashion the land to the use of the farmer. The construction of fields could involve simple clearing of forest but may also involve creating and/or leveling mounded earth, removal or alteration of geological features such as rock outcroppings, construction of walls, digging irrigation and/or drainage ditches, and the construction and use of terraced field systems, such as those found in China, the Philippines, and Peru (see figure 4.2). In some cases, terrace systems can cover hundreds of square miles, as in the Colca Valley of Peru (Denevan 2001; Guillet 1987).

Irrigation systems are common elements in constructed landscapes. Such systems can be very small or quite extensive, with many miles (even thousands of miles) of canals, ditches, and other facilities being constructed. Again, even nonurban small-scale societies have created many such systems, as in Luzon (Philippines) and much of Indonesia. Dams can flood large areas, creating lakes and swamps and eliminating portions of rivers, streams, and valleys, such as Aswan in Egypt and Three Gorges in China. Resulting irrigation can transform landscapes from arid regions to lush agricultural areas.

Other large-scale constructions can transform landscapes. Many groups have built large ritual centers, altering the local terrain and even influencing much larger regions. The construction of cities, especially the giant ones of the twentieth century, have drastically altered landscapes with their housing, transportation, water, and waste management systems.

FIGURE 4.2
A constructed landscape: systems of terraced fields in Peru (photo by E. N. Anderson).

Passive Environmental Manipulation

Ritual activities designed to maintain the environment in its domesticated state are considered **passive environmental manipulation**. Such activities include world renewal ceremonies, such as fertility rituals and even human sacrifice. The Mexica (the cultural group that included the Aztecs) conducted both of these practices to ensure that the sun would continue to rise.

One way to ritually control and maintain the environment is **stewardship**. In Australia, the land and its resources were formed during Dreamtime. Certain places are very special and contain power, and certain people are responsible for the maintenance of those places. The places are not owned; people are caretakers rather than owners. Failure to properly maintain these places could result in catastrophe. Not only can sacred punishment (such as illness) occur, but very real problems develop when the land is not burned, tilled, pruned, and otherwise managed; Australia was supposedly nonagricultural before Anglo settlement, but in fact the land was managed quite intensively. Similar responsibilities are set out in the Bible, where Adam was charged as the steward of the land (Genesis 2:15) and the consequences of bad land management were detailed (Isaiah 34:11).

Resource Management

The management of specific resources is called **resource management**. Such activities are generally on a smaller scale than environmental manipulation, but there can be some overlap. For example, burning may be conducted to manage a specific resource, but it could affect a larger system. Conversely, pruning of tobacco, as practiced by a number of groups, affects a small area, notably the plant itself. Like environmental manipulation, the management of resources can be either active or passive.

Active Resource Management

Some specific resources are **actively managed** or controlled to ensure productivity, that is, some physical action was taken to control the productivity of the species, although some resources are managed for their beauty rather than for food or materials. Most species were managed such that they remained wild, but some were managed so intensively that they were eventually domesticated (see chapter 6).

Plants could be actively managed using a variety of techniques. Burning, often considered to be environmental manipulation, could be considered resource management if conducted as a management technique for one or two plants. Pruning was also a management technique. Tobacco, important to many Native American groups for ceremonial purposes, was monitored and pruned so that it would produce larger leaves. Storage of harvests, such as pine nuts, grass seeds, acorns, and the like, is a form of resource management.

In Nevada and elsewhere, Indians made bows from staves of juniper wood (see Wilke 1988). These staves were taken from special juniper trees that had unusually straight trunks free of knots and twists. Trees with such trunks were purposefully shaped, not merely found and then used. Planning far ahead, trees would be selected, pruned, managed, and nurtured to grow straight and knot-free trunks that could provide bow staves, a process that could take decades. Once the tree was ready, a bow stave would be cut in outline on the tree, left to dry, and removed (already cured) a few years later. It would take many years for the tree to fill in the resulting gap, and it would be monitored and managed to make sure that no branches grew in the stave area. Another bow stave could then be removed, and some trees had many staves removed. These trees were very valuable resources that were constantly monitored, maintained, and reused over hundreds of years. The same was done with yew trees in the Pacific Northwest and probably in old England.

Animals were also actively managed. Everyone knew that females gave birth and that it was important to maintain some level of females in animal populations. In some cases, there were rules about killing female or young animals, with adult males being preferred prey. There are such rules in the contemporary United States for hunting deer; one must have a license, a "deer tag," and cannot kill female or young animals.

Another way to manage a resource, such as a water hole, is to limit access to it. Sometimes access is limited only by formality. For example, among the San of the Kalahari Desert in southern Africa, water holes are owned by bands, and one must have permission to use them (Lee 1984). While permission is always granted for the asking, it is still a way in which to exercise some power over the resource. In other cases, access is more seriously limited, such as a water hole being defended by force. Such control could influence the adaptation of other groups by preventing travel through an area.

Passive Resource Management

Resources can also be managed through passive means, those that do not involve direct physical contact with the resource, and all groups employ some sort of passive management. Several approaches to **passive resource management** are discussed below.

Ritual Management.   Rituals, as part of religious activities, can function as a form of resource management in a number of ways. All known human groups believe in some sort of supernatural power that has control over major elements of the environment, such as gods that control rain or the movement of the sun. Rituals, including prayer, ceremonies, and even some art, are used to influence these deities so that the sun will rise and the rain will come. These rituals, then, serve to manage the environment to the advantage of the people, and so manage the environment.

Other practices can *function* as resource management, even if that was not their original intent. One example is the ritual ownership of an important resource (or sometimes even an area or locality) such as a spring, a common custom in many groups. Such ownership may be passed through generations and would encourage stewardship. Ownership may also function as a conservation technique, a way to discourage the use of the resource by others. It is also a way in which to control resources, wealth, and power, even if ecological management is not a goal.

In many groups, individuals or social entities like families or clans may have a special relationship with some entity in the natural world. These entities are often called totems. In some cultures, there are rules about their utilization by persons or groups claiming the relationship. For example, let us say that the totem of one person was deer, so they would not consume deer as part of their normal diet. The totem of another person was elk, and that person could not eat elk. This practice would possibly (but controversially!) serve as a passive resource management technique to reduce hunting pressure on both deer and elk because fewer people would be eating them.

Another example of passive management of game was put forward by Moore (1957:71). To determine where to go to hunt caribou, the Naskapi Indians of eastern Canada used a caribou scapula to divine the location of the herds rather than using past experience and knowledge. Moore suggested that the divining would have sent the hunters off in different directions and so may have served to randomize the selection of hunting localities. This in turn would lower hunting success and so reduce the pressure on game.

Certain resources, such as meat or milk, may be avoided at specific times. In some cultures, menstruating females are not allowed to eat meat. Other resources might be consumed only during ritual activities. This type of taboo would function to lessen the demand for certain resources and could be viewed as a management technique.

Other ritual behavior might include resource renewal ceremonies. Throughout most of native North America, if an animal is killed for food, it may be necessary to ritually thank its spirit. Failure to do so may result in the animal becoming angry and refusing to allow itself to be killed in the future. If this were to happen, the people would starve. In Western science, such behavior would not be considered resource management, as a connection would be denied. However, in the science of the culture practicing the custom, it may be a very real and important technique of ensuring the continued availability of the resource. In fact, such "respect" for animals does make people think twice about killing them and certainly has a conservation function in at least some groups (Anderson and Medina Tzuc 2005; Nadasdy 2004). This same type of behavior could be extended to general world renewal rituals.

Knowledge Retention. Knowledge itself is a resource, managed both actively (through learning and experience) and passively (encoded into ritual). Most people around the world possess a very considerable knowledge of their environment and use those skills in their everyday activities. These skills center on the use of resources currently in the environment. If the environment occupied by a certain group contained many different ecozones, the number of skills and amount of knowledge needed to exploit those ecozones would be huge. By gaining some understanding of the amount and types of knowledge a group has, one could learn a great deal about how that group adapted.

The retention of knowledge regarding the exploitation of resources that are no longer actively used may be a safeguard against bad times. People might retain knowledge of the use of certain resources not needed in good times so that they could be exploited when and if necessary, for example, the survival techniques taught to contemporary armed forces. Such knowledge might not be present in everyday practice but retained in oral tradition. The recent popularity of relearning the traditional practices of eighteenth- and nineteenth-century America is a related example. One reason for human longevity may be the value of elders' memories of epidemics and famines of the past, and of what was done to survive those. Contemporary Maya carefully teach their children what to eat if crops fail, and this knowledge is still vital when hurricanes pass over.

DECISION MAKING

Another way to analyze environmental manipulation and resource management techniques is through studies of decision making. All groups and all individuals make decisions regarding their actions in any given situation. As all systems are dynamic, constant adjustment is necessary, usually minor, but sometimes major. In all cases, however, decisions regarding what to do and when to do it are required. We somehow assume that the process of decision making is rational and well thought out.

However, bad decisions are made, particularly (it seems) by humans. People make poor decisions for a number of reasons, such as having incomplete information, giving too much weight to emotion, or just plain error. Some poor decisions are annoying while others can be catastrophic, such as invading Russia (just ask the French or Germans). If a culture makes too many bad decisions, it could result in evolutionary failure (extinction). A decision that seems good in the short term may be very bad in the long term (and vice versa), and it is important that a balance be reached. The theory of decision making is, in itself, a field of study within anthropology, and no effort will be made here to explore it in any detail (see Gladwin [1989] for methods of study, Young and Garro [1994] on medicine, and Mithen [1990] for a discussion of hunter-gatherer decision making). However, there are several important points to consider.

Information

Decisions are based largely on information (new or old). However, no one can possibly take account of all the things in one's immediate environment. Economic theory assumes that humans act from "perfect information," but of course this is never true. Perhaps the farthest galaxies and the smallest dust particles influence us somehow, but we normally overlook them. Even much more important things, such as the long- and short-term consequences of our actions, often get ignored.

Anthropologists, therefore, must consider decision making under the assumption of imperfect information (following the ideas of Simon [1960]). This, in turn, involves studying our simplifying premises: humans simplify, generalize, and assume that other people are more like us than they really are. In dealing with people, we routinely believe that they will do about as we would, even if their circumstances are different (Piatelli-Palmarini 1994). Two major realms of study have emerged from this more general concern with "information processing": explanation (inference, attribution) and classification. The former has been largely the domain of social psychologists (see review by Fiske and Taylor 1991), while the latter is the domain of anthropologists (see below).

To make the optimal decision, complete and accurate information is required. However, these conditions are rarely, if ever, met, and a truly optimal decision cannot be made, except by accident. Poor information will likely result in deleterious decisions. It is unrealistic to believe that humans will always have perfect information, and bad decisions must be expected even if the information is good. Information is communicated in several ways, including speech, gesture, smoke signals, and material culture (Mithen 1990:70–71). It can be used in the immediate future or stored for future use through oral tradition and the teaching of the young (through past experience).

The knowledge base of traditional peoples is usually very impressive, often greater than that of professional biologists working in the same area. This is particularly true of remote, poorly studied areas. For example, the Aché of Paraguay hunt flat-headed peccaries (*Platygonus* spp.) as a main staple food, an animal that zoologists had believed to be long extinct. But even well-known areas have surprises. The Sahaptin Indians of Washington State have recognized, for thousands of years, certain root-crop species that biologists only recently realized were there (Hunn 1991).

A hunter or gatherer must not only know how to recognize a species, but know how to use it. Consider a wild seed crop. The gatherer must know where it grows, when it sets seed, and whether it is worth seeking out in a good or bad year. For some years, one of us (ENA) monitored a patch of chia (*Salvia columbariae*), an important wild food in California. The yield of seeds from this patch varied from year to year. In most years, it is not worth the time to gather. Only with moderate, well-distributed rain did it provide much seed. A gatherer would have to decide whether it was worth the effort to utilize the patch.

Traditional peoples possess a great amount of knowledge about their environment, but the sheer quantity of information presents a major problem in systematizing, storing, and retrieving information. The solution lies partly in religion. Religion provides powerful emotional and social involvement. Knowledge is given the absolute value of a sacred text. Moreover, it is encoded in oral tradition (legends or myths)—exciting stories, often well laced with sex and violence! In areas as disparate as Aboriginal Australia (Gould 1969) and southeastern California (Laird 1976, 1984), anthropologists have found that children in deserts learn the location of water sources through stories. The hero travels from water hole to water hole. At each one, dramatic adventures occur. The story is exciting and united by its coherent and orderly development. Therefore, it is much more easily remembered than a simple list of water holes.

Moreover, moral rules are learned along with basic survival knowledge. Most hunting and gathering peoples have rules about sharing resources and about taking only what is needed so as to leave some for others. These rules—along with other rules the group may have—figure prominently in the stories. The hero or villain always suffers by failing to observe them. This provides a united worldview. Religion, ethics, and practical knowledge are not separated. Indeed, no hunting-gathering group seems to have a concept of "religious" as separate from "secular." Some have claimed that for such groups, everything is sacred. The truth is that for these people, everything is both sacred and secular. Everything is religious, but almost everything is practical.

Before information can be used to make a decision, it must first be obtained, classified, and then shared with others. Many hunter-gatherer groups are constantly out in the landscape for various reasons. While moving around, information on a variety of things is obtained and stored in memory, including animal spoor (tracks, dung, sounds, and/or smells), weather information, environmental parameters (e.g., the condition of one species may reflect the condition of another), and the activities and movements of other people. This knowledge is used and/or shared, even with other groups, as needed. To people who make their living on such resources and who depend on good decisions being made, resource information is a very high priority.

One specific method of information procurement is **resource monitoring**, a technique that virtually everyone uses. People pay attention to the status of what is around them, the condition of resources, presence and absence of things, and opportunities. For example, when driving anywhere, you will notice the price of gas at various stations and remember where the best bargain is. You will pay attention to what new restaurants are being built, noting for future reference where they are and what kinds of food they serve. All people monitor their environment for the resources they use.

In many cases, people will gather information on specific resources. When it comes to deciding which pinyon (pine nut) stand to go to in the fall, several years of monitoring data on the various stands may be utilized in the process. In addition to the data on the actual resource, one could consider information on travel time, social opportunities, and the like. The decision on which pinyon stand to visit would be based on all these factors.

Information is gathered constantly, both as an adjunct to what one is doing or by conscious effort. Even when traveling to a specific place, hunter-gatherers will rarely travel in a straight line. By meandering, information regarding a variety of resources, such as the condition of plants and the movement of animals, can be gathered and processed.

A route a hunter-gatherer might take from one place to another is shown in figure 4.3. The actual direct route would miss many of the areas that contain resources used by the group, so the traveler would meander across the landscape to check out things along the way. He or she would first visit resource patch A to determine animal density and inspect the progress of seed maturation to determine whether the seeds there would be worth collecting when they finally become ripe

FIGURE 4.3

A generalized hunter-gatherer travel route to gather information and monitor resources. (See text for explanation.)

in the future. The person would then begin to travel to resource patch B, gathering information on the general condition of the land along the way to access whether rabbits might be worth hunting there. Once at resource patch B, the person would examine the condition of that group of resources, again to access whether they should be gathered in the future. A visit to the water hole would be made to make sure it was productive, and if clogged or dirty, some maintenance might be performed. Next, a game trail would be examined to check on the movement of animals—their numbers, frequency of movement, and direction—so that decisions on when and where to hunt might be made. A visit to resource patch C would then be made to assess the condition of the pinyon crop, the number of cones per tree, the number of trees with cones, and the probable timing of cone opening. The traveler would finally arrive at the destination, having taken more time to get there, but with a wealth of useful information. Such resource monitoring is constant for each member of the group, and the quantity of information obtained is staggering.

Thus, the hunter makes a series of decisions that make up a flowchart or route map. Decision making in agriculture is conceptually similar, but even more complicated (Gladwin 1989). The farmer decides when to clear a field, what to do first, what to plant when the field is prepared, when and what to weed, when to harvest, and so on. The whole process can be studied as a flowchart by asking the farmer what he or she does first, what next, what after that, and so on—at every step asking about the full range of choices. This can get complicated and is best done while actually observing the process over time.

Decision making is what people *do*. It is where the rubber meets the road—where cultural knowledge is translated into individual action. It integrates cognition, motivation, and interaction with the world. It is thus a key matter for cultural ecologists to examine.

Scheduling

Scheduling, the planning of when to move and which resources to exploit, also requires good information. To obtain the seeds of plant X, one must have knowledge of the life cycle of the plant, information on where it is, its condition, and when and where the next resource is to be used. Sometimes a schedule might be very tight and leave little room for error; other times this may not be so critical. If two resources are available at the same time, a decision on which one to use may have to be made. If schedules are not adhered to, serious problems could result. If it is too late to get resource Y, one could be placed under considerable stress (putting the system out of equilibrium), and drastic measures may be required to adjust.

A CONCLUDING THOUGHT ON MANAGEMENT

Cultural ecologists have shown a broad concern with various strategies for managing the environment. On the one hand, this involves looking at soils, fisheries, wildlife, and pests, as well as simple food gathering and farming. On the other, it involves expanding from classical concerns of agriculture and agricultural economics to look at the social framework of food procurement: social systems and their religious and ideological representations, individual decision making and its psychological roots, and how these interact.

Broadly, the central question of resource management is: how can resources be managed to provide optimum benefit over time? This involves questions of allocation, and above all the trade-off of long-term and widespread interests and short-term, narrow ones. Every culture struggles with this question of how to manage resources, and some cultures and individuals within them make better decisions than others.

CHAPTER SUMMARY

While the study of human biological ecology can tell us much about human adaptation, the cultural aspect of adaptation must be examined through cultural ecology. The flexibility of human adaptive responses requires the study of human learning, sociability, intelligence, and basic needs to help understand how people and cultures deal with their everyday problems. Cultural ecology is about explaining how and why cultures adapt in one way and not another.

In essence, culture itself is an adaptive mechanism. Cultures contain a number of elements, such as social and political systems, settlement patterns, and technology and storage that are adaptive in their form and evolve as environments change.

Knowledge is also part of these adaptive cultural elements. Each culture practices science in some form, and each retains and classifies knowledge of the various abiotic and biotic components of their environment. These knowledge systems, collectively called ethnoscience, contain the accumulated knowledge of thousands of cultures over hundreds of thousands of years and constitute a resource of immense value to humanity. For example, much of the knowledge of drugs in contemporary Western medicine was derived from traditional pharmocologies.

Each culture expends some effort to control, or domesticate, its environments and the resources within them. Environmental manipulation entails the regulation of large-scale entities, such as landscapes, while the control of individual resources is called resource management. Both types of practices are done by both active (e.g., physical alteration) and passive (e.g., religious) methods.

Decisions about what resources to use and how to manage them are made through a process that includes using the knowledge of the environment. This knowledge is obtained, classified, and stored in oral tradition and religion for future use. In addition, up-to-date information is obtained through resource monitoring. Once obtained, information has to be interpreted, a task completed by each group using its own cognitive system.

KEY TERMS
active environmental manipulation
active resource management
anthropogenic
archaeoastronomy
cognition
domestication
environmental manipulation
ethnobiology
ethnobotany
ethnoecology
ethnomedicine
ethnopharmacology
ethnoscience
ethnozoology
feng-shui
passive environmental manipulation
passive resource management
resource management
resource monitoring
stewardship
storage
subsistence

5

Hunting and Gathering

Anthropologists often classify cultures based primarily on general subsistence strategy, generally the most visible or important aspect of how they obtain their living, a definition primarily based on ecology rather than social criteria (although these are related). Thus, those cultures that make their *primary* living from obtaining and using "wild" foods are classified as **hunters and gatherers**. In addition, hunter-gatherers are characterized by "the absence of direct [active] . . . control over the reproduction of exploited species" (Panter-Brick et al. 2001a:2). Until about eleven thousand years ago, all the people in the world practiced a hunting and gathering economy, and for most of human history we were hunters and gatherers. Much of our culture and biology is still adapted to that basic lifestyle (e.g., Barkow et al. 1992; Eaton and Eaton 1999).

The term *hunters and gatherers* has become an anthropological cliché. It has been used so much that some anthropologists have sought to find alternatives, such as foragers, collectors, or preagricultural peoples. Some of this classificatory manipulation is to account for political and social complexity; to distinguish small, relatively simple hunter-gatherer groups from large, complex ones. While it is true that an environment may limit the carrying capacity of some hunter-gatherers and so necessitate small groups, it is not necessarily true that small groups must have simple social and/or political systems. The term *forager* is now commonly used as a substitute for hunter-gatherer to avoid "privileging the hunting side of hunter-gatherer" (Kelly 1995:xiv), and the term *gatherer-hunters* (e.g., Bird-David 1990) has been used for the same reason.

The use of the single classificatory term *hunter-gatherer* presupposes that the technological and economic similarities between all hunter-gatherers unifies their cultures to a sufficient degree that they can profitably be compared with one another. This is a significant assumption (see Testart 1988) because other cultural institutions, such as kinship systems, can vary widely, as seen by a comparison of the Australian Aborigines and Inuit (this is also true of other such classifications). Nevertheless, in this book, we classify groups that make their principal living from wild resources as hunter-gatherers, irrespective of resource particulars (seeds or fish, large game or small) or sociopolitical details. We do not believe that we can simply substitute the terms *foraging* and/or *collecting* for hunting and gathering, as we view these categories as subsets of hunting and gathering (see below).

Hunter-gatherers exploit "wild" resources rather than "domesticated" ones as their primary source of food. Resources often have two dimensions: time (when they are available) and space (where they are located in the landscape). Like all groups, hunter-gatherers must solve the problem of getting resources and people together. Herein lies the major complexity in the study of hunter-gatherers. Hunter-gatherers would more likely be tethered to certain resources, such as springs, due to their technology and transport capability.

Hunter-gatherers manifest a vast range of structures, forms, and adaptations (see Bettinger 1980, 1987, 1991; Price and Brown 1985; Thomas 1986; Cashdan 1990; Burch and Ellanna 1994b; Kelly 1995; Lee and Daly 1999; Binford 2001; Panter-Brick et al. 2001b). Their villages and towns may reach populations in the thousands, as they did in the Northwest Coast and in coastal California just prior to contact with Europeans, and probably in the European Mesolithic between twelve thousand and seven thousand years ago. The social networks of hunter-gatherers may extend over an entire continent, or at least a good portion of one, as is seen in Australia. Their religions, literature, art, and music can be as complex as those in some state-level societies. Of more direct relevance to the present book, their ecological adjustments are extremely varied and fine-tuned. The nonagricultural peoples of the world most often depend on the same types of staples that agriculturalists do—seeds and root crops, greens, fruit, meat, and fish—and often in the same basic proportions: mostly seeds and roots, with meat significant and other things less so.

As noted by Winterhalder (2001:13), four basic generalizations can be made for hunter-gatherers. First, they tend to "underproduce": to not exploit all that is exploitable, and to have relatively few material possessions. Second, they routinely share food. Third, they tend to be egalitarian (this is less true of those with larger settlements). Finally, they commonly employ a division of labor where men do much of the hunting and women do much of the gathering.

HUNTER-GATHERER CLASSIFICATION

Most hunter-gatherer cultures are classified based on a description of the basic lifestyle or settlement/subsistence system practiced by the group. A popular view of hunter-gatherers, even among some anthropologists, is that they are nomadic, wandering about the landscape aimlessly in an endless search for food. This is simply not true. No hunter-gatherers wander aimlessly as a normal part of their economic pattern. Individuals may wander a bit, but cultural groups do not. Groups entering a region for the first time, such as the initial colonists entering North America or Australia, may have wandered about until they learned the landscape, but it would have been a short-lived practice. The formal term *nomad* is generally used by anthropologists to refer to mobile pastoralists, but the term has also been applied to hunter-gatherers (e.g., Krader 1959:499). Even very wide-ranging groups like the Inuit do not wander aimlessly; they are aware of the locations (specific or general) of resources and move around to utilize them on a regular basis, though it may be that a great deal of adjustment is needed in their schedule to accommodate changes in local conditions.

It is sometimes problematic in neatly classifying hunter-gatherers separately from agriculturalists, because the former routinely manage wild plant resources, and all of the latter were/are dependent on hunting and gathering for at least some resources. This is still true of modern industrialized culture; we still use some hunted and/or gathered foods, such as deer killed by hunters on vacation or wild berries gathered on the weekend. In some rural areas, wild resources may be very important, and as much so in times of severe stress, such as in the Great Depression of the 1930s, when some Americans even adopted hunting and gathering full time.

Resource Procurement

Defining the various procurement activities generally subsumed into hunting and gathering is not a simple task (see discussion in Ingold [1987:79–100]). Most humans are omnivores, and most hunter-gatherers live primarily on seeds and roots (or tubers). This is especially true in warmer parts of the world. In far northern regions and in some other habitats, such as the thorn-scrub of the South American Chaco, very little of the plant material is edible. Here, people tend more toward the carnivore side of subsistence. If they are anywhere near water, they live primarily by fishing and sea mammal hunting. Only in the deep interior, away from abundant seeds or roots and rivers or seas, do we find actual terrestrial hunters. The best-known cases are the Aché of Paraguay, whose favorite prey is the armadillo (Hill and Hawkes 1983; also see Hill and Hurtado 1996), and the Indians of sub-Arctic Canada.

Plant collectors include specialists who rely heavily on one type of plant food. Some San groups of the Kalahari Desert in southern Africa are dependent on mongongo nuts. Other groups are generalists who eat a great variety of things. Fishing specialists exist along most coasts and major rivers and may live primarily on fish, shellfish, or sea mammals.

Gathering

Gathering has been defined as the collection of "wild plants, small land fauna and shellfish" (Lee 1968:41–42). Key components of the definition include gathered resources being small and relatively nonmobile, plus the common use of some technology for resource extraction and transport, such as digging sticks and containers (see Ingold 1987:82, 84–85). Ambiguity with the inclusion of small fauna in gathering exists because some are quite mobile and unpredictable. The term *collecting* is sometimes used as a synonym for gathering. However, collecting generally implies that resources are in known and predictable locations, such as many plants and shellfish, and that little searching is required. Thus, the predictability of a good yield is high, generally much higher than in hunting. The term *collecting* has now come to define a specific type of hunter-gatherer adaptation (see below).

Hunting

The term **hunting** generally refers to humans actively looking for, killing, butchering, and consuming animals. However, a key part of the definition is that the animals are mobile species pursued and captured by some method (see Ingold 1987:80), with no real guarantee of success. Domesticated animals would not be pursued and so are not hunted. Most definitions of hunting exclude fish, seemingly because they do not have to be pursued across the landscape and/or are generally captured in traps or nets. Sea mammals are also sometimes excluded from hunting and included in a fishing category (Murdock 1969:154).

Lee (1968:42) defined hunting as the pursuit and procurement of wild "land and sea mammals," a definition generally agreed upon herein. However, this definition excludes nonmammals, such as birds, reptiles, shellfish, and insects. Most would include birds (but not bird eggs) and reptiles as being hunted and shellfish as being gathered. Insects have rarely been considered at all, but probably should be classified within gathering (McGrew 1981:45; Ingold 1987:88).

Fishing

Fishing is not an obvious separate category in hunter-gatherer subsistence. Lee (1968:42) defined fishing separate from both hunting and gathering as "obtaining of fish by any technique." The distinction between hunting and gathering was one of basic method: collection or pursuit. However, fishing seems to be distinguished by type of animal rather than by method of procurement (Ingold 1987:80). This distinction remains confusing.

Fishers are obviously rather tightly tethered to certain aquatic ecozones. In large terrestrial biomes, fishers may be tethered to sea coastlines, lakeshores, or rivers and streams (see case study 5.1) with relatively little attention given to other ecozones. In island settings, there may be no other ecozones of any size, resulting in a specialization in fishing.

Scavenging

In anthropology, **scavenging** generally refers to people obtaining animals that are already dead, such as a gazelle killed by a lion, rather than hunting and killing the animals themselves. A number of species will scavenge the carcasses of animals that have died naturally or were killed by other animals, and some, such as hyenas and vultures, make their primary living by scavenging. Humans will also scavenge, but only opportunistically. People will butcher and eat a beached whale and even chase away a large carnivore from a carcass so that they can take the remaining meat. In one sense, this activity could be classified as gathering because the resources are nonmobile. From another angle, it could be seen as hunting because most scavenged carcasses are those of large game, and one would have to look ("hunt") for such opportunities.

Some researchers have argued that the strategy of scavenging preceded the strategy of hunting by early hominids, or at least formed an important aspect of early hominid subsistence (see Shipman 1986; Blumenschine et al. 1994; Rose and Marshall 1996; Speth 2002), but others do not agree (e.g., Wolpoff 1999:222–223). It seems more likely that early humans both scavenged and hunted, much as chimpanzees do today (Stanford and Bunn 2001). If scavenging was an early niche and humans changed to a hunting niche, this could help in understanding the evolution of the ecology of humans. Scavenging is still important in some hunter-gatherer groups.

An Evolving Ecology

Part of the ongoing argument over these terms has to do with trying to understand the adaptational processes that led to becoming human. For a long time, researchers believed that hunting was what distinguished humans from nonhuman primates (e.g., Laughlin 1968:318–319), that many animals foraged for food but only humans hunted other animals with the aid of a technology. Having to carry tools for hunting and then carry the meat back to the family was seen as the reason hominids adopted bipedalism. The evolution was seen as being from forager-predator (without technology) to forager-hunter (with technology) (see Ingold 1987:85).

Subsequently, it has been argued that the initial development of food extractive technology revolved around gathering rather than hunting (Zihlman 1981:108–109). Zihlman (1981:109) suggested that digging sticks and plant-processing tools developed first and that hunting tools such as spears came later. Thus, the forager-predator would have first evolved into a gatherer-predator and only later into a gatherer-hunter (Ingold 1987:85). Still, foraging, predation, scavenging, and other methods of procurement remain in the inventory of the hunter-gatherer.

THE HUNTER-GATHERER STEREOTYPE

Anthropologists and the public have formed a stereotypic view of hunter-gatherers (see Ember 1978). This view includes the idea that hunter-gatherers are nomadic, wandering about the landscape on the edge of starvation, are primitive and not fully evolved, behave like many other animals, and are at the bottom of just about any scale of culture anyone can generate. An oft-cited example of this stereotype is the Great Basin Shoshoneans, the very culture(s) studied by Julian Steward (i.e., 1938). Thomas (1983:59; also see Thomas 1981) examined this stereotypic view of the Shoshoneans, noting that they had neither the simplest technology nor lived in the harshest environment. Through a series of historical and interpretational processes, Steward's "fundamental ethnographic description of a few very simple hunter-gatherers [primarily the Western Shoshone] ultimately escalated into a theoretical statement of major anthropological importance" (Thomas 1983:62). In reality, the Western Shoshone are not typical of the Great Basin groups, nor is Great Basin culture typical of hunter-gatherers.

A common misconception regarding hunter-gatherers is that they were always egalitarian, that they lacked significant social distinctions and status. As hunter-gatherers manifest a diversity of adaptations, they also have a diversity of social complexity. Some groups, such as the Inuit and San, were largely egalitarian, but others, such as the Nuu-chah-nulth (see case study 5.1), had complex class systems where social ranking was very important.

Early cultural ecologists, notably Steward (1955), saw the simplest hunter-gatherers as being organized in small, nomadic, and unstructured "bands." Such bands would have consisted of a core of elders, typically males, who made informal decisions. Everybody would have done more or less what they wanted, and group size would have rarely exceeded forty or fifty people. (Studies suggest that humans evolved in groups of around 50–150 people; Dunbar [1996].) Little authority would have been exercised, and formal social institutions would not have existed.

Societies of this sort very possibly existed in pre-*sapiens* or early *sapiens* phases of human evolution. However, it is highly questionable whether such societies have existed in recent millennia. Steward's model for this social type, the Great Basin Shoshone, are now known to have had much more complex societies. Steward knew these people well, but he knew them after smallpox, tuberculosis, and Euroamerican settlers had severely impacted them.

Other groups that initially appear to be socially simple emerge on inspection to be fragments of larger social orders. For example, some of the San of the Kalahari Desert in southern Africa, often viewed as "pure" hunter-gatherers, were longtime trading partners with their agricultural Bantu neighbors. The Tasaday of the Philippines were almost certainly an agricultural group who lost their land—but their simplicity and isolation were romanticized and/or outright misrepresented in early studies (Headland and Reid 1989). The Aché mentioned above, or at least groups close to them, are descended from agricultural groups missionized by the Jesuits in the eighteenth century but then driven off their land after the Jesuits were expelled from Latin America in the 1750s. Groups like the Mbuti of Africa and the Agta of the Philippines are specialized hunters, trading meat to farmers for grain and other goods.

Hunting and gathering societies that appear to have been isolated from agriculturalists (e.g., the Australian Aborigines) and that had their lives recorded fairly accurately before recent cultures changed them beyond recognition show a far different pattern. Leadership was usually informal, but hereditary chiefs with real power over large tracts of land did exist. Groups broke up into small bands for foraging purposes but aggregated into orderly settlements of hundreds or thousands when resources were concentrated and plentiful. The Great Basin Shoshone came together in such groups for pine-nut gathering and for fiestas. Networks of kinship could be even more wide-flung. Thousands of people over thousands of square miles of land could trace relationships that allowed them to claim friendship, protection, and support during difficult years. Cycles of ceremonies and rituals maintained kinship and political links, and these cycles could be coordinated over vast areas. Trade links extended over these areas and often spread even more widely.

Nonetheless, the concept of the band remains important in the study of hunter-gatherers (Testart 1988:4) and has formed the basis for the common hunter-gatherer stereotype, even though it is recognized that many other hunter-gatherers had more complex political organizations. A different approach might be to diverge from the band, tribe, chiefdom categories (defined in chapter 1) and to classify hunter-gatherers based on other criteria, such as being fishers or mounted hunters (Murdock 1968), or to distinguish between storage-based and nonstorage-based hunting and gathering economies (Testart 1988; also see discussion below on foragers and collectors). The struggle to deal with these issues continues.

BIAS IN HUNTER-GATHERER STUDIES

There have been (and continue to be) several factors resulting in a biased view of hunters and gatherers. The first is that there is an overemphasis on the role of males and, so, on hunting rather than gathering. Another is that anthropologists come from an industrialized agricultural society that tends to look down on hunter-gatherers. Third is the fact that most hunter-gatherer cultures are extinct or have been severely impacted by agriculturalists, and the biomes that they occupied are largely gone. Thus, now we have few real examples to study.

Hunter-gatherers are often viewed as the "most ancient of so-called primitive society" (Testart 1988:1), living fossils, archaic, and representative of preagricultural life (see critique in Headland and Reid [1989:49–51]). This view may have some limited usefulness as a general analogy in certain cases, but in all cases, hunter-gatherers survived because they were adapted to their environment, demonstrating evolutionary *success*, not failure. True, some anthropologists construct models of ancient life using hunter-gatherers as ethnographic analogy, and a great deal can be learned from this. However, contemporary hunter-gatherers are alive *today* and cannot be identical to ancient societies (Testart 1988).

Sexual Bias

There has been a tendency for hunter-gatherer researchers to emphasize the hunting aspect of the system to the detriment of understanding the gathering component. There are at least several reasons for this. First is the initial working assumption that hunting was a male activity and gathering was a female activity. This, coupled with the fact that most of the people working with hunter-gatherers have themselves been male, led to an emphasis of hunting in research. Second is that the hunting of animals is "sexier" and attracts more attention from both the native people and the anthropologists studying them. A third reason is the anthropological view that hunting was such an important factor in the evolution of early humans.

The view is expressed in the title of the then state-of-the-art treatise on hunter-gatherers published in 1968, *Man the Hunter* (Lee and DeVore 1968). While the term *man* was meant to mean "human," it was not long before the role of females in hunter-gatherer societies became a focus of major research. The book *Woman the Gatherer* (Dahlberg 1981) reflected the reaction to the male bias in hunter-gatherer studies. Beginning in the 1970s, with the recognition (or admission) that the gathering was as important, usually more important, to the success of ethnographic hunting and gathering groups as hunting, considerable work has been conducted on the role of women in such societies (e.g., Linton 1971; Begler 1978; Leacock 1978; Dahlberg 1981; Hunn 1981; Tanner 1981; Kurz 1987; McCreedy 1994). This work continues but is somewhat complicated by the emerging understanding that sex roles are not set in stone. Women do some hunting and men do some gathering.

Ethnocentrism

Anthropologists are the people who study hunter-gatherers. Virtually all anthropologists grew up in societies that are agricultural and industrialized. Few anthropologists were raised as hunter-gatherers. The result of this is that the view of the anthropologists is biased toward agriculture. When studying a particular area, there is an inclination to judge it based on agricultural standards. For example, deserts are viewed as being "harsh," based in large part on the lack of greenery and the perception that agriculture would be difficult or impossible. Thus, hunter-gatherers in such environments "must" be living on the edge.

In addition, the notion that hunter-gatherers are primitive (a very poor choice of words) and somehow inferior is implicit in their classification based on unilinear evolutionary principles. This notion is ethnocentric and erroneous. Many also tend to believe that the life of a hunter-gatherer is (was) very difficult, that it is (was) very hard to make a living. This has led to the notion of hunter-gatherers eking a meager living from a hostile land or walking around, picking things up off of the ground, and putting them in their mouths, and subsisting on the edge of starvation.

The Marginal Environment Problem

At one time, hunter-gatherer cultures occupied the entire planet (most terrestrial ecosystems); all peoples made a living hunting and gathering. With the domestication of plants and animals, those areas that were suitable for domesticates were colonized by the agriculturalists, and the hunter-gatherer groups were generally either expelled or assimilated. Over the past ten thousand years, most of the areas formerly occupied by hunter-gatherers have been appropriated by agriculturalists. Thus, contemporary hunter-gatherer groups are limited to those areas not (yet) desired by agriculturalists, those areas currently unsuitable for agriculture (and thus "harsh" in the view of agriculturalists).

As a result of this phenomenon, many believe that the extant hunter-gatherer groups studied by anthropologists are those that have survived in environments that are considered marginal, at least by farmers. Those hunter-gatherers then become the analogs for hunter-gatherers everywhere, throughout time, and so could be very misleading. Recent research, however, suggests that this may not be the case (Porter and Marlowe 2007) and that extant hunter-gatherers still inhabit favorable habitats. Neverthelsss, the fact remains that at least some very productive hunter-gather habitats are now occupied by farmers (e.g., the Great Central Valley of California).

Affluence

It has been argued (Sahlins 1972) that hunters and gatherers were "the original affluent society" because they had abundant resources to satisfy their relatively limited wants and needs (also see Koyama and Thomas 1981; but contrast with Shnirelman 1994). Affluence refers to the amount of free time an individual has and is based on studies that suggested hunter-gatherers worked only four to six hours per day to meet their subsistence needs. While it may be true that hunting or gathering took place for a limited number of hours per day, the calculation did not consider the amount of time spent back in camp processing, repairing, and/or manufacturing things. In reality, then, contemporary hunter-gatherers probably spent much of the day conducting a variety of tasks, although they still probably worked less than most agriculturalists do. However, for hunter-gatherers once located in more productive environments, this may not have been the case. For example, in Northwest Coast groups, a very considerable amount of spare time not required for basic subsistence was available for other pursuits, mostly in the winter after the salmon-fishing season.

There may be a bias in the other direction as well. It may be that some view hunter-gatherers as the perfect society, the original ecologists living in harmony with the environment and having few cares or worries. In truth, like any group of people, hunter-gatherer groups have problems that have to be solved.

POPULATION

Like all cultures, hunters and gatherers must stay within the carrying capacity of their environment (see Baumhoff 1981). Unlike many agricultural groups, they cannot easily manipulate the system to create long-term food increases and must pay closer attention to population control.

Hunter-gatherers have developed (as we all have) a number of mechanisms for demographic control (Cowgill 1975). Obvious ones include migration and celibacy. Resource shortages or other factors may lead to warfare, but such small-scale warfare generally has little impact on population. Other, less obvious methods for population control are used. In San groups that move frequently, for instance, mothers nurse their babies for a long time—up to three years or more. Because nursing reduces the likelihood of conception by about 50 percent (at least in the first several months), San births are kept more or less spaced.

Population can be regulated more directly through birth-control methods, abortion, and infanticide. Inuit groups once employed all of these practices during hard times. They also had a tradition in which old people would go off by themselves to die if conditions became extremely difficult. In the absence of such methods, even disease and warfare are not effective at holding down population growth, and a hunter-gatherer population will soon outgrow its resource base. It is, then, not surprising that all well-studied hunters and gatherers have reported knowledge of abortion and birth-control techniques, and most (if not all) have histories of migration and land conflict.

SETTLEMENT AND SUBSISTENCE

Groups are further divided based on the particular way in which they pursue hunting and gathering. Hunter-gatherers leave their camp or village and venture into the landscape to obtain resources. These trips are most often patterned and planned.

Seasonal Round

If a group is dependent upon wild foods, its members must be well versed on the seasonality of the various resources they exploit. Different resources become available at different times and places. To obtain these resources, the groups (or at least portions of them) have to move to the resource. The same principle actually is true for agriculturalists as well, but most of their food resources are located in the same place, meaning that the people do not have to move very far. The system of the timing and movement of groups across the landscape is called a **seasonal round.**

A seasonal round might be regular or irregular. A very simple regular seasonal round (figure 5.1) might be one in which the group goes to resource area A in the spring to use particular resources. In the summer, it moves to resource area B, to resource area C in the fall, and to resource area D in the winter. The next spring, it would move back to resource area A, the same location and resource(s) that it used the previous spring. Thus, the cycle would begin anew. Native Californians, for example, often moved from winter villages to foothill areas that had rich crops of seeds and roots in spring, then to the mountains for summer hunting and acorn gathering, then back in fall to winter villages.

A more complex round would be an increase in the number of locations and resources used and/or a decrease in the repetition of the use of specific locations. If the group were to go to a *different* location every spring, instead of the same

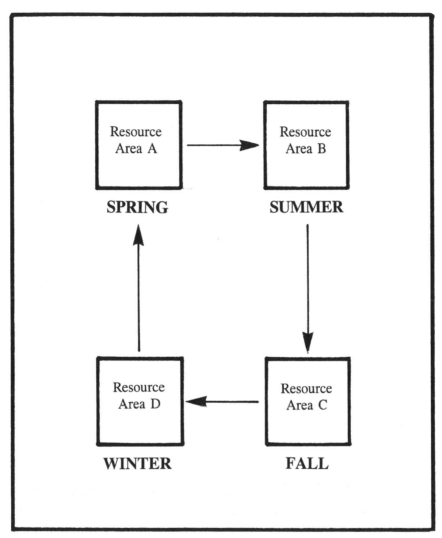

FIGURE 5.1
A very simple seasonal round. Arrows indicate the direction of movement.

place every year, the round would be more diverse (see figure 5.2). This example could be stretched out infinitely, but whatever the case, the group would always know where it was going.

Fission-Fusion

Groups may change their size and distribution depending upon conditions. If a group splits up into several smaller groups that separate from the larger group,

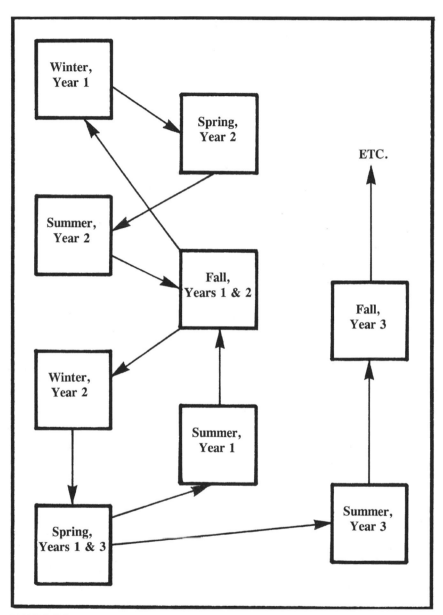

FIGURE 5.2
A fairly complex seasonal round. Arrows indicate the direction of movement. Note seasonal and yearly changes.

this is called fission (splitting). If the groups come back together again, it is called fusion (joining). Some groups practice splitting and joining as a regular part of their seasonal round. If the resources at location A are not abundant enough to support the entire group, it may split, with some of the group going to location 5 at the same time as the rest of the people are at location 1. Later, they will all meet at location 2 to exploit resource B (figure 5.3). This **fission-fusion** tactic may serve to mitigate seasonal resource shortages (e.g., as with some Inuit), allowing for a flexible response to changing conditions.

Fission-fusion may also be used to resolve disputes between members of a social unit. For example, the various hunter-gatherer groups in the forests of central Africa (see case study 5.2) simply leave a particular social unit (village or camp) when there are too many people or if conflict becomes too great. The departing people may join other groups or may form their own. Membership in these groups is very fluid.

Opportunism

As discussed below in greater detail, hunter-gatherers have a planned economic system; they do not do things in a haphazard way. However, they do take advantage of opportunities that may present themselves. If a person exploits a particular resource and happens to encounter another useful one, the person likely will take advantage of the situation and exploit the second resource as well as the first (or perhaps instead of the first).

Many hunting expeditions are conducted to obtain specific prey: a rabbit drive or a bison hunt. However, some hunting excursions do not have a particular prey in mind; any (culturally acceptable) prey encountered will be taken. This is opportunistic in some sense, but there is still planning and knowledge of general prey locations (e.g., around water) and not a random operation.

Flexibility

We have already discussed information systems and resource monitoring. To hunter-gatherers, these factors are central to their success during the year. A group may have a set seasonal round, but that round is dependent upon conditions in the environment. If conditions change, so must the group's response. If resource 1 did not ripen or has moved from location A, a decision must be made regarding where to go and what resource to use instead. Such a decision would involve the consideration of a variety of factors, including which resources were where, the location of other social units, group boundaries, and/or kinship networks. Information derived from resource monitoring would be critical to the

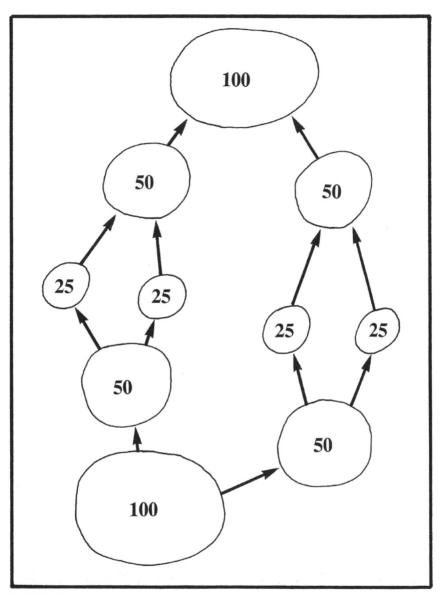

FIGURE 5.3
A very simple fission-fusion model for a culture of one hundred people.

decision. The gathering and sharing of such information enhances the ability to be flexible in times of stress, as does the retention of knowledge, the maintenance of kinship networks, and the ability to use fission-fusion. In times of stress, the greater the flexibility, the greater the chances of success.

Foragers and Collectors

Anthropologists have generally defined two basic hunter-gatherer strategies: foraging and collecting, sometimes also called travelers and processors (Bettinger and Baumhoff 1982:487; see discussion below). Most anthropologists recognize a forager-collector continuum, that a group is more or less of one than the other. However, groups tend to become pigeonholed by their strategy, and the use of these terms belies the complexity inherent in the way that hunter-gatherers make a living. Their flexibility usually is ignored, even if inadvertently.

The terms *foraging* and *collecting* have common or literal meaning, even though they may have been operationally defined differently by anthropologists. However, even if operationally defined differently, the use of a term still implies its literal meaning, particularly to those not aware of the operational definition. We tend to fall into a rut in our thinking, as it is limited by the terms we use.

Foragers

The term *forage* generally means to wander in search of food (or other resources), as in the actions taken by armies supplying themselves in the countryside (Burch and Ellanna 1994a:4). Wandering implies that there is no specific route and no set destination. Thus, when people actually forage, they have no specific goal or resource in mind, they just wander about until some resource is encountered.

The operational anthropological definition is different. **Foragers**, in the most useful definition, are seen as people who have a seasonal round, occupy a series of camps as they move about the landscape, and have no permanent home. They move their residences from place to place depending upon the season and condition of resources, relying on monitoring (although some groups may not have great seasonal variation in resource availability and so may not move often for that reason). Forager groups are viewed as being generally small and mobile and as having a relatively meager material culture (because they carry most of their possessions with them). Thus, foragers move people to the resource (see figure 5.4). In sum, "foragers generally have high residential mobility, low-bulk inputs [gather small quantities at a time], and regular daily food-procurement" (Binford 1980:9). The daily food-gathering trips (represented in figure 5.4 as the

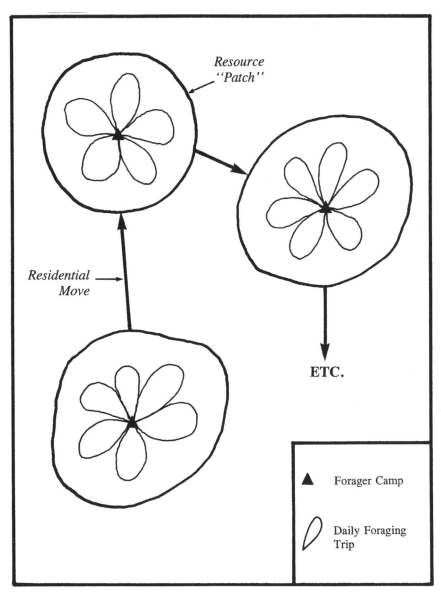

FIGURE 5.4
A very generalized forager settlement model.

"daisy") result in the people gathering information on resources as well as the resources themselves. They often live in deserts (the San, for example). Many exist at the margins of agricultural societies; fully independent hunter-gatherer groups tend to have stable homes for at least part of the year.

Collectors

Collectors is a term employed (see Binford 1980:10) to describe hunter-gatherers that use specially organized task groups to exploit specific resources, often in bulk. In this strategy, the resources are moved to the people (different from the forager approach). Groups practicing a collector strategy would have permanent or semipermanent residences, with many smaller activity locations used briefly by specific task groups to obtain resources (figure 5.5). The native peoples of the Pacific Coast area of the United States and Canada fall into this category. Moving less frequently would allow for a larger population and a greater and more complex material culture. Because the resource would be moved to the people, storage of certain staple resources would be common. This would tend to limit the mobility of the groups, as they would be tethered to the storage facilities. As with foragers, the short-term movements of task groups serve the purpose of information gathering as well as resource procurement.

As defined above, foragers tend to occupy smaller camps, have generally less material culture and a less specialized material culture, rely less on storage, and have a smaller population than collectors. Specialized task groups are present in a collector group but not in a forager group. Also part of the definition of these strategies is settlement, whether villages or camps, and behavior, such as types of social systems and the use of resources. Using these criteria, cultures are classified by strategy as either foragers or collectors. The classification may be based on limited information, and once assigned, a culture is assumed to manifest all criteria, a situation that can mask diversity and confuse analysis.

Strategies and Tactics

As noted above, strategy is a commonly used term, in a classificatory sense, with hunter-gatherers (see Sutton 2000). A **strategy** is a broad, overall plan, a way of reaching long-range goals (e.g., making a living), not short-term practices (e.g., one's current job). Short-term practices are called **tactics**; they differ from strategy in that they are the methods used to execute or accomplish the strategy. Cultures practice a wide variety of tactics to make a living. They possess and retain an inventory of tactics, some of which are used often (even daily), some of which are not but are still retained in the inventory (part of the retention of knowledge and flexibility discussed above).

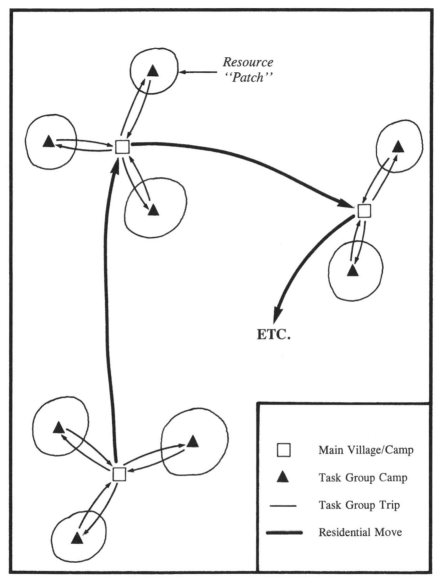

Resource "Patch"

ETC.

Main Village/Camp

Task Group Camp

Task Group Trip

Residential Move

FIGURE 5.5
A very generalized collector settlement model.

Hunter-gatherer cultures frequently are classified as practicing one of the two primary broad classes of strategies, foraging or collecting, based on a few observed criteria, such as having villages or traveling to resources. Once classified, it is commonly assumed that they adhere to the other, even though theoretical, criteria of that strategy as well, such as if they have camps, they must have a small population. Once these assumptions are made, they somehow become "facts," and the variability within the adaptation of the culture is overlooked.

The actual strategy of a hunting and gathering group is to find the resources for making a living. The methods employed to accomplish that end are tactics. A wide variety of tactics are used to make a living, and these tactics vary, depending on the situation. This argument regarding strategy and tactics applies to all cultures, including agriculturalists. If foraging means going out and getting wild foods, then all cultures, including Western cultures, do some foraging, such as fishing, hunting, or picking wild berries. The same is true with collecting. No culture is totally isolated from hunter-gatherer tactics; it is only a matter of degree. One could argue that there is a hunter-gatherer/agriculturalist continuum as well as one from forager to collector.

If the focus of analysis becomes tactical inventories (or adaptations) rather than strategies, perhaps we can better understand the variety of responses and behaviors. Each culture employs a wide range (or repertoire) of tactics, many of which will overlap with those of other groups. It is this diversity of response that is central to their adaptation. Without understanding this diversity in tactics, one cannot understand the adaptation of the culture or the culture itself. The use of strategies as pigeonhole categories limits our understanding.

This way of looking at hunter-gatherers is, perhaps, more important from an archaeological standpoint. In ethnographic situations, we can (in theory) observe the diversity of responses by the people and understand their settlement/ subsistence system as an integral unit. In archaeological contexts, we observe (i.e., excavate) one segment of a system (an archaeological site) and use that to infer the system as a whole. One could easily find a collector camp that "looked" like a forager camp and so classify the cultural system in question as foragers. Based on our theoretical construct of how a forager system is organized and behaves, we might reconstruct the ancient culture in a completely erroneous way. While this error might be corrected in the light of additional archaeological work on that system, the error might have been avoided altogether if we were less myopic about the strategies.

ENVIRONMENTAL MANIPULATION AND RESOURCE MANAGEMENT

Many hunter-gatherer groups practice relatively little active environmental manipulation, as large-scale changes in the landscape were not always required. However, when such methods were used, burning was the most commonly employed method (as discussed in chapter 4). Cultivation and even planting of root crops and sometimes other food plants is widespread, especially in western

North America and northern Australia. Many hunter-gatherer groups live near farmers. Some cultures span the transition by planting and cultivating in favorable areas or years while hunting and gathering otherwise; this is well known for the Kumeyaay of southern California (Shipek 1989) and the inhabitants of the dry belt of southwestern Madagascar. Passive environmental manipulation through the use of ritual was a much more common practice. Such methods included ritual control of weather and places of power, such as the stewardship of Dreamtime places in Australia. Like all people, hunter-gatherers strive to exert at least some control over both abiotic and biotic elements of their environment.

The management of particular resources was common among hunter-gatherers. Active methods included taking adult male animals instead of juveniles or females where possible (but this seems rare; cf. Kay and Simmons [2002]), the pruning or sowing of specific plants (e.g., tobacco) to enhance productivity, and the use of some religious taboos. The intensity of management varied greatly, and in some cases, resources were monitored only as to their availability and condition. At the end of the Pleistocene, some cases of the intense active management of animals and plants ultimately led to the genetic domestication of those species, giving rise to agriculture.

Passive management of many other resources was also conducted. A common practice was a ceremony to thank the soul of the animal that allowed itself to be killed. Failure to thank the animal would anger it, impacting future hunting success.

RELATIONS WITH OTHER GROUPS

Hunter-gatherers always had some contact with other groups. Until about ten thousand years ago, these others were always hunter-gatherers. Such contact often resulted in peaceful relationships, but it is very difficult for two hunter-gatherer groups to occupy the same territory because they would fill the same basic niche in a common habitat. Sharing habitat with pastoralists, who have a different niche, would be easier as long as the seasonal rounds of the two groups did not conflict and the hunter-gatherers did not burn the grass too often.

However, it is generally difficult for hunter-gatherers to coexist with agriculturalists (e.g., Spielmann and Eder 1994; Layton 2001). The farmers generally alter the landscape in a significant manner, and in doing so, they disrupt the hunter-gatherer system to such a degree that the latter are usually forced either to move or be absorbed. Resistance to the farmers usually results in the hunter-gatherers being defeated.

Agriculturalists enter a region and appropriate certain lands for crop production. It may be that these lands were also highly productive for wild foods such as grass seeds or animals. The farmers will claim ownership of the land, sometimes fence it, and always defend it. This practice, in effect, removes that land and its former resources from the seasonal round of the hunter-gatherers, changing the geographic distribution and availability of their resource universe. The hunter-gatherers must adapt by altering their use of resources, seasonal round, and territory, or they will be either killed or absorbed by the farmers. Many times, the farmers appropriate such a large portion of the hunter-gatherer resource base that adjustment is impossible and there is no choice but to acculturate.

There have been, however, cases where hunter-gatherers have expanded against agriculturalists, usually with warfare as an important mechanism. The Apache expansion into the American Southwest during the past five hundred years is a good example. The Apache always knew where the sedentary farmers were located, raided their fields as they would exploit any productive resource patch, and generally created so much havoc that the farmers had to move. Thus, the Apache took control of the region, driving out even the Spanish settlers in north-central Mexico.

Mutualistic Relationships

Despite the problems noted above, some hunter-gatherers have developed a mutually beneficial relationship with their agricultural neighbors. This may include the trade of domesticated foods for wild ones and/or labor exchange. A good example of such a mutualistic relationship is that of the Mbuti and Bila in the Ituri forest of central Africa (see case study 5.2).

CHAPTER SUMMARY

Hunters and gatherers, often referred to as foragers, are those people who make their primary living by exploiting wild plants and animals, and until fairly recently, all human groups were hunter-gatherers. Even today, all cultures rely to some extent on wild foods. Hunter-gatherers display a vast array of structures, forms, and adaptations, from very small, simple groups to very large and complex ones. Gathering primarily involves the collection of plant resources while hunting primarily involves the procurement of animals. Scavenging does not fit neatly into either of these practices but may have been an important early strategy.

Hunter-gatherers are widely misunderstood, often viewed as small and simple groups barely surviving in some hostile environment. Understanding hunter-gatherers is clouded by an analytical overemphasis on hunting, ethnocentrism by researchers, and the fact that all contemporary hunter-gatherers live in marginal environments not yet occupied by agriculturalists, giving rise to the perception that all hunter-gatherers lived in marginal environments.

Most hunter-gatherers move about the landscape to resource localities, a seasonal round, and may employ some sort of fission-fusion. Those who move their populations to resource localities may be classified as foragers while those who bring resources back to their settlements may be classified as collectors. Whatever their strategy, each group operationalizes that strategy through the use of tactical actions.

Hunter-gatherers generally do not make intensive efforts at environmental manipulation or resource management, although there are important exceptions. Relationships with other groups, now mostly agriculturalists, are typically strained, and many hunter-gatherer groups are now under intense pressure to drop their livelihood.

KEY TERMS
collectors
fission-fusion
foragers
gathering
hunters and gatherers
hunting
scavenging
seasonal round
strategy msp
tactics msp

CASE STUDY 5.1

THE NUU-CHAH-NULTH OF BRITISH COLUMBIA

This case study on the Nuu-chah-nulth shows that hunter-gatherers can develop complex political and economic institutions and have dense populations, all features fairly atypical of hunter-gatherers. We also illustrate some of the variability in hunter-gatherer complexity and provide an example of a group that made its living primarily from fishing.

The Nuu-chah-nulth are hunter-gatherers living in an area containing abundant resources along the Northwest Coast of North America. They live on the west coast of Vancouver Island, a large island off the west coast of British Columbia (figure 5.6). The island is mountainous, cold, rainy, and covered with dark, dense forests (figure 5.7), areas where

FIGURE 5.6
Location of the Nuu-chah-nulth along the northwestern coast of North America.

CASE STUDY 5.1

FIGURE 5.7
The forest along the shore of Vancouver Island (photo by Mark Q. Sutton).

hunting and gathering was difficult and unprofitable. The waters, however, teem with life. In the 1770s, the Nuu-chah-nulth numbered perhaps ten thousand people. By 1900, due primarily to European
diseases, their population had shrunk to around five hundred but has
since substantiallyi recovered. Today, the culture remains vigorous.
The most recent summary of the Nuu-chah-nulth was presented by
Arima and Dewhirst (1990), who used the term Nootkan to refer to the
group (see the note at the end of this case study).

THE NATURAL ENVIRONMENT
The western coast of Vancouver Island has an irregular coastline with
many small islands, inlets, and fjords. The terrain is rugged, with high
mountains, thick forests, many watercourses, and narrow beaches. The
climate is mild but very wet, with the rainy season extending from October through April.

The Nuu-chah-nulth exploit four basic ecozones: the forest, the many
riparian zones, the littoral zone, and the open ocean. The forest consists
mostly of cedar, hemlock, spruce, and fir. Many animals living in the

forest, including deer, bear, and elk, were utilized, as were a number of forest plants. The rivers and streams that ran through the forest to the sea were the primary sources of salmon, the most essential of the fish taken by the Nuu-chah-nulth.

The ocean, including the littoral zone, was the main source of food, avenue of travel, and the foundation of identity for the Nuu-chah-nulth. Shellfish were the primary resource of the littoral zone, while the open ocean was home to a number of marine mammals, including seals, sea lions, sea otters, porpoises, and whales. These animals were very abundant and formed important resources. Many species of fish, including some salmon, were also taken from the ocean. The ocean produced vast quantities of fish and sea mammals until the devastation of those resources by the contemporary fishing industry.

SOCIOPOLITICAL ORGANIZATION

The Nuu-chah-nulth once comprised a number of small, politically independent, bands whose primary political unit was the permanent winter town. Groups were designated by the name of their town or sometimes by their principal food (as in *Mowichaht*, "people of the deer"). Life revolved around these winter towns, which might contain up to a thousand people. In the summer, the towns were almost deserted, as the people broke into small groups and traveled to hunting and berry-picking areas. The various groups intermarried and recognized that they had a common language and culture. While the Nuu-chah-nulth had no formal political unity, they were united by ties of kinship, ceremonial interaction, and trade.

The Nuu-chah-nulth were stratified into three social classes: the nobility, commoners, and slaves with lineages, clans, and moieties being important. A complex series of ranks was recognized, with each person occupying an individual rank in the family, each family occupying a rank within the lineage, each lineage having a rank in the clan, each clan being ranked in the moiety, and each moiety being ranked in the town. The positions of rank were often hereditary, but the system required that the person acquiring the rank validate that position through sponsoring a potlatch (see below). The inheritance of property, including titles, rights, and power, was a critical element in maintaining rank.

Religion among the Nuu-chah-nulth was heavily focused on maintaining the social order. Myths and religious texts reinforced the social system and its key values. They also focused on maintaining the ecosystem. The social world did (and still does) not stop at the borders of the human species; all things were involved. Everything, living or not, had spirits that had to be treated as one would treat a human. Thus, virtually all things in the environment were subjects of passive resource management.

ECONOMICS

The Nuu-chah-nulth were hunters and gatherers, and many resources were obtained by a variety of tactics. However, fishing was the most important pursuit. They cultivated wild roots but practiced no agriculture, except perhaps some local raising of tobacco, until the late 1770s, when Europeans introduced the potato—virtually the only crop that thrives in the cold, wet climate.

Aquatic Resources

The principal resource was salmon. Five species of salmon (*Oncorhynchus* spp.) and two closely related species of sea-running trout occur in the area. The five salmon species are lumped together into one category by outsiders, but the Nuu-chah-nulth have quite different names for all of them and regard it as strange that anyone could lump them together. Local English speakers have now adopted this view. They do not use the Nuu-chah-nulth names, but they do use different names for the five: chum, pink, sockeye, and so on. The word *salmon* is never used in ordinary conversation. Thus does ecology affect language.

Each of these fish has very different characteristics. Sockeye has the richest meat, but the young mature only in lakes, so sockeye does not exist except in river-and-lake systems; here they used to occur in the millions. Chum, which spawns only in the lower reaches of rivers, has the leanest meat and is thus ideal for drying in the damp climate; it was the staple for storing and so became the staff of life in winter. Pinks once ran in the millions, but only every other year, and they do not store well, so their usefulness was limited.

The processing of salmon (usually by smoking) presented a logistical problem. Salmon runs tend to be brief, and a vast number of fish swim up the river in a few days. Large rivers have several separate runs. Of particular concern was the chum run, because the lives of the people largely depended on how many chum a group could store for the lean season. Runs sometimes fail. The Nuu-chah-nulth coped as best they could by monitoring fish populations and artificially stocking streams (Sproat 1868). When genuine famine threatened a particular group, it dispersed, to live with relatives or to comb usually neglected areas.

Whales were also a major food source. Migration routes and breeding grounds lie close inshore. The huge animals often come into the large bays of the coast to rest during their travels. Here they become quite tame. The Nuu-chah-nulth were superb whalers and could easily harpoon them in the bays and even in open sea. Sea lions, seals, seabirds, shellfish, and many other resources provided a rich supplement. Additionally, despite the relative poverty of the land, terrestrial resources such as berries and other plant foods were fairly abundant, and hundreds of species were known and used, with the major species being managed (Turner and Efrat 1982). There were even a few places, in the northern and central portions of the island, where rich inland pastures fed large numbers of elk and deer, permitting a few groups to live largely on venison.

These resources were not evenly distributed, however. Shellfish were concentrated on the outer coasts, where open-sea currents brought nutrients to them. However, there is not much else on the outer coasts, and residents of these areas were teased as "eaters of dead minnows on the beaches" (Drucker 1951). Whales were primarily confined to the great bays. Salmon ran best in major rivers with lakes. The prime location for a winter town, then, was a sheltered island, in a bay with a major river system draining into it. Such localities were considered highly desired prizes and were often fought over.

Terrestrial Resources

Animals hunted on land were less important than those taken from the ocean. The most significant land mammal was the deer, which was not abundant on Vancouver Island. Some mammals, including bears, marmots, and elk, were taken for food, while others, such as beaver, mink, and ermine, were taken for their fur. Some seabirds were also taken, along with their eggs. The only domestic animal was the dog.

Hundreds of plants were known and used as food, including many roots and tubers, ferns, numerous kinds of berries and fruits, and some greens, as well as some ocean plants. Other plants were used as material in the manufacture of basketry, cordage and rope, and for woodworking. Red cedar was particularly important for wood and fiber.

Seasonal Round

The primary residence locality is the winter town, occupied for much of the year. However, in the summer the residents of the town disperse to a series of smaller settlements to hunt and gather various resources distributed across the landscape in a generally patchy fashion. Thus, the Nuu-chah-nulth employ fission-fusion in their seasonal round.

The Potlatch

The potlatch is an integral component of Nuu-chah-nulth politics and economy; it is a complex cycle of gift-giving ceremonies whose primary function is to validate title. Potlatching could also elevate a low chief; he could rise higher than a chief that started well but failed to potlatch often. A friend of one of us (ENA) was the eldest successor to a chieftainship of the Clayoquot. He was no power seeker, so he declined to potlatch, in favor of his younger brother who held the potlatch and thus had the position. He tired of it, and our friend decided to potlatch for it after all, thus gaining it for the nonce. Potlatching was highly competitive, especially in the nineteenth century, when trade with the whites was successful for the Nuu-chah-nulth.

This was not mere self-aggrandizement. A chief attracted followers by giving them potlatch gifts. He was not just paying them to join him—he was displaying his success at obtaining and amassing wealth and his generosity in sharing it. In war, in fishing, and in trade, these followers supported him. If he lost the physical prowess and spiritual power that were believed to give him success, he lost the followers. Nuu-chah-nulth society is not fluid or unstructured, but it is a society in which kinship links are far flung and close knit. Everyone is related to everybody else. A man disappointed in his chief can easily find another chief to whom he is more or less equally closely related.

CASE STUDY 5.1

In the mid-nineteenth century, several factors accelerated the potlatch cycle. First, the introduction of guns had made warfare a far more dangerous activity but far more profitable for the winner. Second, trade injected vast new wealth into the system. Third, disease had decimated the population, leading to an abundance of unclaimed land and chiefly titles. Fourth, social disorganization probably led to heightened competition. The result—among the Nuu-chah-nulth as among their neighbors—was an increase in warfare and in potlatching. Enterprising chiefs embarked on ambitious military conquest. The Ahousaht conquered several islands. The Clayoquot (more accurately Tla'okw'aht) took over most of the sound now named for them. The area around Alberni was taken from speakers of an unrelated Salishan language; their descendants are now assimilated into the Nuu-chah-nulth linguistic and cultural world. In short, potlatching was not "just a ceremony," nor was it a pathological waste of material goods. It was a way of mobilizing followers in a war-torn society (Drucker and Heizer 1967).

The potlatch exists in one form or another among all the Northwest Coast peoples and has frequently been a subject for study in anthropology. Initially, anthropologists were influenced by local missionaries, who condemned it as a pagan ceremony that was nothing but a waste of valuable goods. Ruth Benedict, in her famous book *Patterns of Culture* (1934), saw the potlatch of the neighboring Kwakiutl as "megalomaniac paranoid." Others saw it primarily as a way of shoring up the kinship system.

Much of this literature was based on the mistaken belief that the Northwest Coast was so rich an environment that resources were always lavishly abundant. This mistake arose from two sources. First, early scholars did not realize the enormous extent of population reduction due to disease. They saw five hundred Nuu-chah-nulth and several million salmon and could not imagine a time of want. But ten thousand to fifteen thousand Nuu-chah-nulth were a very different matter! Second, these early scholars did not realize the frequency of failure of the critical salmon runs. Many Nuu-chah-nulth groups depended on chum for stored food; even if other salmon were abundant, there was no way to store them, unless exceptionally hot and dry weather permitted successful drying. If the chum run failed, the community faced severe food shortages.

CASE STUDY 5.1

Finally an ecological explanation was devised. Wayne Suttles (see Suttles [1987] for the original paper and his further views on the subject) argued that potlatching among the Straits Salish (southeastern neighbors of the Nuu-chah-nulth) served to spread the food around evenly and thus reduce the risk of famine in bad years. A group that was blessed with an exceptionally rich run of salmon could potlatch. When they hit a bad year, they could collect on their potlatch debt—they could be fed by the people they had fed before.

Stuart Piddocke (1965), a student of Suttles at the time, generalized this hypothesis to cover the entire Northwest Coast. This view was adopted by Harris (1985), but he added—correctly—the observation that social breakdown in the late nineteenth century caused the system to get out of hand. In a classic paper, Orans (1975) showed that there was no good evidence presented for the Piddocke hypothesis and indicated that anyone claiming it would have to show that potlatches were organized that way—that they could and did actually serve that function.

Subsequent research has shown that they did not generally do so. In the old days, a number of years might be required to organize a potlatch. It was thus impossible to predict whether the final year would be a good or bad one (if it was a bad one, the potlatch was delayed a year or so). Moreover, people who were fed in a potlatch were usually called on for more immediate services—labor, help with chiefly duties, or war. Suttles accumulated data that showed how ordinary feasts helped even out the resource picture, but potlatches were a different matter—both ecologically and socially.

Drucker and Heizer (1967) criticized Suttles's theory, reviewed the literature, and concluded that potlatches were related to warfare (also see Ferguson [1984]). For the Nuu-chah-nulth, at least, Drucker and Heizer's theory is definitive. Potlatches did improve the ecological picture for the most powerful chiefs, but not directly. Potlatches did not just provide goods; they provided allies.

ENVIRONMENTAL MANIPULATION AND RESOURCE MANAGEMENT
The Nuu-chah-nulth practiced considerable environmental manipulation, including burning intended to open the landscape to attract deer and enhance the growth of berries and cultivation of root gardens (see Deur and

Turner 2005). They also practiced some passive techniques aimed at controlling bad weather (one of the abiotic elements of the environment).

Passive management was practiced on virtually all resources and all things. Animals, trees, and rocks had spirits that had to be treated as one would treat a human. For example, in stripping the bark from a tree, a person had to ask permission from the tree and explain that the bark was necessary to him and those for whom he was responsible (Drucker 1951; Turner and Efrat 1982). Anyone falsely claiming this was subject to deadly punishment; a tree would soon fall on him, or other disasters would ensue. Whales had to be placated by months of ceremony. The salmon were believed to be people under the sea; if they were treated politely, they would sacrifice themselves for their beloved friends on the land. When Europeans first appeared on the west coast, some Nuu-chah-nulth thought they were the salmon, arriving in their undersea houses (ships; Kirk 1986). To this day, whites are called *mamalni*, "floating house people."

People made sure these ethical messages were enforced because they believed that natural disasters, such as storms and failures of salmon runs, were often punishments for failing to observe these ethical standards. Exhaustion of a stream from overfishing, for instance, was caused by the anger of the salmon people at humans who took more than their share. The strong tendency to see the land as holy, natural entities as "people," and the world as spirit guided is still very pronounced on the west coast of Vancouver Island. Not only has it not died out among the Nuu-chah-nulth, but some of the belief system has been adopted by some local whites! Ceremonies reinforced this view. The simplest was the brief apology and prayer uttered when taking a piece of bark or root. At the other extreme were the months-long, secret, terrifying ceremonies associated with whaling.

NOTE

A word about names is necessary here. The Nuu-chah-nulth had, until recently, no name for themselves. They are known in older literature as the Nootka, from a mistake made by James Cook when he landed among them in the 1770s. He asked the name of the landing place. According to the most believable story (Kirk 1986), the Indians thought he was asking whether he could sail around it and replied, "You can go around," which sounds like *nootka*. For obvious reasons, this name is not used by the people themselves. In Vancouver Island English, they are the "Westcoast People." In the nineteenth century, they were called the Aht, from a suffix that means "people of" (like the "-ian" in "Californian"; *Ahousaht* means "people of Ahous.") The name *Nuu-chah-nulth*, roughly meaning "people on our side of the mountains," was coined in the twentieth century. All of these names are still in use; no one name has universal acceptance. Finally, in 2001, the Nuu-chah-nulth agreed to a treaty with the governments of British Columbia and Canada that would give the groups self-rule, cash, and shared control of much land. The treaty is awaiting final approval and implementation.

THE MBUTI OF THE ITURI FOREST

This case study on the Mbuti provides an example of a mutalistic relationship between hunter-gatherers and agriculturalists interacting within ecological and cultural ecotones, with all of the difficulty in maintaining such a relationship. In addition, the Mbuti have developed a unique inventory of hunting tactics, one that effectively creates multiple human hunting niches within a single habitat.

The Mbuti are one of a number of groups of hunter-gatherers living in the Ituri Forest of central Africa (figure 5.8) and are of short stature, generally under 4.5 feet in average height, and have relatively short legs. This small body size is thought to be an adaptation to humid equatorial forests, as other people of small stature are found in other such forests worldwide. Historically, such people have been called "pygmies," although many now use the term *Twa*, a Bantu word meaning something like "short people." The people of the African rainforests have been known to the outside world since the time of ancient Egypt, but early European characterizations made them out to be sub-human monsters, mythical flying creatures, and the like.

FIGURE 5.8
Location of the Mbuti in the Ituri Forest of Central Africa.

It is not clear how long people have inhabited the Ituri Forest. Some believe that the carrying capacity of the forest was fairly small until the arrival of agriculturalists about four thousand years ago (Bailey et al. 1989). As the Bantu farmers entered the region, they cut down sections of the forest for agricultural fields. Over time, the fields were abandoned and the forest regrew, creating a mosaic of old and secondary growth forest. This use of the forest by the Bantu continues, and their old fields go through a series of succession stages, each of which is utilized by the Twa for different suites of resources.

A number of different Twa groups live in central Africa and have been the subject of numerous studies. Two of the best described groups are the Efe (see Bailey 1991) and the Mbuti. Each of the various groups lives in a different specific environment, and their adaptations vary. This case study considers the Mbuti only as they were in about 1900, when some thirty-five thousand Mbuti lived in the Ituri Forest and interacted with the Bila, their agricultural Bantu neighbors. Much of the information on the Mbuti discussed below was derived from the work of Turnbull (1961, 1983), Hart and Hart (1986), and Duffy (1996). Other Twa and Bantu groups also share similar mutualistic relationships, each tailored to their specific conditions.

THE NATURAL ENVIRONMENT

The Ituri Forest is located in the Congo Basin along the equator in the approximate center of Africa (figure 5.8). It is the forest of Henry Stanley and Dr. David Livingstone, where the American stereotype of "darkest Africa" was born, and covers about fifty thousand square miles. The climate is warm all year, and there is considerable rainfall. Being located at the equator, there are few major seasonal environmental fluctuations in the Ituri Forest, although the winter is generally dryer than the rest of the year and has an impact on adaptations. Seasonal differences in the availability of some resources exist, such as honey and insects.

The forest contains abundant game. However, it has been argued that many of the animals have relatively little body fat in some seasons and that eating lean meat alone could result in malnutrition (Hart and Hart 1986; also see Speth and Spielmann 1983). It is not clear how important a factor this is in the Mbuti economy. Still, plants provide most of the food, with meat being eaten but mostly traded to farmers in exchange for agricultural products. Interestingly, many of the wild plants utilized as food by the Mbuti are obtained from secondary forest, those areas cut down by farmers and later reforested, rather than the old-growth forest. In this sense, the Mbuti are dependent on farmers not only for traded foods but for their cutting of old-growth forests so that secondary forests containing food plants can grow.

Prior to the arrival of farmers, the Ituri was a dense and largely unbroken expanse of old-growth forest. Farmers have cut down portions of the forest for fields, but the forest has grown back over old fields (secondary forest). Many hundreds of tree species grow in the forest, and it is home to many other plants and animals.

The forest is central to Mbuti life. The forest is called "mother," and the Mbuti consider themselves to be the "children of the forest." The forest is viewed as a deity that provides food and materials to support the Mbuti, to which the Mbuti ask for help and offer thanks in ceremony.

Both the Mbuti and the Bila believe the Mbuti to be the original inhabitants of the forest. The Mbuti are thus thought to have special rights in, and/or magical power over, the forest. The forest holds few fears for the Mbuti, although they rarely travel alone and make noise when they walk to avoid being attacked if they surprise an animal. Material possessions are of little concern to the Mbuti; well-being and happiness are much more important. The Bila are afraid of the forest and enter the forest only for specific reasons, such as the very productive annual caterpillar harvest and puberty ceremonies. The Mbuti reinforce this fear to maintain their social and economic distance from the Bila.

SOCIOPOLITICAL ORGANIZATION

The Mbuti are organized into a number of bands, and there is no formal leadership or larger polity. Each band has at least one camp, usually fairly small but with at least six to seven families. Bands have generally "pie-shaped" territories, with an associated Bila village on their outside, other band territories on their sides, and an area in the center defined as being off-limits to hunting, perhaps to provide a sanctuary (a conservation technique) for pursued game. However, hunting territory is not owned, and bands hunt in each other's territory with no problem. Bands are very mobile and practice a fission-fusion settlement system. When game is depleted in an area, the decision will be made to move the camp to a new area within its general territory. However, if an elephant is killed, the camp will be moved to the kill site rather than trying to bring the meat back to the original camp.

The Mbuti are patrilineal and have extensive kinship networks. Having so many relatives in different bands, the Mbuti bands have generally peaceful relationships with one another. Mbuti youths reach sexual maturity at a young age and get married at about the same time. People are expected to marry someone from a different band, the farther away the better, as this establishes and maintains the extensive kinship network. The women move away to live with their husband's band, and a few men have more than one wife. An ideal marriage arrangement is the exchange of females between bands.

Small-scale disputes are settled by the offended individuals shouting at each other and showing contempt and ridicule for each other. Social control of small infractions is enforced in the same way. If a dispute or other problem becomes major, a band will split into two new bands, thus ending the dispute.

While there is no hard-and-fast division of labor, men are the ones who tell the stories and conduct the ceremonies while women have the responsibility of cooking and building houses. In food-getting activities, the work is often shared, with men helping to gather plants and women and children helping in hunting.

ECONOMICS

The primary subsistence pursuits of the Mbuti are hunting the game of the forest, gathering wild plants, and trading for agricultural products, such as bananas, corn beer, yams, manioc, and tobacco, used to supplement their diet. Hunting the various small to large game remains a focus of the Mbuti, but like most hunter-gatherers, hunting provides a minority of the food consumed. Other important food resources include honey and caterpillars.

The Mbuti have two basic hunting adaptations, net hunting and bow hunting. The net hunters live mostly in the west and south of Mbuti territory while the bow hunters mostly live in the east, but the two adaptations do overlap as related to terrain and ecozone. In the area of overlap, one could argue that there are two niches within same habitat.

Hunting

The Mbuti are excellent and stealthy hunters and have an intimate and detailed knowledge of the forest, its travel routes, dangers, and resources. Many kinds of animals are hunted, but duikers (a small antelope) form the major prey species. Elephants are also hunted, being

CASE STUDY 5.2

speared in the belly from ambush on jungle trails. Meat is shared within the group via a very complex system of reciprocity and is traded to the Bila. In sum, there is—or at least used to be—plenty of food available in the forest, and the Mbuti say that "the only hungry Mbuti is a lazy Mbuti."

Net Hunters

One hunting approach is the use of nets to capture game (see Noss [1997] for some comparative data). Net hunting is cooperative, requiring a fairly large number of participants to be effective, and the resulting catch generally includes a broad variety of species. Within groups of net hunters, each family will own a net, generally between one hundred and three hundred feet long. A number of families (at least six or seven are needed) will join together and connect their individual nets into a single net that may be as long as two thousand feet. This large net will be placed in a U shape so that game can be driven into the trap (figure 5.9). In addition to the men, women (who are considered equal partners) and children will also participate, providing logistical support, holding the net, driving game (sometime with the aid of dogs), or processing carcasses. The meat obtained is shared by all the participants.

Net hunts are conducted on an "as needed" basis when a sufficient number of families with nets can be assembled and an agreement is reached regarding the place and timing of the hunt. The net hunters prefer to operate in areas where plant foods are available so that the women can also gather. The animals obtained by net hunting are usually small to medium in size and of many species. Large game, such as buffalo, would run through the nets, ruining them, and are rarely captured using this hunting method.

Bow Hunters

The other basic approach is hunting with the bow and arrow, an effort largely undertaken by solitary men or small groups of men. Game is generally hunted on an opportunistic basis, with the hunters leaving in the morning and returning in the evening, although overnight hunting trips are sometime undertaken. Any meat obtained by the hunters is shared with the community. Mbuti arrows are small, but poison is used on the tips of the arrows, making them lethal.

CASE STUDY 5.2

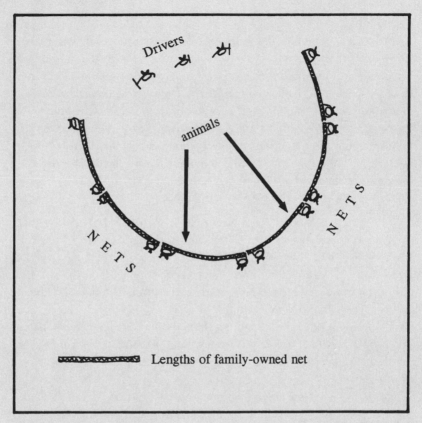

Lengths of family-owned net

FIGURE 5.9
A schematic of the Mbuti net-hunting tactic, with some people driving the animals into the large U-shaped configuration of nets.

The animals obtained by bow hunters are generally larger than those obtained by net hunters, with medium to large animals being the major prey. Bow hunters will take some of the same animals as net hunters, but larger animals, such as buffalo and elephants, are more likely to be sought using spears and traps, and many of the smaller animals captured by the net hunters are not pursued by the bow hunters. With the use of different technologies and with differences in the species taken, bow and net hunters can hunt in the same area (two niches in the same habitat).

CASE STUDY 5.2

Gathering

The Mbuti, generally the women, gather a number of wild plants. However, the number is fairly small compared with the number of plants they know and classify, and wild plant foods are less important to the diet than agricultural products, although this may be a pattern developed only within the past several hundred years. The old-growth forest apparently contains relatively few species used for food, so much of the plant gathering is undertaken in secondary forest. Thus, it could be argued that the Mbuti are dependent on farmers generating secondary forest as they abandon fields.

ENVIRONMENTAL MANIPULATION AND RESOURCE MANAGEMENT

The Mbuti themselves do little to actively manipulate their environment. They try to keep the Bila out of the forest as much as possible, and that helps to maintain and manage the forest. However, the Bila utilize the forest to some extent, practicing some slash-and-burn horticulture. The Mbuti take advantage of this, monitoring the forest succession and utilizing wild resources that colonize the abandoned fields. The Mbuti manage the forest through ritual, maintaining a ceremonial relationship with the forest to ensure its continued productivity and protection.

The Mbuti employ several interesting techniques to manage the game they hunt. First, it could be argued that the bow- and net-hunting adaptations target different animals, preventing overexploitation of game through the reduction of capture rates by any group of hunters. The use of these techniques could be viewed as having separate niches in the same habitat. Second, the Mbuti and their Twa neighbors recognize a central area where hunting is not conducted, thus providing a game refuge.

RELATIONS WITH THE BILA

A relatively large percentage of the plant foods consumed by the Mbuti are domesticated species obtained in trade with the neighboring farmers, the Bila. The Mbuti will travel to the Bila villages to trade, and most speak the Bila language. The Mbuti provide meat to the Bila in exchange for goods, such as bananas, corn beer, manioc, and tobacco. If

CASE STUDY 5.2

they do not have meat to trade, the Mbuti will provide labor in exchange for these products.

The Bila consider themselves as "owning" the Mbuti and want to "rescue" them from a life in the forest. Mbuti will "hunt" (cheat, trick, and/or steal) things from the Bila and feel that the Bila are "stupid" villagers, deserving to be taken advantage of. However, the Bila are usually aware of the Mbuti actions but excuse them as the acts of poor and desperate people. In addition, the Bila do not want to offend the Mbuti by making an issue of their actions.

Individual Bila farmers will develop a close trading relationship with individual Mbuti, whom they regard as poor hunter-gatherers requiring assistance. The Bila thus "adopt" Mbuti, feel responsible for them, sometimes consider them to be property, and will even bequeath them from generation to generation. The Bila want the Mbuti to settle down and become sedentary farmers so that they can be controlled. To accomplish this, the Mbuti are offered land and females. Much to the dismay of the Bila, few Mbuti accept the offers (being ethnocentric, the Bila find it hard to believe that the Mbuti would actually prefer the forest). However, the Bila know that if they become too oppressive, the Mbuti will simply move to a new location, leaving the Bila with no trading partners.

The Bila are dependent on the Mbuti and so avoid offending them. In addition to the very important resources of meat and honey traded to the Bila, the Mbuti include Bila boys in their male initiation ceremonies. The Bila lack the ceremonial expertise to conduct such initiations and so must rely on the Mbuti. If the Mbuti do not perform this service for the Bila, Bila boys will not become men, and the society will not be eligible for marriage.

DISCUSSION

There are four interesting points to be made here about Mbuti ecological adaptations. First, the Mbuti and Bila maintain a mutalistic relationship. The Bila need the Mbuti for meat and labor, and the Mbuti need the Bila for agricultural products. Second, the Bila need the Mbuti for religious reasons: to conduct the initiation ceremonies on Bila boys. Third, the Bila use of some parts of the forest for farming creates the secondary growth where many of the wild plant foods used by the

Mbuti grow. Last, the Mbuti do their best to reinforce the Bila fear of the forest, both to retain their monopoly on providing forest products and initiations to the Bila and to reduce the hunting pressure on the forest animals.

Thus, the Bila and Mbuti share a mutualistic relationship. The Mbuti get agricultural products and trade goods, and the Bila get labor, meat, honey, and their males initiated. Both parties benefit, and neither wishes to offend the other: both are dependent on the relationship. Several of the reasons the system can work is the fact that the two groups have mostly different niches and generally occupy different habitats.

RECENT DEVELOPMENTS

In recent times the people of the Ituri Forest, including the Mbuti, face a number of challenges. Over the past hundred years or so, the government has tried to resettle the Mbuti into villages outside of the forest so as to "free" the Mbuti from their bleak existence as hunter-gatherers. These efforts failed since the Mbuti were adapted to a mobile life and a diet of forest products rather than a sedentary life eating agricultural products.

Today, increased logging of the forest is resulting in the extinction of game and a reduction in habitat, both for the game and for the people. In addition, the expansion of farming and mining in the forest is resulting in its being cut down at an increasing rate, further reducing the habitat of the Mbuti as more and more farmers and miners enter the region. The increasing Bila demand for meat from the Mbuti is steadily increasing, and the supply is beginning to be overexploited. It is possible that the mutualistic system of the Mbuti and Bila, apparently in place for thousands of years, is imperiled.

Perhaps a larger problem is the civil war raging in the region since 1994 (see Hooi 2002). In this war, the Twa have been pressed into military service and find themselves fighting their former neighbors and trading partners. Services, such as education and health care, and supplies have been disrupted or stopped, and the infrastructure of the region has suffered. Trade has been suspended in many parts of the forest.

CASE STUDY 5.2

Ironically, the disruption caused by the recent civil strife has strengthened the mutualistic relationships between the Twa and the Bantu, who rely on each other even more with the erosion of outside support. Thus, the relationship between the two groups is actually quite flexible and adaptive to stressful conditions on their exteriors.

6

The Origins of Food Production

Beginning about twelve thousand years ago, the relationship between humans and the environment changed dramatically. Until that time, all people were hunters and gatherers. At the end of the Pleistocene, or Ice Age, the climate shifted, and in some regions people began a process of intensive control over certain plant and animal species that ultimately led to their domestication. As part of this process, people became dependent upon those domesticated species for food, and the domesticates became dependent upon humans. It further involved major changes in social and political organizations. In addition, the use of land also radically changed, with the clearing of fields and the diversion of rivers and streams. In essence, the development of farming created a new niche for humans. (The most current world review is by Barker [2006].)

The process of domestication seems to have first begun in the Middle East, possibly in the Jordan Valley or neighboring northern Syria and southeastern Turkey. The first domesticated species were dogs, sheep, goats, wheat, and barley. Neolithic villagers began to raise these species between about ten thousand and twelve thousand years ago, although dogs may have been domesticated earlier (Zohary 1982; Zohary and Hopf 1988; Bar-Yosef and Meadow 1995). Wheat and barley grains are attached to the stalk by a thin stem, the rachis. In wild stands, the rachis is brittle and shatters when the grain is mature. The grain falls to the ground and serves as seed for the coming year. Occasionally a wild plant occurs whose rachis is tough and does not shatter. When early harvesters cut wild grain with sickles, the ordinary heads would shatter and scatter grain, but these few exceptional heads would not. The tough seed heads could be carried back to the village with no fear of loss. Probably, over time, stands of these unusual grains arose around the villages. Here, people harvested them and encouraged them to grow.

Deliberate seeding became necessary because the shatterproof heads do not naturally scatter their seeds (Wilke et al. 1972). Thus, agriculture was born.

Animals also were domesticated, including dogs, sheep, cattle, and goats. Biologically, dogs are wolves (see Serpell 1995). The ancestor to the dog was the small southwest Asian wolf, which was something of a scavenger, and presumably was familiar around camps and villages. Families probably kept young ones as pets—as many hunter-gatherers around the world today keep pets. The most docile animals lived the longest; fierce ones were soon killed. Probably many of these dogs escaped to live around the village in loose symbiosis with humans. Eventually, the docile ones began to breed in captivity, and "man's best friend" emerged. Domestic dogs developed smaller teeth and jaws.

Sheep and goats also grew smaller and tamer. Originally sheep did not have wool—that was not to come for thousands of years—but their fleeces probably grew softer over the generations. Cattle were bred to be smaller and tamer than the fierce wild strains. Cattle were apparently domesticated at least three separate times, in the Near East, in India, and in north-central Africa; the strains from these areas remain genetically quite different. Milk did not become a focus of breeding and effort until perhaps seven thousand to eight thousand years ago.

Later, beans, lentils, and tree crops were domesticated. Bitter and poisonous chemicals were bred out of some of them. From among the stony, sour, wild fruit, the least stony and sour were picked to grow, and they interbred. Their least stony and sour progeny were then selected again. It took thousands of years of this artificial selection and breeding for the almost inedible wild pears and apples of the Middle East to become the large, sweet ones of today. By the time tree crops were coming into view in the Middle East, agriculture had arisen independently in several other parts of the world.

By ten thousand years ago, villagers in northern China were raising foxtail millet (*Setaria italica*)—one of several small grains indiscriminately called "millet"— and villagers near Shanghai were raising both short- and long-grain rice (Liu 2004; Loewe and Shaughnessy 1999:46). By six thousand years ago, agriculture was well established all over north and east China. Pigs, dogs, sheep, chickens, and Chinese cabbages had been added to the crop roster. The pigs and sheep were probably domesticated independently of the Middle Eastern center. Sheep tame themselves, as visitors to Banff National Park (Canada) well know; you have to drive them away to keep them from living with you. Chickens are native to south China and southeast Asia and must have come from the more southerly parts of the agricultural zone. They too tend to self-tame, making it easy to domesticate them.

At about the same time, and certainly by seven thousand years ago, people in what is now Mexico domesticated squash (*Cucurbita* spp.), chiles (*Capsicum* spp.), and millet (*Setaria viridis*)—ironically, the American form of the same plant used by the Chinese. By at least five thousand years ago, domesticated corn appeared on the scene, replacing millet; millet is more nutritious, but corn has greater yields. When corn was introduced to China in the sixteenth century, the same process began, and corn has now replaced millets in most of the world.

Common beans (*Phaseolus vulgaris*) and avocados (*Persea americana*) were also domesticated in Mexico, along with many other crops (see Fedick [1995] for a recent review of New World agriculture, as well as the general worldwide review by Barker [2006]). When the Spaniards conquered Mexico, they were astonished at the incredible variety and productivity of the indigenous agricultural scene. There was nothing like it in Europe.

In South America, meanwhile, people domesticated lima beans (*Phaseolus lunatus*)—appropriately first appearing near the city of Lima. It is probable that potatoes (*Solanum tuberosum*) and other crops were domesticated by six thousand years ago. At about the same time, the llama and alpaca were domesticated from their wild forms. In the lowlands, people were probably cultivating manioc (*Manihot utilissima*, tapioca) and yuca (not to be confused with yucca, a different plant). Eventually, they began to grow peanuts (*Arachis hypoglauca*), sweet potatoes (*Ipomoea batatas*), and countless other crops. Like the Mexicans, the South Americans proved to be outstanding plant breeders and agricultural system developers. Their ideas and crops are only now coming to be appreciated (National Research Council 1989).

Archaeological work in New Guinea has disclosed ancient fields that may have grown taro (*Colocasia antiquorum*) or something similar. These fields date as early as six thousand years ago and reveal another independent source of agriculture, either in the highlands of New Guinea or somewhere in mainland or insular Southeast Asia.

It is possible, even probable, that agriculture was independently invented in other areas as well. For example, it began very early in eastern North America (Smith 1995), and the crops found there are markedly different from those of Mexico, where early agriculture was roughly contemporary. Other proposed areas of independent origin include northern Southeast Asia and northeastern South America. For further information and discussion on agriculture, refer to Anderson (1988), Barker (2006), Cowan and Watson (1992), Denham and White (2007), Harris and Hillman (1989), Harlan (1992), MacNeish (1992), Piperno and Pearsall (1998), Price and Gebauer (1995b), and Whittle (1996).

AGRICULTURAL DOMESTICATION

Domestication can be defined at a number of levels (see Rindos 1984; Hayden 1995). As discussed earlier, one might define domestication to mean a general control, such as over landscapes, through active or passive management. A more specific definition is an active process through which the genetic makeup of an organism is purposefully altered by humans to their advantage. Many would make the definition even more narrow to include making the species dependent on humans. In the case of agriculture, we favor the latter definition.

People had always manipulated and interacted with plants and animals. This interaction always resulted in the genetic alteration of the species, even if the alteration was not planned. For example, when deer are hunted, the gene pool of their population is changed, and this will influence their evolution to some degree. In other cases, people purposefully altered some plants, such as the pruning and weeding of native tobacco. However, such alterations were minor and/or incidental, and no serious attempt was made to control genetics (see Rindos 1984:154–158).

Agricultural domestication involves a process in which people purposefully and selectively breed for more of what they want and less of what they do not want. People have long been aware of the combination of traits, selective breeding, and other aspects of basic genetics, although the details of the specific mechanism were not discovered until the mid-twentieth century. Hunter-gatherers also understood this basic biology and took advantage of it by way of environmental manipulation and resource management. Sometime about ten thousand years ago, however, people began to focus on specific plants and animals, developing sets of tactics to enhance the productivity of these species. The seeds of the largest and most succulent fruits were planted so that the next generation of fruits were even larger and more succulent. Animals that were aggressive were killed and eaten before they could reproduce, leaving the tamer individuals to parent the next generation, which would be even more tame. Over many generations, grains became bigger, fruits larger, animals more tame, and all became dependent on humans.

Domestication often involves breeding out some of the natural defenses of the species. Wild sheep are fast, tough, and armed with large horns and can defend themselves well. Tame sheep are notoriously helpless. In fact, after people had domesticated the sheep, they had to breed specialized dogs to care for them!

Taking care of crops involves labor and skill. The more the natural defenses are bred out of crops, the more the farmers have to work. Thus, two choices are available. First, one can retain the natural defenses. This means less need for care in the form of human labor, chemical pesticides, or other things. Second, one can breed single-mindedly for desired traits. This results in more effort being devoted to chemicals, fences, guard dogs, and so on.

These processes are exemplified by two Mexican crops: avocados and corn. Avocado trees have been bred to bear much larger fruit than any wild avocado tree could manage, but otherwise, they are not very domesticated. They contain a number of interesting chemicals that deter insects, herbivores, and diseases. They thin their own fruit, prune their own branches, and sprout with glorious exuberance from their own seeds.

Corn is an extremely domesticated plant. Its tassel, cob, huge and numerous seeds, tall and succulent stalk, and numerous husks are all unnatural traits that do not occur in wild corn. The tough husks protect the cob, but otherwise corn has major problems taking care of itself. It is simply a free lunch counter for insects, fungi, and wild animals. It cannot seed itself because the dense husks prevent scattering of the seed. Seedlings will come up from fallen ears, but they crowd each other to death. Contemporary domesticated corn requires people to plant it, harvest it, and protect it. The domestication process had resulted in a genetically narrow species susceptible to disease. In 1973, one-third of the United States corn crop was wiped out by a single fungus in a couple of months. We now have to breed fungus resistance into corn from wild or primitive strains.

People do not always breed for food values. Within the past few years, it has been discovered that as early as four thousand years ago, some groups along the coast of Peru domesticated cotton to manufacture nets with which to catch fish (Moseley 1975). In this instance, early domestication was undertaken for technological purposes rather than as a direct source of food.

In the United States, sorghum (*Sorghum vulgare*) is used for grain for animal feed, while the stalk is relatively useless. Therefore, sorghum has been bred for short stalks. In China, the stalks are used for firewood and thatch; thus, the sorghum is bred for long stalks. In both cases, the grain yield is kept as high as possible, but the Chinese trade off grain yield against stalk yield, while the American breeders have reduced the stalk to the bare minimum necessary to keep the grain off the ground.

THE TRANSITION TO FARMING

Hunter-gatherers were not instantly transformed to agriculturalists once they began to domesticate plants and animals. In fact, it was a transition (see Price and Gebauer 1995b) in which hunting and gathering became less and less important while domesticates became more and more important. One could say that domesticated species and farming cultures developed a mutalistic relationship and evolved or co-adapted together. This process is still ongoing, as virtually all contemporary cultures are dependent to some degree on agricultural products and all still utilize at least some wild resources. This fact sometimes makes classification of certain cultures difficult, because subsistence strategy is usually defined based on the most visible or important aspect of the economy, and this is sometimes not clear.

Hunter-gatherers and farmers utilize their environment in fundamentally different ways. Hunter-gatherers "largely live off the land in an *extensive* fashion, exploiting a diversity of resources over a broad area, [while] farmers utilize the landscape *intensively* and create a milieu that suits their needs" (Price and Gebauer 1995a:3–4). In that sense, farmers intensify their use of the environment and resources, and in doing so become more narrow and less diverse with lower adaptive flexibility. In most cases, the scale of environmental manipulation and resource management increased with farmers, and there began a general increase in the ritual management of resources. Farmers have manipulated environments on such a scale that much of Europe was deforested during the Neolithic, much of North America during the past five hundred years, and an increasing proportion of Amazonia today.

The evolution of food production has been a process of reducing the land area needed to feed an individual. Hunting and gathering required many acres to support a person; incipient agriculture (agriculture in which crops are raised, but only a few, and those not significantly modified from wild-type ancestors) supported very few more people per square mile. Every change and modification of agriculture allowed more people per square mile to flourish. Today, agricultural development and agricultural intensification are basically directed toward the same goal. This is not to say that the amount of land dedicated to agriculture has not increased; it certainly has. Today, about one-third of the land surface of the earth is under cultivation.

Granted that agriculture only rarely increases the amount of food available to the cultivator, there are two logical reasons for intensifying agriculture. First, an elite might order the peasants to grow more to support the elites' lifestyle. Thus, while the elite would have been better off than the average hunter-gatherer, the peasants would have been worse off. This in turn presupposes intensive agriculture, because most hunting and gathering and simple agricultural economies cannot support elites. Second, there could be a need to get more food per acre even if it does not mean more food per person. This can occur when population increases, when food is sold or traded, when land becomes scarcer, or when extra food can be used for some special reason, for example, fattening animals.

The next logical thing to recognize is that agriculture requires some inputs besides land. Specifically, labor and crop varieties are obviously vital to all agriculture. Fertilizer, pest control, and improving technology are not vital but are very useful indeed. Contemporary agriculture would not support so many people without them, but they also have their negative ecological consequences, such as pollution.

In the end, the average human cultivator may be worse off now, in regard to food and general welfare, than the average person of ten thousand years ago if our knowledge of contemporary hunters and gatherers is any guide. It is common to believe that agriculture is much more productive than hunting and gathering. However, most of the world's population consists of peasants and poor cultivators in the developing world, often malnourished and racked by disease. Agricultural intensification has probably never benefited the majority of mankind. It has permitted more people, and even more rich people, but it has not necessarily made most people better off.

ON THE ORIGIN OF AGRICULTURE

Theories of the origin of agriculture abound (see Barker 2006; Harris and Hillman 1989; Price and Gebauer 1995b; Rindos 1984; and table 6.1). People had been dependent on wild plants and animals for millions of years. Why, then, did hunter-gatherers abandon a relatively stable and productive adaptive strategy to take up agriculture, an economic pursuit that requires more labor and is subject to catastrophic crop failure? The process may have been partly unintentional and even accidental (Rindos 1984). However, it is also possible that people deliberately strived from the beginning to improve plants and animals upon which they depended, making deliberate choices toward desired traits (e.g., larger cobs on corn). They certainly did so later.

Either way, once people became dependent on domesticates, they tended to congregate and make sedentary life the rule. These transformations resulted in a whole series of other changes, including a decreasing dependence on wild resources, much greater emphasis on land ownership, an increase in political complexity, population growth, and specialization. Why and how all this happened is still unclear, but there are many ideas. As domestication occurred in at least several different places at the same time, it may be that each of the models, a combination of them, or one as yet unknown, are correct. An up-to-date review with skeptical commentary was presented by Barker (2006). Factors believed to have led to agriculture fall into three basic categories: environmental change, population pressure, and changes in organization (Price and Gebauer 1995a:4). Each of these three factors is interrelated, and all may have had some influence on the

Table 6.1. Some Theories of the Development of Agriculture

General Theories	Summary	References
Environmental Change		
Oasis theory	Environmental changes at the end of the Pleistocene forced people into a close association with certain plants and animals, leading to their domestication in some instances	Childe 1936, 1942
Hilly flanks theory	Intensive exploitation of the native grasses along the hilly flanks of the Tigris-Euphrates river valley led to domestication of those species in some areas	Braidwood 1960
Marginal environment	Due to increasing need for efficiency, people living in marginal environments would have been forced to intensively manage their plants and animals, resulting in their domestication in some instances	Binford 1968; Flannery 1969
Food crisis	Due to the loss of Pleistocene species hunted by people, people were forced to manage their remaining animals more efficiently, leading to their domestication in some instances	Cohen 1977
Wet and stable	Dry and unstable environment prevented agriculture during the Pleistocene, but environment became wetter and stable afterwards, leading to plant intensification, domestication, and agriculture	Richerson et al. 2001
Population Expansion		
Population growth	As populations began to expand and demand for food increased, the exploitation of certain species intensified and led to their domestication	Cohen 1977
Changes in Organization and Management		
Efficient hunter-gatherers	A particular efficient group of hunter-gatherers increased the yield of a particular resource, perhaps to the point of increasing dependence and ultimate domestication of that resource	Winterhalder and Goland 1997
Scheduling changes	Changes in scheduling in the exploitation of wild resources created an overreliance on some resources, eventually leading to domestication	Flannery 1972

process. While the origin of agriculture is not at all clear, most now agree that agriculture initially developed in areas with relatively abundant resources among relatively complex groups.

Environmental Change

It is clear that there was a major environmental change at the end of the Pleistocene, when the climate became hotter and drier. Many species went extinct, and many others moved to other regions. No one questions that these changes impacted human populations. While the details of human adaptation to these changes are not fully understood, all known agriculture began at about the same time in many regions of the world. This timing coincidence is highly suggestive of climatic change having a major role in the development of agriculture.

The Oasis Theory   *Climate, Location*

V. Gordon Childe (1936, 1942) put forward the oasis theory, in which he argued that as the environment generally dried up at the end of the Pleistocene, people, plants, and particularly animals were forced into close association in areas of remaining permanent water, or oases. He argued that this geographic association led to a close symbiotic relationship between people and certain species and eventually to the domestication of some of those species. Childe held the view that farmers were superior to hunter-gatherers, that an evolution to farming was natural and desired, and that people would adopt farming at their first opportunity (see Watson 1995:24).

Striking support for this theory has recently emerged from the Middle East. The earliest known agriculture occurs in the Pre-Pottery Neolithic A period, in and around the huge earthquake-riven zone that includes the Jordan river valley. The Younger Dryas climate change made the region suddenly much drier around eleven thousand years ago. Human populations shrank and concentrated around permanent water sources. Here they apparently began to sow the crops they had previously harvested wild but now had to produce (Leslie Quintero, Philip Wilke, personal communication based on their ongoing research). In general, agricultural development takes time, requiring thousands of years to reach fully productive levels (Sauer 1952; MacNeish 1992), but the Jordan valley case indicates that Childe's concept of spatial manipulation and oasis survival may have been critically important.

The Hilly Flanks Theory   *Location, Technology*

In 1948, Robert Braidwood, motivated by the oasis theory, began a concerted effort to identify the location and date of the earliest farming. He found the earliest evidence (to that time) of agriculture along the hilly flanks bordering the

Tigris-Euphrates river valley. Braidwood (1960) argued that there had not been the catastrophic climatic change that Childe had thought and that the grasses that would become wheat and barley thrived in the prime grass habitat that surrounded the valley. Living amid the dense stands of grasses, people eventually developed the technology to domesticate those species (see Watson 1995:24–26), and the practice then spread elsewhere. To date, no early agriculture has been found so far in the hilly flank zones, but sheep and goats may have been domesticated there.

Margin Theories *environmentq climate*

Binford (1968) and Flannery (1969; also see Redding [1988]) later argued that domestication should not occur in areas rich with resources but in marginal environments, where people had to work harder to make a living. It was argued that in regions where resources were less abundant, people would pay closer attention to the species, manage them better, maintain a more intimate relationship, and eventually domesticate them.

A Food Crisis *Resources / climate*

Cohen (1977; also see Boserup 1965) suggested that the mass extinction of giant animal forms due to climatic change at the end of the Pleistocene caused a "food crisis" that led to agriculture. In essence, when the large animals that hunters relied on died off, people had little choice but to farm. There are many problems with this theory. First, it seems clear now that reliance on large animals in the relevant areas was less than once believed. Second, if the idea were correct, one would expect evidence of malnutrition among the hunter-gatherers of the time, but there was no such evidence. Malnutrition became common only after agriculture was widespread—when reliance on one or two staple grain foods led to unbalanced diets and susceptibility to famines when crops failed (Cohen and Armelagos 1984).

Most recently, it has been suggested (Richerson et al. 2001) that the climate of the Pleistocene, arid and highly variable, made agriculture impossible. Further, they argued, as the climate changed to conditions more favorable to agriculture (wetter and more stable), plant intensification began and inexorably led to domestication and agriculture, although sooner in some places than in others. This fits available evidence well. *population / Resources*

Population Expansion

In an argument related to the food crisis, Cohen (1977) also argued that by the end of the Pleistocene, the human groups had occupied all of the terrestrial habitats, and population growth had reached a critical point that required a larger and more stable food supply. It was argued that agriculture was the only way to support the growing populations. However, many hunter-gatherer populations were large and growing without agriculture. Some sort of population size and pressure may have been a precondition or an effect, rather than a cause, for the development of agriculture (see Price and Gebauer 1995a:7).

Changes in Organization and Management

Particular groups are organized in particular ways, presumably in some general accommodation with their environment. However, if conditions changed, various aspects of adaptive organization would also have changed, some of which could have initiated the process of domestication. These conditions could include environment, population, technology, and/or religion, to name a few.

Efficient Hunter-Gatherers

Hunter-gatherers differ in their efficiency, at both the individual and group level. If a particular group was unusually efficient or developed a new and productive technology, that group may have been able to increase the yield of a particular resource, perhaps to the point of increasing dependence and ultimate domestication of that resource. Further, it has been suggested that individual groups made key decisions about resource use and risk management that led to dependence and ultimately domestication (Winterhalder and Goland 1997).

Scheduling environment

It has been proposed (Flannery 1972) that simple scheduling changes could send a group down the road to an overdependence on a specific resource and ultimately to the domestication of that species by that group. For example, if the seasonal round of a group brought them to resource patch A at a certain time and they stayed too long at that patch, it may have become too late to move to the next patch if the resources there were short lived. Under those circumstances, the group may have been forced to stay in patch A and to increase the intensity of the use of the species there. If this were a recurring circumstance, the resource in patch A may have eventually become domesticated, with the group dependent on the resource and devoted to its cultivation.

Trade resources

Another theory, advanced by R. S. MacNeish (1992), took a different tack. MacNeish's theory is complex, but it includes a recognition that agriculture arose independently in several areas that are ecologically very complex, with many different zones of altitude and moisture. They are also in the central parts of large regions where trade was active. Under these conditions, agriculture grew out of trade or exchange. People exchanged products in their local zone with others in other zones, nearby or far away. One can imagine that these traders wanted to maintain a secure supply of their trade goods. This theory too has been criticized, largely on evidential grounds (Watson 1995). The debate is not over (see also Rindos 1984; McCorriston and Hole 1991; Blumler 1992; McCorriston 1992).

TYPES OF AGRICULTURE

For general purposes, agriculture can be defined as the cultivation and/or raising and use of domesticated plants and animals. Within this general definition can be placed the three major forms of agriculture: horticulture, pastoralism, and intensive agriculture. The differences between the three are largely a matter of scale (table 6.2).

Within cultures emphasizing plant cultivation, **monoculture** (single-species planting) and **polyculture** (multiple-species planting) are the primary systems used. Monoculture results in a greater yield but is highly susceptible to pests, disease, and soil exhaustion, which can result in catastrophic crop failure, such as the Irish potato famine. In contrast, polyculture seems to be more stable (with greater diversity) but has less yield. **Silviculture** is an agricultural system using domesticated trees. All of these systems have relatively low biodiversity and usually replace systems with much greater biodiversity, like turning rainforests into cornfields.

Horticulture

Horticulture (discussed in detail in chapter 7) is agriculture involving relatively small-scale fields, plots, and gardens. Of some importance is the fact that hunter-gatherers can employ horticulture on a part-time basis without abandoning hunting and gathering. While horticulture does involve tilling, planting, and harvesting, it does not necessarily require an irrevocable commitment to do-

Table 6.2.   Types of Agriculture

Type	Emphasis	Characteristics
Horticulture	Plants, but some animals, hunting and gathering Often remains important	Small-scale individual production, only human labor
Pastoralism	Animals, but some plants, some hunting and gathering	Small-to-large-scale, generally mobile
Intensive agriculture	Plants, but animals are sometimes raised intensely	Large-scale, use of labor supplements (animals or machines)

mesticated species. It is normally understood as agriculture without plowing. Horticulture is sometimes defined as simple or low-intensity agriculture (e.g., Kottak 2008), but this would surprise the American Horticultural Society, devoted to the exceedingly intensive and sophisticated flower and vegetable gardening and tree crop production of the modern United States.

Both plants and animals can be raised in horticultural systems. Such a system generally does not involve the use of heavy equipment (e.g., plows), draft animals, or mass labor. The food is raised primarily for personal or local consumption rather than being widely traded or given to a central authority. Being small scale, horticultural systems include those that support smaller (and/or dispersed) populations and have generally less complex political systems than intensive agricultural systems. However, small-scale, local, and smallholder farming in highly complex societies is also usually horticultural.

Pastoralism

Pastoralism (discussed in detail in chapter 8) involves the herding, breeding, consumption, and use of domesticated (or managed) animals such as sheep, cattle, reindeer, camels, horses, llamas, and yaks, sometimes called **animal husbandry**. (That term also includes intensive animal rearing in settled systems, e.g., dairy farming.) Plant cultivation generally is not part of this adaptation, but such goods may be obtained from other groups. Pastoralists, sometimes called **nomads**, may either be sedentary or practice a seasonal round based largely on the availability of forage for the animals.

Intensive Agriculture

Intensive agriculture (discussed in detail in chapter 9) involves a full commitment to domesticated species, although wild resources remain in the economy. Intensive agriculture is the large-scale cultivation of plants, often with the use of animal labor, equipment such as plows, and irrigation or other water-diversion techniques. Some pastoral activities also may be a part of intensive agricultural systems. It usually happens that horticultural techniques are employed by intensive agriculturalists, as seen by the small personal gardens that are common in Western societies.

THE IMPACT OF AGRICULTURE

All organisms interact with and affect their environment. Humans, with their culture, impact it on a much greater scale than do other organisms (see treatments of human impacts to the environment by Goudie [1994], Meyer [1996], Redman [1999], and Chew [2001, 2007]; also see Fagan [1999]). The practice of agriculture involves the genetic modification of plants and animals, and so impacts to those natural populations is substantial. Further, agriculture involves the manipulation and management of landscapes on a scale typically much greater than that practiced by hunter-gatherers. This almost certainly includes changes in technology and the intensity of use of specific areas. These impacts increase as agriculture intensifies, with the greatest effects coming with intensive agriculture and industrialization (see table 6.3).

Impacts on the Natural Environment

Perhaps the most significant impact of agriculture on the natural environment is the transformation of landscapes that results in the overall decrease in biodiversity (Vitousek et al. 1997:495), especially in the past one hundred years (see Matson et al. 1997). As agriculture expands into new areas, the relatively diverse and generalized natural ecosystems are destroyed and replaced with much

Table 6.3. Summary of the Environmental Impact of Agriculture

Category	General Impacts
	The Natural Environment
General	Loss of biodiversity and habitat, pollution by chemicals
Plants	Loss of habitat for most species, extinction of some species, domestication and proliferation of a few species
Animals	Loss of habitat for most species, extinction of some species, domestication and proliferation of a few species
Water	Loss of fresh water for natural habitats, pollution of most water sources
Soils	Erosion of topsoil in agricultural lands, exhaustion of soils
Landforms	Alteration of landforms resulting in habitat loss
Atmosphere	Pollution
Climate	Long-term global warming through loss of forests and development of industrialized cultures
	People and Cultures
Population	Huge long-term increase in population, subsequent sedentation and urbanization
Resource dependence	Ongoing trend for reliance on a fewer number of resources, populations more frequently subjected to famine due to crop failure
Workload	Increase in workload for most, decrease for some (elite and/or wealthy)
Disease	Dramatic increase in crowd diseases affecting billions
Health	Increase in general health for many people, little change for others, generally longer life expectancy
Warfare	Increase in scale of warfare, with increasing effects on population and environment
Knowledge	Loss of traditional knowledge, increase in specialized agricultural knowledge, explosion in overall knowledge

less diverse and specialized agroecosystems. This process often results in the loss of entire natural ecosystems and the destruction of habitat of many species. This loss of habitat constrains species, eventually leading to their extinction. It has been variously estimated that current extinction rates are between one hundred and one thousand times faster than in the recent past (Vitousek et al. 1997:498). Sponsel and colleagues (1996b:3) reported that

> By 1989 the annual rate of [tropical] deforestation had reached 142,200 square kilometers [in 2008, it was approximately 130,000 square kilometers per year], which represents 1.8% of the 8 million square kilometers of remaining forest, and the rate of deforestation is even accelerating. . . . Current rates of deforestation exceed 0.4 hectares [about one acre] per second. . . . As a result of habitat destruction as many as 10,000 species may become extinct each year, a level unprecedented in all of geological history. . . .

As a whole, biological diversity is decreasing, and any loss of diversity has long-term negative effects. One of the benefits of anthropological work with a culture is the recordation of biodiversity and its preservation through contemporary conservation programs (e.g., Western and Wright 1994; Orlove and Brush 1996). Interestingly, domesticated species are also subject to extinction with the increasing specialization and homogenization of agriculture. Of the many domesticated livestock breeds that once existed, many are now extinct, and the diversity among the animals used for food is decreasing.

A second major impact, a serious problem only after World War II, is pollution, from both agricultural and industrial sources. Agricultural pollution includes dust and pesticides in the air, chemical fertilizers and pesticides entering water systems through runoff from fields, and an increase in silt washed into rivers and streams by erosion of fields—silt that clogs waterways and destroys habitat.

Impacts on Plants and Animals

The biggest problem for most plants and animals is the loss of habitat that comes when natural lands are converted to agriculture. Land is cleared, and individuals are either killed (plants) or have to move (many animals). Eventually, there is nowhere to move, and extinction is possible. About 80 percent of the deforestation in the world is done to make land for agriculture.

Impacts on Water

Today, more than one-half of the accessible fresh water on the planet is used for human purposes, primarily for agriculture (Pimentel et al. 1994:204; Vitousek et al.

1997:494; Gleick 1998; Smil 2000). Much of this water is diverted from rivers and streams into reservoirs and irrigation systems. The construction of reservoirs results in the loss of terrestrial habitat but results in the creation of freshwater aquatic habitat. River flow is often decreased below the irrigation systems, with a resultant loss of riparian and wetland habitats.

In addition, in the United States, groundwater is being pumped 25 percent faster than it is being replenished (Pimentel et al. 1994:205), with the result that water tables are being lowered at an alarming rate The lowering of water tables can cause the ground surface to subside (indeed, portions of the San Joaquin Valley of California have subsided more than thirty feet since 1925) and natural water sources, such as springs, to dry up, thus killing species dependent on groundwater.

Impacts on Soils

Agriculture has a number of impacts on soils. First, the removal of vegetation and plowing breaks up soils and allows them to erode more easily. Water erosion can be serious, but wind erosion can be a major problem, as demonstrated by the Dust Bowl in the central United States in the 1930s. An inch of topsoil takes about five hundred years to form, and in the United States, it is being lost at rates sixteen to forty times faster (Pimentel et al. 1994:203).

Second, agriculture will eventually result in soil exhaustion, where the loss of organic matter and nutrients in the soil precludes further crop production. To avert this, fields have to be allowed to lie fallow and/or crops have to be rotated. However, the pressure for short-term crop production sometimes precludes these options, resulting in rapid exhaustion.

Last, the absence of soil deposition can be a problem, as exemplified by the situation in Egypt. For thousands of years the agricultural system in Egypt relied on the natural yearly flooding of the Nile to provide irrigation water and a fresh layer of topsoil, a system in which soils were not exhausted. With the construction of the Aswan High Dam in the 1960s, the Nile no longer floods, and no new soil is deposited. Today, Egyptian farmers are forced to use chemicals to maintain the fertility of the soil, an additional expense and a source of pollution with impacts on the fish populations that served as food.

Impacts on Landforms

Humans have altered between about 40 and 50 percent of the land surface of the earth, and this transformation is the "primary driving force in the loss of biological diversity worldwide" (Vitousek et al. 1997:495). Land is cleared, burned, leveled, terraced, and built upon. Rivers are rerouted, valleys flooded behind dams, and wetlands drained. Today, between 10 and 15 percent of the land surface is occupied by crop agriculture or urban centers and another 6 to 8 percent by pasture. All of these landforms have been drastically altered.

Impacts on People and Cultures

The impact of agriculture directly on humans has been considerable. With the increased carrying capacity that resulted from food production, population began to grow and has now reached a rate of 2 percent per year. As the population of agriculturalists grew, they began to settle together, to build cities, and to clear more and more land for farming. Agriculturalists expanded their territory into lands suitable for farming, displacing the hunter-gatherers that had lived there. The hunter-gatherers were forced to move, be assimilated, or be killed. Many groups were just eliminated.

Farming is a difficult profession, and people generally had to work longer hours to get the same number of calories as hunter-gatherers. Competition for resources, particularly land and water, increased, and warfare to control those resources also increased. As a result, a great investment in resources (human and otherwise) has been made in military matters in the name of preserving lifestyle.

Crowd diseases began to kill millions of people packed into dirty urban centers; at least twenty million died from the Black Death in Europe between 1346 and 1350 (Cantor 2001:7), and more than twenty million more from the flu in 1918 (Crosby 1989:207). Even for the living, the misery was immense.

Agriculture had the further effect of narrowing the human food resource base from hundreds or even thousands of species in some societies to only a few dozen in agricultural societies. Today, wheat, rice, corn, potatoes, sugar, soybeans, and cotton account for most of the world's agricultural production, and a handful of other grains and legumes account for most of the rest. Animal raising depends primarily on cattle, pigs, chickens, and sheep. This is a dangerously narrow base, and it continues to narrow. Supermarkets may have a few exotic species in their produce racks, but the human diet is becoming increasingly dependent on fewer plants. Some of these unused species became extinct, and the knowledge required to use others was lost. Being reliant on a few species made crop failure an ever-present and very serious problem, and famine could result.

One could argue that agriculture provided the food necessary to allow humans to develop the complex cultures seen today, to pursue science and art, and to improve the quality of life for all humanity. While it is true that the quality of life has improved, that benefit is enjoyed by a minority; most people still live in poverty and in conditions worse than the hunter-gatherers they replaced.

CHAPTER SUMMARY

When people began to manage certain species so intensively that they began to manipulate and control their genetics, those species became domesticated, and food production began. This process originated in a number of places at about the same time, and those people and societies involved in the process began to shift toward farming lifestyles and new organizations.

The reasons behind the shift to food production are not fully clear. Ideas include environmental changes that created opportunities or forced people to alter their subsistence practices, growth of population requiring new food supplies, and changes in organization and management enabling the shift.

Several types of agriculture can be defined: horticulture, pastoralism, and intensive agriculture. Horticulture is low-intensity agriculture involving relatively small-scale fields, plots, and gardens cultivated with human labor. Pastoralism involves the herding, breeding, consumption, and use of domesticated (or managed) animals. Intensive agriculture is the large-scale cultivation of plants, often with the use of supplemental labor and irrigation.

The practice of agriculture has significant impacts on both the natural and cultural environment, including loss of biodiversity, loss of habitat, extinction of species, erosion, and pollution. Impacts on people and cultures include growing populations and resource pressures, increasing disease, increasing workloads, increasing lifespan, more war and associated suffering, and a loss of some knowledge but a gain in other knowledge.

KEY TERMS

animal husbandry
horticulture
intensive agriculture
monoculture
nomad
pastoralism
polyculture
silviculture

7

Horticulture

Horticulture is small-scale agriculture involving the use of relatively small fields, plots, and/or gardens. Groups practicing horticulture will often have populations in the many thousands, live in one place all year, and frequently have a tribe-level political organization. Some hunter-gatherers will employ aspects of horticultural practices as a minor part of their subsistence system.

Horticulture generally involves the use of individual human labor and small hand tools such as digging sticks or shovels rather than mass labor, draft animals, or equipment such as plows or tractors. Crops are grown for mostly personal consumption, although some of them might be traded or given to a central authority, such as the chief. Intensity ranges from the tiny plots of some primarily hunting-gathering groups to the extremely intensive and sophisticated systems of the Maya and Polynesians.

HORTICULTURAL TECHNIQUES

Both domestic plants and animals are raised by horticulturalists, but the emphasis is on the production of plant crops. Crops are mainly grown in small fields, called gardens, and such gardens may be solitary or part of a larger system of gardens. In addition, various small domesticated animals, such as pigs, chickens, and dogs are often raised by horticulturalists. Wild resources may also form an important component of a horticultural economy.

Gardens

Gardens are small fields cultivated by individuals or small groups of people. The specific size of a garden is limited by the available labor. Some gardens are expedient, just small plots of land cleared and planted with little investment of time and labor. However, most gardens are used repeatedly and tend to be located in the same place over time, with techniques such as crop rotation, fallowing, and the use of fertilizer being used to maintain fertility. Thus, most such gardens require a large investment in labor but a relatively small investment in land.

Well-managed gardens can be highly productive and can sustain high population densities. For example, some root crop gardens in Highland New Guinea can support as many as 160 to 200 people per square kilometer (Brookfield and Brown 1963:119-122). Three basic types of sustainable gardens, chinampas, terraced gardens, and slash-and-burn, are discussed below. Any or all of these types can be incorporated as components of intensive agricultural systems. For example, small personal gardens in the backyard are commonly used by many Americans today.

Chinampas

Chinampas are small, raised fields or gardens used in a number of regions, but extensively in Mesoamerica. They were built within, on, or surrounded by water, and many types of plants could be cultivated on them. A single chinampa could be viewed as a small-scale garden. However, a number of chinampas were generally constructed in combination and integrated into a much larger, intensive agricultural system, such as the one used by the ancient Maya (see chapter 9).

The classic form of chinampa (figure 7.1) was constructed within a lake. First, long stakes were driven into the lake bottom to create a "form." Soil from the lake bottom was then dredged up and piled within the stakes. Layers of different types of soil were placed upon one another until the field had been raised up above the level of the lake. Once formed, willow trees were planted along the edges of the chinampa to help control erosion. Crops could then be planted. New soil was constantly dredged up and added to the chinampa, maintaining its fertility and productivity. As it was surrounded by water, the chinampa was self-irrigating, with the different layers of soil serving the purpose of drawing water to the plant roots. Additional chinampas would be built and arranged in a pattern that created a system of canals between them. The construction and maintenance of such a field require a great deal of labor.

The Mexica employed this form of chinampa on Lake Texcoco as a major component of their intensive agricultural system. The Mexica chinampas around their capital city of Tenochtitlán have been erroneously referred to as "floating" gardens. A remnant of that system, the Floating Gardens of Xochimilco (see figure 7.1), is a tourist attraction in Mexico City today (see Werner 1992).

A similar form of chinampa was constructed in swampy areas, such as the lowland Yucatan. These raised fields were created by digging ditches around a

FIGURE 7.1
Modern chinampas at Xochimilco near Mexico City (photo courtesy of Claudia García-
Des Lauriers).

small patch of land and placing the soil in a pile in the middle. This raised the
small field up a few feet out of the water and created ditches around it. A series
of such fields would be constructed in a wafflelike pattern, with the ditches being linked to form a system of canals, probably connected to a major body of water, such as a river or lake (figure 7.2). As the ditches/canals slowly silted in, they
were cleaned and dredged, with the resulting silt and organic debris being added
to the fields. Thus, soil renewal was continuous, and the fields were self-irrigating
and very productive. Like the other chinampas, the construction and maintenance of these fields also required a great deal of labor. We are now beginning to
realize that the ancient Maya made extensive use of these chinampa-like systems,
as did past peoples in other regions such as South America (see Bray 2000; Whitmore and Turner 2001).

The canals present in both types of chinampas were purposefully created and
served three major functions. First, they were transportation routes, with small
boats being used in them to move people and products. Thus, the canals had to
be maintained with the proper width and depth for boats. Second, the canals
served as passive irrigation systems, with water saturating the soil and so watering

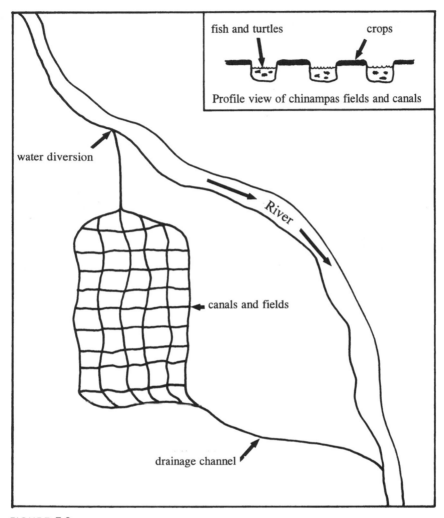

fish and turtles   crops

Profile view of chinampas fields and canals

water diversion

River

canals and fields

drainage channel

FIGURE 7.2

A plan-view schematic of a system of raised chinampas, fed by a diverted water source with a profile view of the raised fields and interconnecting canals (no scale). The crops are grown in the raised portion with fish, turtles, and aquatic plants being harvested from the canals.

the crops. Last, the canals created habitat for a variety of other resources. Fish, shellfish, turtles, frogs, waterfowl, and other aquatic animals inhabited the canals and fed on pests and agricultural debris from the fields. In addition, reeds grew along the edges of the canals and were harvested and used for a variety of purposes, including matting and thatch. These various wild resources formed an important addition to the economy and were encouraged to inhabit the canals.

Although not under direct genetic control, such resources could be considered domesticated in the broad sense of the term (see the discussion in chapter 4) as their habitat and populations would be created and controlled.

In highland Bolivia, an ancient system of chinampa-like raised fields was also used to regulate the air temperature of the fields (Erickson 1986). It was suggested that the water in the system stored heat during the day and the gradual release of that heat during the night kept the crops warm enough to prevent freezing. Thus, the use of chinampas, rather than traditional fields, extended the already short growing season and permitted the raising of crop species not otherwise possible. Clark Erickson has reconstructed such fields, and similar fields, called *waruwaru*, are in local use today.

It has recently been discovered that ancient cultures in the Amazon created very fertile plots of soil in the rainforest, called "dark earth" (*Terra preta* in Portuguese), in which they grew crops (Tennesen 2007). The plots of soil were created by mulching trash, including plant and animal remains and charcoal (from the burning of cleared vegetation but not burned to ash). Understanding this system is important for two reasons. First, such a system of fertile plots in the rainforest may have supported a larger population than is possible using current agricultural techniques and so may have direct and practical application to contemporary overpopulation of the forest. Second, it is possible that the addition of charcoal, rather than ash, into the soil could result in the sequestering of carbon and a lowering of carbon emissions.

Terraced Gardens

Terraced gardens are small fields usually constructed on sloping terrain. Small retaining walls of rock would be built to impound both soils and water. Such fields are not to be confused with larger, much more extensive systems of terraced fields, such as those used in rice agriculture. Terraced gardens generally served three functions: (1) production of level planting surfaces, (2) erosion control, and (3) creation of deep soils (Smith and Price 1994:175).

Terraced gardens were, and are, widely used by many cultures. The Chinese (see case study 9.1) employed small terraced gardens around their towns, and these gardens produced the majority of their vegetables. The rice was produced in much larger and more complex terraced fields. The use of terraced gardens was widespread throughout Mesoamerica. In addition to the small terraced gardens on slopes, Mesoamericans also utilized small raised gardens, made by building small enclosures from low rock walls and filling the enclosure with soil (Smith and Price 1994). Terraced gardens could be very productive, and managed properly with the addition of new soil and organics, they could remain so for a long time. Some of the most spectacular terraces are in South America, where slopes up to two miles high are terraced with intricate stonework that is often many centuries old (Denevan 2001).

A number of other gardening techniques were also employed. For example, aboriginal farmers in the American Southwest employed a variety of small gardens (see Forde [1931]; Hack [1942]; Kennard [1979]; and Bradfield [1995] for descriptions of the Hopi system). Expedient gardens would be used anytime a sufficient amount of water could be captured from a thunderstorm. Small check dams would be constructed across washes to capture both sediment and water. Water would rush down the wash, be slowed or trapped behind the dam, and drop its load of wet soil, instantly forming a ready-made field of wet and fertile soil in which crops were planted. If a stream overflowed and created a patch of wet soil, crops would be planted. Sand dunes that had been rained on were planted with special types of long-rooted corn to take advantage of the mulching capabilities of the dune. Such single-use gardens were spread across the landscapes, and the crops in them would often fail. However, the investment in them was small, and their number and dispersion across the landscape served to reduce general crop failure. More permanent gardens were built and maintained around areas with more reliable water, such as permanent streams or springs.

Slash-and-Burn

Slash-and-burn, sometimes called shifting cultivation, is a technique used to create a garden or small field within a forested environment. Slash-and-burn is practiced in areas of poor soil, primarily in forests and woodlands, as many forested regions, particularly rainforests, have poor soil due to the constant rain washing away topsoil and nutrients and preventing the formation of rich soils.

As soils are often poor, slash-and-burn fields are usually productive for only a short time. People generally grow crops in a field for a couple of years or so, then abandon the field and move to a new one. Otherwise, a huge amount of time, labor, and organic fertilizer must be invested to maintain crop yields. It is just easier and more cost effective to move on. Even in areas of good soil, the combination of soil restoration and valuable forest products often makes forest fallowing a good idea.

Slash-and-burn fields are generally small, sometimes several acres in size, and are created by one or a few people clearing a small patch of forest. The technology utilized in clearing is usually limited to axes, bush knives, and fire, with fire doing much of the work in reducing the vegetation. Nevertheless, a considerable amount of labor is required to make a field, and the successful use of slash-and-burn as a system (see the swidden system, below) requires a great deal of land since fields are abandoned after a year or two.

At the beginning of the process of creating a field, the trees must be dealt with, as their canopies cause too much shade for crops. The trees can be killed (by girdling) and left standing, cut down and burned, or cut down with the wood being used for other purposes, such as firewood and house construction. Next, the brush is cleared, or slashed, from the field (figure 7.3). The resulting dead vegetation is allowed to dry and then burned. The burning is done at a time of year when the climate is dry enough to allow burning the slash, but not dry enough to allow the fire to spread into healthy forest. Alternatively, firebreaks can be made. The field is then not only cleared, but also fertilized by the ash, with the logs too large to completely burn being left in the field to retard erosion. Crops are then planted with digging sticks.

Crop Choices. It is common to practice polyculture as yields and results are better and more reliable than with monoculture, which is highly vulnerable to flooding, pests, and diseases. However, sometimes just the staple crop is planted, particularly by the transient farmers of today.

FIGURE 7.3
A slash-and-burn field within a forest in the Yucatan of southeastern Mexico. Note that the palm trees were not killed, presumably because they do not cause enough shade to worry about (photo by E. N. Anderson).

Traditional farmers often plant their fields with many different plants, creating a forestlike environment, with grain crops, root crops, vegetables, herbs, fruit trees, cotton, and much else, perhaps as many as one hundred species or varieties in a single plot. Multiple crops complement one another: some thrive in shade, others in sun; some like bare soil while others do not; some fix nitrogen, others need more nitrogen; some grow on others (vines on small trees); and some harbor insects that eat the pests of the others (Conklin 1957; Geertz 1963). Root crops provide safety in case fire or hurricane devastates the field. This sort of mixed planting is an insurance policy. If one or more crops fail, the plot is not a total loss.

If the field itself is not a mixed system, there is inevitably a relatively large and diverse garden around the home. That garden would have the multilayered structure of the forest. It also would have plants and animals occupying many different niches: sun or shade, thin soil or good soil, or wet and dry places.

Weed and Pest Control.   The control of weeds is more difficult with single crops than multiple crops because the crop occupies only a single niche, leaving all the others open for weeds. With many crops, more of the niches are filled and unavailable for weeds. In many cases, little or no weeding is needed. Maize, for instance, needs intensive weeding, but if squash is planted between the rows of maize, the squash plants outcompete the weeds. Traditionally, beans are also planted in this multicrop system; their root nodules fix nitrogen and thus fertilize the other two crops.

Pests are also easier to control with multiple crops. Single pest species have fewer targets and can do only limited damage to any one crop. With insect pests, some of the other crops may harbor other insects that prey on the destructive species, thus providing some built-in insect control. Some larger pests, such as deer, are controlled through hunting, a process that provides needed animal protein in the diet.

Moving Fields.   The major problem in slash-and-burn fields is soil exhaustion. Soils are generally poor to begin with, and the choice of crops can influence the speed of exhaustion. For example, seed crops such as corn are more demanding on soil nutrients and wear out the soil faster than root crops. When a field reaches a point of declining production, it is abandoned and a new field is created. It will take some time, depending on local conditions, for the plot of land to regain its fertility. If a sustainable system of field use, fallowing, and eventual reuse is developed, it is called a swidden system (discussed below).

Small plots are easily reclaimed by the forest if a sufficient amount of forest is left nearby to serve as a source of colonizing plant and animal species. This is often not the case in the large-scale forest clearing now occurring around the world, where too little forest is left in place, land becomes overgrown with weeds, and it takes a very long time for the forest to recover.

Current Problems with Slash-and-Burn.   Although slash-and-burn agriculture has been practiced for thousands of years with a relatively minor impact on the forest, the greatly increased use of slash-and-burn by increasing numbers of people has made it a major problem. In all cases, slash-and-burn results in the elimination of the forest within the boundaries of the field. However, if the field is small relative to the remaining surrounding forest, the field is quickly reclaimed by vegetation, and the forest suffers no real permanent damage. It may even be improved by constant renewal of small patches. However, if too much of the forest is subjected to slash-and-burn at any one time, the forest cannot recover and can be permanently degraded or even destroyed, the situation in many of the rainforests today. Slash-and-burn agriculture can totally destroy valuable tree species, so the technique is hated by loggers, but on the other hand many valuable tree species (including mahogany and teak) like to grow in small burned-over plots and are thus favored by long-fallow swidden systems.

Moreover, though it has been said that slash-and-burn cultivation is energy efficient, this is true only of the human labor component. Fire does most of the work but consumes a great deal of energy in the form of biomass. Today, when energy sources are running short and greenhouse gases are causing concern, this consumption of wood represents another problem—though a minor problem in comparison with burning forest and brush to create cattle pasture and plantations.

The Swidden System

The **swidden system** is an integrated system of sustainable agriculture, or **permaculture**, that incorporates the slash-and-burn technique as its major component (e.g., Conklin 1957; Spencer 1966). Alone, slash-and-burn is a method that creates a one-time field, but a swidden system is sustainable. Swidden is often referred to as "slash-and-burn cultivation" and is known by other names as well, including shifting cultivation and various local names. Using swidden, slash-and-burn fields are left fallow long enough to recover and are then reused in a regular and sustainable cycle. Small gardens may also be an important component of a swidden system.

A swidden system requires a great deal of land, most of which is fallow at any given time. For example, if a farmer uses five-acre fields, each producing for one year, and each requiring ten years to regain its fertility, the farmer will have to have fifty acres fallow with five in production, plus some land for the house and gardens (figure 7.4).

The management of a swidden system—such as deciding when to burn, where to put the next field, when to plant, and what to plant—is a fantastically complex and difficult undertaking. To properly manage a swidden system, farmers must be highly skilled and have an incredible knowledge of local plants, animals, soils, weather, and cultivation methods. Studies in the Philippines (Conklin 1957), Mexico (Berlin et al. 1974; Alcorn 1984; Breedlove and Laughlin 1992), and Brazil (Balée 1994) show that people using the swidden system often know literally thousands of plant and animal species—not only how to identify them, but how to use them and when to find them at their best. This has led to a great deal of research on swidden systems (e.g., Anderson 1990; Dove 1993a, 1993b; Balée 1994), and most studies show that the use of swidden is very efficient and highly adapted to local forest environments. It is a reasonable way to use the forest— probably the best for some. However, this is true only so long as population density remains low and proper plot rotation persists.

Knowledge of forest succession, knowing when a former field can be reused, is an integral part of swidden management, and each individual system must be managed under its own unique circumstances of water, soil, and species. Within the system at any one time, most of the fields are in varying degrees of recovery, each having a slightly different biotic community. In effect, then, the presence of a whole series of fallowed fields in different succession stages greatly increases the biotic diversity within the field system and provides increased opportunity for resource exploitation.

When population density is high, people may be forced to recut their fields before full fertility has been regained. Weeds, pests, and soil exhaustion eventually combine to ruin the yields, as in Thailand and the Philippines. Rampant logging on top of slash-and-burn cultivation greatly decreased the once-valuable forests of these countries. This led, in turn, to massive flooding of more productive farming areas downstream.

In some areas—the temperate forests of the eastern United States for one— the use of swidden gave way to more intensive farming methods. In tropical areas of poor soil and hilly relief, however, no other method works, except restoring an artificial forest of commercial and subsistence tree crops. This sort of tree cropping is locally practiced but is not a perfect solution. For example, coffee is

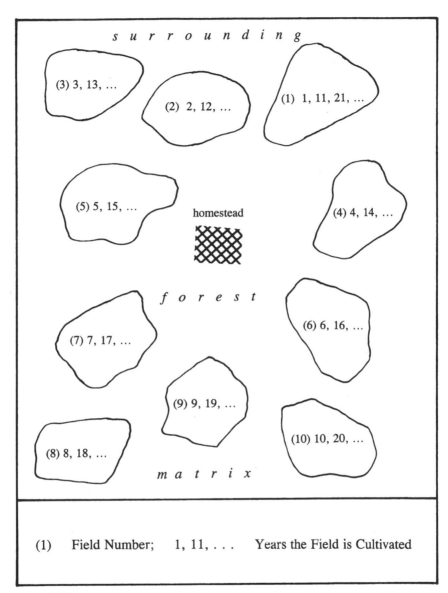

surrounding

(3) 3, 13, ...

(2) 2, 12, ...

(1) 1, 11, 21, ...

(5) 5, 15, ...

homestead

(4) 4, 14, ...

forest

(7) 7, 17, ...

(6) 6, 16, ...

(9) 9, 19, ...

(8) 8, 18, ...

(10) 10, 20, ...

matrix

(1)   Field Number;   1, 11, . . .   Years the Field is Cultivated

FIGURE 7.4
An example of the land requirements of a swidden system with a ten-year cycle.
Field 1 is cultivated in year 1 and then left fallow until year 11; field 2 is cultivated in
year 2, left fallow and cultivated again in year 12; and so on. Thus, the system requires continual control and management of one active and nine fallow fields, with
only 10 percent of the land under cultivation during any particular year.

the most successful tree (or bush) crop in many cool, tropical mountains, and so was promoted as a great way to intensify; therefore, almost every nation with any tropical mountain lands began to grow it. The result was overproduction and a worldwide crash in coffee prices.

Field Rotation

One of the keys in a successful swidden system is properly managed field rotation. When the crop yield from the existing field falls below a certain point (always dependent on the local conditions), the farmer abandons the field and opens a new one. To do this, one has to be able to judge both the fertility of the existing field and the potential fertility of the new field under consideration. The condition of each of the fields in the system has to be monitored and considered in the overall field rotation plan. As long as field rotation is properly managed and population density remains, a swidden system can be used over the long term, with the farmers living in small permanent villages and utilizing the surrounding forest on a rotating basis.

Another approach is to use a much larger-scale rotation system, with large tracts of land being rapidly used and exhausted. In a short time, the entire village would be moved to an entirely new location, leaving the original area to recover and to be reused generations later (see Carneiro 1960). In some cases, however, the movement of settlements may be related more to social factors or availability of animal protein or firewood rather than land exhaustion.

However, if a group moves but keeps expanding into virgin territory rather than reoccupying past field complexes, a predatory society may develop, with warfare being practiced to drive other groups out of potential farmland, as the Iban did in Borneo.

USE OF WILD RESOURCES

Most horticulturalists utilize a wide array of wild resources. Hunting and gathering is done in areas away from the fields and gardens to obtain supplemental foods and materials for manufacture and medicine. Fallow fields are also exploited, as different species of wild plants and animals will colonize them during the various stages of forest regrowth.

Hunting is often better in abandoned fields than in mature forests because new growth is attractive to browsing animals such as deer. In Mesoamerica, a great many deer are hunted in such fields, and these animals form an important source of meat for the farmers. Thus, even "abandoned" fields are still used for some purposes.

Intensive horticulture is typical of Oceania. Grain crops do poorly or are susceptible to typhoons, so root crops such as taro and yams are preferred. Tree crops such as breadfruit, pandanus, and coconuts make up most of the rest of the vegetable food base. The horticultural systems on some islands became extremely intensive over time, with terracing of whole mountainsides, control of streams, and excavation of low wet areas for marsh-loving crops. Fishing is extremely intensive and usually managed in a very careful fashion; sustainable management is often compelled by taboos (*tabu* is a Polynesian word) and other religious mechanisms (Johannes 1981; Ruddle and Akimichi 1984). A fishing expert in a Micronesian island may know details about the habits and ecology of hundreds of species of marine life.

An interesting pattern emerges from the archaeology of Polynesia. In island after island, initial settlement led to wasteful and destructive use of resources, followed by a population crash; then, use of resources gradually became wiser and more constructive, allowing population to rebound and become even greater than before (Kirch 1994, 1997). This is a clear case of something North Americans know from the history of European settlement: a pioneer fringe tends to be characterized by carelessness with nature's bounty, but ultimately reality catches up, and people have to economize and cultivate intensively.

ENVIRONMENTAL MANIPULATION AND RESOURCE MANAGEMENT

Horticulturalists do actively manipulate the environment, such as in the construction of gardens and rotating fields. However, the scale and impact of such alterations is less degrading to the environment compared with clear cutting forests for cattle ranches. In some cases, specific localities can be significantly altered, with very substantial changes being made. Examples of this would include terraced fields and uncontrolled and unmanaged use of slash-and-burn fields.

Passive environmental manipulation is probably more important to horticulturalists than to many hunter-gatherers. The control of weather, water, and sun (abiotic elements) are critical to agricultural success, and some efforts are commonly made in ritual to manage those forces.

Horticulturalists do actively and intensively manage the specific domesticated species that they rely on. Some management of wild species may also be conducted, such as the hunting of deer in fallow fields.

RELATIONS WITH OTHER GROUPS

In general terms, it is possible for horticulturalists to share habitat with hunter-gatherers and pastoralists, if scheduling of land use and details of resource competitions can be worked out (see case study 5.2). However, it seems that such accommodations are relatively uncommon. Horticulturalists cannot coexist with intensive agriculturalists because the two occupy too close a niche, with fertile land and water being critical resources.

CHAPTER SUMMARY

Horticulture is small-scale, low-intensity agriculture conducted using only human labor. Horticulturalists generally grow food, primarily plants but a few animals, for their own consumption. Many horticultural groups have relatively large populations and fairly complex sociopolitical organizations.

The primary type of field used by horticulturalists is the garden, a small field cultivated by one or a small group of individuals. Types of gardens include various kinds of raised fields called chinampas, terraced fields built on sloping terrain, and slash-and-burn fields in forested environments. Construction and maintenance of gardens requires a great deal of effort, and in the case of slash-and-burn fields, gardens must be frequently abandoned and new ones created. Decisions on what kinds of crops to plant, crop rotation, or field abandonment are critical elements of horticulture. Groups will often utilize different garden types, both for diversity and to utilize different landforms.

In some cases, people will utilize gardens in an integrated system, such as a large group of chinampas connected by canals. A number of groups employ the swidden system, a coordinated use of the slash-and-burn fields designed to rotate through a series of specific areas where the fields are used, allowed to recover, and then used again in a sustainable system. Proper management of a swidden system requires good crop and field rotation and leaving fields fallow long enough to recover. Without good management, a swidden system will fail.

Horticulturalists also utilize wild resources to some extent, often as a major component of the economy. Environmental manipulation and resource management is common but is usually small-scale.

KEY TERMS

chinampa
garden
permaculture
slash-and-burn
swidden system

CASE STUDY 7.1

THE GRAND VALLEY DANI OF HIGHLAND NEW GUINEA

This case study presents an interpretation of Grand Valley Dani ecology that emphasizes warfare and pig consumption. This interpretation goes beyond a simple model of adaptation to interconnect economic, sociopolitical, and ritual behaviors into a single ecological system.

The Dani comprise a series of related groups of horticultural people living in the central highlands of Irian Jaya, the eastern portion of New Guinea controlled by Indonesia (figure 7.5). One of these Dani groups, the Grand Valley Dani (hereafter called Dani), became famous in ethnographic and ecological literature through the films and books that resulted from the work of the Peabody Museum of Harvard University Expedition between 1961 and 1963. A number of studies of the Dani has been conducted (Matthiessen 1962; Gardner and Heider 1969; Heider 1970, 1979), and several movies about the Dani have been produced,

FIGURE 7.5
Location of the Grand Valley Dani in New Guinea.

including the well-known 1963 film, *Dead Birds*. The pursuits of the Dani were summarized by Heider (1970:10) as being "war, farming, and pigs." The people of highland New Guinea were not discovered by the outside world until 1933, when a group of Australian gold miners entered the interior of the island. They encountered about a million native people living in a large number of small horticultural societies. The gold miners carried a movie camera with them and filmed the astonished natives. That film footage was made into a film, *First Contact*, and a book by the same name (Connolly and Anderson 1987).

THE NATURAL ENVIRONMENT

The heart of Dani territory is the wide and fertile Grand Valley, lying more than five thousand feet above sea level and surrounded by the great mountains that form the spine of New Guinea. The Balim River flows through the valley, only occasionally overflowing. Located just south of the equator, the valley receives about eighty inches of rain per year with a moderate temperature. The Dani do not recognize any distinct seasons.

The land was, at one time, densely forested, but thousands of years of horticulture have converted much of it into fields, grasslands, and second-growth scrub. Few wild animals remain in the valley itself, having been hunted out long ago, but a relatively pristine forest surrounds the valley and is occupied by a large array of wildlife.

SOCIOPOLITICAL ORGANIZATION

About fifty thousand people live in the Grand Valley, all speaking the same language and having a similar culture. They are organized into about fifty separate groups, or confederations, and there is no united political organization in the valley. Each of the confederations has well-defined territories with guarded borders. Some confederations join together to form temporary alliances, and each confederation/alliance is always at war with at least one other.

The people live in small settlements or compounds of a number of families, which are protected by fences and gates (figure 7.6). Among the compounds are "Big Men," males of influence but of little real power. The political and social organization is centered on the compound, with little overall complexity.

CASE STUDY 7.1

FIGURE 7.6
Aerial view of a village and garden complex, highland New Guinea, about 1938
(photo courtesy of Bill Richardson).

ECONOMICS

The primary focus of Dani horticulture is the growing of yellow sweet potatoes, what Americans call "yams," and about 90 percent of the Dani diet is derived from this tuber. Yams are rich in vitamin A, have good-quality protein, and have a fair amount of B vitamins, although they are short in minerals and vitamin C. However, the leaves of the yam are eaten and supply adequate amounts of vitamin C, as well as some other vitamins and minerals. Even so, the Dani had to depend on other sources for much of the nutrient value in their diet, and they were chronically short of protein, calcium, and iron, even though they ate pork. They were short in stature, probably (in part) as a result of this.

The primary type of garden is located in the valley bottom and consists of raised fields providing drainage from excess water. Yams grow best in these well-drained gardens, and much of the Grand Valley has been converted into a vast system of these fields, carefully engineered to be the perfect environment for the yam (see Gardner and Heider 1969; Heider 1970:37). The raised fields are surrounded by ditches that not only drain the water, but protect the fields from pigs. The fields were constructed by cooperative work parties, using digging sticks and other simple tools. Under such cultivation, yams can produce many tons of food per acre, and given the climate of the valley, yams can be grown all year. About one-half of the valley fields are fallow at any one time.

Yams and other crops are grown in the two other types of gardens used by the Dani. Small gardens are located behind most houses. Some men will use slash-and-burn fields on nearby hill slopes, abandoning them after a few plantings. The valley is located just at the upper range of bananas and pandanus, both of which are also used as food.

Much of the Dani language is devoted to agriculture. They recognize dozens of varieties of yam, and even more variety names, and have countless words evaluating them. Heider recorded more than seventy variety names in one small community. Another vocabulary details the processes and methods of yam cultivation.

Interestingly, the yam is native to South America, apparently having reached New Guinea only a couple of centuries ago, give or take a century. Before that, the Dani and the hundreds of other New Guinea mountain groups grew other root and tuber crops, notably taro (*Colocasia esculenta*) and perhaps kudzu (*Pueraria montana* var. *lobata*). More important in the lowlands, but also common in the highlands, were the native large, whitish yams of the lily family, very different from the late-arriving yam species. These roots have been grown for more than six thousand years, very possibly for ten thousand years, in the New Guinea highlands, making New Guinea one of the original and ancient homelands of domestication. Taro and white yams are still grown in a small way by the Dani.

Some other highland groups grow many species of vegetables, but the Dani seem to be content with growing only a few species of vegetables in addition to the versatile, tractable yam. Some tobacco and gourds are also grown, and some of the gourds are used as penis sheaths, much valued as male apparel.

In addition to their primary horticultural practices, the Dani also raise domestic pigs (an example of sedentary animal husbandry; see chapter 8). Pigs supply the vast majority of the animal protein in the diet. Pigs are tended close to the village by children and are fed the garbage and other materials that people generally do not eat. Pigs are butchered and eaten almost exclusively on festive occasions, but these were frequent in traditional times, and so pork consumption was common.

The Dani practiced some hunting of animals in the forest, including wild pigs, and a number of wild plants were gathered. However, most of the valley has been stripped of forest to make gardens, and so wild foods are fairly rare. Trips to the forested mountains are uncommon.

WARFARE

When not cultivating, the Dani were apt to be fighting. Highly ritualized combat, the sort portrayed in the film *Dead Birds*, took place frequently but caused few casualties. Less common, but more dangerous, were ambushes of isolated individuals who were cultivating or hunting far from home. Much less common and far more serious was a nighttime raid in which enemies would infiltrate a village and try to kill everyone.

To defend against the enemy, the border was constantly guarded, with watchtowers being built along the border. Constant vigilance was part of daily life. Warfare was not conducted for land, food, or other resources but to avenge earlier deaths. The Dani believe that death is not natural and is always caused by the action of the enemy, either directly in battle or other violent confrontation, or through witchcraft. The souls of the dead require that they be avenged; otherwise, the village will be haunted by ghosts. The other side also believes this, and so there is never any balance; one or the other side is always seeking revenge for the last death.

This pattern of warfare is more or less widespread in the New Guinea highlands (see Meggitt 1977; Ember 1982), and one of the primary reasons for the intensive, labor-demanding cultivation of the valley floor was the extreme danger of going more than a mile from home to cultivate. This presumably explains the presence of intense horticulture in an area of relatively simple technology and low population density.

CEREMONIES

Throughout the year, the Dani put on a series of large ceremonies or festivals, in which rituals are held and food is consumed, particularly

CASE STUDY 7.1

pigs. These events are sponsored by important men for a number of reasons, including the celebration of the death of an enemy and to mourn the death of someone from one's own group. They also can function to make peace between conflicting groups or to marshal support for one particular group. The ceremonies also provide a reason for intensive food production. For one reason or another, such ceremonies are held frequently, at least one every few weeks.

AN ECOLOGICAL INTERPRETATION OF DANI WARFARE

Rappaport (1984; also see Ember [1982] and Dwyer [1990]) argued that among the Tsembaga Maring, a group very similar to the Dani, ceremonies were timed to get rid of excess pigs, when they became numerous enough to be damaging the gardens. Alternatively, the Tsembaga may actually let pig populations build up when they want a festival. The Dani have more intensive pig rearing; all are carefully raised and tended, whereas the Tsembaga pigs are semiwild. Thus, the Dani control the process better and seem not to worry about pig population cycles.

It has also been argued (Rappaport 1984) that the pattern of warfare can be linked to the system of ceremonies and pig consumption. Pork is the primary protein source but cannot be eaten daily, as there are not enough of them. So their consumption has to be somehow controlled in such a way as to provide the needed protein on a regular basis. Because the pigs are eaten only at ceremonies, the frequency of the ceremonies would serve to regulate pork, and so protein, consumption. The ceremonies are tied, at least in part, to the regular cycle of warfare, which would serve to regulate the frequency of ceremonies, and so pig consumption. At each death, each of the warring groups would hold a ceremony, one to celebrate and the other to mourn, and everyone would get some pork to eat. Given the nature of Dani warfare, ceremonies could be expected every few weeks. The argument is that protein consumption is regulated so that people get enough but the resource base (pigs) is not overexploited. Although this is obviously a materialist and functionalist interpretation, it does have merit. However, it has been criticized for appealing more to plausibility than to evidence; Andrew Vayda, an expert on highland New Guinea, has called

CASE STUDY 7.1

for establishing firm causal chains in explaining New Guinea ecology (Vayda 1989).

When the Dani were forced by the Indonesian government to give up warfare in the mid-1960s, they apparently did so with little resistance. Heider (1979:112) thought that Dani life did not change much; men still sat around talking, and "frequent occasions were still found to eat pigs."

CASE STUDY 7.2

THE LOZI OF WESTERN ZAMBIA

The Lozi case study illustrates two important aspects of adaptation. First, the political organization of the Lozi divides the culture into halves yet ensures the equitable distribution of resources throughout the land. Second, the agricultural system is intensive and complex but still involves a seasonal movement of people and an adoption of seasonally specific agricultural tactics. The resulting system is unique.

The Lozi live along the Zambezi River in western Zambia (figure 7.7) and have an economy that emphasizes horticulture, cattle, and fishing. They consist of some twenty-five separate tribes, four of which are the Lozi proper, with the others being groups assimilated into the Lozi culture. The Lozi are also known by a number of other names, including the Barotse and Luyana. In 2000, the overall Lozi population was about five hundred thousand, some seventy thousand of which were the Lozi proper. This case study describes the group as they were in the early 1900s.

The Lozi moved into the region sometime during the seventeenth century and imposed their rule over the local inhabitants. By the early 1840s, they were conquered by the invading Kololo but regained their independence in 1864. In 1896, the British took control of the region and formed the colony of Northern Rhodesia. In 1964, the country gained its independence and was renamed Zambia.

The Lozi occupy some 150,000 square miles of western Zambia (now called the Western Province) and live primarily on the floodplain of the

FIGURE 7.7
Location of the Lozi in southern Africa.

Zambezi River. Each year, these villages are flooded (figure 7.8), and the people are forced to move into the nearby forest until the water recedes. They then move back to the villages and reestablish their gardens for the next year's crops. Thus, they have a seasonal round that includes two separate systems of settlement and subsistence. Some basic information on the Lozi can be found in Gluckman (1941, 1951), Turner (1952), and Caplan (1970).

THE NATURAL ENVIRONMENT
The broad, sandy floodplain of the Zambezi River in southwestern Zambia is called the Barotse Plain. The plain lies below 3,500 feet, but the surrounding forested regions rise to a maximum of 7,000 feet in elevation. The area has relatively warm temperatures all year, with highs

FIGURE 7.8
A Lozi village isolated by flooding (photo courtesy of Philip Silverman).

between sixty and one hundred degrees Fahrenheit. Rainfall is variable, but the headwaters of the Zambezi River receive about forty inches of rainfall per year. The plain is treeless except for some planted for fruit or shade. The grasses on the plain can grow as high as six feet.

The Barotse Plain is flanked by forest. The soils in the forest are poor quality, consisting mostly of sand. The forest is traversed by a number of small tributaries of the Zambezi, and their small valleys are also inhabited by Lozi. The forest consists of teak and other trees plus many shrubs that form a relatively dense undergrowth.

At the southern extreme of this area, the Barotse Plain narrows significantly and the Zambezi River changes direction to flow eastward to the Indian Ocean. One of the great natural wonders of the world, Victoria Falls (known locally as *Musi-o-tunya*, "the smoke that thunders") is located in this area.

The region has three major seasons, dry, rainy, and hot, with the rainy season beginning about October/November and lasting until March/April. During the rainy season, the Zambezi River floods most, and sometimes all, of the Barotse Plain. In wet years, a lake some twenty to thirty miles wide, one hundred to one hundred twenty miles long, and fifteen feet deep is formed.

Lozi life revolves around the flood. The flood "covers and uncovers gardens, fertilizing and watering them, fixes the pasturing of the cattle, and conditions the methods of fishing. All life in the Plain moves with the flood: people, fish, cattle, game, wildfowl, snakes, rodents, and insects" (Gluckman 1951:11).

SOCIOPOLITICAL ORGANIZATION

The Lozi have a social system with classes, including royalty, the wealthy, the poor, and prior to British rule, slaves. Most people live in small villages of between fifty and seventy-five inhabitants, and each village has a headman appointed by the ruler. Many of the Lozi villages are located on the Barotse Plain, but a number of Lozi live permanently away from the plain. The villages on the Barotse Plain are built on high ground, either on mounds especially built for that purpose, or on old termite or ant mounds. Houses are constructed by plastering mud and cow dung over a wooden framework, a technique called wattle and daub.

The Lozi had a hereditary monarchy divided into two halves, north and south, although the actual territories of the north and south were geographically intermingled. Originally, each half was ruled by a king who was assisted by a council of local leaders to advise him and lived in a capital, a large village also on the Barotse Plain. Each king ruled his half but also had considerable influence in the other half. After 1864, the ruler of the south was a female, always a daughter of the king of the north. Each monarch had a council, and the governments of both the north and south functioned as a single body to make important state decisions.

Each monarch controlled land and resources throughout Lozi territory and collected taxes (in resources rather than cash) from all over his and her lands. These resources would be redistributed as needed. This dual system served to ensure that resources were evenly distributed throughout Lozi territory and that no one had a monopoly.

When the floods came, the monarchs would move their royal courts to the forest in a large public pageant called Kuomboka. On the date of

CASE STUDY 7.2

Kuomboka, each small village on the Barotse Plain moved to its temporary village at the forest edge. The two monarchs coordinated their move to the forest so that all of the Lozi could move at the same time.

ECONOMICS
The economic system consists of three primary components: horticulture, cattle raising, and fishing, although some hunting and gathering is also important. Most of the gardens used by the Lozi are located on the Barotse Plain, as is most, and the best, cattle pasture. The main crop is corn (maize), but they also grow cassava, millet, sorghum, squash, tobacco, beans, and sweet potatoes, as well as bananas and mangos. Cattle provide meat, milk, leather, and fertilizer and there are also several small domesticated animals, such as chickens and goats. Dogs are kept and survive as scavengers. Fishing is a major activity, and some other hunting and gathering is also done. In addition, the Lozi maintain a substantial trade with other groups living in the forest. A detailed description of the Lozi horticultural systems was provided by Peters (1960).

THE SEASONAL ROUND
The Lozi live in small villages located on high ground on the Barotse Plain for most of the year. However, when the Zambezi River floods, the Barotse Plain becomes a large lake, and the people have to move to higher ground in the forested areas on either side of the plain. Thus, the Lozi employ a simple and regular seasonal round, one that has them in their primary villages on the plain for about nine months and in their secondary villages on the edge of the forest for about three months each year. Each of these villages is usually occupied year after year.

Once the waters begin to rise, the cattle are moved to higher ground, with the herders living in small camps. About a month later, when the water gets high enough to flood most of the area and the insects become unbearable, the royal families move to the forest, a signal for the rest of the people to also move. The villagers pack what they need into their canoes and move to their forest villages to reestablish their households and begin work on their gardens in the forest. Some materials and food are left stored in the plains villages, and the people return by boat to obtain those materials as necessary. The forest villages consist of the same basic number of houses constructed in a similar, though less substantial, manner as the plains houses.

The cattle are moved back onto the plains as soon as the water recedes, to take advantage of the new grass and to fertilize the agricultural fields. The land is dry enough for cattle but still too wet for people and planting. The people return to their plains villages about a month after the cattle. Upon their return, they must repair the flood damage done to their mud houses and prepare the fields for planting.

Gardens

The Lozi employ a number of different types and variants of gardens for the diverse conditions on the Barotse Plain and the forest. Most of the gardens are less than an acre in size, and the important conditions for the location and type of gardens are soil type and available water. Corn is the primary crop for the gardens on the plain, while cassava is the most important crop grown in the forest gardens.

The Barotse Plain Garden System

The soils on the Barotse Plain are generally good and fertile, being renewed almost annually by new alluvial sediments dropped by the floodwaters. Most of the gardens are not purposefully irrigated; in fact, most have to be drained to be used. However, a few plots are supplied with irrigation water from a small system of canals, which are also used as transportation routes for canoes. Decisions on what and where to plant on the Barotse Plain are made depending on the level of flooding, amount of new sediment, soil moisture, and other factors.

The most desirable garden, called *lizulu*, is located on small mounds or ridges, often old anthills. However, these are the same places where villages are built, and there is competition between the two uses. Lizulu are cultivated all year if they remain above the floodwater, and during the flood season they are tended by people commuting from the forest in boats.

The most common garden types on the plains are similar to chinampas. The first type, called *mikomena*, are constructed in relatively poor soils by digging trenches around a small plot of land and piling up the soil in the middle to form a raised field. Some mikomena are dry, but groundwater seeps into the trenches surrounding others. The mikomena are usually planted with sweet potatoes, then broken back down and planted with corn, then left fallow for at least six years.

The second form of garden, called *li-shanjo* (figure 7.9), is similar to a chinampa, built in the same general manner as the mikomena, but in swampy areas where peat is a common soil constituent. Relatively large tracts of land might be covered with these gardens, and the various channels dug around them would be connected to some natural water course to allow the water to drain. The gardens are prepared by burning the weeds and debris left from the last planting. Corn is the most common crop in these gardens, but sweet potatoes will be planted first in new or renovated gardens to increase the fertility of the soil for corn.

FIGURE 7.9
A woman tilling a Lozi *li-shanjo* garden, ca. 1966 (photo courtesy of Philip Silverman).

Litongo gardens are those placed in the relatively steeply sloped, sandy soils on the edge of the plain, or in the forest, and are essentially located in the ecotone between the plain and the forest. They come in several forms, dry, moist, and plains, depending on their location and water content. Most contain poor soils and are not highly productive. However, the moist litongo gardens are located on lower slopes of the plain, where water constantly seeps in, and are more productive. The Lozi mostly grow root crops in these gardens.

The last major garden type is the small *ndamino*, the kitchen garden, and is often placed on a moist litongo located near the village. The ndamino receives a "good deal of [household] refuse and the droppings of small domesticated animals" (Peters 1960:16). These gardens are quite fertile and used for corn and sorghum.

The Forest Garden System

The Lozi also farm the forests that ring the Barotse Plain, mostly during the three months that they live in the forest. The soils in the forest are generally poor and leach badly. Most areas have a covering of trees and thick brush. The primary type of garden in the forest is called *matema*, or bush gardens, and are slash-and-burn fields. The vegetation on a matema is cut between April and June, left to dry, and then burned in September. Because of the low soil fertility, cassava is the primary crop of the matema, although millet is also planted when the rains come, usually in October. The matema system seems to have been adopted relatively recently but has been used long enough that most of the forest surrounding the Barotse Plains is now mostly secondary forest.

Livestock

Cattle are the primary domesticated animal, and the Lozi keep a fairly large number of them. For most of the year, cattle are grazed on the Barotse Plain. In April, when the waters begin to rise and about a month before the people move to escape the rising waters, the cattle are moved off the Barotse Plain to pastures on the edge of, or in, the forest. The cattle are tended by herdsmen who often live in separate camps for the season. The animals are moved back to the Barotse Plain in June, about a month before the people return to their villages. The manure is used to fertilize the various gardens before the farmers return to begin cultivation for the year.

Use of Wild Resources

A number of wild resources were used by the Lozi, several of which were very important. Some of these resources were obtained by the Lozi themselves, while others were obtained by trade with other groups in the forest. Wild plants formed a relatively minor aspect of the Lozi economy.

Fish from the Zambezi River were the most important animal and were a major protein source. Fish were taken year-round by a variety of methods, including traps, nets, and spears. Game animals were hunted both on the plain and in the forest. Antelope, elephants, hippopotami (still a favorite as the meat is thought to have aphrodisiac properties), crocodiles, and a number of small mammals and birds were hunted using spears, harpoons, and pit traps. When the water began to rise on the Barotse Plain, animals trapped on high ground were driven into the water and killed by men in canoes using spears. Today, few game animals survive on the Barotse Plain.

ENVIRONMENTAL MANIPULATION AND RESOURCE MANAGEMENT

The Lozi manipulate their environment in a number of ways. Active manipulation includes the construction of some artificial mounds on the Barotse Plain on which to build villages, which then generally survive the annual floods. Flooded villages require a considerable amount of rebuilding. A number of other fields and facilities are built on the plain, but they are commonly washed away by the floods and have to be reestablished. Thus, much of the Lozi activity on the plain has little long-term impact. The slash-and-burn system in the surrounding forest, however, has resulted in the conversion of the original forest into secondary growth.

The Lozi actively manage both abiotic and biotic resources, including soil, livestock, crops, and some wild animals. Of interest is the soil management. Soil fertility is of great concern and efforts are made to maintain fertility by the addition of animal dung, rotation of crops of sweet potatoes and corn, addition of ash from the burning of detritus, and a system of fallowing. Water is also managed; however, primarily this revolves around draining flooded fields.

CASE STUDY 7.2

DISCUSSION

The Lozi have developed a complex system of adaptations to the changing seasonal conditions. In the dry season, they occupy one ecozone (the valley) and practice irrigation agriculture on the valley floor. In the wet season, they move to a different ecozone and adopt a different subsistence system that revolves around forest gardens. This adaptation involves a regular movement of villages and required a dual land base. Thus, each village uses both valley and forest ecozones plus the ecotone between them each year.

The sociopolitical system is adapted to this seasonally fluctuating economic system. The overlapping power of the dual monarchs ensures the distribution of resources throughout Lozi territory. The pomp and ceremony attached to the movement of the villages out of the plain and into the forest reinforces the social nature and ecological necessity of the move.

As so often happens, modern changes have not been kind to the Lozi. Dams and development projects have displaced them (see Scudder 2005), and modern states have altered their political situation.

8

Pastoralism

Pastoralism is that form of agriculture in which its practitioners specialize in, and obtain their primary subsistence from, the husbandry of one or a few domesticated animal species. These species are invariably herbivores such as cattle, horses, sheep, llamas, alpacas, goats, camels, reindeer, and similar animals. Plant cultivation often forms one component of pastoralism but is not generally dominant. In some cases, however, such as reindeer, the species of focus is not domesticated.

A precise definition of pastoralism is elusive, with the primary disagreement centering on the proportion of horticulture/agriculture in the economy and degrees of mobility (see Krader 1959:499; Khazanov 1984:7, 15–17; and Cribb 1991:15–17, 20; also see Spooner 1973; Goldschmidt 1979). The term *nomad* has generally been used by anthropologists to refer to mobile pastoralists and should not be applied to hunter-gatherers (see Krader 1959:499). A brief history of the study of pastoralists was presented by Dyson-Hudson (1972:2–7; also see Waller and Sobania 1994).

Pastoralists and their animals have developed a long-term mutually beneficial relationship (see Krader 1959:501). Animals provide humans with products such as meat, milk, hide, dung, wool, labor, and services such as companionship and the transportation of people and goods. Humans provide animals with protection from predators, a steady food supply, health care, an expanded habitat, and assured reproductive success.

Pastoralism requires a great deal of land as a pasture base. It is generally more productive (calories per acre) than most hunting and gathering but less productive than farming. However, pastoralism can be very efficient in areas unsuitable for farming. Pastoralists utilize their animals to convert unusable biomass from

225

one trophic level to usable products in another trophic level: grasses that humans cannot digest are converted into milk and meat that they can eat. Even though using the animals involves an additional trophic step, it is highly efficient in such circumstances because people cannot use the grasses anyway. However, the use of supplemental feed, such as corn, that humans could directly consume, is a very inefficient use of resources, and few pastoralists do that.

Domesticated animals also serve as efficient storage facilities, food resources "stored" on the hoof (making them mobile as well!). In many cases, they could also be considered examples of social storage, wealth "stored" in animals owned by individuals.

GENERAL SOCIOPOLITICAL ORGANIZATION

There really is not a typical pastoral sociopolitical organization, varying from loosely organized tribes to almost state-level societies. The Mongols of central Asia were loosely organized groups of families and lineages until Genghis Khan united them into an imperial state. After his time, they reverted to their former organization within a few generations. However, many pastoral groups maintain a loose tribe-level sociopolitical organization, one that preserves the independence of individual herding groups but ensures some overall control of the system of pastures.

The household, consisting of either a nuclear or extended family, is the usual primary unit of social organization, and most are patrilineal. Social units have to be flexible in size and membership to be able to adjust to the shifting size and composition of herds. People tend to marry someone from a nearby family, both to maintain animal ownership and to cement alliances. Most groups maintain at least two major settlement types, villages where most people live and stock camps where the herders are tending the animals.

The population of pastoral groups can vary greatly, from a few thousand to hundreds of thousands, but pastoralists usually have a lower population density than plant cultivators, because pastoralism is often less productive per acre than farming. However, in some areas such as the central Andes, and in Iran and central Asia, pastoralists, supplemented by some agriculture, have maintained fairly large and stable populations for long periods of time (see Yamamoto 1985).

In a pastoral society, most, if not all, of the population is engaged in animal husbandry. Most groups have a fairly strict sexual division of labor, with the men generally tending the animals, often at stock camps. The women are often left in the village to maintain the household and tend the lower-status animals.

TYPES OF PASTORALISM

Here, we define three basic types of pastoralism (table 8.1) in which animals form the basis of the economy (roughly following Khazanov [1984:17–25]). These types form a continuum from what many consider to be "real" pastoralists, those who are highly mobile and completely reliant on their animals, to **sedentary** or "village" pastoralists, those who are settled and where agriculture forms an important aspect of the economy. Individual groups will alter their adaptations depending on conditions, and so the categories must remain flexible.

The first type is **nomadic pastoralism**, where animals and their products form virtually the only resource. Some gathering of wild plant resources would be conducted, but no agriculture would be practiced. Such societies would consist of small, highly mobile groups that follow their livestock across the landscape.

Table 8.1. The Basic Types of Pastoralism

Type	Major Features	Mobility and Settlement Pattern	Examples
Primary Pastoral Systems			
Nomadic	Almost all of the resources produced are derived from animals and their products, with some trade for other products	Highly mobile, seasonal round with few permanent settlements	Saami
Seminomadic	The bulk of the resources used come from animals and their products, supplemented by some horticulture, hunting and gathering, and trade	Generally mobile, seasonal round but with some of the population remaining in permanent or semipermanent villages	Maasai
Semisedentary	Animals and their products provide many of the resources used, but horticulture, hunting and gathering, and trade are very important	Some mobility by specialized task groups, most of the population in settled villages	Navajo
Pastoral Components of Larger Agricultural Systems			
Herdsman husbandry	Animals important but farming the dominant activity	Animals are raised in pastures distant from the main agricultural centers, task groups tend animals and move them seasonally	Basque, ranchers in the United States
Sedentary animal husbandry	Animals important but farming the dominant activity	Animals raised in a static location	Dani, dairies in the United States

Nomadic pastoralists are uncommon, but the Saami (or Lapps) reindeer herders of far northern Scandinavia are a good example (see Spencer 1978; Beach 1988).

Seminomadic pastoralism is the second major type of pastoralism. Seminomadic groups have a seasonal round, and animals are moved from pasture to pasture, a pattern called **seasonal transhumance**. In some groups, the entire population, human and animal, will move to new pastures, meaning that the new pasture must be of sufficient size and quality to support all of the people and animals. In other groups, just the men will move the animals while the women stay in a permanent village tending gardens. In this system, animals are by far the most important resource, but some horticulture may be practiced to supplement the animal products. Trade of animal products to other groups would also be common. This is the most common form of pastoralism (see case study 8.1 at the end of the chapter).

The third major type is **semisedentary pastoralism**, sometimes called agropastoralism. In this type, the animals are still the main resource, but horticulture forms a major aspect of the economy. Many of the people in such a group would live in a permanent village and grow crops. The animals would have to be moved around from pasture to pasture, but a relatively small number of specialized herdsmen would do that work. An example of this type of pastoralism is the Navajo of the American Southwest (see case study 8.2).

Two other types of pastoralism have been defined (see Khazanov 1984:17–25), but these are really pastoral components of agricultural systems. In **herdsman husbandry**, animals are important but agriculture is the predominant economic activity, and the majority of the population are sedentary farmers. The animal herds are tended by herdsmen in pastures distant from the main community. Examples of this type of pastoralism are the Basque in France and Spain (see Ott 1993).

Sedentary animal husbandry is also a pastoral technique that forms a component of an agricultural system. This form is more accurately described as agriculture with some stock raising, because it consists of full-time farmers who also raise some animals. A small-scale example is the Dani, described in chapter 7. The dairy industry in the United States is a good example of a large-scale practice.

THE GEOGRAPHY OF PASTORALISM

Until recently, pastoralists occupied a large portion of the Old World, extending from East Africa east to China and north to Siberia. Spooner (1973:6–7) defined five broad ecological zones occupied by pastoralists in the Old World, characterized by the primary types of animals raised. Pastoralists relying primarily on single species of animals occupy four broad regions of the Old World (figure 8.1): (1) northern Eurasia, where reindeer are the primary stock; (2) the eastern Mediterranean region, where sheep are the major animal; (3) portions of North Africa and the Arabian peninsula, where camels are the primary stock; and (4) sub-Saharan Africa where cattle are the main stock. The fifth general region, where pastoralists work multiple stock, including horses, occupies the broad arid region extending from North Africa east across southwest Asia and to Mongolia.

There are only a few native pastoral groups in the New World. The Navajo herd sheep and some cattle in the American Southwest (see case study 8.3). A number of groups herd llamas and alpacas in the mountains of South America. Other local pastoral economies in South America include the gaucho economy of Argentina and neighboring countries and the Goajira of the Goajira Peninsula on the Venezuela-Colombia border. The gaucho way of life developed as cattle ranchers moved out onto the pampas, the vast, dry plains of Argentina. Gauchos

FIGURE 8.1
A general geographical distribution of pastoralists in the Old World by broad ecological zones.

were, originally, cowboys of mixed Spanish/Native American ancestry who developed a unique way of life following the herds of cattle across the unfenced ranges.

The Goajira are a Native South American people who adopted herding soon after contact. They raise cattle, horses, and small stock in their arid and isolated peninsula. Until recently, they maintained a strikingly distinctive way of life, but, as elsewhere, the old ways are now changing fast.

The areas occupied by pastoralists are shrinking all over the world due to constant and increasing pressure for them to adopt more sedentary lifestyles. This is due partly to a loss of pasture to expanding agriculturalists and to a desire by governments to exercise control of the pastoral populations within their borders. National governments now seek to regulate and "help" pastoralists by forcing them to settle in villages and adopt agriculture. A discussion of pastoral sedentarization processes is presented in Salzman (1980).

THE ORIGIN OF PASTORALISM

It is generally believed that pastoralism evolved from an agricultural base (see Lees and Bates 1974; Smith 1992). Perhaps some early farmers decided to specialize in animals, either by choice or because there were too many people for too small a grain harvest. Perhaps the first pastoralists were outcasts from agricultural communities, forced for some reason to live with the animals on the fringes of the town. Whatever the specific reason, it seems that early pastoralists were probably people who left farming and began moving their animals around the landscape to take advantage of areas not used by the farmers. It is probable that pastoralism emerged as a standard way of life soon after the domestication of sheep and goats.

SOME PARAMETERS OF PASTORALISM

Pastoralism is a complex endeavor that requires a great deal of knowledge about both animals and the environment, including the availability of water and pasture and the presence of competing groups (Bates and Lees 1996b:153). The important considerations include pastures, types of animals, herd composition and size, movement of herds, and products.

Pastures

The primary land resource for pastoralists is the pasture, a general area where animals can find the foods they need. Thus, like farmers, pastoralists are usually tied to specific plots of land. Many people equate a pasture with a grass-covered area where animals such as cattle or horses graze. However, a pasture is just a place where food for a particular animal is present. Pastoral animals occupy two general dietary niches: grazing and browsing. **Grazers** primarily eat grasses and low-growing plants while **browsers** primarily eat the foliage from bushes and trees. If the animals are browsers, a good pasture would consist of bushes and trees, not grasses. Nevertheless, the term *grazing* is commonly used to refer to the feeding behaviors of both grazing and browsing domesticated animals.

In all cases, pastures must be properly managed to prevent overgrazing. The primary issue is the carrying capacity of the pasture. The determination of carrying capacity is based on water availability, pasture type and quality, and the type(s) of animals to be herded, all of which can vary by season. One must be careful not to put too many animals or the wrong animals on a pasture or keep them there too long. As many pastoral groups move their entire livestock populations to new pastures, they must ensure that the pasture is capable of supporting all of the animals. In essence, then, the herders must monitor the nature and condition of pastures and note the succession stages of the various plant species in them to know when to have animals on them and how long the animals can be there. Another consideration is the slope of the pasture, as the herders do not want to excessively tire their animals on steep-sloped pastures.

If pastures are owned or controlled by individuals, the decision-making process would rest with that person. If, however, pastures are communally owned, some sort of centralized control would be needed. Among the pastoralists of Persia (now Iran), Barth (1964) showed that while individual households owned and controlled their own herds, the tribal chiefs generally regulated the assignment of those herds to pastures. This served to prevent overexploitation of the pastures by any one segment, as overgrazing could endanger the pasture system of the entire group. In addition to the regulation of grazing, pasture assignments also functioned to control animal population, which in turn helped to control human population by limiting the food supply.

However, pastures are sometimes poorly managed. If an individual limits herd size for the good of the community so as to not overexploit a pasture, he depends on the owners of other herds to do the same. If everyone does not cooperate, there is little incentive for individuals to limit their herds, and short-term gain is put ahead of long-term stability (not a good situation). In such cases, the total population of livestock may crash in response to overgrazing, drought, disease, or other conditions that change the carrying capacity of the available pastures. The animal population will fall below the carrying capacity of the pastures, and the human population will follow suit. As the pasture recovers, both the animal and human population will grow until the next crash, and a boom-and-bust cycle will result. The recent drought in eastern Africa that so severely affected the Maasai is a good example of this phenomenon (see case study 8.1).

Types of Animals

Ecological conditions influence the types of animals that can be raised in certain areas. The availability of proper pasture, water, and accessibility to land limit and tether both animals and their herders. The choice of which animal(s) to herd is also greatly influenced by tradition. Some domesticated animals, such as pigs, chickens, and dogs, are not herded in a pastoral manner and are not considered as pastoral species.

Grazers

Cattle (*Bos* sp.) are primarily grazers and require fairly good pasture and a great deal of water to do well. Cattle eat the blades of the grass and leave the roots in the ground, allowing the grass to rapidly regrow and be eaten again. However, cattle will also do some browsing and eat the leaves of trees and bushes. Domestic cattle require considerable human labor, particularly in areas with snow, because cows will not dig through even shallow snow to the grass below and have to be fed. Well-fed cattle will produce milk, a major product, in quantity. Yaks (*Poephagus grunniens*) are related to cattle (both are bovids) and behave in a similar manner, except that yaks live at very high altitudes in central Asia and will paw through snow.

Horses (*Equus caballus*) have the same basic habits and needs as cattle but generally require less human labor than cattle. Horses do less browsing than cattle and so have a greater impact on grasses. Cattle and horses can share pasture as long as the total number of animals does not exceed the overall carrying capacity of the pasture. Like cattle, horses can be used for meat, skin, and milk, but are more highly valued for transportation.

However, horses and cattle cannot always be in the same pasture. In the Yucatan Peninsula, the Spanish had a very difficult time grazing their horses, as there was little suitable grass. However, they eventually found that horses would eat the leaves of the ramón plant (*Brosimum alicastrum*), *ramón* being Spanish for "horse fodder." Cattle in the same region would eat the waxim plant, but horses could not, as waxim contains a chemical that makes the hair of the horses fall out. The cattle can eat it as their four-chambered stomachs can detoxify the chemical.

Sheep (*Ovis aries*) are also grazers and will eat many types of vegetation. However, when sheep eat grass, they will often pull up and eat the roots, killing the plant and leaving the land bare. Thus, rather than just quickly regrowing, the entire grass plant is removed and new plants must colonize the pasture. This process takes time, and so pasture recovery is more difficult. Thus, sheep are more likely to overgraze and do not share pasture with other grazing animals well (having an overlapping niche and habitat). This is one of the problems that led to the enmity between cattle herders and sheepherders in the Old West and remains a problem in the United States today.

Llamas (*Lama glama glama*) and alpacas (*L. g. pacos*) are the two species of domesticated camelids herded in the mountains of South America (see Flannery et al. 1989). Both animals are grazers, but the llama is more tolerant of differing habitats (e.g., elevation) and is widely used as a pack animal and for meat. Alpacas need to remain above three thousand feet of elevation and are valued more for their fine wool than their meat.

Browsers

Goats (*Capra* spp.) can both graze and browse, making that species very versatile and adaptable to most pasture types and able to take advantage of ecotone pastures. In that sense, goats are excellent secondary animals that can complement any herd. Goats produce milk that can be made into cheese. Goats, eating almost all vegetation, tend to seriously overgraze pastures and must be carefully managed.

Camels (*Camelus* spp.) are browsers. The one humped camel (*C. dromedarius*) is native to the Middle East and Africa, while the two-humped camel (*C. bactrianus*) is native to central Asia. Camels can get along well on poor pasture and with relatively little water. Both water and fat are stored in the hump(s), and camels can survive in severe conditions for long periods of time. Camels are used for meat, skins, and milk, but the milk has too little fat to be churned into butter. Like horses, camels are most valued for transportation.

Reindeer (*Rangifer tarandus*) browse on the short vegetation of the tundra, primarily lichens. A number of groups in the far north of the Old World herd reindeer. While the herders own the animals and view them as being domesticated, at least in the broad sense of the term (e.g., Ingold 1980), most reindeer are not controlled genetically but are essentially tamed wild animals that are still more or less hunted by people. Small herds of tame animals are kept for milk, meat, and used as decoys when hunting other reindeer. Pasture for reindeer is available all year, and the animals move around the landscape on their own to take advantage of better areas. Some groups of reindeer herders, such as the Chukchi of eastern Siberia, basically track and intercept wild reindeer as they migrate to new pastures, rather than purposefully move them to new pastures.

The distinction between hunter-gatherers and pastoralists is very fuzzy with reindeer herders. Reindeer are actually wild animals and are really hunted. However, the economic focus of the herders is so specific to the reindeer that they function much like pastoralists do.

Herd Composition and Size

A herd is "not simply an aggregation of available animals" (Spooner 1973:9) and a number of things must be considered in deciding on its composition and size. The type(s) of animals herded is dependent on several factors. Initially, the natural environment has to be considered because not all animals can successfully inhabit all ecozones. Even if a species is suited to the ecozone, "the economic expediency and effectiveness of herding them in specific ecological conditions" (Khazanov 1984:27) has to be considered. Once the choice is made, tradition and cultural preference play a major role in continuing the use of the animals. However, as conditions change, groups must be able to adapt by changing herd composition.

The size of the herd is also dependent on a number of factors, with the carrying capacity of the pasture being a primary issue. As different species of animals vary in their ease of control, susceptibility to disease or predators, or attractiveness to raiders/rustlers, the size of the herd may be dependent on the available labor to control and/or defend them. These factors are important considerations because disease and/or theft can instantly decrease the number of animals one has, reducing "a rich household to poverty overnight" (Bates and Lees 1996b:154). In addition, each pasture will have a natural limiting factor that will restrict herd size, and the number of animals cannot exceed that limit (following Liebig's Law of the Minimum).

It may also be desirable to maintain certain sex and age ratios in the herd. In some cases, herds are culled, with most young males being killed for their meat and hides and only a few being kept for breeding purposes. Most of the females are kept to reproduce and to provide milk. In addition, animals will form attachments and relationships with one another. Due to species differences in life span, each species requires a different herd size to allow for individual animals to live together long enough to form these relationships (Spooner 1973:9).

Finally, there are social factors in determining the size of a herd. The requirements of the family owning the herd will greatly influence its minimum size. A herd might be developed to be as large as possible, even if overtaxing the pasture in the short-term, so that it can be split into two herds. Such a split of herds may also be done to allow the human social unit to also split.

The number and types of animals are also status markers. A person might choose to maintain a herd of cattle for status reasons, even if those animals were ill suited to the pasture type. For example, in Mongolia, wealthy families kept larger stock and tended toward sheep, while poorer families had smaller animals and tended toward goats. All families tried to keep as many horses as possible, even if unneeded or uneconomic (see Khazanov 1984:25–26).

Movement of Herds

No natural pasture can support herd animals all year (Spooner 1973:21), and pastoralists must generally move their animals to different pastures depending on the season. The movement of animals from pasture to pasture may be based on a number of factors. If a pasture is exhausted, the animals will have to be moved to a new one. In many cases, pastures in the mountains are used in the summer and the animals moved to pastures at lower elevations in the summer. Movement might also be based on rainfall, with animals being moved from dryer to wetter pastures. A seasonal migration might also be undertaken to maintain political autonomy, to avoid disease or pests, or to exploit other resources (Khazanov 1984:39).

Most pastoral groups are mobile and practice a seasonal round (see figures 5.1 and 5.2 in chapter 5) within a well-defined territory, called **tethered nomadism**. However, all movements are flexible to some extent as conditions change, and people must be able to adapt to them. In some cases, only a segment of the population, such as the herders, move with their animals in a seasonal transhumance system.

The movement of people and animals to different pastures requires careful planning that incorporates information on pasture condition (resource monitoring). Such trips range from as few as ten miles to as many as one thousand miles (Spooner 1973:21). Among the most important decisions made are where to move, when to move, and how long to stay, a decision string similar to that made in patch choice models. In some cases, such as in central Asia, the winters are such that there is nowhere to move the animals. In those cases, fodder is gathered and stored to feed the animals during the winter.

Pastoralists must be able to judge the quality of water and pasture before the animals are moved because one does not want to invest the time and energy to move a herd to a place that cannot support them. Thus, like hunter-gatherers, it is important to monitor pasture areas so that sufficient information can be available when decisions on when and where to move the animals are made.

Pastoral Products

The primary resources derived directly from animals are meat, blood, milk, hides, hair, wool, and dung. The major secondary uses of animals are for transportation of humans and goods and for labor, such as pulling plows.

Animals provide a number of foods used by people. Meat is a major animal product, but obtaining it results in the death of the animal, a "one-time" use. If meat were the major goal, it would be most efficient to butcher most of the males for their meat and hides, keeping a few for breeding purposes, and retaining the females for reproduction and milk production. As the females died naturally, their meat and hide would then be utilized. This is the approach taken by the cattle industry in Western countries.

A more efficient use of the animals and their products is to utilize them without killing them, ultimately getting more food value from each animal. One example of this approach is the production of milk as the major product, called **milch pastoralism**. Milk is obtained from females and is consumed or made into butter, cream, or cheese. If the product goal is just milk, females and only a few males are needed, as in the contemporary dairy industry.

Blood is another major product that can be obtained without killing the animal. About a quart of blood can be taken from a cow of either sex about once a month without damaging its health. If females are being milked, the blood extraction might be primarily from males. The blood can be consumed alone or can be mixed with milk for consumption. Thus, some pastoral groups will not butcher healthy animals but milk and bleed them, using those products, along with meat from aged animals, as their main foods. In East African pastoral groups, the primary component in the human diet is milk, with meat second and blood third (Khazanov 1984:64; also see Galvin et al. 1994).

Like meat, the procurement of skins or hides requires that the animal be killed. Hides can be used for a large number of products, including covers for shelter, clothing, shoes, and a variety of other leather products. Hair and wool can also be made into many products, but unlike hides, hair and wool can be removed from live animals and so are renewable resources.

Dung can be a major animal product. Dung can be used as fuel, in the construction of houses, walls, or other structures, or for a number of other purposes. Dung also serves as a fertilizer and helps to maintain the productivity of the pasture. In addition, dung can be traded to farmers for use in their fields. In some cases, farmers will arrange for pastoralist's animals to be grazed in their fallow fields so that they can be fertilized.

USE OF NONPASTORAL PRODUCTS

No pastoralists can subsist exclusively on pastoral products, and all depend to some extent on plant products in their diet. Such products are obtained through hunting and gathering, horticulture, and/or trade. Interestingly, some pastoral groups tend to disparage the consumption of nonpastoral foods, seemingly as a mechanism to retain their image of superiority over farming groups.

Most pastoralists practice some horticulture or agriculture, and all trade animal products for agricultural crops, usually some type of grain, and/or tools. Depending on the type of pastoralism practiced, horticulture might constitute a major activity. Gardens might be tended full-time by a portion of the population, or crops might be planted, left unattended, and harvested when the group passed through the area again in the seasonal round. In the Middle East, dates are important crops. Dates have to be pollinated and harvested at specific times but can be left unattended most of the year.

Some pastoralists, such as the reindeer herders in the far north, do not utilize any agricultural products but supplement their pastoralism solely by hunting and gathering wild resources for food and other purposes (see Ingold 1980).

Pastoralists rarely live in areas where fish are a significant resource. Some groups, such as the Navajo, taboo fish outright. A few coastal groups in the Middle East use fish, but worldwide, the only significant pastoralist-fishers are the reindeer herders of North Europe and Siberia; many of these live near rivers and rely heavily on fish, often dried (as "yukola") for storage.

ENVIRONMENTAL MANIPULATION AND RESOURCE MANAGEMENT

Large-scale environmental manipulation is very common in pastoral groups, primarily through the actions of burning to create pasture and of grazing to maintain it. Without active grazing, much of the pasture would revert to woodlands or forests. Most pastoral groups, particularly the more mobile groups, generally invest their labor in their animals (Bates and Lees 1996b:154), rather than invest time and effort into capital improvements. However, water and pasture are also critical resources, and both are managed and manipulated to some degree. A frequent project is the construction and maintenance of water sources, some of which can be quite elaborate. A less common manipulation is pasture modification and improvement. However, the investment of time and material in pastures tends to tie groups to a piece of land and decrease mobility. For more sedentary groups, such capital improvements are more common, with water sources, pastures, agricultural fields, and settlements receiving more investment.

Intense resource management, specifically of animals, is a hallmark of pastoralists. Most groups will utilize natural landscapes for pastures and so will invest relatively little time in environmental manipulation, preferring instead to invest their labor in increasing the number of animals and/or their products (Bates and Lees 1996b:154). Controlling animals, their movement, the kinds and amounts of food eaten, and timing and circumstances of death, are important management goals.

Exercising control of breeding is also a major management goal. One can prevent certain animals from reproducing by killing them before they can breed, castrating the males, or keeping the various animals isolated from potential mates. The purpose of controlled breeding is to maximize desired traits and to minimize or eliminate undesired characteristics. Desired traits might include increased production of products, such as milk or hair, or an ability to flourish in poor-quality pasture.

RELATIONS WITH OTHER GROUPS

Pastoralists often occupy and/or utilize at least two ecozones, one where they live for most of the time, and another where they pasture their animals. Usually, pastures are located at some distance from the main habitation area, and the regions between the pastures are occupied by other people, whether hunter-gatherers, other pastoralists, or agriculturalists, the latter being the most common.

To move their animals, pastoralists must often traverse the territory of these other groups (Khazanov 1984:33) and so must maintain good relationships with them. During those occasions, products will likely be traded between the two groups. If the second group are farmers, the pastoralists may graze their animals in the fallow fields so that the dung can be used as a source of fertilizer.

Pastoralists may also share some ecozones with other groups, particularly farmers, rather than just traverse them. This sharing is sometimes done on a seasonal basis, with each group being in the area at different times with no conflict. In some cases, the pastoralists will live intermingled with the farmers, grazing their animals in fallow fields, along roads, or wherever they can until it is time to move to new pastures. One could argue that the two groups occupy different niches within the same habitat (Khazanov 1984:34). However, Bates (1971) argued that the patterns of shared land use should be viewed as a function of the balance of power rather than of ecology.

A NOTE ON THE IMPACT OF GRAZING

It is probable that grazing (here meant to include both grazing and browsing) has damaged the environment from the beginning of animal domestication. Devastated forests and woodlands in the early Middle East seem to have resulted from herding activities (Köhler-Rollefson 1988), though fire and agriculture have also contributed.

Throughout the world, sheep, goats, and cattle have eaten their way through the plant communities of local ecosystems. Unless carefully managed, those animals overcrop their favorite foods. This is serious when the foods in question are one of the dominant species in the local environment. Cattle eat willow and cottonwood shoots in the western United States, leading to elimination of these forests that are the homes of many species of wildlife, and to massive erosion of streambeds once held in place by these trees.

As with the swidden system, grazing has been studied by many cultural ecologists, and the general conclusion is that light grazing with frequent moving of stock does little damage. Herding peoples in East Africa, for instance, have maintained a stable and balanced relationship with their environment for a long time (Dyson-Hudson and Dyson-Hudson 1980; Netting 1986; see case study 8.1). When a given area is grazed to the point where cattle cannot find their preferred forage, the herders move on. The East African "cattle complex" (Herskovits 1926) is an ancient and complex system, tied to local agriculture and beautifully adapted to the East African environment (for a history of its development, see Marshall [1990] and Mace [1993]). Unfortunately, population growth and political restrictions on grazing and mobility have devastated this equilibrium (see McCabe et al. 1992; Campbell 1995).

Alpine herders in Switzerland (Netting 1981) maintain equilibrium under more populous surroundings by carefully moving the herds to summer pasture, then winter-feeding them on hay. Many other systems around the world practice intensive stock raising without environmental damage. By contrast, most of the Middle East has been turned into a desert in which nothing lives except shrubs too spiny for even goats to eat. Normally, this process involves the cutting of firewood, random burning, war, and so on, as well as herding, but herding was the final death stroke in the Middle East (e.g., Harlan 1992; MacNeish 1992; Williams 1996).

In the United States and much of Latin America, grazing was and is utterly uneconomical. It is, however, financed by government or international subsidies and so ranchers are often politically powerful. Much of the western United States, as well as Latin America, has been deforested or turned from lush grassland into unproductive scrub by badly managed grazing (see Gillis [1991] for a brief, balanced treatment; Jacobs [1991] and Tucker [2000:285–341] provide antigrazing positions; Kaus [1992] and Hedrick [2007] provide more pro-rancher treatments, showing how government policies may help or hinder reasonable grazing practices).

In some cases, though, ranchers can be the major protectors of the local ecosystem rather than the local destroyers (e.g., Kaus 1992), depending on local conditions and economic incentives. Where cattle production is not subsidized, and where other uses of the land are recognized as valuable, ranching often does relatively little damage to the landscape. Where ranchers are paid by the taxpayers to overgraze at the expense of all else, they will do so.

Grazing has been subjected to all-out attack (e.g., Rifkin 1992) as a purely destructive use of the land. However, grazing is, after all, a natural thing. Hundreds of species of grazing animals exist, and grass has evolved a mutualistic relationship with them. Humans cannot use grass or woody vegetation for food. To get any food benefit from grasslands and brushlands, humans have to cycle some of the productivity through herbivorous animals. It seems that creating and maintaining stable, sustainable grazing systems are not beyond human ability. Indeed, some seemingly technologically simple societies manage it very well. Present serious problems with overgrazing are not due to any innate evil of grazing, but to corrupted or badly conceived management.

CHAPTER SUMMARY

Pastoralism is the form of agriculture in which domestic animals are emphasized, sometimes to the exclusion of other resources. In pastoralism, humans and animals have formed a long-term mutualistic relationship where animals are guaranteed reproduction and protection and humans get food and other products. Many pastoral groups maintain a loose tribal organization, but the household is generally the primary organization.

Three major types of pastoralism can be defined. These are (1) nomadic, where groups are very mobile and depend almost entirely on their animals; (2) seminomadic, where groups are less mobile and animal products are supplemented by horticulture; and (3) semisedentary, where groups are not very mobile and horticulture forms a major component of the economy. Two other forms, herdsman husbandry and sedentary animal husbandry, are pastoral components of larger agricultural systems.

Pastoralists specializing in one species occupy four broad regions of the Old World, including northern Eurasia (reindeer), the eastern Mediterranean (sheep), the Arabian peninsula (camels), and sub-Saharan Africa (cattle). Pastoralists working multiple stock occupy the broad arid region extending from North Africa, east across southwest Asia and to Mongolia. All of these groups are under pressure to abandon pastoralism and take up farming.

The primary components of any pastoral system include use and maintenance of pastures, the types of animals (grazers or browsers) herded, composition and size of herds, and the movement of herds. To be successful, pastoralism must make good long-term decisions in all of these areas. Pastoral products include meat, blood, milk, hides, hair, wool, and dung, In addition, most groups supplement these materials with other domesticated products, either grown or obtained by trade. Wild resources are also widely used.

Grazing, properly managed, does little damage to ecosystems and some, such as the plains of North America, developed concurrently with grazing animals. However, poor planning, bad decisions, or other factors can result in overgrazing that can alter ecosystems until they are virtually destroyed. The modern practice of turning diverse forest ecosystems into pasture is causing considerable damage.

KEY TERMS
browsers
grazers
herdsman husbandry
milch pastoralism
nomadic pastoralism
seasonal transhumance
sedentary
sedentary animal husbandry
seminomadic pastoralism
semisedentary pastoralism
tethered nomadism

CASE STUDY 8.1

THE MAASAI: PASTORALISTS IN EAST AFRICA

This case study on the Maasai shows how pastoralists can operate even when the populations of both humans and animals are large. The Maasai employ milch pastoralism, where the products of live animals, rather than their meat, are the primary foods. In addition, the Maasai example illustrates how an environment can adapt to humans to form a natural and stable system.

The Maasai are seminomadic pastoralists living in southern Kenya and northern Tanzania (figure 8.2), both former British colonies that gained their independence in the early 1960s. Today, the population of the Maasai is about 350,000 people. To the Maasai, cattle form the basis of life. In addition to their use as food and materials, cattle are used as currency, to legitimize marriages, and to solidify social relationships.

FIGURE 8.2
Location of the Maasai in eastern Africa.

The Maasai are one of the pastoral cultures defined by Herskovits (1926) as part of the "East-African cattle complex," and summaries of Maasai culture are available in Saitoti and Beckwith (1980), Spencer (1988), and Spear and Waller (1993).

THE NATURAL ENVIRONMENT
The Maasai occupy a region in eastern Africa that contains two major ecozones: a relatively arid plain and better-watered mountain areas. The large plain lies at an elevation of about four thousand feet and contains an extensive grassland. In northern Tanzania, this plain is called

the Maasai Steppe, with the famous Serengeti Plain being just to the west. The plains generally receive less than twenty inches of rain per year. To the west of the plains, the elevation increases, there is more water, and forest intermingles with the grasslands. These highlands are mostly occupied by farmers.

SOCIOPOLITICAL ORGANIZATION

The social and political systems of the Maasai are flexible, with the elder men having most of the political authority. The Maasai have some fifteen primary territorial groups whose members have priority rights to use pastures. The use of the pastures by others must be negotiated with the owners.

The status and wealth of a man is determined by how many cattle he owns and by what grazing rights he controls. Cattle are handed down from father to son. A man wants to marry as many women as he can afford, and cattle are given as gifts to the family of the bride. Children, especially male children, are also important as status markers, and a man who owns cattle and has male children is considered very wealthy.

Maasai society is organized around age grades, a group with persons passing from one status to another as they age. Males tend livestock until they are about age twenty, when they become warriors and eventually get married. At this time, they generally stop tending herds but will continue to do so if they do not have younger brothers. Later, the males will become elders and possibly the political leaders of their family groups. Cattle are rarely killed, but a cow will be slaughtered to celebrate the passage of an individual from one age grade to another. Traditionally, males had to kill a lion as a passage to manhood. As those animals became more scarce, the rite of passage has become more ritualized, with lions not being killed so often, although in some areas, they are still killed when they menace herds.

A number of related families live in a small village, designed and constructed to protect the cattle. The village has a perimeter fence built of thorn bushes, and the small houses, built from bent poles covered with grass and plastered with cow dung, are constructed along the inside of the fence. The center of the village is reserved for the cattle. Smaller camps are made by the young men when they are herding cattle away from the village.

At one time, warfare was an important aspect of Maasai culture. Males were raised to be warriors, and once they had achieved that status, they generally stopped herding cattle themselves. The primary function of a Maasai warrior was to protect the cattle from rustlers and to rustle cattle from other, non-Maasai people.

ECONOMICS

Although the primary economic pursuit of the Maasai is cattle herding, some horticulture is also practiced, supplemented by the gathering of wild plants. The cattle herds are tended by young males on foot. If the herds are located in pastures away from the village, small temporary camps are used by the herders. If the cattle are close, males take care of the animals during the daytime and women are responsible for the herds at night. Women are also responsible for milking and helping cows give birth.

Pastures

Pasture is a critical resource, particularly in the relatively dry lowlands. Animals must be moved fairly often, and a complex system of who can have how many animals in which pasture is controlled by the local leaders. Pasture condition has to be constantly monitored, and animals are closely watched as to their general health and ability to produce milk to determine the quality of the pastures.

Types of Animals

Cattle are clearly the most important animals to the Maasai, and most of the effort made in stock raising is expended for cattle. In addition, however, several smaller species, such as sheep and goats, are included with the cattle herds. These other animals occupy the same habitat but have slightly different niches, and so provide the herder with a greater efficiency of pasture and water utilization.

Herd Composition and Size

Herds of cattle consists mainly of females and a few bulls. Most male cattle are castrated when young and kept for meat and labor or sold. The bulls in a herd are of different ages to prevent them from fighting. The size of a herd is dependent on the available pasture and water, but the constant goal is to have as large a herd as possible.

Movement of Herds

The movement of livestock is based on a number of factors and is carefully planned. A principal factor in the decision is the seasonal variation in rainfall, with animals generally being moved to the highlands during the dry season and to the lowlands during the wet season. Decisions cn livestock movement must also involve other local conditions and negotiations with other groups for access to their lands. This system is designed to ensure that livestock are dispersed so as to not overgraze regions and so reduce the risk for any one group.

Many animals are lost each year to a variety of diseases, and disease control is a major factor in deciding when and where to move animals. One such example is malignant catarrh fever (MCF), a disease fatal to cattle (see Evangelou 1984:77). For centuries, the Maasai believed that MCF was carried by the wildebeest and spread when the animals had their calves. To reduce the exposure of their cattle to MCF, the Maasai planned their seasonal movements to keep their cattle away from the areas used by the wildebeest while calving. Thus, through careful planning, the Maasai were able to utilize the same range as the wildebeest, but at different seasons. Recently, it was confirmed that MCF was indeed carried in wildebeest placentas.

Pastoral Products

The Maasai utilize all parts of their cattle. The primary products are milk, blood, and meat for food, urine for medicinal purposes, dung for fuel and for building houses, horns for containers, and hide for clothing, shoes, and rope. Milk and blood are most commonly eaten as doing so is the most efficient use of the animal. To obtain blood, the jugular vein of a cow or bull is pierced and about a quart of blood is removed. Typically, the neck of the animal is lightly tied to make the vein bulge out, and it is then shot with a tiny bow and arrow. The blood runs into a cup. Bark is often added to prevent coagulation and spoilage, and many barks have the ability to reduce cholesterol in the blood—useful for this high-cholesterol food. In a healthy animal, blood can be removed about once a month. The blood is often mixed with milk for consumption. If a cow dies or is injured or sick, it will likely be butchered for the meat and other products.

Horticulture

Plant foods are important to the Maasai, and they practice some horticulture in specific and confined localities. Small gardens are maintained around the villages, and women tend to eat more plants than men. In addition, the Maasai trade animal products for grain from their neighboring farmers.

Hunting and Gathering

The Maasai collect many wild plants for food, medicine, and other purposes and have a great deal of knowledge of regional botany. However, the consumption of wild game is frowned upon and for all practical purposes, the Maasai do not hunt game for food, and look upon people who do with contempt. Nevertheless, the Maasai do hunt a number of animals, such as lions, that prey on their herds and retain substantial hunting skills. In bad times (e.g., severe drought), some individuals or small groups of people might have been forced into the niche of hunting wild animals for food. More recently, those people who, for whatever reason, cannot make a living as pastoralists, have immigrated to the cities to find work.

ENVIRONMENTAL MANIPULATION

In general, the Maasai practice relatively little large-scale manipulation of their environment. An exception is the controlled burning of tracts of land to eliminate brush and to encourage grass for better cattle pasture. This has had the effect of also encouraging some wild species of large grazers to increase their numbers in Maasai pastures and has had a negative domino effect on much of the other, smaller wildlife.

In some areas, the Maasai have been prevented from burning with the idea that the burning was detrimental to the large game. Without burning, the brush took over and the big herbivores moved away, making the land less productive for cattle and for tourists. Without the Maasai managing those areas, the wild game left, and the tourist industry declined.

RESOURCE MANAGEMENT

The Maasai basically have three major resources to manage, their animals, their pastures, and water. The animals are very intensively man-

CASE STUDY 8.1

aged, with selective breeding and castration being important techniques used. Poor-quality animals are culled, and the proper mixture of sex and age is maintained in the herds. The animals are also closely monitored to prevent or limit diseases.

The pastures are the second critical resource. Their condition is constantly monitored so as to have sufficient information to make decisions of where to go, when to move, and what to use. A complex system of pasture assignment strives to prevent overgrazing.

Water is the third important resource as cattle require a considerable amount of water. Water holes are important places and are owned by individuals, who modify and maintain them. Access to the water is open to all for the asking. Drought is always a concern, and the worst recorded drought was in 1960 and 1961, when the Maasai cattle population declined from 630,000 to about 200,000. The cattle population had recovered to its predrought numbers by 1968, a recovery accelerated by Maasai herd management practices (Evangelou 1984:20).

RELATIONS WITH OTHER GROUPS

The Maasai believe that pastoral life is the best, and they have little but contempt for neighboring nonpastoral groups, especially hunters and gatherers. The surrounding pastoral groups are also considered inferior, and in the past, those groups were raided for cattle.

DISCUSSION

The Maasai illustrate a number of important issues regarding pastoralists. To be successful, the Maasai must maintain a carefully coordinated and efficient system of management of animals, pasture, and water. They generally operate within a single ecosystem, the plains, but can adapt to the highlands if necessary. Through careful management, the Maasai are able to herd animals with different niches (e.g., cattle and goats) within the same pasture habitat. The Maasai also illustrate the efficient use of animal resources, store their animals live to consume their milk and blood, rather than their meat, as the primary product. In this way, a relatively smaller number of cattle can support a larger human population.

CASE STUDY 8.1

In recent times, the governments of Kenya and Tanzania have put pressure on the Maasai (and other pastoralists such as the Ariaal of northern Kenya; see Fratkin 1998) to become settled farmers. In 1973, the government of Tanzania, where most of the Maasai live, required all people to move into "developmental villages" to get them out of the landscape and force them into farming. Due to pressure from herders, the policy was changed in 1974 to include "livestock developmental villages," thus allowing pastoral groups to continue their economies. Nevertheless, the trend away from pastoralism to settled farming is increasing.

In the past several decades, the Maasai have lost some 75 percent of their traditional lands and have been largely relegated to reservations (Olol-Dapash 2002). Some of this land has been taken by farmers while large tracts have been set aside as wildlife preserves and game parks. The Maasai cattle have been excluded from such preserves so that the wild animals would return and boost the tourist trade. Interestingly, without the cattle and land management by the Maasai, the brush began to take over the land, and the game that did live there began to leave, just the opposite of what the governments wanted. Today, the Maasai are slowly being allowed to return to many such lands to reintroduce cattle and resume burning, in the hope that the wild game will return.

CASE STUDY 8.2

THE NAVAJO: PASTORALISTS OF THE AMERICAN SOUTHWEST

This case study on the Navajo illustrates a pastoralist adaptation within a desert biome. While successful, the Navajo have their share of problems with overgrazing, drought, and neighbors. In particular, the very success of the Navajo has brought them into conflict with the Hopi, a sedentary agricultural group. Here we see some issues of incompatible subsistence strategies and a clear illustration of cultural conflict.

The Navajo are semisedentary pastoralists living in Arizona and New Mexico in the American Southwest (figure 8.3). They have the largest reservation and the second largest population (ca. 300,000; only the Cherokee are more numerous) of any Indian group in North America. The

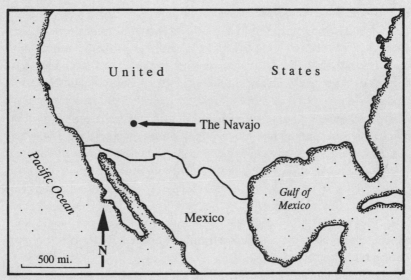

FIGURE 8.3
Location of the Navajo in southwestern North America.

Navajo generally call themselves *Diné*, meaning "people of the surface of the earth." They moved to the Southwest about 500 years ago and adopted various Pueblo, Spanish, and other traits, forming the present Navajo culture. The Navajo reservation overlaps that of the Hopi Indians, who are horticulturalists, and this relationship is quite interesting. Recent descriptions of Navajo culture are available in Ortiz (1983), Iverson (1990), and Parezo (1996). This section describes a Navajo lifestyle that is slowly disappearing as Navajo are increasingly being employed in the larger American economy.

THE NATURAL ENVIRONMENT

The Navajo reservation is located in fairly rugged country with mountains, deep canyons, many small mesas, and numerous valleys. Elevations range between three thousand and nine thousand feet. About half of the reservation is desert but contains grasses important for sheep grazing. The remainder of the reservation consists of mountains, mesas, and valleys that contain forests of pine and juniper, along with a great many other plants, including cottonwoods, willows, and many grasses.

SOCIOPOLITICAL ORGANIZATION

The Navajo are organized into a relatively large number of small, autonomous social and political units, sometimes called bands. Each band has a male headman to deal with outsiders, but the females are dominant in politics, with the family matriarch making most of the family decisions.

The primary social unit is the nuclear family, centered on the mother and her livestock and fields. Husbands generally move to land near the wife's mother and form a new family unit, or homestead. A number of these families related through a matriarch live in the same area, forming an extended family unit. These families are very mobile and move around to exploit changes in the availability of water, firewood, and grazing areas. The families will frequently move to new lands, and sheep camps are often established at some distance from the home during the summer.

Women do the household work and herd the sheep when they are close to the home, mostly during the winter. Males will herd sheep during the summer when they are located in distant pastures. Males also tend to the horses and cattle, do most of the heavy agricultural labor, and conduct most of the ceremonies. Everyone assists in collecting water and firewood and in planting and harvesting crops.

Marriage is mandatory, as only married people are considered adults. The most important aspects of mate selection are economic and political considerations. Wealthy males might have two or three wives, who generally live in separate households near their mothers.

ECONOMICS

Prior to the 1860s, agriculture and raiding to obtain goods and livestock were major elements of the Navajo economy. After being defeated by the Americans in 1864, the Navajo reservation was established in 1868. At that time, the Navajo adopted herding, mostly of sheep but some cattle, as their primary economic focus. The number of livestock increased rapidly and by the 1930s, overgrazing by sheep had become such a problem that the government forced the Navajo to significantly reduce their sheep herds and encouraged them to increase the number of cattle.

All of the sheep owned by individuals within a homestead unit are kept in a common herd, and all of the homestead members share the responsibility for their care (Witherspoon 1983), with shearing and dipping being community efforts. The size and well-being of the sheep herd is the main factor in the status and power of the family or individuals within it.

Pastures

Pastures are generally located fairly close to the homestead, and the pastures, residences, and gardens of a family are called a "traditional use area" (Downs 1972:43). The pastures are controlled by families who share them with other members of the local residential unit. Each family unit is responsible for only its own livestock and the specific pasture used at any one time. If nearby pastures are not sufficient, as determined by the availability of water, families may move their animals to more distant pastures where there is more water.

Types of Animals

The main domestic animal is sheep, a grazer easily adapted to a variety of ecozones that provides meat and wool for weaving. Wealth is measured by the number of sheep an individual owns. Other animals, including cattle, are also kept but are much less important than sheep. Horses are also important for transporting people and materials and for social standing as everyone is expected to own at least one horse. Goats are often kept with the sheep herds and are used as a source of milk and cheese. Some chickens are also kept.

Herd Composition and Size

The primary animal is the sheep. It is the general desire that sheep herds be as large as possible, but this has led to serious overgrazing and land degradation through loss of plant cover and erosion. Today, the federal government closely monitors pasture condition and so regulates herd size. Cattle and horses are also raised but do not have to be herded as sheep. Nevertheless, they require care, the job of men.

Movement of Herds

Four major factors govern the movement of sheep herds: (1) availability of water for the animals; (2) location of gardens; (3) availability of firewood; and (4) season (Downs 1972:44–46). If possible, sheep are kept near the homestead. During those times, the sheep are usually kept in pens for the night, driven to nearby pastures for the day, and then driven back to the pens for the night. Dogs are used to help herd the sheep and to guard the herd from packs of wild dogs.

If water becomes a problem, both the homestead and herds might be moved to locations with better water, although permission has to be obtained to use water in other pastures. A shortage of firewood might also prompt a homestead to move, the sheep being moved with it. On the other hand, people may opt to stay near their gardens and move the sheep to other pastures without moving the homestead. In these cases, young men would move and tend the sheep and might be away from the homestead for extended periods.

Pastoral Products

Sheep provide the major source of meat and all of the wool needed for clothing and weaving. Cattle provide only cash, because the Navajo do not butcher their cattle but sell them to others. Horses provide cash and transportation.

Horticulture

Domestic crops are much less important than the animals, but some horticulture is practiced. Each homestead has one or more agricultural fields, tended by one or more women. Corn is the primary crop, but beans and squash are also grown, along with wheat and oats. Fruit orchards are also common. In more recent times, with overgrazing and livestock reduction, horticulture is becoming more important in the economy.

Hunting and Gathering

Hunting is not a very important source of food, although a few small animals, particularly rabbits and rodents, are hunted for meat. Although a minor part of the economy, hunting by young males is encouraged and serves to acquaint them with the landscape and the animals in it, and to develop many of the skills needed for livestock herding. Some wild plants are gathered for food, but most plant gathering is for the purpose of obtaining herbs and materials for rituals, dyes, and medicines.

ENVIRONMENTAL MANIPULATION AND RESOURCE MANAGEMENT

The Navajo conduct very little environmental manipulation. However, the sheep cause a considerable amount of damage to pastures through overgrazing. The sheep strip the vegetation, which produces considerable erosion, delaying pasture recovery. So much topsoil has been lost on the Navajo reservation that the federal government has been concerned about the silt clogging the Colorado River.

The Navajo manage their herds fairly intensively, with cattle and horses receiving less attention than sheep. Although sheep breed all year, the Navajo try to control the breeding so that lambs are born in the spring, when they have a better chance of survival. Otherwise, the sheep are managed to produce wool and meat.

The Navajo have not been pastoralists for very long (several hundred years) and have tended to manage their pastures for maximum short-term production of sheep. They allowed their livestock to seriously overgraze pastures, and then they moved on to new pastures. This practice allowed them to have artificially large numbers of animals and to constantly expand their territory, which, one could argue, has been to their distinct advantage. However, since the 1930s, the federal government regulates the number of animals the Navajo can have and has limited the expansion of Navajo territory. Today, the government conducts considerable monitoring of pasture condition to gather information for making decisions of how many animals the Navajo can have.

The relationship between the Navajo and the U.S. government over grazing impacts has played a major role in Navajo ecology. When the Navajo reservation was formed in 1868, the Navajo brought with them a large number of grazing animals, mostly sheep. Overgrazing became an immediate problem. By the 1930s, overgrazing had become such a problem that the government forced the Navajo to significantly reduce their sheep herds and encouraged them to increase the number of cattle. Sheep were sold (at very low prices during the Depression) and sometimes even destroyed by the government without compensation to the Navajo. This stock reduction forced many Navajo out of ranching and into other work, transforming their entire economy. In addition, the wealth and status of women was lowered, since it was they who owned most of the livestock (see Shepardson 1982).

The Navaho, who love their sheep, reacted extremely negatively to federal reduction of sheep herds in the 1930s; they have never subsequently trusted the government to regulate grazing. This has led to accusations of bad faith on both sides, and range management has all too often been a casualty of the conflict.

RELATIONS WITH THE HOPI

The Hopi are horticulturalists living in the same general area as the Navajo. The two cultures occupy basically different niches within an overlapping habitat. The Hopi claim that the Navajo have taken up residence on lands that the Hopi consider their traditional territory. After its establishment in 1868, the Navajo reservation was expanded several times and, by 1934, surrounded the Hopi reservation.

The Hopi have made a number of claims and suits to force the Navajo to stop encroaching and to force the removal of those who moved onto the Hopi reservation since 1882, when it was established. The Navajo argued that the land is traditionally Navajo and the Hopi were not using it anyway. The Hopi counter that the land has been Hopi for thousands of years, that the Navajo are trespassing, and that Navajo livestock are overgrazing and damaging Hopi land. The discovery of considerable coal and oil reserves in the region prompted the government to seek a settlement so that leases could be obtained (see Lacerenza 1988).

The Navajo-Hopi Land Settlement Act of 1974 partitioned the disputed lands between the Navajo and the Hopi, required a reduction in Navajo livestock (see Wood 1985), and mandated the relocation of Indians on the wrong side of the line, mostly Navajo who were on Hopi lands. The relocation of Navajo families began in early 1981, but some families remained very resistant, feeling that they had a strong tie to the land because many were born in the places they were being told to leave (see Schwarz 1997). Some people then argued that the Navajo have always been mobile, did not have a problem moving onto Hopi lands, and so should not have a problem moving off them (see Prucha 1984:1178).

Congress made a new effort to settle the issue and passed the Navajo-Hopi Land Dispute Settlement Act of 1996. This allowed Navajo families still in the disputed areas to sign seventy-five-year leases with the Hopi and to live under Hopi jurisdiction. A majority of families did so, but a few did not. These families sued but lost, appealed, lost again, and appealed again to the U.S. Supreme Court, who told everyone involved to settle out of court. So the two tribes resumed negotiations, and no action was taken on the families. In April 2001, the Supreme Court dismissed the Navajo case; however, the situation on the ground remains unchanged.

The Hopi and Navajo have a number of issues regarding the land dispute, including access to places of religious significance, royalties for coal and gas, and general frustration in losing lands to outsiders. Still, the degradation of Hopi lands by overgrazing Navajo livestock remains a key problem. More information on Navajo/Hopi land issues can be obtained from Kammer (1980), Feher-Elston (1988), Parlowe (1988), Clemmer (1991), Benedek (1992), Brugge (1994), and Schwarz (1997).

DISCUSSION

The Navajo adopted pastoralism in fairly recent times, acquiring sheep and focusing their economy on that animal. Sheep treat pastures notoriously poorly, rapidly overgrazing them and making their recovery difficult. As long as the Navajo could expand into new territories and pastures, this short-term disadvantage was not a problem. Today, however, the Navajo do not have easy access to new lands and must adopt a long-term solution to finite and fragile pastures. Part of this solution is a reduction of the number of sheep, and part is the replacement of some of the sheep with cattle. As these two animals occupy at least partly different niches, the pasture habitat can be better managed.

Also of interest is the competition between the pastoral Navajo and the horticultural Hopi. Although one could argue that the two groups occupy different niches within the same habitat, there is enough overlap (e.g., access to water and pasture for the lesser number of Hopi animals) that conflict has ensued. The solution to this issue will be political, but there is a great deal to learn about the interaction of the two lifeways.

CASE STUDY 8.3

CATTLE RANCHERS IN THE AMERICAN WEST

By Kimberly Hedrick

This case study of Eastern Sierra corridor cattle ranchers shows that food producers in modern agricultural systems can have distinctive economic and social patterns from the broader population and face unique challenges in both household economy and resource management compared with most citizens in a developed nation-state. The Eastern Sierra ranchers also demonstrate a complex system in which land tenure is held by both public (federal government) and private (ranchers) owners at the same time.

The Eastern Sierra corridor is a narrow valley located between the Sierra Nevada in California and the White Mountains, which straddle the California-Nevada border in the United States (figure 8.4). The land was originally occupied by the Paiute, hunter-gatherers who also cultivated wild foods using irrigation. The ranching families currently in the valley first arrived in the mid-1800s, generally practicing multicropping, including growing vegetables, planting orchards, and raising cattle and sheep. Families obtained land through the Homestead Act, settling near rivers and streams and using uplands as pastures. During the Great Depression, the City of Los Angeles, in search for a water source for the growing city, began to buy the land in the corridor in order to obtain the water rights to the Owens River, the river into which all the tributaries fed by snow-pack from the mountains gathered. By the 1940s, most of the water had been diverted to Los Angeles, diminishing the capacity to grow crops other than native grasses for pasture, and hay was diminished and mixed-use farmers switched to ranching.

NATURAL ENVIRONMENT
Flanked by two high-altitude mountain ranges, the Eastern Sierra corridor runs from Olancha, California, to Bridgeport, California, a span of approximately 170 miles along the sole highway. The valley is high desert, with summer temperatures topping one hundred degrees and frequent drought years, and winter lows often dipping well below freezing. Precipitation in the valley is infrequent due to rain shadow ef-

CASE STUDY 8.3

FIGURE 8.4
Location of the Eastern Sierra corridor in California and Nevada.

fects, and water for irrigation is dependent on the many streams and rivers that bring melted snowpack from the surrounding mountains. Ranchers use the valley pastures, upland shrublands, and mountain meadows for pasture at different times of the year.

SOCIOPOLITICAL ORGANIZATION

The ranchers cooperate with the federal, state, and local governments in rangeland management, as well as the City of Los Angeles and various nonprofit organizations (such as land conservancies and environmental activist groups). Ranchers form local cattlemen's associations that serve to discuss issues of local and national importance to cattle ranching, elect leaders to coordinate with state and federal government on agricultural policy, and to gather informally to share information about ranching. The ranching community is a very tight-knit social group, primarily due to long-standing networks among families and the necessity of cooperative group efforts in the face of challenges such as fluctuating markets, rising production costs without substantially increased gross incomes, and pressure from environmental organizations.

The primary unit for decision making, labor organization, and residence is the extended family, though nuclear family units are not uncommon. Generally, a ranch will consist of a senior husband and wife and one or more of their adult children and their spouses and children; each nuclear family is housed in its own house or trailer, but they live together on the family's land. Land ownership and tenure in the corridor tends to be discontinuous, so nuclear families within the extended group may not live in the same town and yet be living on the same ranch, each occupying a separate piece of property but running all the property together as a single enterprise. Gendered labor organization is highly variable, with some families' women and girls taking a large role in animal husbandry and related tasks and other families having a more gendered division of labor in which the women prepare food, look after the household, and often hold wage-labor jobs outside the home and the men care for the animals and land.

Due to labor shortages, ranchers often cooperate during times of peak labor demand. During branding in the spring and weaning in the fall, families often gather together to meet work demands. School-age and college-age children often take some time off and return to the ranch in order to assist their parents. Additionally, some ranchers work with cowboys who are retired from other careers and settled in the area. These strategies cut production costs.

ECONOMICS

Family cattle ranching in the western United States is very tenuous as an enterprise. Most family ranchers make very little profit (about twenty-five thousand dollars per year is common in the American West), but they must manage expansive pastures (often twenty thousand to fifty thousand acres or more) and capital investments (their land, equipment, and cattle are often worth over one million dollars) to obtain this small income. Because of this, the family exists as both wealthy (in terms of assets) and working-class (in terms of income) people. It is a challenge to meet both family needs and enterprise needs. When the family faces economic hardship, in cases of medical need, for example, it can be very difficult to obtain cash resources without selling critical assets such as land or cattle.

Pastures

On either side of Highway 395 are the valley pastures, irrigated with water from the Owens River, which runs down the center of the valley. These are the pastures that are most reliable year to year due to the irrigation, and ranchers rely on these for winter forage as well as limited summer use. Flanking these are the mountain uplands, which are predominantly owned and managed by a federal agency, the Bureau of Land Management (BLM). These uplands are accessible to the ranchers through long-standing permits that are renewed annually for a small fee. The ranchers use the BLM pastures only in years with heavy rainfall, as most of them do not produce adequate forage under regular precipitation conditions. Finally, there are mountain meadow pastures. These are fairly reliable barring severe drought, forest fire, or grasshopper infestation, and these are used for summer pasture. When the temperatures in the valley exceed one hundred degrees, many of the cows and calves can be accommodated in the small but cool meadows. Cattle are supervised by cowboys who stay in high elevation "cow camps," old cabins and canvas tents with limited plumbing and propane.

CASE STUDY 8.3

Animals

Most ranchers in the Eastern Sierra corridor are cow-calf ranchers, keeping a herd of mother cows and a limited number of bulls year-round and producing weanling calves each fall that are generally shipped to a feedlot to be fattened. A few ranchers who have a shortage of winter pastures have "stocker" cattle, calves that are gaining weight on grass. Cow-calf ranchers are more limited in their response to natural fluctuations in precipitation and other parameters, because mother cows must be continually cared for year-round, even through drought or other forage shortages. When a forage shortage occurs, ranchers who cannot supply hay to their mother cows must sell them on a market that is generally swollen with many other ranchers' cattle for the same reason, and prices are quite low. Later, when they are ready to buy the cows back to replace their herd, prices are often high as other ranchers attempt to do the same thing. Thus, there is a consistent problem of buying high and selling low in cow-calf ranching, with limited options in times of drought or other resource shortage. However, cow-calf operations operate on a wider profit margin than do stocker operations, and so most ranchers choose them as their primary herd composition, adding stocker cattle only when there is extra forage and the possibility of additional profit.

Herd Composition and Size

Most ranchers compose their herds of Black Angus cattle (as well as a smaller percentage of Beefmaster) in order to meet the higher market demand for these breeds. The majority of ranchers raise their own ranch horses, and some supplement their income by selling high-quality registered horses for pleasure horse owners. Horses are generally pastured separately from cattle as they must be more closely monitored due to their more damaging grazing habits.

A ranching family needs at least three hundred mother cows, a small but viable herd, in a cow-calf operation to produce a sustainable income. Some ranchers have as many as one thousand mother cows located on several ranches, all owned and managed by a single extended family. Ranchers either purchase their bulls independently or with guidance from companies through which they engage in contract farming, such as Harris Ranch. Bulls are very carefully selected to en-

CASE STUDY 8.3

hance the herd's genetic pool, with a priority placed on calf health, weaning weight, and quality (premiums are paid to ranchers with prime-grade calves), and with an eye for the reproductive potential of the bull. The process of selecting bulls is a highly complex and carefully considered endeavor due to the cost and impact to the rancher's potential profits, and the rancher is guided by reviewing statistics provided by feedlots and veterinarians for each bull. Ranchers need far fewer bulls than mother cows, and the bulls run with the herd during only part of the year. The rest of the year they are pastured separately.

Movement

Cattle are housed in lower-lying high desert valley pastures along the Owens River and in pastures across the border into Nevada near Bridgeport in the winter. The harsh temperatures and deep snow in the higher country makes keeping cattle there through the winter impossible. Furthermore, the mother cows must be housed close to the ranchers' homes in the winter so that they can closely monitor first-time mothers and assist them in giving birth. Cows begin giving birth in early spring, and by late spring the calves are branded and the ranchers begin to drive them to the mountain meadows. Some ranchers use trucks to transport the cattle, while others continue the traditional method of horseback drives. This choice rests on factors such as the cost of trucking, the ability of the ranchers to drive the cattle to their summer pastures on horseback without encroaching on other non-ranching landowners (such as those that would need to go up the highway or through a city), and the accessibility of the summer pastures to trucks (some are inaccessible by large rigs).

The majority of the cattle are housed in cooler mountain meadow pastures leased from the United States Forest Service as temperatures in the low-lying valleys soar to over one hundred degrees. In fall, when the temperatures begin to drop below freezing at night in the mountains, the cattle are driven back to the valley pastures (figure 8.5), which by that time have recovered from earlier grazing, and build up a store of winter forage. In this way, all pastures are rested during part of the year. Additionally, many ranchers divide their irrigated pastures into relatively small blocks, rotating cows through them to maximize productivity and allow the land maximum capacity for regeneration of forage.

CASE STUDY 8.3

FIGURE 8.5
"Moooving" out. Cattle beginning the trek from mountain pastures to the valley below (photo by Kimberly Hedrick).

Ranchers read professional publications in agricultural and range science, attend conferences, and participate in university-sponsored studies to improve their range management techniques for maximizing productivity and minimizing negative impacts to the land.

Pastoral Products

Cow-calf ranchers sell their calves at weaning weight each fall to feedlots (figure 8.6), which then grow the cattle to slaughter weight before they are distributed to grocery stores, restaurants, and the global market. Ranchers in the Eastern Sierras are primarily trying to produce for a niche market—many produce natural beef (raised without hormones and antibiotics) and prime-grade beef (the highest quality, which generally goes to fine steakhouses rather than grocery stores). Each calf takes approximately the same amount of forage and other resources to produce; by increasing the value of each calf through its

CASE STUDY 8.3

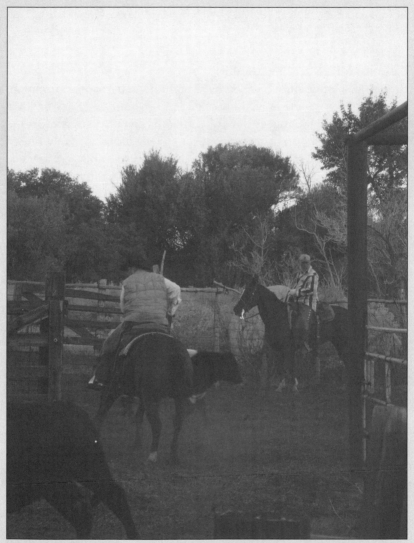

FIGURE 8.6
A cowboy separating a calf from its mother (photo by Kimberly Hedrick).

CASE STUDY 8.3

quality and weaning weight, the rancher can increase profitability without increasing herd size.

ENVIRONMENTAL MANAGEMENT

While ranching is often viewed by urban and suburban environmentalists as having a negative impact on the environment, the reality is that environmental impact can be positive or negative and almost entirely depends on a rancher's priorities, knowledge, and management techniques. Many ranchers participate in controlled burning, a practice that was common among indigenous peoples in California and that generally assists native species propagation. Furthermore, ranchers continue irrigating valley pastures, a practice begun by the Paiute and to which the native grasses are adapted. Finally, ranchers work to eradicate invasive, nonnative, species that threaten to outcompete native plants. Without someone monitoring and controlling invasive species, plants such as Russian thistle could rapidly outcompete native plants, reducing biodiversity. Most ranchers keep careful records of climate, plant community composition, and other observations (including wildlife populations and stream information) over time and seek to manage their lands for both profit and conservation of traditional plants and wildlife.

RESOURCE MANAGEMENT

Ranchers must properly manage cattle, land, and water in order to produce a profitable calf crop. Cattle movements are carefully monitored in order to maximize productivity (to move cattle before they stop gaining weight) and sustainability (to move cattle before they cause harm to the land or water sources). Cattle are managed both through frequent observation by cowboys and by fencing pastures in ways that facilitate a sustainable and smooth-running operation. Land resources are monitored primarily for forage use and composition; forage monitoring is conducted not only by ranchers but also (for public lands pastures) by range conservationists who work with the Bureau of Land Management and the Forest Service. Wildlife populations are monitored by federal biologists. Natural water resources are perhaps the most difficult resource to manage, as without management, cattle will often trample a stream or lake and cause significant damage. Ranchers evaluate each water source and determine how to best use it in a sustainable manner: to fence it, to monitor the cattle more closely, to lower stocking rates, or to add water improvements (such as troughs) to distribute cattle differently on the landscape. Ranchers frequently conduct informal and even university-led experiments in their management plans to find an optimal strategy for both production and long-term sustainability.

RELATIONSHIPS WITH OTHER GROUPS

Ranchers have an interesting and varied relationship with other groups around them. Having a distinctive culture and community, they also exist in a broader local (with many nonranchers in town) and national context (only 2 percent of the United States population is agrarian). Because most people have little or no experience with the challenges of ranching life, ranchers are often portrayed by the media in either a romanticized light or as villains of the environment, neither of which is generally true. Ranchers are often viewed by the general public as living in the past, whereas they have modernized their production and conservation efforts, both financially and environmentally, as science and finance has marched onward. Many environmental organizations view ranchers negatively but fail to address the real complexity and challenge of sustainably and productively managing the arid landscapes of the American West. Such land is often thought of as "wilderness" in the imaginations of urban and suburban peoples, which implies that if it were left alone, it would sustain native plants and wildlife indefinitely.

The reality is that much of the West was managed by indigenous peoples, and native plants and wildlife would struggle without careful management and encouragement. There is currently little funding for federal, state, or local government to adequately monitor and manage the vast open spaces of the Western states; ranchers fill this need, and with adequate support have seen improvements in the rangelands of the Eastern Sierra corridor. Despite these victories and obvious efforts to promote education (most ranchers had college degrees in agricultural or range science and participated in university-led studies), nonfood producers in

California often view ranchers with suspicion due to their direct economic stake in land and water management. Often misunderstood and facing bias against food producers, ranchers organize into associations to lobby for the agricultural community, attempt to use their limited human resources to attend meetings related to land and water management (which in the Eastern Sierra corridor can be as frequent as biweekly), and retain a cautious optimism that, with time and education, Americans will cooperate with agrarian people to preserve open space and food security.

DISCUSSION

Most ranchers entered the Eastern Sierras relatively recently (in the past 150 years). Prior to that time, Paiute hunter-gatherers utilized the land in ways that caused native species to adapt to human management. In the early days of ranching, overgrazing was frequent as ranchers learned about long-term drought cycles in California and sustainable levels of production. Rangelands have been steadily improving in most areas of the Eastern Sierra corridor as ranchers have created better management techniques through experiment and observation. Ranchers are now the primary caretakers of the native plant communities, often managing tens of thousands of acres and hundreds of cattle in extended family groups. Facing limited profit and increasing political, financial, and natural (due to global warming) challenges, ranchers attempt to hold onto their land and lifeway because it is essential to their identity. Therefore, rangelands are often politically contentious issues, as environmental organizations and agrarian producers dispute the best way to conserve land and water resources in the West. Agricultural productivity and food security aside, the substantial and potentially costly challenges of curbing invasive species, encouraging native plant growth, watching over public lands (for poaching, dumping, and other misuses), and other such environmental management will continue to be key issues in discussions about how to best conserve the open spaces of the American West.

9

Intensive Agriculture

Intensive agriculture is a large-scale and complex system of farming and animal husbandry often involving the use of animal labor, equipment, water diversion techniques, and the production of surplus food. Intensive agriculture represents a significant shift in the scale and scope of agriculture and reflects a fundamental change in the relationship between people and the environment. The use of animals and machines to supplement human labor is significant in intensive agriculture, although there are a few intensive systems that rely solely on human labor.

The changing scope and scale of intensive agriculture, coupled with increasing social and technical complexity, increases the range of options that humans have in adapting to the environment. Given a sufficient reservoir of potential action, some intensive agriculturalists have developed a worldview that places them above nature, in which they are not as bound by nature as their less complex neighbors. This belief system may generate a feeling that nature can be, and so must be, controlled and/or conquered. However, this is a flawed view because all cultures are integrated with their environment and cannot escape the consequences of their actions (Flannery 1972) unless they relocate or exploit resources of distant places through trade or conquest.

Intensive agricultural systems tend to rely on a more narrow range of domestic species than horticulturalists, with increases in both productivity and risk. They will employ components of the other subsistence strategies—hunting and gathering, horticulture, and pastoralism—but these tend to be minor components of the system. A consequence of the increased productivity of intensive agriculture is an enormous increase in human carrying capacity (assuming food is the limiting factor, following Liebig's Law of the Minimum) and so huge increases in population. With population increase comes greater sociopolitical complexity, reduction of mobility, nucleation of settlements, and the eventual evolution of state-level societies. While this cause-and-effect relationship between agriculture, population increase, and state development is overly simplistic, the trend is generally true.

CHANGES IN SCALE

The most dramatic difference between horticulture and intensive agriculture is that of scale. Intensive agriculturalists generally cultivate larger quantities of land, have larger populations, and impact the environment to a much greater degree. The use of animals to supplement the labor of humans significantly increased the scale and intensity of agriculture. The introduction of agricultural machines based on the internal combustion engine changed the scale again, this time in a massive way, ushering in contemporary industrialized agriculture.

Labor Supplements

In horticultural and pastoral societies, humans provide the vast majority of the labor needed to produce food, including the clearing of land, constructing fields, and planting and harvesting crops. People, by themselves, can do only so much. However, as animals and machines began to supplement human labor, the scale of agriculture increased dramatically, and ecozones previously too difficult for agriculture could be colonized by farmers, who often displaced other groups already in those ecosystems.

Animals were incorporated into some agricultural systems early on and quickly became an integral component of those systems. Human labor still remained important, but animals are able to do the work of many people by carrying heavy loads and pulling plows through heavy soils. The use of animals as labor requires a support system of feed and care. In some instances, animals were fed food that people might ordinarily eat but in many cases, the animals ate substances, such as grasses, that people could not, making efficient use of those resources.

While domesticated animals had been around for a long time, large animals were required to be useful for agricultural labor, as animals such as dogs are too small to pull plows. However, large domestic animals were not available in all societies. The few present in the New World, such as llamas in the Andes, were used as pack animals but not for agricultural labor. Thus, the intensive agricultural systems in the New World, such as the Maya system (see case study 9.2), were all based on human labor.

The use of machines is a recent development. Early machines were water or steam powered and did not have a dramatic impact on agricultural systems that still relied on animal and human labor. Those machines did, however, have dramatic effects on industrialization and transportation that later affected agriculture. While some machines had previously been used in agriculture, it was the internal combustion engine that, after about 1900, really initiated the mechanization of farming, a process still going on today. Human labor is still important in mechanized agriculture, but to a much smaller degree than before.

Unlike animals, machines do not compete directly for human food. However, like animals, machines require a support system. The machines and parts for them must be manufactured, repaired, and fueled. All of this requires a complex industrial infrastructure.

Technological Changes

Technological change has been an important aspect of the development of intensive agricultural systems. Technology has increased the efficiency with which farmers can grow crops and has opened new ecozones to agriculture. A number of simple technological changes had significant impacts on farming, including the use of metal axes, which allowed forests to be cleared much faster than with stone axes. To illustrate the point further, Europeans initially had little interest in colonizing the Great Plains/Prairies of North America, as the grassland sod was too thick to be penetrated by the plows of the time. In the early to mid-1800s, the Great Plains/Prairies were known as the "Great American Desert," and white settlers passed through them to California and Oregon without major colonization. However, after the American Civil War, the development of heavy steel plows enabled farmers to penetrate the sod of the prairies and to plant fields. These farmers became known as "sodbusters," and they colonized large areas of the prairies. The innovation of the heavy steel plow opened the prairie ecozone to intensive agriculture and hastened the replacement of the Indians with white American settlers.

More dramatic change can be seen with the development of machines powered by fossil fuels. Clearing a section of forest that would have taken many men a year with metal axes and horse-drawn wagons can now be done in a matter of days by a few men with gasoline-powered chainsaws and diesel-powered bulldozers. The machines changed the speed and efficiency of these activities and in doing so also changed the scale of environmental manipulation.

Finally, our technology is on the verge of allowing us to purposefully reshape an entire biosphere. Plans are being developed to send machines to Mars with the intent of creating an atmosphere breathable by humans, warming the planet, melting the polar ice, and creating oceans. We are fairly certain that this can be done, as we have inadvertently done the same basic thing to our own biosphere through the pumping of carbon dioxide into the atmosphere. Once this was accomplished, in several hundred years time and at huge expense, Mars would be colonized by all manner of life from Earth.

Changes in Organization

As carrying capacity and population increased, social organizations became more complex. While there are large and complex groups of hunter-gatherers, horticulturalists, and pastoralists, even the most complex of these groups fall within the sociopolitical category of chiefdoms, and none developed a state-level organization. On the other hand, a number of intensive agriculturalists did evolve sociopolitical organizations classified as states.

A state (early states are sometimes called archaic states) is a society with elaborate social stratification (at least classes of rulers and commoners) and a hierarchical and complex political system that was highly centralized and internally specialized (Marcus and Feinman 1998:4; also see Adams 2001). Many earlier researchers (e.g., Childe 1942; Steward 1955) used the term *civilization* and included a number of other criteria, including urban centers, writing, monumental architecture, craft specialization, bureaucracies, large populations living in urban centers, codified law, and a central authority with the ability to use force following the law. Each of the various criteria used to define a state is intended to demonstrate the sociopolitical complexity of the society and the ability of the rulers to call on the populace to do things. For example, if a group has cities, it follows that they must have had a complex infrastructure, a bureaucracy that can control the population, sufficient resources to support many people who are not farmers, and other complex organizations. The same logic is true of the other criteria.

All agricultural economies are based on a stable carbohydrate source, such as some sort of tuber or grain, and the agricultural systems of all state-level societies are based on some sort of grain crop. While grain crops provide a much greater caloric return per pound than root crops (table 9.1), root crops generally yield much more per acre, offsetting the grain advantage. However, tubers are difficult to store in the quantities needed by states.

Theories on the Origin of the State

The reasons why people evolved such complex state-level sociopolitical organizations has long been of interest to anthropologists (e.g., Steward 1955; Flannery 1972; Feinman and Marcus 1998; Sanderson 1999; Johnson and Earle 2000;

Table 9.1. Nutritive Value of Various Foods, per 100 grams

	Calories	Protein (g.)
Grains		
Corn	361	9.4
Amaranth	358	12.9
Rice	357	7.2
Barley	348	9.7
Sorghum	342	8.8
Wheat	330	14.0
Roots and Tubers		
Manioc (bitter)	148	0.8
Manioc (sweet)	132	1.0
Sweet potato	116	1.3
Yam	100	2.0
Taro	92	1.6
White potato	79	2.8

Source: USDA 1963.

Lamberg-Karlovsky 2000). All contemporary state organizations have their roots in past states, and so some comprehension of the origin and development of the state can add to an understanding of ourselves.

We are concerned here with "primary states," that is, states that arise where no states were before. "Secondary" or "reflex" states develop when primary states expand, forcing the neighbors to organize in defense. Eventually the neighbors are usually forced to create states of their own. Often these reflex states end up conquering the primary ones, as happened when the Babylonians took Mesopotamia (now Iraq) from the Sumerian city-states before 2000 BC. The famous fall of the Roman Empire was a similar case; Rome was originally a secondary state in itself, but as it expanded it became by far the biggest power in the Western world. Eventually the "barbarians" developed states of their own and slowly encroached on Rome (Heather 2006).

Managerial Models

Several models argue that state-level organizations developed out of the need to manage people, resources, or both. Agricultural surpluses, trade requirements, warfare, population expansion, and water were at various times all seen as prime movers in the cultural evolution of states.

Wittfogel (1957) proposed the "hydraulic theory" in which water for irrigation was a critical resource. Wittfogel argued that in some instances, such as in large river valleys, competition for water for agriculture led to the development of irrigation management systems and even warfare between some groups. The model proposed that due to the need to manage and protect water, these societies evolved state-level political structures. Not all groups that used irrigation evolved state-level societies, and many researchers have rejected the hydraulic model (see Hunt 1988). Price (1994), using Mesoamerican data, argued that while some small-scale societies that used irrigation, called hydroagricultural by Wittfogel, did not evolve into states, others, called hydraulic by Wittfogel, did develop state-level organizations. However, further research shows that in at least some of these cases—notably in East Asia—the state came long before the large-scale irrigation works, while in others the irrigation came so long before the state that the connection is hard to maintain. Thus, the theory in its pure form has been substantially abandoned. However, large-scale irrigation works certainly do provide one way for a state to achieve legitimacy and power, and the association (perhaps especially in Mesoamerica) remains under study.

Conflict Models

Conflict, in the form of competition or outright warfare, can be seen as a powerful incentive to organize. Warfare between political entities, particularly over critical resources, may have had a major influence on the development of complex organizations (Carneiro 1970; Cohen 1984). However, all state-level societies practice some warfare, and it is not clear whether warfare is a cause of, or a result of, states.

The Circumscription Theory

Robert Carneiro (1970) suggested that states might have arisen in very rich but very sharply circumscribed environments—usually fertile river valleys bordered by desert. Here, highly productive agriculture tempted conquerors and rulers, and the peasants had nowhere to run. State power would have been aided by the natural barriers of desert and mountain. This refreshingly simple theory is almost totally predictive and seems to be a genuine component of any explanation of state origins.

Multivariant Models

A number of researchers (e.g., Adams 1966; Butzer 1976) have suggested that causality in state formation was probably the result of a number of factors, with no single prime mover. Such a multivariate cause would involve a very complex set of interactions, with warfare, irrigation, and trade being major factors. The complex social and political organizations that characterize the state would have developed (selected for, as in an evolutionary sense) from these interactions (on this and other aspects of early state dynamics, see Chase-Dunn and Anderson [2005]; Turchin [2003, 2006]).

TECHNIQUES OF INTENSIVE AGRICULTURE

Intensive agriculture is cumulative in its use of techniques, employing all of the primary methods used by all other groups, with intensive agriculture being much larger in scale. The major new techniques used by intensive agriculturalists are plow cultivation and irrigation. Plows do not necessarily intensify anything—they merely create opportunities—but irrigation is generally not worth doing unless it pays off in high yields. Some groups, however, irrigate wild plants (as Julian Steward knew; see Lawton et al. 1976). Many irrigate very small-scale plots, such as vegetable gardens. Well-watered crops produce much greater yields than unirrigated crops. Higher crop yields can support more people, whose labor can help intensify agriculture to support even more people, and large numbers of people are a condition for the development of complex sociopolitical entities.

Irrigation

Irrigation generally involves the purposeful diversion of water from its natural source onto agricultural fields to provide water and any nutrients it may contain. Irrigation can be small-scale, such as the simple diversion of a small spring-fed creek onto a patch of grass, to very large scale, such as the construction of hundreds of miles of canals. With irrigation comes the need to control water sources, a fact that inspired the hydraulic theory of state development (see the discussion in chapter 6). Some 40 percent of the food produced in the world comes from the 16 percent of the agricultural land that is irrigated (Matson et al. 1997:506).

A number of different types of irrigation systems are known. The first system is flood irrigation, also called natural or basic irrigation, and involves the use of floodwaters to cover and soak fields. While this methods results in the irrigation of fields, it is not true irrigation because no human constructions are used. Much of the irrigation of the Egyptian culture, from ancient times to the completion of the Aswan Dam in 1970, was flood irrigation. However, the Egyptians supplemented the natural flooding with pot irrigation and with the construction of basins to store floodwater.

Genuine irrigation involves the construction of some facilities, such as dams, diversions, canals, wells, or other methods to purposefully divert water to fields. Rivers and/or streams might be diverted, channeled into canals, and delivered to fields many miles distant. For example, between 1,300 and 500 years ago, the Hohokam in the Sonoran Desert of the American Southwest employed a vast network of irrigation canals to support a large population and complex culture (see Bayman [2001] for a review of the Hohokam). The ancient state-level societies of the Tigris-Euphrates and Indus river valleys also relied on extensive canal systems.

The current Central Valley Project of California involves moving water from northern California some four hundred miles to the south in a massive aqueduct.

In addition to surface water, people also made use of subsurface water. This water was extracted from the ground with the use of wells, pots, and more recently, pumps. Such methods may constitute the primary irrigation system or supplement others.

Dry Farming

Dry farming, somewhat of a misnomer, is the production of crops relying on water from rainfall, and no constructed irrigation systems are used. Farming irrigated lands may have been the most important approach in early states, but today, about 84 percent of the world's agricultural land, including pasture, is dry farmed. In many areas, rainfall is quite sufficient as a water source, and in some areas, fields have to have systems to drain excess water. In other regions, such as the central United States, crops are utterly dependent on rain, and a dry year can result in crop failure.

The Use of Other Subsistence Techniques

Hunting and Gathering

All cultures do some hunting and gathering, but such activities are usually much less important in intensive agricultural economies than in horticultural or pastoral groups. Most intensive agriculturalists use very small amounts of wild resources, but some, such as ocean fish, are now extracted on a vast scale, using fishing fleets and industrial complexes. The economies of some countries, such as Japan, Iceland, and even the United States, are highly dependent on ocean fish. In a number of instances, certain wild species, such as trout, have been domesticated and are now raised on farms.

Horticultural Techniques

Small-scale agricultural plots and gardens still form an aspect of intensive agriculture, as can be seen by the numerous backyard gardens in the United States. Some intensive systems largely or entirely comprise an assorted combination of horticultural techniques, used intensively and in combination. An example of this is the Maya system described in case study 9.2.

Pastoral Techniques

Most farmers raise some animals for food, usually small species such as dogs, pigs, chickens, and guinea pigs. Intensive agriculturalists tend to raise much larger animals, such as cows, and while these are generally used for food, they are also used for a number of other purposes. These include production of various products such as leather, for prestige purposes, and for labor, including use as pack animals and for pulling plows.

Most intensive agriculturalists employ a component of pastoralism. Those using herdsman husbandry are sedentary farmers whose animal herds are tended by herdsmen in pastures distant from the main community. Those using sedentary animal husbandry are really full-time farmers who also raise some stock. This latter technique is widely practiced in the United States.

CONTEMPORARY INDUSTRIALIZED AGRICULTURE

The agricultural system used in the United States and some other industrialized nations is relatively new, really coming into its own after World War II. This system is highly specialized, focusing on a relatively few species, with corn being the most important of the crops. The vast majority of labor in this system is provided by machines powered by fossil fuels, and new machines to replace human workers continue to be introduced. Fields are very intensively used, and their fertility is usually maintained through the use of chemical fertilizers. Diseases and pests are controlled by chemical pesticides. Large-scale storage facilities and refrigeration allow crops to be stored for years, and so mitigate fluctuations in productivity due to drought or other conditions. A complex transportation and trade system allows these crops to be moved around the world with little difficulty.

While this system is highly productive, it is also very polluting and inefficient. Chemical fertilizers, herbicides, and pesticides pollute water supplies and unintentionally kill many other plants and animals. The system also results in the large-scale alteration of habitat and in the loss of biodiversity. Further, the system is ultimately unsustainable. In the United States, in addition to the human labor, it takes about three hundred calories of fossil fuel to produce one hundred calories of food, including the energy expended in packaging, transportation, and refrigeration (Pimentel et al. 1994:203). If the supply of fossil fuels became too costly or difficult to obtain (such as during a war in the Middle East), the entire system could collapse (the rise in the price of oil and the economic events of 2008 illustrate this danger). Part of the solution may be to eat foods that are grown locally in order to increase efficiency by decreasing transport costs (recall that this is one of the elements in any optimal foraging model) (Schueller 2001).

Some recent trends seem hopeful. For example, there is a growing market for organically grown fruits and vegetables, those raised without the use of chemicals for fertilizer or pest control. One could view this as another form of species modification or intensification of resource management. Part of this trend is the small but growing use of biological pest controls, having "good" bugs eat the "bad" bugs rather than using chemicals to kill all the bugs.

Contemporary Use of Traditional Systems

Given the propensity of contemporary agriculture to destroy land and pollute water, many people are searching for alternative methods of food production. It is slowing being realized that some traditional techniques of agriculture can be highly productive and valuable, or even necessary, in many areas (Marten 1986; Wilken 1987), and ethnographers and agronomists are working together to document the vast storehouse of traditional agricultural knowledge (Atran 1993). For example, the system utilized by the ancient Maya (see case study 9.2) could be adapted for use in rainforests and could support large numbers of people without the destruction of the forest.

Part of the problem is an arrogance on the part of Western development agents who believe that their practices must be superior. For example, on the island of Bali in the southern Pacific Ocean, traditional water management practices were replaced with contemporary techniques. However, these proved so much less successful than the traditional system that the contemporary innovations had to be abandoned (Lansing 1991; Lansing and Kremer 1993). The traditional Chinese wet rice system (see case study 9.1) is exceedingly efficient and productive, utilizing virtually all of the available resources within an area, but is being replaced by industrialized agriculture. This will result in a short-term increase in productivity but will ultimately make the land less productive.

James Fairhead and Melissa Leach (1996) showed that West African agriculture was not only far more sophisticated than had been assumed, but that it had actually created many of the groves that outsiders were trying to "protect" from "underdeveloped" farming. Johan Pottier (1999) established a wider context for this, describing the ways in which African agriculture is fine-tuned to a continent of poor soil and frequent drought, where development often means disaster. The geographers A. Grove and Oliver Rackham (2001) filled a large (and beautiful) book with ways in which Mediterranean peasants, often despised and regarded as land abusers by national elites, have actually maintained and efficiently cropped their rather hostile landscapes, often by intensive tree cropping (e.g., olives and almonds) and tree management (e.g., various ways of cutting branches, which can regrow, rather than sacrificing whole trees). Similar examples might be provided worldwide.

ENVIRONMENTAL MANIPULATION AND RESOURCE MANAGEMENT

The rate and scale of environmental manipulation are much greater in intensive agriculture than in other systems, and one of the hallmarks of intensive agriculture is the active large-scale alteration of landscapes. Entire ecozones have been so modified that they have little resemblance to their natural state. Whole valleys are flooded behind dams; entire forests are removed; rivers are rerouted; lakes are drained and plowed under; cities fill floodplains; plant and animal species continue to be driven to extinction; entire cultures are absorbed. The list of impacts is long.

In addition, systems of passive manipulation of the abiotic environment also increased considerably, with maintenance of the cosmos and control of the weather being major goals. Many of these systems required the commitment of considerable resources, such as the construction of temples and support of priests, and in some cases, the sacrifice of humans to the gods. In those belief systems, failure to adequately appease the supernatural powers could result in an environmental catastrophe.

Intensive agriculturalists generally practice more intense resource management than horticulturalists. The dependence on domesticated plants and animals is greater, but they focus on fewer species. Nondomesticated species are usually unimportant.

RELATIONS WITH OTHER GROUPS

Intensive agriculture is generally incompatible with other systems of subsistence and rapidly replaces them. This occurs for a number of reasons, including the fact that intensive agriculturalists have a very different relationship with the land, being more intensive and possessive. Most intensive agriculturalists tend to simplify their ecosystems (see Flannery 1972:399), through, for example, the use of monoculture. Such practices so alter landscapes that the other groups find their former areas unusable. Finally, intensive agriculturalists can successfully expand into the territories of other groups because they generally have larger populations and sociopolitical organizations that can support a full-time military, often the vehicle of expansion.

CHAPTER SUMMARY

Intensive agriculture is large-scale farming, often involving the use of animal labor, equipment, water-diversion techniques, and the production of surplus food. Intensive agriculture represents a fundamental shift upward in the intensity of land use, increases in population, growth in the complexity of sociopolitical systems, and increases in the human impact on the environment.

The change in agricultural intensity resulted in the growth in population, an increasing complexity in social and political organization, and eventually in some groups developing state-level societies. The processes by which this occurred are unclear, but a number of models have been proposed, including those based on management, conflict, and a combination of factors.

Intensive agriculture employs all of the techniques of horticulture and pastoralism, plus supplemental labor and irrigation, all combined into a complex and interrelated system. Such systems are quite flexible and resilient and can support billions of people.

After World War II, Western agriculture became increasingly industrialized and mechanized, with machines powered by fossil fuels providing much of the labor and manufactured chemicals much of the fertilizer. This type of agriculture is highly productive and has rapidly expanded to replace many traditional systems and to take over ecozones previously unoccupied by farmers.

Intensive agriculture has had a significant impact on the environment, much more than horticulture or pastoralism alone. Ecosystems become simplified, landforms significantly altered, and food economies more narrow. Ultimately, issues of pollution, dependency on fossil fuels, and population growth will make contemporary industrialized agriculture unsustainable in the long term.

KEY TERMS
dry farming
irrigation

CASE STUDY 9.1

MOUNTAINS AND WATER: THE TRADITIONAL AGRICULTURAL SYSTEM ALONG SOUTH COASTAL CHINA

The traditional system of Chinese rice agriculture is highly productive and fine-tuned to their environment. This case study illustrates how the Chinese utilize every possible food source within a sustainable system. The encroachment of modern agriculture threatens to disrupt the traditional system and to replace it with one that is more productive in the short term but not sustainable in the long term.

CASE STUDY 9.1

The Chinese word for "landscape painting," *shan-shui hua*, means, literally, "painting of mountains and water." Indeed, much of China's landscape is divided into mountainous land and well-watered river and stream valleys. This is especially true in the southern part of the country. North China's most populous region is the flat North China Plain, but the plain does not extend south of the Wei, Huai, and Yangtze rivers that traverse the center of the country. South of these rivers, the ancient continental shield is highly dissected and, from the air, this portion of China appears like a choppy sea. Rainfall is intense, and almost all of it falls in summer. The climate is monsoonal: hot, wet winds blow during the warmer months from the South China Sea, while cold winds blow all winter from the dry interior of Asia.

Here, in south coastal China (figure 9.1), thousands of years of experiment and innovation by local peasants have produced an agricultural system well adapted to local realities. This system supports about two-thirds of China's vast population. It produces about one-third of the world's rice, and perhaps most of the world's pigs, as well as enormous

FIGURE 9.1
The region (lined) of traditional Chinese wet rice agriculture.

quantities of corn, sweet potatoes, peanuts, and many fruits and vegetables. The major sources of information regarding the traditional
Chinese agricultural system are available in King (1911), Buck (1937),
Anderson and Anderson (1973), Bray (1984), Chao (1986), Wittwer et al.
(1987), Anderson (1988), Ruddle and Zhong (1988), and Dazhong and
Pimentel (1984, 1986a, 1986b). For archaeological information, see Ho
(1975, 1988), Chang (1986), and Liu (2004).

THE TRADITIONAL SYSTEM

We present here a somewhat generalized description (see note at
the end of this case study) of the way south China's rice production
system functions on the ground (see figure 9.2). Let us consider a
typical valley on the south China coast just before Western agricultural techniques (chemicals and mechanization) were brought to the
region.

FIGURE 9.2
An idealized model of traditional Chinese wet rice agriculture (drawn by Blendon
Walker).

This system is based on exquisitely fine-tuned choices of what to grow. The plant and animal production processes fit into each other neatly. They have come, through the millennia, to an accommodation. At every point, recycling and composting maintain or increase soil fertility and quality. Everything is composted: dung, old rope, agricultural wastes, ashes, and household debris. Even pottery, mud bricks, and tiles were ground up in the old days and added to the pile. Proper composting kills parasites, breaking their cycles of transmission and reducing risk of infection for people.

Geography

Each valley centers on a large stream or river. Ninety percent of the watershed of the stream is mountain land, too steep to cultivate on any significant scale. Now and then someone creates a dry field or terraces the few patches of soil in this zone, but it is more often left in forest, brush, and grass. These areas are important, as they are where people hunt, gather herbs and other plants, and obtain firewood.

Farther down the valley, the hills become less steep, permitting the terracing of some of the slopes. Eventually, the stream begins to develop a floodplain, forming some land suitable for fields. As one travels farther down the valley, the terrain flattens out, and freshwater lakes and swamps are located there. As the stream reaches the ocean, estuaries form. At the ocean, a beach and littoral zone, and eventually open ocean, are encountered.

Feng-Shui: Manipulation and Management

The Chinese employ the approach of feng-shui ("wind and water") in dealing with their environment. Feng-shui is a broad system in which humans fit into their environment, interact with it, and remain in some general balance with it (Anderson 1996). Among the many feng-shui practices are land and crop management tactics intended to maximize the benefits of wind and water while minimizing the damage to the land, and these practices have many important applications in the system of traditional agriculture. Feng-shui regulates the placement of most things, including roads, towns, fields, and forests to ensure harmony. Feng-shui is also used within homes to properly place furniture and other items.

CASE STUDY 9.1

Feng-shui has a strong magical or religious component. It is believed that good or evil fortune follows from one's choices of habitation. The siting and orientation of a house affect the health and wealth of the inhabitants. The placement of a grave affects the fate of the descendants of its occupant. Cutting down the trees (the feng-shui grove) associated with a town would bring disaster to the town, and the older and more well-grown a tree is, the more good luck it radiates.

Thus, whatever mystical beliefs it may have accumulated over the years, feng-shui is based on solid, pragmatic observation. Its magical overtones make it more persuasive—persuasive enough to convince millions of peasants to sacrifice short-term personal gain for long-term community benefit. Without the magic, the ecosystems in south China will degrade or collapse. Rational self-interest does not adequately motivate people to consider the long-range consequences of their behavior (Anderson 1996).

Hills and Forests

The hills are often burned, either to clear land or destroy dangerous animals, or due to an accident. This frequent burning releases ash, which washes down the streams, helping to restore the fertility of the farmlands downstream. Thus, though this burning is unfortunate—it would be much better if the land were left in forest—it does have its advantages. It releases, in the ash, mineral nutrients pulled up by tree roots from deep rock and soil layers. Also, many hill plants have, in their roots, large concentrations of bacteria that can take up nitrogen from the air and fix it as organic nitrates—something no higher plant or animal can do.

Of all of the nutrients that plants derive from the soil, nitrates are the ones needed in the most quantity, and they tend to be the great limiting resource for agriculture and plant growth (recall Liebig's Law of the Minimum). The plant cover of an area thus depends on its nitrogen-fixing bacteria. As they burn or decay, most of the nitrogen goes back into the air, but a good portion gets washed down to the fields below. In southwestern China, though not in the southeast, some communities deliberately plant alder trees on fallow land. When the trees are tall, they are cut for lumber, and the land can then be farmed, taking advantage of the enormous quantities of nitrogen that are released as the leaves and roots decay.

The greatest problem with traditional south Chinese environmental management is its destructive effect on the tree cover. Much of the forested areas of southern China have been cut down but because of feng-shui, large groves of trees are left around and above towns and constitute most of what little forest cover survives. Nevertheless, a chronic shortage of wood persists.

Without the deeply religious involvement of feng-shui, the temptation to deforest is too strong. Where modernization has meant the loss of belief, feng-shui groves have disappeared. All the predicted disasters have therefore come to pass: erosion, water shortages and droughts, fertility loss, and the other well-known consequences of massive deforestation. Thus, feng-shui, slighted by many contemporary Chinese as mere *mixin* (superstition), proves its value—whatever the skeptic may think of "good influences" and the mythical dragons that are often said to send them. It provides a classic case of the use of religion to sanction good ecological management, confirming the theory of Rappaport (1984) that ecological information and management practices could be encoded into religion to ensure that they were followed.

Towns

Most people live in towns and houses located in the upper part of the valley, on land that cannot be used for fields. They are sited on a comfortable, sunny slope above the streams, preferably near the junction of two streams, and just below the tops of the ridges that shield them from typhoons. The roads leading to the towns are winding to discourage evil spirits and other evils such as soldiers, tax collectors, and robbers. Buildings are located near reliable water sources, but above areas that flood. Graves are located on high, steep slopes, where they do not compete for land used for food production. Feng-shui groves are left around and above the towns and provide shade, firewood, erosion control, fruit, some construction timber, and similar benefits.

The use of feng-shui succeeds in keeping towns away from flood plains. This has the double value of protecting the towns and preventing the urbanization of critically needed rice-producing land (the Western world has yet to learn this lesson). In the great floods of June 1966, one of us (ENA) observed that all the traditionally sited buildings in the western New Territories of Hong Kong were above water, and almost all the new buildings were below it. Also observed were the contemporary construction sites in which the builders had cut too deeply into the hill slopes. With intense rain, the slopes failed and destroyed the sites and many buildings. The peasants said the cuts had "cut the dragon's pulse." Whether one believes in the dragon or in the equally mysterious geological concept of "angle of repose," the effects are the same: undercutting a slope brings disaster.

Gardens

Available land around the town is terraced for vegetable gardens. The vegetables are grown nearest the towns for several reasons. First, they need the good drainage—they do not grow well in the bottomland where the rice grows. Second, they are heavy, and they need a lot of fertilizer, and carrying everything to and from the vegetable fields is difficult. Third, they demand intensive care—constant weeding, pest control, watering, and harvesting, and people need to be close.

Rice Paddies

Below, in the valleys, most of the land has traditionally been dedicated to producing the great staple food: rice. Peanuts and sweet potatoes are grown on land unsuitable for rice. In south Chinese dialects, as in most southeast Asian languages, the word for "cooked rice" is often used to refer to food in general. Rice has to be irrigated to yield well. This demands good control over water. The better managed the water levels are, the higher the yield. A difference of a couple of inches in water level can affect production. Moreover, rice has to start growing when water is shallow, finish growing in deeper water, and then be dried off before harvesting.

Every tract of land with adequate drainage and water supply is terraced and diked to catch and control water (figure 9.3). Fields are plowed in winter—the dry season—but often again in summer. With the spring rains, the fields are flooded to very shallow depths. Rice is grown in seedling nurseries and transplanted out to the fields. Rice grows better and produces more grain if it is transplanted. As the rice grows, more water is added. When the grain starts to mature, the fields are drained so that the rice will not rot. Harvest takes place, and the cycle starts again. Most fields produce two crops of rice per year;

CASE STUDY 9.1

FIGURE 9.3
Rice paddies in China, 1978 (photo by E. N. Anderson).

some produce three. Mulberry trees are grown on dikes between rice fields to stabilize the dikes and prevent erosion. The trees do double duty as their leaves are used to feed the silkworms grown to make silk.

Lakes and Marshes

Lower in the valley, there comes a point at which rice cultivation is no longer economical because the water is too difficult to control; it ponds up too deeply and/or stays too long. Crops that need more water, such as lotus, water spinach, and other greens, are grown here. In addition, water buffalo and ducks are raised in these areas.

Still lower in the valley, where permanent fresh water in the form of lakes or marshes exist, wild and domesticated fish are intensively farmed. If quality fish are desired, ponds produce about a ton of fish per hectare (2.47 acres), but if buyers are satisfied with small, rather lean fish, yields can go up to seven or eight tons. The fish raised are species of carp, along with some catfish and mullet. Most of them eat vegetation and small animal life. The pond stocking system includes a number of different fish so that they can utilize every niche in the pond: floating vegetation, bottom fauna, microplankton, and even grass and weeds cut from the bank. The ponds are fertilized with night soil (human waste), soybean wastes, and other by-products of the land economy. A detailed account of this amazing system was provided by Ruddle and Zhong (1988; also see Anderson 1988).

At the mouth of the stream or river, there is usually an estuary and brackish swamp. Soil erosion from the deforested mountains expands the alluvial fan, extending the land outward into the water; much of south China's rice land is of recent origin, having been created from new alluvium over the past thousand years. Silt or sand is deposited; mangroves and reeds grow, preventing further erosion. Eventually the inner fringe of this new land can be drained and cultivated. Thus are born the "sand fields" (sha-tian) commemorated in many place-names along the south coast. In the meantime, the swamp is used for catching fish and shrimp. Brackish swamps are the most productive of all landscapes, enriched as they are by input from both land and sea.

The Sea

Out to sea, cultivated oyster beds continue the range of aquiculture in the littoral zone. Oystermen own long strips, aligned between landmarks on the coast. They create oyster habitat by dropping tiles, bricks, or stones for the spat (floating oyster larvae) to attach themselves to. Each oysterman knows his attachments and his landmarks, so theft is difficult. Oysters are phenomenally productive but subject to predators, so management must be careful and continual.

Finally, the ocean is fished intensively by professionals. Living in their boats, they are a different class from the shore people. They rarely fish from shore; the land people rarely fish from boats. The fishers have their own songs, traditions, customs, and classificatory systems. However, they rely on the land people for a variety of products, such as rice and vegetables. Likewise, the land people rely on the fishers for fish and other ocean products. In a very real sense, the two groups (land and fishers) have formed a mutualistic relationship in a cultural and natural ecotone (the shore) much like the Mbuti and Bantu of the Ituri Forest (see case study 5.2).

About Rice

Rice is the foundation of the traditional Chinese agricultural system. The first known domesticated rice comes from the Yangtze Delta,

CASE STUDY 9.1

where both long-grain and short-grain varieties were grown by 8,000 years ago (see Liu 2004). Soon rice dominated the food production system of the region. Today, rice is the staple food of perhaps two billion people, the vast majority of them in monsoonal Asia.

Nowhere is rice more dominant than in south coastal China. Here it provided, until recent times, 90 percent of the calories for the ordinary person. Fields produced two or even three crops per year. The lowland landscape was a solid sheet of brilliant gold-green—the color of plants photosynthesizing at maximum efficiency. Even in cloudy monsoon light, they are trapping the energy of the sun, using it to drive the chemical reactions that turn air, water, and mud into the world's most productive grain crop.

Under traditional conditions, paddy (i.e., wet-grown) rice yields one thousand to three thousand pounds per acre. Thus, a triple-cropped field could theoretically produce almost ten thousand pounds per acre, though it is doubtful whether such yields have ever been achieved. The best figures are from Taiwan, where average yields of paddy rice increased from about 1,300 pounds per acre at the turn of the century to twice that by 1961 (Chinese-American Joint Commission on Rural Reconstruction 1966:26). The second figure indicates about the limit of what was possible for a regionwide average with traditional techniques; after that date, improved varieties and agricultural chemicals became widespread, and yields soared. Rice now yields up to ten thousand or even twelve thousands pounds per acre per crop.

Rice responds very well to fertilizer and to control of water amount and quality. Lower figures (one thousand pounds per acre) are typical where fertilizer is not used or where the water or soil is salty (as on new "sand fields"), or where water levels are not well regulated. But at least it produces under such conditions. Few grains will produce at all in brackish water, but specialized rice varieties flourish there.

No other grain produces so well under traditional conditions. In China, however, corn, wheat, and millet approach it. All were grown on the drier uplands where rice does not yield well. Wheat was often grown during the winter in areas where water could not be made adequate for rice or in areas too cold for a winter rice crop.

At these yield levels, it is possible to feed six or more people per hectare—around two thousand per square mile (this is about the density of an American suburb). Densities of this level are common in river deltas and other especially favorable localities. Even higher population densities have been recorded in areas where people could produce high-value handicraft items such as silk (Huang 1990).

Other Resources

Rice is mostly starch and alone does not provide adequate nutrition for people. Supplementary protein, vitamins, and minerals must come from other foods. In southern China, these foods include soybeans, peanuts, and other beans, whose protein complements that of rice. They also include vegetables, especially Chinese cabbages, which are among the richest in vitamins of all greens. Chiles, tomatoes, eggplants, squash, sweet and white potatoes, and dozens of lesser vegetable crops abound, providing further supplementation. All these are high yielding under south Chinese conditions. The land is too scarce for wasteful uses. Chinese cabbage, for instance, produced about eleven thousand pounds per acre under traditional conditions in Taiwan (Chinese-American Joint Commission on Rural Reconstruction 1966:100). Other vegetables were similarly productive.

The shortage of calories is not as limiting as deficiencies of protein, calcium, and iron. The Chinese recognize a condition ("cold *qii*," what we call anemia) and have developed a specific and effective treatment: feeding the sufferer pig livers (the addition of "warm *qi*"). Although the Chinese do not know that it is iron deficiency they are treating or why pig livers are an effective treatment, it works.

The domestic animals grown by the Chinese are those that can most efficiently turn farm and food wastes into meat: dogs, pigs, chickens, and ducks. Pigs and chickens were domesticated in China by seven thousand years ago (Underhill 1997:121), and ducks perhaps as early. These animals not only eat garbage, waste, and scraps—they eat weeds and pests. Chickens and ducks are often the insect and weed control in the fields and paddies. Some duck owners rent their ducks to other farmers for the ducks to eat the pests; the renters also get to keep the duck manure generated while on their fields (in the United States, "weeder geese" are now being used for weed control in some situations). Thus, dangerous pests are turned into good meat. By contrast, cattle are rare and are mostly plow stock. Sheep and other less efficient meat producers are very rare. Unlike Western livestock systems, no animal is raised if it requires food humans could eat. Wild animals are encouraged but are cropped for food.

Many of the wild animals also have a pest-control function. When pesticides came to southern Asia, frogs were exterminated in many areas. This not only deprived the peasants of an important food source—it also accompanied an explosion of insect pests. The frogs had been more efficient insect killers than the chemicals. The pesticides also killed fish and birds that were eaten by people. It was better to lose some of the rice to the fish and birds and get to eat them.

Wild resources include not only timber for firewood, but also herbs for medicine and game for food. Even insects are eaten, and the giant waterbug is a delicacy in parts of south China and northern Thailand (Pemberton 1988). Vines for tying, leaves for fertilizer, flowers for decoration, water plants for pig fodder, and countless other products are derived from wild and weedy plants.

Cultural traditions have evolved to fit well with the overall system. Cooking, for example, has come to be based on processes that require very little fuel: stir-frying and steaming instead of baking and long boiling. Food preferences run to vegetables and fish, not the meat and potatoes of Western diets. Choice vegetables cost more than meat in the markets of China.

Nutrients through the System

Consider the fate of a nitrogen atom in this system. It is trapped and incorporated into a nitrate molecule by bacteria in the root nodules of a hill plant. Eventually, as the plant burns or decays, this particular bit of nitrate happens to wash downstream. The water is channeled into a vegetable garden, and the nitrogen is picked up by a radish. Picked and carried into town, the radish is eaten, and the nitrogen atom is eventually excreted. The night soil is composted, mixed with other composted waste items, and returned to the land as fertilizer.

The nitrogen atom might simply cycle forever between vegetables and town, but eventually most nutrients escape downstream into the rice paddies. Here they are caught up in yet another cycle: rice to town, compost back to the land. The rice is consumed by humans. The rice straw is eaten by cattle and water buffalo. Straw too tough to eat is

CASE STUDY 9.1

made into ropes and sandals, and when these wear out they, too, are composted.

In the rice paddies, more nitrogen is fixed. Blue-green algae, often growing on small floating ferns of the genus *Azolla*, are excellent nitrogen fixers. Chinese and Southeast Asian growers have long known that rice paddy pond scum makes excellent fertilizer. Vietnamese peasants even learned to transplant *Azolla* to new paddies.

Eventually escaping the paddy cycle, our atom washes on downstream and is cycled several times more through the fish ponds. Finally it leaves via the swamp (and more cycling) into the ocean. Here it becomes part of the outflow that fertilizes the marine waters and produces a rich fishery. Eventually it is incorporated into a fish. The fish is caught, dried, and traded back up to the town at the top of the valley—and the entire story begins again.

Thus, a given bit of nitrate passes through many plants and many digestive tracts on the way to the sea. Few nutrients escape this system. Because new ones are constantly being incorporated into the system as they erode from the surrounding rock, it follows that the system keeps getting richer. Indeed, many of the valleys of south China have become more extensive and fertile, in spite of the enormous nutrient drain caused by exporting food to cities and other far places.

DISCUSSION

This broad-spectrum use of the environment is ecologically healthy. The whole south Chinese landscape is cropped. Its productivity is maximized, and virtually everything is used. By contrast, Western-style agriculture normally eliminates most natural biota and sets up an artificial system producing a very few crops. This system is productive for a short while but is unstable. Soil degradation, crop diseases, and changing economics that make a crop suddenly unprofitable can all be devastating in short order. The long-term result is desertified, abandoned land.

The diet produced by this system is also healthy—if one can avoid waterborne diseases and parasites. Living on rice, fish, and vegetables, Chinese males have one-sixteenth the heart disease rates of American males, and the cholesterol level of the average adult is 127 (it is over 180 in the United States). The people in southern China have less can-

CASE STUDY 9.1

cer than those in the north who consume more wheat and meat. Life expectancy in China is almost as high as in the United States, although until recently China had only 1 percent as much wealth per capita (see Chen et al. 1990; or summary in Lang 1989).

This is not to say that China's system is, or was, perfect. Plants are tougher and more adaptable than they are productive—they have to be. Famine was always a possibility if rice crops failed. In recent times, improved pest control and the adoption of more productive rice strains resulted in higher production. Animals also need better disease control and better feed than they usually get in traditional China.

Moreover, Southeast Asia developed an even better system, based on extensive tree cropping, as well as rice, vegetables, and fish. Forests are left on the hills but are often converted to economically useful species. Large orchards and tree plantations maximize use of dry, thin soil, not well-used in south China. The Southeast Asian system is better adapted to the tropics, where tree growth is faster and more tree varieties occur, but it is locally found in south China. The real problems with tree cropping in China are the slow growth of the trees, the pressure to feed an increasing population immediately, and the danger of warfare. Trees, once cut in war, regrow very slowly.

Other superior systems have been devised and tested, but only on a small scale. So far in the world, only China and Southeast Asia have shown an ability to feed an extremely dense population for thousands of years without destroying the resource base (but consider the Maya system).

The south Chinese system, and its close relatives or variants in Vietnam and Java, feed more people per unit of area than any other on earth. Even the United States' much-vaunted agricultural system does not do so well, because so much of the land is taken up with less productive uses: extensive cattle ranching, wheat production, specialized but nutritionally worthless sugar growing, and the like. Also, Americans prefer more meat, which takes much more area and feed to produce.

But in ecology, as in other walks of life, "there ain't no free lunch." People must pay in labor. China's agriculture is fine-tuned, more like home gardening than American field cropping. Individuals lavish vast quantities of skill and knowledge, as well as sheer hard work, on the land. They must know when and where to grow everything. They must work to plant the next vegetable crop among already-growing crops—planting the seeds among the maturing leaves. They must know exactly what mix of varieties is ideal for their particular fields. Rice under traditional conditions requires fifty person-days of work per acre per crop in southeast China, and more in some other areas (Buck 1937:302). In California today, rice is seeded by airplanes and cultivated by tractors, and the labor requirement is a few hours per acre.

The sheer population growth in south China created problems (Huang 1990). In the absence of rapid growth in urban employment, peasants had no alternative but to stay on the land. Even immigration to America and southern Asia was not enough to relieve the pressure of population. Thus, the system had even greater labor assets and became ever more fine-tuned and skill intensive.

This also resulted in a form of development that was overwhelmingly focused on crop varieties and cropping patterns rather than on machines and chemicals. While the Western world was inventing threshers, harvesters, tractors, gang plows, artificial fertilizers, and thousands of other high-tech mechanical innovations, China was perfecting an organic or biological system. American agriculture, with all its machines, is intended to get the most production per *worker*, because the United States is well supplied with land but not always with labor. China must get more per *land* unit by lavishing labor upon it (Hayami and Ruttan 1985). The system did not stand still; it continued to innovate, and continues to do so today. When people face a limit, they breed a new variety, domesticate a new species, or develop a new and more intensive cropping pattern.

Agricultural development does not just happen; it is helped or hindered by government (Hayami and Ruttan 1985). The Chinese government, throughout history, has favored agriculture and tried to help the farmers. Land taxes were usually low and occasionally waived altogether.

The Chinese imperial government, as early as two thousand years ago, performed experiments, issued extension manuals, recognized productive farmers, distributed superior planting stock, had international missions bring back useful plants, and in many other ways helped the agricultural process (Bray 1984; Anderson 1988). What

CASE STUDY 9.1

Hayami and Ruttan (1985) showed for the recent past was in fact true throughout history: the government favored biological technology as opposed to mechanical or chemical. Heavy taxes on industry, and lack of encouragement for technological innovation, often inhibited mechanical progress. Thus, China's agriculture was profoundly shaped by government policy.

Moreover, the Chinese government was perhaps the first in the world (before recent times) to organize charity and famine relief, both by distributing food and by working to develop agriculture (Will 1990; Will and Wong 1991). There were also private charitable societies that worked with the government on this (Handlin Smith 1987). This, too, helped agriculture, but it also allowed rampant population growth. Thus, in spite of the best efforts of the government, the fortune of the farmers did not improve. Their numbers increased; their income did not. It is a story all too familiar in the world today.

In China, as in all state societies, the "invisible hand of the market" is simply another imaginary supernatural being. In the real world, agricultural development takes place because of conscious choice by government officials and farmers. These people must choose in response to political, social, ecological, and personal factors as well as narrowly economic ones. The price of farm products must be considered along with charitable famine relief, population pressure, religion, ethnic traditions, and the fads that so often affect food buyers. The apparent irrationality of feng-shui turns out to lead to rational site planning; the apparent rationality of Western monocrop agriculture leads to irrational destruction of millions of acres of land. Agricultural systems are more complex than they appear at first sight.

Many authorities think that this has led to technological stagnation or even decline in China (Elvin 1973; Chao 1986). With peasants growing poorer and harder working all the time, there was no incentive to devise machines. There was also no incentive to mass-produce consumption goods—the peasants could not afford them. At best, the farm sector did not prove to be the driving force toward modernization that it became in the United States, England, and elsewhere.

Having said all that, agriculture in China is rapidly changing to a system modeled after the West, one that emphasizes chemical fertilizers, pesticides, and machines powered by fossil fuels. In the years since

CASE STUDY 9.1

1955, there has been a hundred-fold increase in the use of fossil fuels in Chinese agriculture (Wen and Pimentel 1986a, 1986b), and the use of chemicals is also rapidly increasing. The change is partly motivated by an attempt to obtain short-term increases in productivity and to the overall effort by the Chinese to reduce population growth. By allowing families to have only a limited number of children, the labor pool needed to maintain traditional agriculture is shrinking, and the need to use other methods is increasing. Nevertheless, the shift away from traditional techniques, developed and perfected over thousands of years, will have a serious long-term impact on the environment.

CASE STUDY 9.2

THE MAYA AGRICULTURAL SYSTEM

This case study on the ancient Maya shows how a complex state-level society with a large population can adapt to a rainforest environment without totally destroying it. The lessons to be learned from the Maya can be employed by contemporary people living in rainforests and can slow, or even prevent, rainforest destruction.

The agricultural system developed by the ancient Maya was able to support a large population living in urban centers within a rainforest. The ancient Maya system incorporated a series of horticultural techniques that, when used intensively and extensively, made the entire system one of intensive agriculture. (It might be considered strictly horticulture, except for the size of the landscape modification, with terracing, raised fields, drainage, and other large-scale influences. Today, of course, plows, integrated livestock management, and other European agricultural techniques have been added.) While the ancient Maya are no longer extant, the contemporary Maya still employ most of the elements of the old system. An understanding of the ancient Maya system, which was actually quite variable from lowlands to highlands, could lead to the development of techniques and systems that could be utilized in contemporary rainforest settings, perhaps supporting large populations without the outright destruction of the rainforest. This is an important goal. Additional general information on the Maya

CASE STUDY 9.2

agricultural system can be found in Anderson (2005b), Redfield and Rojas (1934), Kintz (1990), Wilk (1991), Fedick (1996), and Faust (1998).

THE ORIGINAL VIEW OF MAYA AGRICULTURE
Upon its discovery in the mid-1800s, the ancient Maya were thought to have a relatively small and widely dispersed population living in small villages. The large Maya sites with monumental architecture (pyramids) were believed to be ceremonial centers, constructed by the people living within the jurisdiction of its priests. It was thought that only a small population of priests and other specialists lived in these centers.

Given the belief that the Maya population was relatively small and dispersed, it was thought that a relatively simple swidden system, which is used by a dispersed population, was capable of supporting the Maya. Thus, little research was done on the agricultural system, but it was hypothesized that some sort of a failure of the swidden system had led to the downfall of the ancient Maya (see, e.g., Diamond 2005).

A NEW UNDERSTANDING
Beginning in the 1970s, researchers began to realize that the forest contained an unusual distribution of certain plants, shrubs and bushes not native to the area, certain tree species clumped together, such as the seed-bearing ramón (*Brosimum alicastrum*), the fruit-bearing sapodilla (*Manilkara sapota*), mamey sapote (*Pouteria sapota*), various species of citrus, and the mahogany (*Swietenia macrophylla*), desired for hardwood. People began to look more closely at the ethnobotany of the contemporary Maya for clues on the ancient Maya system.

A bit later, archaeologists began investigating areas outside of the large sites with the impressive architecture, and they began to discover small, low house foundations that had previously gone unnoticed in the thick jungle. Large numbers of houses were discovered, and it was soon realized that the sites originally thought to be ceremonial centers were actually cities with large urban populations.

It quickly became apparent that if these centers were actually cities and the Maya population was much larger than previously believed, a reevaluation of the Maya agricultural system was needed. It was clear that the swidden system originally thought to have been used by the

CASE STUDY 9.2

Maya was not capable of supporting the three hundred to four hundred people per square mile that lived in the Maya region.

Researchers began looking much more closely at the agricultural system and discovered the archaeological remains of a number of non-swidden field systems. Large numbers of small stone-walled enclosures, the remains of small terraced gardens called *pet kot* (round wall of stone) by the Maya, were discovered on the sides of small hills. These features are very subtle and difficult to notice in heavy undergrowth. In other areas, systems of raised chinampas were found in a number of swampy places, the best studied being Pulltrouser Swamp in southeastern Yucatan and northern Belize (Turner and Harrison 1983; Sharer and Traxler 2005; also see Gidwitz 2002). These were constructed by digging ditches in the swamp and piling the soil up in a wafflelike pattern (see figure 7.2), raising the fields up out of the water, and creating canals between them. The canals were dredged with the soil added to the field to maintain its fertility. The canals between the fields were colonized by turtles and fish, both of which were eaten.

While our understanding of the Maya agricultural system is still incomplete, it is now clear that they utilized at least four major approaches. The first was a complex system of orchards integrated into the forest (agroforestry). These trees were utilized for food, lumber, and beauty. Second, large numbers of small terraced gardens were constructed where possible. Third, the Maya constructed complex systems of chinampas in areas not normally thought by Westerners as being suited to agriculture. Last, of course, the Maya extensively utilized a swidden system. The combination of these techniques into a unified system was highly productive and is classified as intensive agriculture. In addition, the Maya utilized a number of wild resources as part of their overall economy.

Environmental Manipulation

The Maya extensively manipulated the forest and, as a result, virtually remodeled it to suit their needs. Native trees were removed and replaced with other species, creating a mosaic that can still be seen today. Water was rerouted into fields and canals, altering the natural system. Finally, sections of forest were cleared for the construction of the many cities, towns, and other facilities used by the Maya. In spite of all of their extensive modification of specific areas, the Maya managed to maintain the overall diversity of the forest.

The Maya also conducted extensive passive manipulation of the cosmos to ensure continued good harvests. These practices included a wide assortment of ceremonies, and recently it has been determined that some of these ceremonies incorporated human sacrifice.

Resource Management

The Maya practiced intensive management of their various domesticated crops. They also intensively managed their trees, planting them at various places in the landscape, even in areas outside their natural habitat.

Intensive management was also practiced on a number of wild species. The fish, turtles, and other species in the canals of the chinampas were controlled as to their numbers and locations and their habitat being expanded or reduced, depending on the conditions. However, as far as is known, these species were not genetically domesticated. There was also some management of other wild animals such as deer. The animals were attracted to the vegetation of fallow swidden fields, where they were hunted. Proper management of those fields and of the hunting could ensure a continued supply of deer.

Collapse

The culture of the ancient Maya did eventually collapse in the central lowlands, though it survived in the northern and southern parts of the Maya world. Drought was a factor, probably a major one (Gill 2000; Peterson and Haug 2005). Deforestation, chronic warfare, shortening of swidden cycles, erosion, and/or silting in of chinampas are all candidates for causal factors (Demarest 2004; Webster 2002). Whatever the cause, there is much to learn and apply from the Maya example.

THE CONTEMPORARY YUCATEC MAYA SYSTEM

As the ancient Maya culture declined, so did their population. The Maya people stayed in the same place but scaled down their agriculture, adopting more of a horticultural-scale system, with swidden being its major component. They retained much of the knowledge of the ancient system and continue to use its various components today.

CASE STUDY 9.2

Most recently, however, components of Western-style intensive agriculture are being adopted, and the Maya region is being adversely transformed much like the Amazon Basin and other rainforests around the world (see "The Rainforest Dilemma" in chapter 10). The Yucatec Maya (see Kintz 1990) are one of a number of contemporary Maya groups that still occupy the same regions as their more famous predecessors.

The Natural Environment

The Yucatec Maya live in the Yucatan Peninsula, in the Mexican state of Quintana Roo (figure 9.4). They live in a communally owned area, known as an *ejido*, of some 14,330 hectares. The ejido, named Chunhuhub (see Anderson 2005b; Anderson and Medina Tzuc 2005), lies in an ecotone between seasonally dry forest and permanently moist rainforest. Three major seasons are recognized. The wet season lasts from mid-May to November. From November to late February, it is cool and relatively dry, but with frequent cool rains. The dry season lasts from March to mid-May. Rainfall averages between fifty and eight inches per

FIGURE 9.4
Location of the Yucatec Maya in the Yucatan Peninsula.

year, depending on location. Temperatures range from fifty degrees Fahrenheit on cold winter nights to around one hundred degrees Fahrenheit in the height of the dry season in April and early May.

Sociopolitical Organization

Traditionally, the Maya were organized by patrilineages, with the leaders of each exercising political power. Today, the primary social unit is the bilateral extended family. The leaders of the various levels, towns, ejido, and *municipio*, are now democratically elected, although family leaders still have considerable say over things.

Economics

The Swidden System

The Yucatec Maya use a swidden system, generally called *sak'aab* after the first stage of forest succession. The system involves the use of rotating fields, called milpas (figure 9.5), an American misuse of the Nahuatl word for "cornfield," and remains highly productive. Like any human activity, the swidden system does impact the forest, but it does not destroy diversity or cause extinctions. The Yucatec Maya continue to manage the forest and maintain a sustainable agricultural system. A concerted effort is now underway to record and preserve as much traditional knowledge as possible so that an intensive agricultural system, sustainable in a rainforest, can be developed.

Light, well-drained soils are preferred for milpas. The favored areas are low hills and valleys covered with dry forest. The wet, less fertile clay soils of the tropical rainforest are not good for milpas—a fact that has protected most of the high forest from frequent cutting. To cultivate a milpa, the family first cuts the forest and then lets it dry. When dry, the vegetation is burned. Any large branches that did not burn completely are gathered up and reburned. The ash is then mixed with the soil.

In cutting the forest for the milpa, the trees are managed. Certain fast-growing trees are cut and then used for firewood and building materials. Slow-growing food and medicine-producing trees are not cut for wood, and some flowering trees are left for aesthetic reasons. Other trees are retained due to their interdependence with other species. For example, some bees depend on certain trees for nectar, so those trees

CASE STUDY 9.2

FIGURE 9.5
A Maya milpa (photo by E. N. Anderson).

would be left and the honey collected at a later time. Cleared lands are then planted.

Men, sometimes aided by women, use digging sticks to poke small holes in the ash and soil. A few corn kernels, often with a bean or two, are placed in the hole and covered with soil. Chiles and so on are planted separately, in the more fertile, low-lying parts of the field. The simple sharpened stick is the only cultivating tool—it is ideal for the purpose; shovels and plows would only disturb the light soil and ash and allow them to blow away. Weeding is done a couple of times as the crop grows; machetes are used today, but in earlier times weeds had to be pulled by hand or mashed down with stone tools. The yields are consistently around one thousand pounds per acre.

Table 9.2. General Maya Forest Succession Stages

General Stage	General Maya Name	Years of Fallow
1	Sak'aab	1 to 2
2	Sak'aab'kool	2 to 5
3	Kambalhubche'	5 to 10
4	Kanalhubche'	10 to 30
5	Kelenche'	30 to 50
6	Kaanal'k'aax	Mature or "tall" forest

Milpas are cultivated for two years and then abandoned. The Yucatec Maya recognize three succession stages of forest. A newly abandoned field is called *sak'aab*; a field two or three years out of cultivation is *hubche'* ("brushwood"); and then the forest grows up to *kaanal k'aax*, "tall forest." The other stages are known (see table 9.2) but not used much by the Yucatec, and some Maya distinguish even more than the six stages.

The success of the system depends on a thorough knowledge of the plants, animals, and soils. Older Maya have an encyclopedic knowledge of the local land. They recognize five or six major soil types, each with many subtypes, and they know what kinds of plants will grow best in each subtype. Some four hundred species of animals and close to a thousand wild plants are known.

Gardens

Dark, moist soils rich in organic matter are favored for orchards and gardens, and houses are built in those areas. The gardens are then placed around the houses, and dozens of species of plants are grown. The yields of fruit and vegetables in the gardens are far higher than in the milpas. The gardens produce up to a quarter of the food of a family, and an even higher percentage of the protein and vitamins.

Crops

The Yucatec Maya grow many types of crops in their milpas and gardens. By far the most important crop in the milpas is corn, as it has been for the past five thousand years. Corn still provides three-quarters of the calories in the diet of the rural cultivators—a figure unchanged for millennia. In contrast to much of Latin America, beans are not very important; they do not grow well in Quintana Roo, apparently due to the poor soil. Squash and chiles, the other famous Mexican crops, are correspondingly even more important than elsewhere, and squash seeds traditionally provided much of the protein in the diet. Today, chickens and pigs have taken over that function, and squash seeds are largely a ceremonial food.

Milpas on light hill soils are usually used to grow corn alone. In better soil, especially in the valleys between the hills, beans, squash, chiles, papayas, tomatoes, and occasionally other foods are grown among the corn stalks. The beans climb the corn and fix nitrogen that fertilizes the soil. The squash covers the soil in between, shading it and killing weeds, and the chiles derive protection from the other plants. Thus, each of these plants depends on the others.

The gardens and houses are protected and shaded by some thirty species of tall fruit trees. More chiles and tomatoes are grown in the garden, along with chives, onions, cabbage, radishes, and medicinal herbs such as rue, mint, and aloe vera. Some enterprising gardeners grow their own coffee and chocolate. Others produce cotton or experiment with plants such as grapes, which do not normally fruit in Quintana Roo. Domesticated chickens and pigs, introduced by the Spaniards, plus native turkeys and Muscovy ducks live in and near the gardens.

Hunting and Gathering

The Yucatec Maya do some hunting to supplement the chickens and pigs raised around the houses. The primary game are deer and peccary (a small wild pig), which are attracted to active milpas and gardens and to recently abandoned milpas. In addition, some wild pigeons are also hunted. The proliferation of shotguns has increased hunting success and put pressure on game populations. As the human population increases, this pressure intensifies, although game birds are adept at escape and their numbers remain high.

A large number of wild plants are gathered and used for various purposes, including over 330 used for medicine, 122 for food, and 103 for construction wood. Firewood alone requires a book's worth of knowledge; each kind of wood is distinctive in specific heat, drying qualities, rate of burning, and usefulness in particular contexts. Another five

CASE STUDY 9.2

species are used for basketry, two as rat poison, and one sticky-leaved plant for catching fleas.

Environmental Manipulation

The Yucatec Maya practice much less environmental manipulation than their more famous ancestors. Today, the population is lower and the major cities are no longer occupied. In addition, some of the agricultural techniques, such as terracing and field/canal systems, are either used less or not at all, reducing the need for manipulation. Still, the forest is managed for purposes of swidden and fruit tree production. The abandoned swidden fields are still managed for their use as hunting grounds for wild game.

Passive environmental manipulation is still important and is accomplished through ceremony. Until recently, these ceremonies were carried out to bring rain and to pray to—and later thank—the spirits of forest and field for the success of the crops. The *chaak* (rain gods) and *yum il k'aax* ("lords of the forest") want to be remembered, and appreciate honey mead, corn gruel, corn bread, and chicken stew offered with appropriate chanting and incense. A detailed round of ceremonies was part of daily life until very recently. Many farmers still hold some or all of these ceremonies, but modernization is taking its toll on the old ritual representation of agriculture.

Resource Management

The Yucatec Maya continue to manage their various resources very well. Some recent "improvements" such as vegetable farming and fruit growing have not worked out, except as changes to already existing practices. The swidden system has been effective at preserving forest and soils. Some areas cleared for more modern agriculture have not done well, losing soil and being overrun by weeds. An expansion of fruit orchards into these areas is one way to reclaim that land. Logging has impacted the forest, and mature mahogany trees have all but been eliminated. Reforestation is a continuing practice, but tree poachers continue to frustrate the efforts.

The Yucatec Maya also continue to employ passive resource management. They are still careful not to offend the spirits of the forest by taking more resources than they need. They also employ prayer and offerings to the spirits to protect the fields and the crops as they approach harvest.

CASE STUDY 9.2

DISCUSSION

The Maya today practice a sustainable agriculture within a rainforest; however, it is well below the carrying capacity of the ancient system. The reasons for this are unclear as it has only recently been realized that this was the case. It seems that the ancient Maya exceeded the carrying capacity of the forest and that the system collapsed catastrophically (a bust cycle) with a drastic reduction in population. It may be that any recovery was interrupted by the Spanish conquest and disease. The Maya population may only now be recovering. With increasing populations, there may be more pressure to adopt ancient techniques.

Current Issues and Problems

As people, we all face a number of environmental issues and problems. The environment is paying a high price for the system of intensive agriculture now widely adopted across the world. Modernization and development have resulted in increasing homogenization of both the natural and cultural environments. Diverse and complex ecosystems are converted into simple ones through monoculture, with an associated loss of habitat and extinction of species. Long-term overgrazing and other mismanagement have turned entire regions, such as the Middle East, into deserts. Fresh water is running out; most human use of it is for agriculture, and efficiency, conservation, and better desalination technology lag behind the rising need for water (Gleick 2008; Rogers 2008). Current land management policies tend to be shortsighted and destructive, committing us to an agricultural system that is ultimately unsustainable. Invasive species, those transported to new areas by ships and planes, are also causing havoc in many ecosystems. Change in planning procedures is clearly in order.

Human activity has also led to global warming, including droughts (see McIntosh et al. 2000). Everyone worries about global warming, but the ecological anthropologist does more, by comparing it with previous periods of warming. The Medieval Warm Period (AD 800 to 1300) was comparably warm with the present—but much less so than the future will be, unless we act now. Brian Fagan (2008) found that it had various effects, according to how the different groups of people in the world coped with it. Its effects ranged from droughts that brought down whole civilizations in the New World to warming that released agricultural potential in Europe.

Deforestation, which dates from at least the Neolithic in Europe and Africa, has resulted in the alteration of long-term rainfall patterns across the region.

While the Romans initiated industrial pollution (e.g., lead), it was a modest beginning compared with the pollution levels of modern industry. Contemporary pollution (mostly the release of carbon into the atmosphere) is in the process of causing global warming, although it is not yet clear what effect it will have. There is little hope, however, that it will be positive. We simply do not fully understand the impact of our actions; however, some consequences are clear but ignored (e.g., the refusal of the United States and some others to reduce carbon emissions). Some developing nations are avoiding the mistakes of the developed countries, but others seem to see those mistakes as necessary to progress. China is in a rush to modernize at all costs, with resulting pollution, loss of farmland, loss of biodiversity, and shortages of everything from energy to water (Smil 2004). Anthropologists have been in the forefront of documenting particular problems for local small-scale communities. Among important summaries of broad problem areas, Thayer Scudder (2005) spent a lifetime documenting the problems caused by large dams. Thomas Dichter (2003) described development so misguided that it has made problems worse rather than better. Johan Pottier (1999) dealt with the human ecology of food security. On a more local note, a particularly useful function of anthropology has been providing a way for local people to get their voices heard. Stuart Kirsch (2006) not only documents the problems of mining in New Guinea, but provides detailed quotations from local people about the matter. West (2006), Agrawal (2005), and many other recent authors have brought in the indigenous voice to varying degrees.

As traditional cultures are altered and ultimately vanish, everyone suffers through the loss of their experience, knowledge, products, and solutions to problems. In the final analysis, the loss of any group weakens us all through the deterioration of our overall diversity and our adaptability. Few people recognize these issues as problems, but consider this analogy (from Ehrlich and Ehrlich 1981:xi–xii). An airplane is held together with thousands of rivets, each one attached to something else, all forming a complex system that keeps the plane from falling apart. What would you do if, just before the plane took off with you on it, you saw someone removing rivets from the wing? Would you just sit back and say, "Oh well, a few rivets don't matter"? As you watched rivets being removed one after another, you should have the very real fear that the wing will fall off and the plane will crash. Think not only of biological species (as in the Ehrlichs' metaphor) but also of other cultures and their adaptations as rivets.

Some things have improved. Today, there is a better understanding by the Western public of many environmental issues and a reduction in ethnocentrism

and racism. Groups such as Cultural Survival have been formed to help indigenous people. Conservation organizations are trying to save portions of ecosystems. Government efforts to improve the environment seem to have increased
through air quality acts, preservation of endangered ecosystems, and the like.
There is much more to do, but there is also reason for hope.

Many of the problems faced by Western groups are also faced by traditional
people. However, it is worse for them since it is *their* cultures that are threatened
with extinction, *their* homes destroyed, *their* lands taken, and *their* children dying. They also have to deal with issues such as global warming (particularly bad
for Arctic peoples because warming is faster and the results more dramatic
there), but only after they get out of the way of the bulldozer. Here we discuss
several of the major problems faced by all of us, but perhaps more directly by traditional peoples. Each of these issues is related in that they form much of the root
causes for many of the specific problems faced by traditional cultures.

THE TRAGEDY OF THE COMMONS

When short-term gain is sought at the expense of long-term return and an overexploitation of a resource results, a "**tragedy of the commons**" (Hardin 1968) occurs. In a tragedy of the commons situation, the resource would be owned by a
large group or not owned at all, resulting in unregulated use. If the resource was
valuable, there would be considerable pressure to exploit it as fast as possible so
as to maximize short-term returns. If only one player took that approach, all of
the others would be forced to join in and get theirs as fast as they could, before
the resource was gone. Thus, a free-for-all develops.

Persons with weak political power—the poor (as in most traditional cultures),
the young, and above all the unborn future generations—are at an enormous
disadvantage. So are downstream users—the upstream people get to pollute the
river unless the downstream users can sue or show force. The powerful, the rich,
and the upstream thus tend to win out, even if their use of the resource base is
suboptimal (Murphy 1967).

In a Tragedy of the Commons, no one can conserve the resource, no one has
the authority to protect it, and each person has to take as much as he or she can.
This leads to destruction of the resource base, because profits accrue to the most
predatory users. Where some try to preserve the resource, they get forced out of
the competition because the users get immediate profits and so prosper, while
the former forgo immediate profits and so go out of business. If those (the rich,
governments, and/or companies) with strictly short-term, cut-and-run interests

have the power, they are apt to destroy the resource, and a much greater long-term payoff is sacrificed (Daly 1993; also see Borgerhoff Mulder and Coppolillo 2005; Repetto 1992; Dove 1993a; Moran 1993a, 1993b, 1996, 2006, 2008).

Many tragedy of the commons examples can be cited, from the overlogging and overgrazing of public lands in the United States, to overfishing the Grand Banks of New England, to the destruction of the world's rainforests by mining, lumbering, ranching, and other activities (also see Tucker 2000). However, many resource crises are managed and planned. People trade off short-term profits against long-term stability and resilience. In these cases, governments and companies unite to exploit the resources; companies act out of very short-term interest and governments out of corruption and/or a need for cash. The common people are pushed out of the way, sometimes by force. Such planned tragedies now outnumber true tragedies of the commons. The latter are emergents, caused by lack of planning. In fact, as Hardin recognized (Hardin 1991), *managed* commons are often very well regulated.

One of the delusions, very important in environmental politics, is the "jobs versus trees" fallacy (Goodstein 1999). Clearly, cutting down all the forests and catching all the fish is bad for the economy in the long run. Even preserving aesthetic resources pays off, in tourism and increased property values.

A new field of social ecology (an aspect of political ecology) has been developed (Guha 1994), and considerable research on the management, or mismanagement, of resources is being conducted within political ecology (Stonich 1993; Alcorn and Molnar 1996; Sponsel et al. 1996a; Stonich and DeWalt 1996; Robbins 2004). Vayda (1996) discussed the complex causation of forestry management schemes on the ground in Indonesia, putting these political-ecological questions in a wider context.

The literature on preventing the tragedy of the commons is more extensive and has recently burgeoned, especially in regard to fisheries. Basically, it has been found that traditional fishermen from Anglo-Americans to Micronesians almost always specify the commons—that is, parcel them out on an ownership basis. "Sea tenure" has boomed as a field of study, just as land tenure did some years ago (see Johannes 1981; Ruddle and Akimichi 1984; Morrell 1985; McCay and Acheson 1987). Anderson and Anderson (1978) studied the opposite case, the breakdown and failure of a system.

AGRICULTURAL INVOLUTION

Clifford Geertz (1963; see White [1983] for critique; Huang [1990] for support using Chinese data), describing the agricultural system of central Java, coined the term **agricultural involution** to describe the pattern in which people work harder and harder to grow more and more on less and less land. In Java, he showed that colonialism was the cause; the Dutch forced peasants off the best land and created a labor demand that led to large families. The result was, of course, more people on less land (see case study 9.1). People were forced to work harder.

Involution is now generally defined as a rise in total production accompanied by a fall in per capita income—because of a rise in population and/or extraction of surplus value by outsiders. The extraction of this surplus sometimes means that the survival needs of the farmers are not met and a number of them starve to death every year.

Agricultural involution has occurred in traditional preindustrial societies suddenly shoved into the modern world (e.g., Indonesia and Mexico). Population increase and oppressive elites force people to work harder and harder, but in conditions of such extreme poverty that they cannot get ahead. Indeed, they tend to fall farther and farther behind, becoming even worse fed and more destitute. These pressures face traditional farmers all over the world.

AGRICULTURAL DEVELOPMENT AND INTENSIFICATION

Both the tragedy of the commons and agricultural involution result from development and intensification. One could view post-Ice Age human history as the history of agricultural intensification, and ecologists often quote Jonathan Swift to the effect that "whoever makes two blades of grass grow where one grew before is the greatest benefactor of man." Grass not only supports grazing animals but, of course, most of our staple foods are grasses—including wheat, corn, rice, and millets. This is because the seeds of grasses are unique in having a particularly efficient balance of starch, oil, and protein for human nutrition, and because they are easily storable and very easy to grow.

This intensification involves an enormous increase in capital and wealth, but no real improvement in the average human condition. A variety of agricultural systems currently exist, each the result of particular circumstances of land, crops, labor, and/or available technology. A variety of models are proposed to explain some general trends in the development of such systems.

Yujiro Hayami and Vernon Ruttan (1985) developed the best model yet, pointing out that people will always work on the part of the system that is of the highest cost. If land is scarce or expensive, people will work to increase the yield per acre. If land is easy to obtain but labor is scarce and thus expensive, people will invent labor-saving tools and machines. Hayami and Ruttan showed that East Asian agriculture developed with abundant labor and scarce land, and thus has achieved the maximum (in terms of balanced diet, though they did not say it that way) out of an acre using a fantastic labor input, while Western agriculture has developed in a world of abundant land (at least in the United States and other bigger countries) and scarce labor and so has concentrated on labor-saving machines. Some countries have both limited land and expensive labor, so they have done both (e.g., the Netherlands and Denmark). Conversely, areas with much land and cheap labor do not have to develop at all. This neatly predicts the observed facts about hunting-and-gathering and many traditional agricultural societies.

However, this model does not always work. There has to be a society willing to work for change (rather than, say, robbing the neighbors). Consider Haiti: very scarce land, but not much improvement in agriculture in five hundred years! Instead of changing the system to support the increased population, outside pressures and local poverty and corruption have led to the Haitian population becoming worse and worse off, to the point of starvation. However, other things being equal, agricultural societies do clearly target their efforts toward reducing the worst problems (or highest costs). The theory that Hayami and Ruttan developed from this insight is, in their terms, the theory of induced development: society induces development in the specific area of highest costs.

The theory of induced development can subsume previous theories, such as that of Boserup (1965) that population growth leads to agricultural intensification. Obviously, population growth does lead to agricultural intensification if society sees food as a limiting factor, has the capability to develop, and is willing to devote resources to development. Otherwise, population growth does not lead to intensification, as in the case of Haiti and other developing countries. In contrast, a society with a static population will intensify agriculture if there are other reasons to do so, such as a desire to increase sales of farm products, or an increase in ceremonial activity leading to greater need for ritual foods (Rappaport 1984). This sort of activity maintains the production of food in New Guinea societies, where agriculture is highly intensified in spite of sparse population, no markets, and no elites—just rituals compelling the people to produce food by means of a sustainable system (Rappaport [1984]; note the final part of this book, in which Rappaport addressed several criticisms of his theory and mechanism).

Current Trends

Agricultural productivity worldwide has increased dramatically over the past two hundred years. There was not much difference between the agriculture of Europe in 1700 and that of the Middle East five thousand years ago—at least not much by comparison with what came after, although the groundwork of the revolution was laid by 1700. Asia was far more advanced agriculturally in 1700, but by 1800 was falling behind, and by 1900 was underdeveloped. Today, Asia is catching up, but Latin America and Africa are still relatively less affluent. The agricultural changes were due to increased trade and commerce (and thus demand), new technological events stimulated by the same expansion of commerce, and other related factors.

The legacy in Europe and, increasingly, the whole world, is an agriculture that relies heavily on machines and land rather than human effort. In other words, capital and land are consumed, even squandered, while labor is conserved. This is due to the relatively high price of labor, although relative to other occupations, agricultural labor is notoriously poorly paid, not just in the United States but everywhere. In east Asia, agricultural innovation caused the price of labor to fall, because the new technologies allowed more people to be supported per acre and per unit of capital input. Thus, it became economical to substitute labor for land and capital.

The result is that a two-track agriculture has developed in the world. "Developed" agriculture uses far more energy and other capital-intensive input, overusing and polluting the land and leading to a rapid decline of the resource base—it is an agricultural system that is unsustainable. "Underdeveloped" agriculture tends to be labor intensive, low in production per worker, but more finetuned to local ecosystems. The two systems lead to and reinforce each other, thus, "the development of underdevelopment." In the extreme forms of this, the rich countries extract resources from the poor ones, so they (the rich) can use resources lavishly and impoverish the poor ones by terms of trade, forcing them to rely on unskilled, poorly paid labor. This is supported by a world system of international trade—the terms much in favor of the rich—and security that permits the repression of the poorer countries.

The richer socialist countries are not significantly better than the capitalist ones in their behavior. Indeed, the countries of the former Soviet Union are the world's great environmental disaster story, a cautionary tale for other countries (Feshbach and Friendly 1992). Ecologically, the deforestation, soil erosion, mining of water resources, exhaustion of genetic stocks as crops become more homogeneous, and buildup of pests that are resistant to current pesticides are now proceeding so rapidly that total ruin of the world's intensive agriculture, and return of the world to an essentially medieval agriculture, is now a real possibility.

Hope for the future lies in developing a way to use the traditional techniques, as well as all the new ones we can find, that are sustainable and that do not massively destroy the environment. Most traditional techniques are sustainable, or they would never have become traditional, though there are some very important exceptions. For example, overgrazing in the Middle East has been endemic and disastrous for some eight thousand years! We must learn and apply all we can, now, before it is too late (e.g., Wilken 1987).

THE RAINFOREST DILEMMA

One of the most serious ecological problems of the world in recent decades has been the disappearance of forests (Williams 2003), and especially tropical rainforests (see Richards and Tucker 1988; Anderson 1990; Croll and Parkin 1992; Moran 1993a, 1993b; Stonich 1993; Sponsel et al. 1996b; Tucker 2000). The destruction of rainforest has reached levels that can only be described as catastrophic. We will thus use it as an example of the problems facing the world today.

Rainforests cover about 16 percent of the earth but are enormously diverse and rich in life; they are home to perhaps 50 percent of all species. The loss of rainforest is not limited to just species, but to entire ecosystems that are very difficult, if not impossible, to reconstitute. Small-scale plots such as slash-and-burn fields are easily grown over by forest with little permanent damage, but large-scale deforestation results in the forest being segmented such that the necessary colonizing species are too far apart to successfully interact and regrow the forest. In past centuries, destruction of tropical forests has occurred on a local scale, as, for instance, in some of the lands of classic societies like the Maya and Khmer. What is new is the rate of clearance.

Until recently, the forests were protected by barriers of disease, remoteness, and the sheer difficulty of clearing. Today, diseases that once frightened people away from the forests can be controlled and the technology of clearing has changed from axes to chainsaws and bulldozers. This has produced something of a pioneer attitude in most of the world. Like the early European settlers of the United States (and even the early people of much of Polynesia [see Kirch 1994, 1997; Meilleur 1996]), local and international interests alike are rushing to clear the tropics with little thought of the future. Before the mid-twenty-first century, all old-growth tropical forest not specifically reserved will be gone.

Issues

The destruction of tropical rainforests is a serious problem for several reasons. First, and most obvious, most of these forests could support long-term exploitation that would produce far more revenue than do the farms and ranches that replace them (a tragedy of the commons). Most groups living in forests have shaped the forest to some degree as a result of their long-term management (e.g., Anderson 1990; Balée 1994) and have often created a fine-tuned, well-managed landscape capable of sustained yield. Even with increased exploitation, forests could still be managed for sustainable yields (Cooke 1999; Robinson and Bennett 2000).

Second, tropical forests produce a large number of products, including food (e.g., Pimentel et al. 1997). One important product is hardwoods, often worth hundreds of dollars per cubic meter. If these woods were selectively harvested rather than clearcut, the forest could produce hardwoods for centuries to come. Countless nontimber forest products could be harvested sustainably (Plotkin and Famolare 1992). These include such things as rattans (tough palm vines used for furniture and baskets), honey, medicinal plants, game meat for local inhabitants, poles for local construction, wild and semiwild fruit and nuts, and ornamental plants for the nursery trade. These, however, cannot replace high-quality timber in most economic situations; they merely add to other reasons to preserve the forest ecosystem.

Third, forests provide watershed and soil protection. Many tropical soils, stripped of their forest cover, dry out and become very hard and difficult to cultivate. Other soils wash away quickly or, due to chemical changes, become too acidic to grow much useful new cover. It is also possible that deforestation reduces rainfall downwind.

Fourth, deforestation releases massive amounts of greenhouse gases, as the trees are burned or allowed to decay. This has been a factor in global warming, producing about 20 percent of the excess carbon, although fossil fuels are a more serious cause.

Fifth, tropical forests are very diverse ecosystems. They hold literally millions of species of animals, plants, fungi, molds, bacteria, and algae. Few of these species have been adequately studied, and many of them have enormous potential as medicines (Plotkin 2000). For example, our most powerful antibiotics—penicillin, chloromycin, and the like—are derived from molds, and many of the few rainforest molds that have been studied also show antibiotic properties. Literally tens of thousands of tropical plants have been reported to have medicinal effect. Thousands have been examined, and many have already produced valuable drugs, ranging from quinine and caffeine to the new cancer drugs (e.g., Plotkin 2000). Other tropical species have enormous potential for producing food, fiber, oil, fuel, and other commodities. But even the less obviously useful tropical species provide such an incredible wealth of beauty, interest, genetic potential, and evolutionary possibility that there are more than adequate reasons for saving them.

Sixth, and perhaps the most serious of all to anthropologists, the tropical forests are home to many hundreds of cultural and ethnic groups whose lives revolve around using the forests in some way. These groups range from bands of scattered hunter-gatherers to the huge, stable, ancient states of the Maya and Khmer. Many groups have been deprived of their forests in recent years. All too many of these groups have suffered from cultural and personal collapse. It is psychologically devastating to any group, be it a group of hunter-gatherers or the workers of an industrial city, to be suddenly deprived of its livelihood and its way of life. Small groups, impoverished by loss of their forest resources, have great difficulty in adjusting to a new world—especially if that world is openly hostile to them and their interests.

Loss of the forests would then be a tragedy for their inhabitants and for all of us. The effects on climate, food production, medicine development, and hydrology, taken together, would amount to a worldwide catastrophe far worse than any ecological crisis that humanity has endured so far.

The Dilemma

The forests have been cleared for a number of reasons, but primarily due to an expansion of grazing and agriculture. Broadly speaking, there are three patterns. First, extensive but not intensive cattle ranching has been the major cause of deforestation in many areas (Downing et al. 1992; Painter and Durham 1995). This often involves clearing the forest, planting grass, and running a few scrub cattle worth far less than the timber wasted in the clearing process. In other situations, with better soil and better facilities, viable ranches with quality stock can be developed, but even in these cases one doubts whether the cattle are worth as much as the forest was.

Second, contemporary commercial agriculture, usually oriented toward export to rich temperate-zone countries, has replaced forests in much of the world. The tropics supply the world's coffee, chocolate, rubber, palm and palm-kernel oil, coconut oil, and bananas plus countless species of specialty fruit. They produce much of the tea, citrus fruit, and rice that enters international trade. On a darker note, the New World montane tropics produce the world's cocaine, and opium flourishes in many tropical and subtropical highlands.

In some areas, wood is the most important of these products. For centuries, forests have been selectively cut for valuable woods, but now whole forests are being clearcut—often for pulpwood, fuel, or cheap throwaway uses such as chopsticks or temporary construction siding. Mining and oil extraction are also local problems of consequence (Rudel 2005).

Third, and the most morally difficult to deal with, is the huge increase in the number of people using slash-and-burn cultivation in the forest to support themselves. Until recently, most of the real tropics were too sparsely populated for this to be a major problem. The relatively few people living in those areas utilized a sustainable swidden system and made little significant impact on the forest. However, recent population growth in developing countries and the migration of unemployed city workers to farms has led to shortening of, and then the elimination of, the swidden cycles. Now, so many people are using slash-and-burn that there is not enough land to lie fallow for eventual reuse. Instead, the field is abandoned and the family moves on to the next patch of forest, with no thought or intention of returning. Like a wave moving across a lake, the forest is cut, farmed for a year or two, abandoned, and a new field cut, leaving nothing but abandoned fields in its wake. Eventually, deforestation, weed invasion, and erosion leads to total ruin of the landscape. Eroded hills, covered with almost impenetrable tangles of worthless grass and brush, replace former forest. Some level lands with relatively fertile soils can be salvaged after years under grass (Dove 1981), but most lands cannot.

The problem is human. The poor farmers have little choice but to continue their farming, however destructive it is in the long term. They have to feed their families now. One cannot just tell them not to farm without providing some alternative way to make a living. Peasants who see their children starving are going to do anything to get land and food—now. This problem is real and serious, especially in densely populated areas like Southeast Asia, but even there its role has been exaggerated (Dove 1993a). In more lightly populated areas such as the Brazilian Amazon, it is less important than corporate and large-scale projects.

A Tragedy of the Commons

One wonders why people destroy million-dollar forests for ten-dollar cows (Painter and Durham 1995). On the whole, there is an economic rationale behind this: the million-dollar return is very slow in coming, but the ten dollars are there now. Sustainable selective cutting of valuable woods produces a steady but modest stream of income, but destroying the forest for quick profit produces more in the short run. If people are in no position to reap the long-run benefits, they will opt for the short term.

The biggest problem of all seems to be the short-term philosophies of many governments and multinational bodies. Multinational firms and international organizations are less than rational: they want results *now*, whether for their stockholders or for press releases to backers back home. The predatory instincts of multinational firms are well known but are often exacerbated by local tax systems and other institutions that virtually force the firms to destroy (Ascher 1999). Stonich (1993; Stonich and DeWalt 1996) has meticulously documented the ways in which government policies and large landlord politics continue to force peasants in Honduras to cut and burn against their better judgment. Probably all anthropologists who have worked in the forested tropics have similar stories. Thus, the old question of whether "the rich" or "the poor peasants" are the worst offenders in clearing the forests is not very useful to ask. We have learned that the poor peasants often are driven to act because of forces unleashed by the powerful. These forces may be simple and straightforward: if the powerful have seized all the good land, the peasants have to do what they can. Or the problems may be much more complex: international coffee-pricing policies, and the response of the Mexican government to these, have affected the smallholder coffee economy of Mexico in negative ways (E. N. Anderson, personal research; Jan Rus, personal communication 1999). There are also market failures. Cattle are easy to sell—the marketing system is there. Local woods and nontimber forest products are not so well marketed. A lack of marketing expertise is possibly the worst single problem for small-scale sustainable production in the tropics.

Perhaps this is understandable in the case of politicians, who may be looking ahead only to the next election or military coup. However, economic theory suggests that large landlords and politicians should be more concerned with long-term profits. They have enough wealth to allow them to look to the long term, and they should be interested in maximizing their overall wealth, not their immediate advantage.

Indeed, many of them are, but others are interested only in making a quick killing and then retiring to enjoy a genteel lifestyle. Still others may simply not understand what they could do with their forests. While indigenous people have an enormous knowledge of forest products, the immigrants often know nothing at all about the forest and thus see nothing better to do with it than clear it for cattle.

Moreover, much of the worst devastation of the tropics has been done by (theoretically) well-meaning international aid organizations, who clear land for pasture, build dams, and otherwise ravage the landscape without needing to concern themselves with the cost-benefit ratios of the projects in question. They have acted from mistaken charity or from a genuine commitment to "progress," or, in some cases, just to show that they are busy. Often, the projects are economically irrational.

In Quintana Roo, Mexico, site of E. N. Anderson's recent research, the government has blown hot and cold. On the one hand, Anderson was shown a huge tract of land that had been cleared by the government to "open up land for cultivation." The government had deforested a very dry tract, scraped off the topsoil in the process, and then left it to the local villagers—and all this without providing any water! Twenty years later, the land was still a desert, and no one could figure out any use for it. On the other hand, and more recently, the state and federal governments have cooperated on some truly exemplary plans for sustainable forest management, local reserves, and wildlife protection. These plans are real models for the world, and one can only hope they succeed (Kiernan and Freese 1997; Flachsenberg and Galletti 1998; Galletti 1998).

Protecting local people from dispossession of their land by multinational mining or logging companies, or by commercial farmers and ranchers, has proved difficult. The multinationals, in particular, have vastly more money and political influence than do small local groups of forest hunters or farmers. In several cases, perhaps especially tragic, local groups have been displaced to create national parks and reserves to "conserve" the forest (Harper 2002; West et al. 2006). Conservation of the forest can thus seriously impact local people, who may have strong proforest and proconservation sentiments but still be unable to deal with large-scale displacement by conservation agencies unsympathetic to their immediate needs. Paige West (2006) not only raised the problem for New Guinea, but usefully quoted long and detailed statements by the people themselves, showing these mixed emotions.

Fortunately, most conservation bodies are now aware that if a group has been using and managing a forest for several thousand years, throwing it off the land is more apt to destroy the forest ecosystem than to preserve it (e.g., Western and Wright 1994).

Alternatives to deforestation have often been proposed (e.g., A. Anderson 1990; Committee on Sustainable Agriculture and the Environment in the Humid Tropics 1993; Dove 1993b). These include forest farming of various kinds, often with native tree crops. However, while these may preserve the structure of the forest and thus save the soil, planting too many trees of the same species could destroy almost as much biodiversity as clearcutting does. The same can be said for the hopeful regrowth of forest in much of the Amazon (Moran 1993a, 1993b). It was feared that the cutting of the Amazon forests would lead to total desertification. This has not yet occurred; much land has gone out of production and has been rapidly reclaimed by forest. Unfortunately, the new second-growth forest has only a tiny fraction of the biodiversity of the original high forest.

Sustainable logging for selected valuable woods remains the best option in many areas and is correspondingly the most widespread option currently. However, it, too, is damaging too many animals. Reforestation, successful in much of the temperate zone and dramatically so in Korea (e.g., Choe 1994), has been less successful in the tropics. The better-quality tropical trees grow slowly; the forest habitat recovers even more slowly. Soil degrades in the process and may take centuries to recover.

In practice, reserves—with traditional management firmly in place, where appropriate—are necessary and will be increasingly necessary in the future. It has been repeatedly pointed out that because the tropical forest is a world resource, the world community must pay to save it.

Tropical forest nations are often among the poorest in the world and cannot shoulder all of the burden. The World Wildlife Fund, Nature Conservancy, Conservation International, the Rainforest Alliance, Cultural Survival, and other nongovernmental organizations (NGOs) interested in conservation have spearheaded the resulting multipronged attempt to unite the world community in saving what is probably its most valuable ecosystem. Cultural Survival has been particularly concerned about indigenous peoples and their problems and interests. Other NGOs have been sensitive to varying degrees to this concern, but most have rapidly improved their awareness—and consequently their behavior—in recent years.

The situation would be cautiously hopeful were it not for the runaway population growth in the tropics and the runaway growth of markets for some tropical products in the rest of the world. As it is, the sheer pressure of needs and wants is increasing so fast that almost no one can plan comprehensively for the long term.

The above is not to be taken as implying that only the tropics face deforestation problems. Destruction of old-growth forests is progressing as fast in the United States and Canada as it is in most tropical countries (see Tucker 2000). This is doubly unpardonable. These rich nations do not need to destroy their resource futures. Moreover, most of the wood they produce is exported, cheaply, to countries that make expensive products from it and thereby reap almost all the profits. Tropical countries often note, pointedly, that at least their forests are being destroyed to feed starving people.

THE GENERAL PROBLEM
In essentially all conceivable cases of resource use, society must deliberately intervene to protect the long-term, wide interests and thus optimize resource use

(while protecting indigenous rights). This can be done legally, via suits and standing to sue, property rights, or conservation laws and enforcement; it can be done politically (via vote or equivalent); it can be done through religion, by cultivating an ethical system that is highly conservationist. In practice these must all be invoked.

Moreover, there has to be education, information flow, research, and communication—in short, knowledge has to be shared. People have to know what their interest really is and be able to make key decisions on the basis of the information they have.

The contemporary world fails at two levels. First, we simply do not have an adequate institutional framework to deal with our rapidly increasing ability to wreck the environment. Second, we are failing more and more at treating the poor, the weak, and the downstream users fairly. Thus, we can profit from examining resource management cross-culturally. Traditional people know a wide range of tactics from which we can learn; and more generally, the comparison will show us what problems are universal and what solutions are most widespread. Research in this, especially into the question of how knowledge is shared and passed on, is only beginning.

Considerable recent work turns on simple matters of what is done that effectively manages resources. Marten (1986) provided a major review of how traditional farmers in southeast Asia manage trees, soil, pests, and other things. Local studies that cover similar ground include Conklin (1957), Stuart (1978), Alcorn (1984), and many others. These address to some extent the question of what is done, how, and why. Special topics include a diversity, from crops that extend the range of cultivation (Harlan 1992) to fire and its role, and the costs of fire suppression in natural brushlands (Minnich 1983). An excellent study of education for traditional food procurement was conducted by Ruddle and Chesterfield (1977).

Literature on common property resource management has expanded greatly in recent years (Conference on Common Property Resource Management 1986; Alberta Society of Professional Biologists 1988; Libecap 1989; Ostrom 1990; Hardin 1991; Oldfield and Alcorn 1987). It now appears that communities can be expected to regulate their resources unless pressures are too numerous or uncontrollable (Burton 1992; also see Ostrom 1990). Management must be carefully tuned, however, to allow maximum local management (Pinkerton 1989). Excessive top-down control that alienates control from the people on the ground is a virtual guarantee of failure and is probably the reason for the breakdown of the world environment recently (Pinkerton 1989; Anderson and Burton 1992).

On the other hand, there must be centralized goal setting. Also, some problems are now worldwide and must be handled on a worldwide basis, which makes the question of community a challenging one (Burton 1992).

Religion was the standard carrier of environmental morality in earlier societies (Anderson 1996; Berkes 1999; Grim 2001; Tiedje and Snodgrass 2008). It still has this virtue in many areas, but religion has lost much ground in this regard, either to secularization or to extremism that sees religion as solely about hatred and conflict. Environmentalists need to find a vehicle for wider social morality that will persuade people to balance human needs against the environment's capacity to satisfy those over time.

The world now has no true wilderness left; all areas, even the Antarctic ice sheet, are occupied and being profoundly transformed by humans. Thus, Daniel Janzen (1998) advocated facing the fact that the world is a garden and that we must therefore treat it as a garden—taking care of it and using it wisely, rather than either preserving it "unaffected by humans"—now a futile effort—or using it destructively and irresponsibly. The slippery concept of sustainability becomes more manageable if viewed this way; we can treat the world as a garden, providing food, fiber, shelter, health, recreation, and beauty.

Needed now are studies of traditional agriculture comparable to those of contemporary developing world agriculture (e.g., Ghai et al. 1979; Hopkins et al. 1979). Some anthropological research related to this approach covers marketing (e.g., Halperin and Dow 1977), nutritional effects of poorly planned modernization (e.g., Bryant et al. 2003), sexual division of labor in agriculture (e.g., Burton and White 1984), the different responses to contemporary stress by traditional groups (e.g., Hayami and Kikuchi 1981), problems of agricultural intensification (Geertz 1984; White 1983), and much more.

In a world where there is plenty of food and many chances for expanding the supply (Avery 1985), there is no excuse for the worldwide poverty, hunger, and waste we actually observe (Brown 1981). The explanation for mismanagement is clearly social, not technological. Thus, studies of how people actually decide what to do have grown apace.

CHAPTER SUMMARY

We all face the challenges of a changing natural and cultural environment. The way individual groups confront and address issues ultimately impacts everyone to some degree. Problems such as the tragedy of the commons, agricultural involution, agricultural intensification, and deforestation should be the concern of everyone.

If there is any truth in the findings of cultural ecology, it is that religion and symbolism greatly inform human uses of the environment (Anderson 1996). People preserve their environment for aesthetic and moral reasons as well as for narrowly economic ones. Insofar as this is the case, we need to study traditional conservation and resource management. We have a great deal to learn—not only about how to manage the earth, but about how to motivate other people to manage the earth better. At best, we will learn from one another. At worst, even the most cursory study of cultural ecology will open our minds to the fact that there are many different ways to see the world.

KEY TERMS
agricultural involution
tragedy of the commons

Glossary

abiotic that part of the ecosystem that is not biological in origin, such as water, minerals, and land forms

active environmental manipulation the purposeful, physical alteration of groups of species and of ecosystems on a large scale

active resource management physical management or control of resources to maintain and/or increase productivity

adaptation modification of the body, species, or culture in response to changing environmental conditions

agricultural involution a pattern in which people work harder and harder to grow more and more on less and less land

anatomical adaptations long-term changes in genotype and phenotype through natural selection

animal husbandry the herding, breeding, consumption, and use of domesticated animals

anthropogenic human-caused, for example, changes in the environment

anthropology the study of humans (biology, culture, language, past and present, etc.)

archaeoastronomy the study of the astronomy of past groups

band a small-scale society without formal leaders; the family is the primary sociopolitical and economic unit

Bergmann's Rule states that body shape is influenced by temperature: surface area to mass ratio for heat retention (short and stocky in cold climates; tall and lean in hot climates)

biodiversity the number and dominance of species present in an ecosystem

biomass the quantity (mass) of living matter within a specified area

biome a large, general, easily defined environmental zone (e.g., rainforest or grassland)

biosphere the global environment and interacting ecosystems

biotic that part of the ecosystem that is biological in origin (plants, animals, etc.)

boom and bust cycle increases in population that exceed the food supply, resulting in a rapid loss of population

browsers animals whose food consists mainly of the foliage of bushes and trees

calorie unit of energy (in food); one calorie is the energy needed to raise the temperature of one gram of water one degree centigrade

carbohydrates compounds in foods, including sugars, starches, and cellulose

carnivore a species that is primarily a meat eater

carrying capacity a measure of the maximum number of individuals of a particular species that can be supported within a specific ecosystem for a specific time

central place foraging an optimization model that assumed that a group stays in one central place, with specialized task teams traveling to the resources

chiefdom a society with a relatively large population, permanent settlements, some central authority, and a stratified social structure, but no formal state institutions

chinampa a small field constructed within or on a body of water

cognition the way in which information from the senses is processed and interpreted, including classification systems, decision making, and planning

collectors a classification of hunter-gatherer groups where the group is oriented toward moving resources to the people. Collector groups are typically viewed as being larger and more sedentary than foragers.

cultural ecology the study of the cultural aspects of human interaction with the environment

cultural materialism a practical, rather simplistic functionalist approach to anthropology, with a focus on the specific hows and whys of culture

cultural relativism the study of culture without any attempt to show scientifically that one is "better" than another; cultures are interpreted nonjudgmentally

culture learned and shared behavior in humans

a [specific] culture a group of humans who share a common set of traits and (usually) identify themselves as a group separate from other groups

culture area a geographic region where environment and cultures are similar

currency a quantifiable unit of measure of cost and benefit used in optimization models

diet breadth model an optimization model that predicts the order in which resources (foods) will be added to the diet

domestication a process by which organisms and/or landscapes are controlled; in agriculture, domestication means that the genetic makeup of an organism is purposefully altered by humans to their advantage

dry farming the production of crops relying only on rainfall to water the crops

ecology the study of the interactions between organism(s) and its (their) environment

ecosystem a bounded community (or communities) that includes both abiotic (basic elements) and biotic (producers and heterotrophs) components and that is tied together in a system

ecotone the intersection of, and transition between, two ecozones, usually a more productive place than either of the ecozones

ecozone an area defined by biotic communities and/or geographic criteria (short for environmental zone)

empirical science knowledge system based on tangible data observable by other scientists ("hard" data, testable, reproducible)

environment the surroundings within which an organism interacts

environmental determinism the view that the environment dictates what a culture must do and how it must adapt

environmental manipulation large-scale alteration of the environment by people to effect changes to the advantage of the culture

environmental zone (see **ecozone**) an area defined by biotic communities and/or geographic criteria

ethnobiology the classification and knowledge of materials of biological origin (plants and animals) by a traditional culture

ethnobotany the classification, knowledge, and use of plants by a traditional culture

ethnocentrism the view that one's own group is superior to other groups

ethnoecology the classification of the various components of the natural world, including both the abiotic (geography, astronomy, soils, etc.) and the biotic (botany, zoology, etc.), by a traditional culture

ethnography the study of a particular group at a particular time

ethnology the comparative study of culture

ethnomedicine knowledge and materials used by a traditional culture for medical purposes

ethnopharmacology the classification, knowledge, and use of materials (plants, animals, and other substances) of a traditional culture for medical or other nondietary purposes

ethnoscience knowledge system (empirical and/or nonempirical) of a traditional culture

ethnozoology the knowledge, use, and significance of animals by a traditional culture

evolution change over time (specific disciplines have more specific definitions)

evolutionary ecology any evolutionary thinking about ecology, but commonly defined as an analytical approach that presumes that cultures behave as biological organisms do, that natural selection processes act on them, and that they adapt and evolve as organisms do

fat lipids that store energy within the body of an organism

feng-shui the Chinese science of proper arrangement of elements in a landscape to ensure harmony

fission-fusion the splitting of a larger group into smaller ones, which later rejoin to reform the original larger group. Fission-fusion may occur for a variety of reasons, including as part of a seasonal round.

food chain the flow of nutrients through trophic levels; the sequence of which organism is consuming which

food web food chains linked together by some common thread

foragers hunter-gatherer groups in which the group is oriented toward moving people to resources. Forager groups are typically viewed as being smaller and more mobile than collectors.

garden a small agricultural plot, tilled by hand

gathering the collection of relatively small and nonmobile resources, such as wild plants, small land fauna, and shellfish

grazers animals whose food consists mainly of grasses and other low-growing plants

habitat the place an organism lives; where its niche is located geographically in the environment

herbivore plant eater; some species may be specialized, for example, fruit eaters (frugivores)

herdsman husbandry a pastoral technique used as a component of an agricultural system, where most members of the group are sedentary agriculturalists but some animals are raised at distant pastures tended by herdsmen

horticulture low-intensity agriculture involving relatively small-scale fields, plots, and gardens; food raised primarily for personal consumption rather than for trade or a central authority

human biological ecology the study of the biological adaptations of humans to their environment

human ecology the broad field of study of human interaction with the environment

hunters and gatherers groups that make their *primary* living from the exploitation of wild foods

hunting actively looking for, killing, butchering, and consuming animals

intensive agriculture large-scale agriculture often involving the use of animal labor, equipment, and water diversion techniques

irrigation the purposeful diversion of water from its natural course onto agricultural fields

Liebig's Law of the Minimum the law that states that some condition or resource will limit carrying capacity (a.k.a. the Convoy Principle)

life expectancy a measure of the average age at death of all the people who died in a particular year

linear programming a mathematical technique of calculating the optimal allocation of resources toward a defined goal in the face of multiple constraints

milch pastoralism the production of milk as the major pastoral product

minerals inorganic substances needed by the body for combination with organic compounds

monoculture primary use of a single species of domesticated plant in a field

multilinear cultural evolution the evolution of cultures along many lines

mutualism a relatiohsip between two species in which they both directly benefit

neoevolution a revival of nineteenth-century unilineal cultural evolution

new ecology the idea that human cultures formed only one of the population units interacting in the environment, placing humans within a unified science of ecology

niche the role an organism plays in the environment; what it eats, where it lives, and how it reproduces

nomads another term for pastoralists

nomadic pastoralism the type of pastoralism where groups are small, mobile, and completely dependent on their animals

nutrition materials needed by the body for proper operation

omnivore species that have very broad diets and can eat a wide variety of foods, animal and plant

optimization the process of getting the best return for the investment made, using resources as efficiently as possible to accomplish goals

optimization models models used to explain some aspects of behavior related to the utilization of resources

passive environmental manipulation nonphysical (e.g., ritual) activities designed to maintain and control the environment

passive resource management nonphysical (e.g., ritual) management or control of resources (often abiotic) to maintain and/or increase productivity

pastoralism the herding, breeding, consumption, and use of managed or domesticated animals, to the general exclusion of plants

patch choice model an optimization model that predicts the order in which patches of resources (foods) will be utilized

permaculture permanent, sustainable agriculture involving complex systems with many species

physiological adaptations short-term biological changes in the body as a result of adaptation, for example, the development of a tan to protect the skin from ultraviolet radiation

political ecology the study of the day-to-day conflicts, alliances, and negotiations that ultimately result in some sort of definitive behavior; how politics affects or structures resource use

polyculture planting multiple domesticated species in a field (thereby increasing diversity)

possibilism the idea that a variety of solutions are present in any environment and that a culture chooses a solution(s) best suited to it

postmodermism a paradigm that holds that human cultural behavior is essentially arbitrary and so can be interpreted in any number of arbitrary ways

protein a complex combination of amino acids, required by the body for its constituent amino acids

rational choice theory a theory that asserts that people decide how to achieve their goals on the basis of deliberate, individual consideration of all available information, and that they are good calculators of their chances

refugia a surviving remnant of a past biome

resource something used by an organism; may be either renewable or nonrenewable

resource management the small-scale alteration of specific resources to effect changes to the advantage of the culture (see active and passive resource management)

resource monitoring the visitation of resource locations to determine present and future conditions

resource universe the resources that were available and utilized by the group being studied using optimization models

scavenging the act of obtaining animals that are already dead

seasonal round a system of movement of people and/or resources about the landscape based on the seasonal availability of resources and their geographic location

seasonal transhumance the seasonal movement of herders and their animals from pasture to pasture while the rest of the population stays in one place; the term is sometimes applied to hunter-gatherers to describe a seasonal round

sedentary living in one place all the time

sedentary animal husbandry a pastoral technique used as a component of an agricultural system, where full-time farmers will also raise some animals in and around their farms. Examples include modern dairy farming and cattle feedlots.

seminomadic pastoralism the type of pastoralism where animals are moved from pasture to pasture but some horticulture may be practiced to supplement the animal products. This is the most common form of pastoralism.

semisedentary pastoralism the type of pastoralism where some members of the group move around seasonally with their animals, but horticulture forms an important aspect of the economy

silviculture agriculture emphasizing tree crops

slash-and-burn a horticultural technique involving the cutting, drying, and burning of natural vegetation from a small plot and planting crops in the field. The field quickly loses its agricultural productivity and another plot must be processed. Sometimes called "shifting cultivation."

state a society with a large population, complex social and political structures, complex record keeping, urban centers (cities), central authority, monumental architecture, specialization, and the legal control of the use of force

stewardship having responsibility for maintaining a resource; being a guardian

storage taking some resource and saving it for later use

strategy an overall plan to achieve a long-term goal; in the context of this book, an overall subsistence system such as hunting and gathering

stress a condition that forces change in a system

subsistence a complex system that includes resources, technology, social and political organizations, settlement patterns, and all of the other aspects of making a living

succession patterned, developmental change in a plant community as it evolves to maturity

swidden system a sustainable horticultural system involving the rotation of fields where slash-and-burn is the primary technique used

symbiotic a long-term, dependent relationship between two species

tactics methods or techniques used to accomplish a goal; the action component of a strategy

tethered nomadism a pastoral group whose seasonal round is limited within a well-defined territory

tether a restriction due to the distribution of a resource, for example, having to stay within a certain walking distance of a spring

tragedy of the commons the tendency of people to overuse a common-pool resource because there is an incentive to use but no way to enforce conservation; a user can overuse without cost, but if the user foregoes consumption others merely expand their take, thus eliminating any benefit to conserving

tribe a society with a relatively large population, a number of villages, and leaders (chiefs) with some actual power

trophic pyramid a description of the levels of relationship between producers, heterotrophs, and decomposers: what is eaten and how many conversions from solar energy have taken place

unilinear cultural evolution the theory that cultures evolved upward along a single line

vitamins organic compounds used by the body to maintain certain functions, but not manufactured by the body and so must be present in food

References

Abrams, Elliot M., and David J. Rue

    1988   The Causes and Consequences of Deforestation Among the Prehistoric Maya. Human Ecology 16(4):377–395.

Adams, Charles C.

    1935   The Relation of General Ecology to Human Ecology. Ecology 16(3):316–335.

Adams, Robert McC.

    1966   The Evolution of Urban Society. Chicago: Aldine.

    2001   Complexity in Archaic States. Journal of Anthropological Archaeology 20(3):345–360.

Agrawal, Arun

    2005   Environmentality: Technologies of Government and the Making of Subjects. Durham, NC: Duke University Press.

Alberta Society of Professional Biologists

    1988   Native People and Renewable Resource Management (symposium volume). Edmonton: Author.

Alcorn, Janis B.

    1984   Huastec Mayan Ethnobotany. Austin: University of Texas Press.

Alcorn, Janis B., and Augusta Molnar

    1996   Deforestation and Human-Forest Relationships: What Can We Learn from India? In: Tropical Deforestation: The Human Dimension. Leslie E. Sponsel, Thomas N. Headland, and Robert C. Bailey, eds., pp. 99–121. New York: Columbia University Press.

Anderson, Anthony B. (ed.)

    1990   Alternatives to Deforestation. New York: Columbia University Press.

Anderson, E. N.

    1972   The Life and Culture of Ecotopia. In: Reinventing Anthropology. Dell Hymes, ed., pp. 264–283. New York: Pantheon Press,.

    1988   The Food of China. New Haven, CT: Yale University Press.

    1996   Ecologies of the Heart. New York: Oxford University Press.

2000   Is It All Politics? Political Ecology within Human Ecology. Paper presented at the annual meetings of the American Anthropological Association, San Francisco, CA.

2005a   Everyone Eats. New York: New York University Press.

2005b   Political Ecology in a Yucatec Maya Community. Tucson: University of Arizona Press.

Anderson, E. N., and Marja Anderson

1973   Mountains and Water: The Cultural Ecology of South Coastal China. Taipei: Orient Cultural Service.

1978   Fishing in Troubled Waters. Taipei: Orient Cultural Service.

Anderson, E. N., and Sharon Burton

1992   Tragedies of the Commons: Malaysia. Paper presented at the Pacific Coast Division, American Association for the Advancement of Science, Santa Barbara, CA.

Anderson, E. N., and Felix Medina Tzuc

2005   Animals and the Maya in Southeast Mexico. Tucson: University of Arizona Press.

Anderson, Leslie

1994   The Political Ecology of the Modern Peasant: Calculation and Community. Baltimore: Johns Hopkins University Press.

Anderson, M. Kat

1999   The Fire, Pruning, and Coppice Management of Temperate Ecosystems for Basketry Material by California Indian Tribes. Human Ecology 27(1):79–113.

2005   Tending the Wild: Native American Knowledge and the Management of California's Natural Resources. Berkeley: University of California Press.

Arens, William

1979   The Man-Eating Myth: Anthropology and Anthropophagy. New York: Oxford University Press.

Arima, Eugene, and John Dewhirst

1990   Nootkans of Vancouver Island. In: Handbook of North American Indians, Vol. 7, Northwest Coast. Wayne Suttles, ed., pp. 391–411. Washington, DC: Smithsonian Institution Press.

Ascher, William

1999   Why Governments Waste Natural Resources. Baltimore: Johns Hopkins University Press.

Ashmore, Wendy

2004   Social Archaeologies of Landscape. In: A Companion to Social Archaeology. Lynn Meskell and Robert Preucel, eds., pp. 255–271. Oxford: Blackwell.

Askenasy, Hans

1994   Cannibalism: From Sacrifice to Survival. Amherst, NY: Prometheus Books.

Atran, Scott

1993   Itza Maya Tropical Agro-Forestry. Current Anthropology 34(5):633–700.

Aveni, Anthony

1993   Ancestral Astronomers. Washington, DC: Smithsonian Institution Press.

Avery, Dennis

1985   U.S. Farm Dilemma: The Global Bad News Is Wrong. Science 230:408–412.

Bailey, Robert C.
    1991   The Behavioral Ecology of Efe Pygmy Men in the Ituri Forest, Zaire. University of
            Michigan, Museum of Anthropology, Anthropological Papers No. 86.
Bailey, Robert C., Genevieve Head, Mark Jenike, Bruce Owen, Robert Rechtman, and Elzbieta
Zechenter
    1989   Hunters and Gatherers in Tropical Rain Forests: Is It Possible? American
            Anthropologist 91(1):59–82.
Balée, William (ed.)
    1998a   Advances in Historical Ecology. New York: Columbia University Press.
Balée, William
    1994   Footprints of the Forest. New York: Columbia University Press.
    1998b   Historical Ecology: Premises and Postulates. In: Advances in Historical Ecology.
            William Balée, ed., pp. 13–29. New York: Columbia University Press.
    1998c   Introduction. In: Advances in Historical Ecology. William Balée, ed., pp. 1–10.
            New York: Columbia University Press.
    2006   The Research Program of Historical Ecology. Annual Review of Anthropology
            35:75–98.
Bar-Yosef, Ofer, and Richard H. Meadow
    1995   The Origins of Agriculture in the Near East. In: Last Hunters—First Farmers: New
            Perspectives on the Prehistoric Transition to Agriculture. T. Douglas Price and
            Anne Birgitte Gebauer, eds., pp. 39–94. Santa Fe: School of American Research
            Press.
Barker, Graeme
    2006   The Agricultural Revolution in Prehistory. Oxford: Oxford University Press.
Barkow, Jerome, Leda Cosmides, and John Tooby
    1992   The Adapted Mind. New York: Oxford University Press.
Barth, Fredrik
    1956   Ecological Relationships of Ethnic Groups in Swat, Northern Pakistan. American
            Anthropologist 58(6):1079–1099.
    1964   Nomads of South Persia: The Basseri Tribe of the Khamseh Confederacy. Oslo:
            Universitetsforlaget.
Bates, Daniel G.
    1971   The Role of the State in Peasant-Nomad Mutualism. Anthropological Quarterly
            44:109–131.
    2005   Human Adaptive Strategies: Ecology, Culture, and Politics. 2nd ed. Boston: Allyn
            & Bacon.
Bates, Daniel G., and Susan H. Lees (eds.)
    1996a   Case Studies in Human Ecology. New York: Plenum Press.
    1996b   Pastoralism. In: Case Studies in Human Ecology. Daniel G. Bates and Susan H.
            Lees, eds., pp. 153–157. New York: Plenum Press.
Baumhoff, M. A.
    1981   The Carrying Capacity of Hunter-Gatherers. In: Affluent Foragers: Pacific Coasts
            East and West. Shuzo Koyama and David Hurst Thomas, eds., pp. 77–87. Osaka:
            Senri Ethnological Studies No. 9.

Bayman, James M.
    2001   The Hohakam of Southwest North America. Journal of New World Prehistory
            15(3):257–311.
BBC News
    2008   Wildlife Populations 'Plummeting.' BBC News Online, May 16, 2008,
            http://news.bbc.co.uk/2/hi/uk_news/7403989.stm.
Beach, Hugh
    1988   The Saami of Lapland. London: The Minority Rights Group, Report No. 55.
Begler, Elsie B.
    1978   Sex, Status and Authority in Egalitarian Society. American Anthropologist
            80(3):571–588.
Belovsky, Gary E.
    1987   Hunter-Gatherer Foraging: A Linear Programming Approach. Journal of
            Anthropological Archaeology 6(1):29–76.
    1988   An Optimal Foraging-Based Model of Hunter-Gatherer Population Dynamics.
            Journal of Anthropological Archaeology 7(4):329–372.
Bender, Barbara, and Margot Winer (eds.)
    2001   Contested Landscapes: Movement, Exile and Place. Oxford: Berg.
Benedek, Emily
    1992   The Wind Won't Know Me: A History of the Navajo-Hopi Land Dispute. New
            York: Alfred A. Knopf.
Benedict, Ruth
    1934   Patterns of Culture. Boston: Houghton Mifflin.
Bennett, John W.
    1976   The Ecological Transition: Cultural Anthropology and Human Adaptation. New
            York: Academic Press.
    1992   Human Ecology as Human Behavior. New Brunswick, NJ: Transaction.
Berkes, Fikret
    1999   Sacred Ecology: Traditional Ecological Knowledge and Resource Management.
            Philadelphia: Taylor and Francis.
Berlin, Brent, Dennis Breedlove, and Peter H. Raven
    1974   Principles of Tzeltal Plant Classification. New York: Academic Press.
Bernard, H. Russell
    2006   Research Methods in Anthropology. 4th edition. Lanham, MD: AltaMira Press.
Bettinger, Robert L.
    1980   Explanatory/Predictive Models of Hunter-Gatherer Adaptation. In: Advances in
            Archaeological Method and Theory, Vol. 3. Michael B. Schiffer, ed., pp. 189–255.
            New York: Academic Press.
    1987   Archaeological Approaches to Hunter-Gatherers. Annual Review of Anthropology
            16:121–142.
    1991   Hunter-Gatherers: Archaeological and Evolutionary Theory. New York: Plenum
            Press.
Bettinger, Robert L., and Martin A. Baumhoff
    1982   The Numic Spread: Great Basin Cultures in Competition. American Antiquity
            47(3):485–503.

Bicker, Alan, Paul Sillitoe, and Johan Pottier (eds.)

    2004   Development and Local Knowledge. London: Routledge.

Binford, Lewis R.

    1968   Post-Pleistocene Adaptations. In: New Perspectives in Archaeology. Sally Binford and Lewis R. Binford, eds., pp. 313–341. Chicago: Aldine.

    1980   Willow Smoke and Dog's Tails: Hunter-Gatherer Settlement Systems and Archaeological Site Formation. American Antiquity 45(1):4–20.

    1990   Mobility, Housing, and Environment: A Comparative Study. Journal of Anthropological Research 46(2):119–152.

    2001   Constructing Frames of Reference: An Analytical Method for Archaeological Theory Building Using Ethnographic and Environmental Data Sets. Berkeley: University of California Press.

Bird, Douglas W., and James F. O'Connell

    2006   Behavioral Ecology and Archaeology. Journal of Archaeological Research 14(2):143–188.

Bird-David, Nurit

    1990   The Giving Environment: Another Perspective on the Economic System of Gatherer-Hunters. Current Anthropology 31(2):189–196.

Birdsell, Joseph B.

    1953   Some Environmental and Cultural Factors Influencing the Structuring of Australian Aboriginal Populations. American Naturalist 87(2):171–207.

Blackburn, Thomas C., and Kat Anderson (eds.)

    1993   Before the Wilderness: Environmental Management by Native Californians. Ballena Press Anthropological Paper No. 40.

Blaikie, Piers, and Harold Brookfield

    1987   Land Degradation and Society. London: Methuen.

Blaustein, Andrew R., and David B. Wake

    1995   The Puzzle of Declining Amphibian Populations. Scientific American 273:52–57.

Bliege Bird, Rebecca L., and Douglas W. Bird

    1997   Delayed Reciprocity and Tolerated Theft: The Behavioral Ecology of Food-Sharing Strategies. Current Anthropology 38(1):49–78.

Blumenschine, Robert J., John A. Cavallo, and Salvatore D. Capaldo

    1994   Competition for Carcasses and Early Hominid Behavioral Ecology: A Case Study and Conceptual Framework. Journal of Human Evolution 27(1,2,3):197–213.

Blumler, Mark A.

    1992   Independent Inventionism and Recent Genetic Evidence on Plant Domestication. Economic Botany 46(1):98–111.

Boas, Franz

    1927   Primitive Art. Cambridge, MA: Harvard University Press.

    1940   Race, Language and Culture. New York: Macmillan.

Bodenheimer, Friedrich S.

    1951   Insects as Human Food: A Chapter of the Ecology of Man. The Hague: W. Junk.

Bodley, John H.

    1999   Victims of Progress. 4th edition. Mountain View, CA: Mayfield.

    2001   Anthropology and Contemporary Human Problems. Mountain View, CA: Mayfield.

Bol, Marsha C.
    1998   Stars Above, Earth Below: American Indians and Nature. Niwot, CO: Roberts
            Reinhart Publishers.
Borgerhoff Mulder, Monique, and Peter Coppolillo
    2005   Conservation: Linking Ecology, Economics, and Culture. Princeton, NJ: Princeton
            University Press.
Boserup, Ester
    1965   The Conditions of Agricultural Growth: The Economics of Agrarian Change
            under Population Pressure. Chicago: Aldine.
Botkin, Daniel
    1990   Discordant Harmonies: A New Ecology for the Twenty-First Century. New York:
            Oxford University Press.
Boyd, Robert (ed.)
    1999   Indians, Fire, and the Land in the Pacific Northwest. Corvallis: Oregon State
            University Press.
Boyd, Robert, and Peter Richerson
    2005   The Origin and Evolution of Cultures. New York: Oxford University Press.
Bradfield, Richard Maitland
    1995   An Interpretation of Hopi Culture. Derby, England: Privately printed.
Braidwood, Robert
    1960   The Agricultural Revolution. Scientific American 203:130–141.
Bray, Francesca
    1984   Science and Civilization in China, vol. 6, part 2: Agriculture. Cambridge:
            Cambridge University Press.
Bray, Warwick
    2000   Ancient Food for Thought. Nature 408(6809):145–146.
Breedlove, Dennis, and Robert Laughlin
    1992   The Flowering of Man. Washington: Smithsonian Institution Press.
Brookfield, Harold C., and Paula Brown
    1963   Struggle for Land: Agriculture and Group Territories among the Chimbu of the
            New Guinea Highlands. Melbourne: Oxford University Press.
Brown, Lester R.
    1981   World Population Growth, Soil Erosion, and Food Security. Science 214:995–1002.
    1994   Facing Food Insecurity. In: State of the World 1994. Lester R. Brown, ed., pp.
            177–197. New York: W. W. Norton & Company.
    1996   Tough Choices: Facing the Challenge of Food Scarcity. New York: W. W. Norton &
            Company.
Brück, Joanna, and Melissa Goodman
    1999   Introduction: Themes for a Critical Archaeology of Prehistoric Settlement. In:
            Making Places in the Prehistoric World: Themes in Settlement Archaeology.
            Joanna Brück and Melissa Goodman, eds., pp. 1–19. London: UCL Press.
Brugge, David M.
    1994   The Navajo-Hopi Land Dispute: An American Tragedy. Albuquerque: University
            of New Mexico Press.

Brush, Stephen B.
    1975   The Concept of Carrying Capacity for Systems of Shifting Cultivation. American
            Anthropologist 77(4):799–811.
Brush, Stephen B., and D. Stabinsky (eds.)
    1996   Intellectual Property Rights and Indigenous Knowledge. Washington, DC: Island
            Press.
Bryant, Carol, Anita Courtenay, Barbara Markesbery, and Kathleen DeWalt
    1985   The Cultural Feast: An Introduction to Food and Society. St. Paul, MN: West
            Publishing Company.
Bryant, Carol, Kathleen DeWalt, Anita Courtney, Jeffery Schwartz
    2003   The Cultural Feast: An Introduction to Food and Society. Florence, KY:
            Brooks/Cole (Cengage).
Buck, J. L.
    1937   Land Utilization in China. Chicago: University of Chicago Press.
Bullard, Robert
    1990   Dumping in Dixie. Boulder, CO: Westview Press.
Burch, Ernest S., Jr., and Linda J. Ellanna
    1994a   Introduction. In: Key Issues in Hunter-Gatherer Research. Ernest S. Burch, Jr., and
            Linda J. Ellanna, eds., pp. 1–8. Oxford: Berg Publishers.
Burch, Ernest S., Jr., and Linda J. Ellanna (eds.)
    1994b   Key Issues in Hunter-Gatherer Research. Oxford: Berg Publishers.
Burger, Kenneth J. B.
    1993   An Ecological Perspective of Feng Shui Landscape. Taipei: Pacific Cultural
            Foundation.
Burton, Michael, and Douglas R. White
    1984   Sexual Division of Labor in Agriculture. American Anthropologist 86(3):568–583.
Burton, Sharon
    1992   Under What Circumstances Will a Commons Resource Management Group Arise?
            Paper presented at the annual meetings of the Southwestern Anthropological
            Association, Berkeley, CA.
Butzer, Karl W.
    1976   Early Hydraulic Civilization in Egypt: A Study in Cultural Ecology. Chicago:
            University of Chicago Press.
    1982   Archaeology as Human Ecology. Cambridge: Cambridge University Press.
Callicott, J. Baird, and Roger T. Ames (eds.)
    1989   Nature in Asian Traditions of Thought: Essays in Environmental Philosophy.
            Albany: State University of New York Press.
Campbell, Bernard
    1995   Human Ecology. 2nd edition. New York: Aldine.
Campbell, Kenneth L., and James W. Wood (eds.)
    1994   Human Reproductive Ecology: Interactions of Environment, Fertility, and
            Behavior. Annals of the New York Academy of Sciences, vol. 709.
Candolle, Alphone de
    1959   Origin of Cultivated Plants (orig. 1886). New York: Hafner.

Cantor, Norman F.
    2001   In the Wake of the Plague: The Black Death and the World It Made. New York: The Free Press.

Caplan, Gerald L.
    1970   The Elites of Barotseland, 1878–1969: A Political History of Zambia's Western Province. Berkeley: University of California Press.

Carkhuff, Robert R., and Bernard G. Berenson
    1977   Beyond Counseling and Therapy. New York: Holt, Rinehart and Winston.

Carlson, John B.
    1993   Rise and Fall of the City of the Gods. Discover 46(6):58–69.

Carneiro, Robert L.
    1960   Slash-and-Burn Agriculture: A Closer Look at Its Implications for Settlement Patterns. In: Men and Cultures: Selected Papers of the Fifth International Congress of Anthropological and Ethnological Sciences. Anthony F. C. Wallace, ed., pp. 229–234. Philadelphia: University of Pennsylvania Press.
    1970   A Theory of the Origin of the State. Science 169:733–738.

Carter, W. E.
    1969   New Land and Old Traditions: Kekchi Cultivators in the Guatemalan Lowlands. Gainesville: University of Florida, Latin American Monographs.

Cartmill, Matt
    1972   Arboreal Adaptations and the Origin of the Order Primates. In: The Functional and Evolutionary Biology of Primates. Russell Tuttle, ed., pp. 97–122. Chicago: Aldine.

Cashdan, Elizabeth (ed.)
    1990   Risk and Uncertainty in Tribal and Peasant Economies. Boulder, CO: Westview Press.

Chang, Kwang-chih
    1986   The Archaeology of Ancient China. 4th edition. New Haven, CT: Yale University Press.

Chao, Kang
    1986   Man and Land in Chinese History. Stanford, CA: Stanford University Press.

Chase-Dunn, Christopher, and E. N. Anderson (eds.)
    2005   The Historical Evolution of World-Systems. New York: Palgrave Macmillan.

Chase-Dunn, Christopher, and Kelly Mann
    1998   The Wintu and Their Neighbors: A Very Small World-System in Northern California. Tucson: University of Arizona Press.

Chayanov, A. V.
    1966   The Theory of Peasant Economy. Homewood, IL: Richard D. Irwin.

Chen, Junshi, T. Colin Campbell, Li Junyao, and Richard Peto
    1990   Diet, Life-Style, and Mortality in China. Ithaca, NY: Cornell University Press.

Cheu, S. P.
    1952   Changes in Fat and Protein Content of the African Migratory Locust, *Locusta migratoria migratorioides* (R. and F.). Bulletin of Entomological Research 43:101–109.

Chew, Sing C.
  2001   World Ecological Degradation: Accumulation, Urbanization, and Deforestation
          3000 B.C.—A.D. 2000. Walnut Creek, CA: AltaMira Press.
  2007   The Recurring Dark Ages: Ecological Stress, Climate Changes, and System
          Transformation. Lanham, MD: AltaMira Press.
Childe, V. Gordon
  1936   Man Makes Himself. London: Watts.
  1942   What Happened in History. Harmondsworth, Sussex: Pelican Books.
Chinese-American Joint Commission on Rural Reconstruction
  1966   Taiwan Agricultural Statistics 1901-1965. Taipei:
Chivian, Eric, and Aaron Bernstein
  2008   Sustaining Life: How Human Health Depends on Biodiversity. New York:
          Oxford University Press.
Choe Chung-ho
  1994   Korea's Landscape and Mindscape. Koreana 8(4):4–9.
Cipolla, Carlo
  1967   An Economic History of World Population. Harmondsworth, England:
          Penguin.
Clarke, Charlotte
  1977   Edible and Useful Plants of California. Berkeley: University of California Press.
Cleland, Charles E.
  1966   The Prehistoric Animal Ecology and Ethnozoology of the Upper Great Lakes
          Region. University of Michigan, Museum of Anthropology, Anthropological
          Papers No. 29.
  1976   The Focal-Diffuse Model: An Evolutionary Perspective on the Prehistoric
          Cultural Adaptations of the Eastern United States. Mid-Continental Journal of
          Archaeology 1(1):59–76.
Clements, Frederic, and Victor E. Shelford
  1939   Bio-Ecology. New York: John Wiley & Sons.
Clemmer, Richard O.
  1991   Crying for the Children of Sacred Ground: A Review Article on the Hopi-
          Navajo Land Dispute. American Indian Quarterly 15(2):225–230.
Clifford, James, and George Marcus (eds.)
  1986   Writing Culture. Berkeley: University of California Press.
Cohen, Joel E.
  1995   Population Growth and Earth's Human Carrying Capacity. Science
          269:341–346.
Cohen, Mark N.
  1977   The Food Crisis in Prehistory: Overpopulation and the Origins of Agriculture.
          New Haven, CT: Yale University Press.
Cohen, Mark N., and George Armelagos (eds.)
  1984   Paleopathology at the Origins of Agriculture, Editors' Summary. In:
          Paleopathology at the Origins of Agriculture. Mark N. Cohen and George
          Armelagos, eds., pp. 585–602. Orlando: Academic Press.

Cohen, Ronald
    1984   Warfare and State Formation: Wars Make States and States Make War. In: Warfare,
            Culture, and Environment. R. Brian Ferguson, ed., pp. 329–358. New York:
            Academic Press.
Cohen, Yehudi A.
    1974   Culture as Adaptation. In: Man in Adaptation: The Cultural Present. Yehudi A.
            Cohen, ed., pp. 45–68. New York: Aldine.
Committee on Sustainable Agriculture and the Environment in the Humid Tropics, Board on
Agriculture and Board on Science and Technology for International Development, National
Research Council
    1993   Sustainable Agriculture and the Environment in the Humid Tropics. Washington,
            DC: National Academy Press.
Conconi, Julieta R. E. de, Jose M. P. Moreno, Carlos M. Mayadon, Fernando R. Valdez, Manuel A.
Perez, Esteban E. Prado, and Hector B. Rodriguez
    1984   Protein Content of Some Edible Insects in Mexico. Journal of Ethnobiology
            4(1):61–72.
Condon, Richard G., Julia Ogina, and Holman Elders
    1996   The Northern Copper Inuit. Norman: University of Oklahoma Press.
Conference on Common Property Resource Management
    1986   Proceedings. Prepared by Panel on Common Property Resource Management,
            Board on Science and Technology for International Development, Office of
            International Affairs, National Research Council, Washington, DC.
Conklin, Harold C.
    1957   Hanunóo Agriculture: A Report on an Integrated System of Shifting Cultivation
            in the Phillippines. Rome: Food and Agricultural Organization of the United
            Nations.
    1959   Population-Land Balance under Systems of Tropical Forest Agriculture.
            Proceedings of the Ninth Pacific Science Congress of the Pacific Science
            Association, 1957, 7:63.
Connolly, Bob, and Robin Anderson
    1987   First Contact: New Guinea's Highlanders Encounter the Outside World. New York:
            Penguin Books.
Cooke, Fadzilah Majid
    1999   The Challenge of Sustainable Forests: Forest Resource Policy in Malaysia,
            1970–1995. Honolulu: University of Hawai'i Press.
Coon, Carleton
    1951   Caravan. New York: Henry Holt.
Cornelius, C., G. Dandrifosse, and C. Jeuniaux
    1976   Chitinolytic Enzymes of the Gastric Mucosa of Perodictius potto (Primate
            Prosimian): Purification and Enzyme Specificity. International Journal of
            Biochemistry 7:445–448.
Cowan, C. Wesley, and Patty Jo Watson (eds.)
    1992   The Origins of Agriculture: An International Perspective. Washington, DC:
            Smithsonian Institution Press.

Cowgill, George
  1975   On Causes and Consequences of Ancient and Modern Population Changes.
         American Anthropologist 77(3):505–524.
Cox, Paul, and Sandra Banack (eds.)
  1991   Islands, Plants and Polynesians. Portland: Dioscorides Press.
Cribb, Roger
  1991   Nomads in Archaeology. Cambridge: Cambridge University Press.
Croll, Elisabeth, and David Parkin (eds.)
  1992   Bush Base, Forest Farm: Culture, Environment and Development. London:
         Routledge.
Cronk, Lee
  1991   Human Behavioral Ecology. Annual Review of Anthropology 20:25–53.
  1999   That Complex Whole: Culture and the Evolution of Human Behavior. Boulder,
         CO: Westview Press.
Cronk, Lee, Napoleon Chagnon, and William Irons (eds.)
  2000   Adaptation and Human Behavior: An Anthropological Perspective. New York:
         Aldine.
Cronon, William
  1983   Changes in the Land. New York: Hill and Wang.
Crosby, Alfred W.
  1989   America's Forgotten Pandemic: The Influenza of 1918. Cambridge: Cambridge
         University Press.
Crumley, Carole L. (ed.)
  1994   Historical Ecology: Cultural Knowledge and Changing Landscapes. Santa Fe:
         School of American Research Press.
Crumley, Carole L.
  1998   Foreword. In: Advances in Historical Ecology. William Balée, ed., pp. ix–xiv. New
         York: Columbia University Press.
Crumley, Carole L., A. Elizabeth van Deventer, and Joseph J. Fletcher (eds.)
  2001   New Directions in Anthropology and Environment: Intersections. Walnut Creek,
         CA: AltaMira Press.
Cushing, Frank
  1920   Zuni Breadstuffs. New York: Museum of the American Indian (Heye Foundation),
         Indian Notes and Monographs, VII:7–642.
Dahlberg, Frances (ed.)
  1981   Woman the Gatherer. New Haven, CT: Yale University Press.
Daly, Herman, and Kenneth W. Townsend (eds.)
  1993   Valuing the Earth: Economics, Ecology, Ethics. Cambridge, MA: Massachusetts
         Institute of Technology Press.
Darwin, Charles
  1859   On the Origin of Species by Means of Natural Selection. New York: D. Appleton.
Davis, Shelton H.
  1977   Victims of the Miracle: Development and the Indians of Brazil. Cambridge:
         Cambridge University Press.

Dazhong, Wen, and David Pimentel
    1984   Energy Inputs in Agricultural Systems of China. Agriculture, Ecosystems &
             Environment 11:29–35.
    1986a   Seventeenth-Century Organic Agriculture in China: I: Cropping Systems in Jiaxing
             Region. Human Ecology 14(1):1–14.
    1986b   Seventeenth-Century Organic Agriculture in China: II: Energy Flows through and
             Agroecosystem in Jiaxing Region. Human Ecology 14(1):15–18.
DeFoliart, G. R., M. D. Finke, and M. L. Sunde
    1982   Potential Value of the Mormon Cricket (Orthoptera:Tettigoniidae) Harvested as a
             High-Protein Feed for Poultry. Journal of Economic Entomology 75(5):848–852.
Demarest, Arthur
    2004   Ancient Maya: The Rise and Fall of a Rainforest Civilization. Cambridge:
             Cambridge University Press.
Denevan, William
    1992   The Pristine Myth: The Landscape of the Americas in 1492. Annals of the
             Association of American Geographers 82:369–385.
    2001   Cultivated Landscapes of Native Amazonia and the Andes. New York: Oxford
             University Press.
Denham, Tim, and Peter White (eds.)
    2007   The Emergence of Agriculture. 2nd edition. Abingdon, Oxon, England: Routledge.
Deur, Douglas, and Nancy J. Turner (eds.)
    2005   Keeping It Living: Traditions of Plant Use and Cultivation on the Northwest Coast
             of North America. Seattle: University of Washington Press.
DeVore, Irven, and S. L. Washburn
    1963   Baboon Ecology and Human Evolution. In: African Ecology and Human
             Evolution. F. Clark Howell and François Bourliére, eds., pp. 335–367. Chicago:
             Aldine.
DeWalt, Billie R.
    1994   Using Indigenous Knowledge to Improve Agriculture and Natural Resource
             Management. Human Organization 53(2):123–131.
Dewar, Robert E.
    1984   Environmental Productivity, Population Regulation, and Carrying Capacity.
             American Anthropologist 86(3):601–614.
Diamond, Jared
    1995   Easter's End. Discover 16(8):62–69.
    1997   Guns, Germs and Steel. New York: W. W. Norton.
    2005   Collapse: How Societies Choose to Fail or Succeed. New York: Viking.
Dichter, Thomas W.
    2003   Despite Good Intentions: Why Development Assistance to the Third World Has
             Failed. Amherst: University of Massachusetts Press.
Diener, Paul, and Eugene Robkin
    1978   Ecology, Evolution, and the Search for Cultural Origins: The Question of Islamic
             Pig Prohibition. Current Anthropology 19(3):493–540.

Dincauze, Dena F.
    2000   Environmental Archaeology: Principles and Practice. Cambridge: Cambridge University Press.

Dissanayake, Ellen
    1992   Homo Aestheticus. New York: Free Press.

Divale, William Tullio, and Marvin Harris
    1976   Population, Warfare, and the Male Supremacy Complex. American Anthropologist 78(3):521–538.

Dobzhansky, Theodosius G.
    1972   On the Evolutionary Uniqueness of Man. Evolutionary Biology 6:415–430.

Doolittle, William F.
    2000   Cultivated Landscapes of Native North America. Oxford: Oxford University Press.

Douglas, Mary
    1966   Purity and Danger. New York: Praeger.
    1970   Natural Symbols. London: Barrie and Rockliff.
    1975   Implicit Meanings. London: Routledge and Kegan Paul.

Dove, Michael R.
    1981   Symbiotic Relationships between Human Populations and *Imperata cylindrica*: The Question of Ecosystematic Succession and Preservation in South Kalimantan. In: Conservation Inputs from Life Sciences. M. Nordin, ed., pp. 187–200. Kuala Lumpur: Universiti Kebangsaan Malaysia.
    1993a   A Revisionist View of Tropical Deforestation and Development. Environmental Conservation 20:17–25.
    1993b   Smallholder Rubber and Swidden Agriculture in Borneo: A Sustainable Adaptation to the Ecology and Economy of the Tropical Forest. Economic Botany 47(2):136–147.
    2006   Indigenous People and Environmental Politics. Annual Review of Anthropology 35:191–208.

Dove, Michael, and Carol Carpenter (eds.)
    2008   Environmental Anthropology: A Historical Reader. Oxford: Blackwell.

Downing, Theodore E., Susanna B. Hecht, Henry A. Pearson, and Carmen Garcia-Downing
    1992   Development or Destruction: The Conversion of Tropical Forest to Pasture in Latin America. Boulder, CO: Westview Press.

Downs, James F.
    1972   The Navajo. New York: Holt, Rinehart and Winston.

Drucker, Peter
    1992   The Ecological Vision. New Brunswick, NJ: Transaction.

Drucker, Philip
    1951   The Northern and Central Nootkan Tribes. Bureau of American Ethnology Bulletin 144.

Drucker, Philip, and Robert F. Heizer
    1967   To Make My Name Good: A Reexamination of the Southern Kawakuitl Potlatch. Berkeley: University of California Press.

Dryzek, John
    1988   Rational Ecology. Oxford: Basil Blackwell.

Duffy, Kevin
    1996   Children of the Forest: Africa's Mbuti Pygmies. Prospect Heights, IL: Waveland Press.

Dufour, Darna L.
    1987   Insects as Food: A Case Study from the Northwest Amazon. American Anthropologist 89(2):383–397.

Duhring, John L.
    1984   Nutrition in Pregnancy. In: Nutrition Reviews' Present Knowledge in Nutrition, pp. 636–645. Washington, DC: Nutrition Foundation.

Duke, J., and E. Ayensu
    1985   Medicinal Plants of China. New York: Reference Press.

Dunbar, Robin
    1996   Grooming, Gossip, and the Evolution of Language. Cambridge, MA: Harvard University Press.

Dunbar, Robin, Chris Knight, and Camilla Power (eds.)
    1999   The Evolution of Culture: An Interdisciplinary View. New Brunswick, NJ: Rutgers University Press.

Durham, William H.
    1981   Overview: Optimal Foraging Analysis in Human Ecology. In: Hunter-Gatherer Foraging Strategies: Ethnographic and Archaeological Analyses. Bruce Winterhalder and Eric Alden Smith, eds., pp. 218–231. Chicago: University of Chicago Press.

Durrenberger, Paul (ed.)
    1984   Chayanov, Peasants and Economic Anthropology. New York: Academic Press.

Dwyer, Peter D.
    1990   The Pigs That Ate the Garden: A Human Ecology from Papua New Guinea. Ann Arbor: University of Michigan Press.

Dyer, Christopher, and J. McGoodwin (eds.)
    1994   Folk Management in the World's Fisheries. Boulder: University of Colorado Press.

Dyson-Hudson, Neville
    1972   The Study of Nomads. In: Perspectives on Nomadism. William Irons and Neville Dyson-Hudson, eds., pp. 2–29. International Studies in Sociology and Social Anthropology, vol. 13.

Dyson-Hudson, Rada, and Neville Dyson-Hudson
    1980   Nomadic Pastoralism. Annual Review of Anthropology 9:15–61.

Earle, Timothy, and Andrew L. Christenson (eds.)
    1980   Modeling Change in Prehistoric Subsistence Economies. New York: Academic Press.

Eaton, S. Boyd, and Stanley B. Eaton
    1999   Hunter-Gatherers and Human Health. In: The Cambridge Encyclopedia of Hunters and Gatherers. Richard B. Lee and Richard Daly, eds., pp. 449–456. Cambridge: Cambridge University Press.

Ebeling, Walter
    1985   Handbook of Indian Foods and Fibers of Arid America. Berkeley: University of
            California Press.

Edwards, Richard
    1979   Contested Terrain. New York: Basic Books.

Ehrlich, Paul R.
    2000   Human Natures: Genes, Cultures and the Human Prospect. Washington, DC:
            Island Press.

Ehrlich, Paul R., and Anne H. Ehrlich
    1981   Extinction: The Causes and Consequences of the Disappearance of Species. New
            York: Random House.
    1996   Betrayal of Science and Reason: How Anti-Environmental Rhetoric Threatens Our
            Future. Washington: Island Press.

Ehrlich, Paul R., and Marcus Feldman
    2003   Genes and Cultures: What Creates Our Behavioral Phenome? Current
            Anthropology 44(1):87–107.

Eisenberg, Nancy
    1986   Altruistic Emotion, Cognition and Behavior. Hillsdale, NJ: Lawrence Erlbaum
            Associates.

Ekvall, Robert B.
    1968   Fields on the Hoof: Nexus of Tibetan Nomadic Pastoralism. New York: Holt,
            Rinehart and Winston.

Ellen, Roy R.
    1982   Environment, Subsistence and System. Cambridge: Cambridge University Press.
    1986   Ethnobiology, Cognition and the Structure of Prehension: Some General
            Theoretical Notes. Journal of Ethnobiology 6(1):83–98.

Elster, Jon
    1987   Rational Choice. Cambridge: Cambridge University Press.

Elvin, Mark
    1973   The Pattern of the Chinese Past. Stanford, CA: Stanford University Press.

Ember, Carol
    1978   Myths about Hunter-Gatherers. Ethnology 17(4):439–448.

Ember, Melvin
    1982   Statistical Evidence for an Ecological Explanation of Warfare. American
            Anthropologist 84(3):645–649.

Engels, Frederick
    1942   The Origin of the Family, Private Property, and the State. New York: International
            Publishers.
    1966[1894]   Anti-Duhring: Herr Eugen Duhring's Revolution in Science. New York:
            International Publishers.

Erichsen-Brown, Charlotte
    1979   Uses of Plants for the Past 500 Years. Aurora, Ontario, Canada: Breezy Creeks
            Press.

Erickson, Clark
    1986   Cómo Construir Waru Waru. Puno, Peru: Proyecto Agrícola de los Campos Elevados.
Etkin, Nina
    1988   Ethnopharmacology: Biobehavioral Approaches in the Anthropological Study of
            Indigenous Medicines. Annual Review of Anthropology 17:23–42.
Etkin, Nina L. (ed.)
    1994   Eating on the Wild Side: The Pharmacologic, Ecologic, and Social Implications of
            Using Noncultigens. Tucson: University of Arizona Press.
Evangelou, Phylo
    1984   Livestock Development in Kenya's Maasailand: Pastoralists' Transition to a Market
            Economy. Boulder, CO: Westview Press.
Evans-Pritchard, E. E.
    1940   The Nuer. Oxford: Oxford University Press.
Evers, Larry, and Felipe Molina
    1987   Yaqui Deer Songs/Maso Bwikam. Tucson: University of Arizona Press.
Fagan, Brian
    1999   Floods, Famines, and Emperors: El Nino and the Fate of Civilizations. New York:
            Basic Books.
    2008   The Great Warming: Climate Change and the Rise and Fall of Civilizations. New
            York: Bloomsbury Press.
Fairhead, James, and Melissa Leach
    1996   Misreading the African Landscape. Cambridge: Cambridge University Press.
Farberow, Norman (ed.)
    1975   Suicide in Different Cultures. Baltimore: University Park Press.
    1980   The Many Faces of Suicide. New York: McGraw-Hill.
Farnsworth, Norman R., and Djaja Doel Soejarto
    1985   Potential Consequence of Plant Extinction in the United States on the Current
            and Future Availability of Prescription Drugs. Economic Botany 39(3):231–240.
Farris, Glenn J.
    1982   Pine Nuts as an Aboriginal Food Source in California and Nevada: Some
            Contrasts. Journal of Ethnobiology 2(2):114–122.
Faust, Betty B.
    1998   Mexican Rural Development and the Plumed Serpent. Westport, CT: Bergin and
            Garvey.
Fedick, Scott L.
    1995   Indigenous Agriculture in the Americas. Journal of Archaeological Research
            3(4):257–303.
Fedick, Scott L. (ed.)
    1996   The View from Yalahau. University of California, Mexus.
Fedigan, Linda Marie
    1986   The Changing Role of Women in Models of Human Evolution. Annual Review of
            Anthropology 15:25–66.
Feher-Elston, Catherine
    1988   Children of the Sacred Ground. Flagstaff: Northland Press.

Feinman, Gary M., and Joyce Marcus (eds.)

    1998   Archaic States. Santa Fe, NM: School of American Research Press.

Feld, Steven, and Keith Basso (eds.)

    1996   Senses of Place. Santa Fe: School of American Research Press.

Ferguson, R. Brian

    1984   A Reexamination of the Causes of Northwest Coast Warfare. In: Warfare, Culture, and Environment. R. Brian Ferguson, ed., pp. 267–328. New York: Academic Press.

Feshbach, Murray, and Alfred Friendly Jr.

    1992   Ecocide in the USSR. New York: Basic Books.

Field, Barry C.

    1994   Environmental Economics: An Introduction. New York: McGraw-Hill.

Finerman, Ruthbeth

    1983   Experience and Expectation: Conflict and Change in Traditional Family Health Care among the Quichua of Saraguro. Social Science and Medicine 17(17):1291–1298.

    1984   A Matter of Life and Death: Health Care Change in an Andean Community. Social Science and Medicine 18(4):329–334.

Firth, Raymond

    1936   We the Tikopia. London: George Allen and Unwin.

    1959   Social Change in Tikopia. London: George Allen and Unwin.

    1965   Economics of the New Zealand Maori. London: Routledge and Kegan Paul.

    1966   Malay Fishermen: Their Peasant Economy. New York: Norton.

Firth, Rosemary

    1966   Housekeeping among Malay Peasants. London: Athlone Press.

Fischhoff, Baruch, Sara L. Lichtenstein, Paul Slovic, Stephen L. Derby, and Ralph L. Keeney

    1981   Acceptable Risk. Cambridge: Cambridge University Press.

Fiske, Susan T., and Shelley E. Taylor

    1991   Social Cognition. 2nd edition. New York: McGraw-Hill.

Flachsenberg, Henning, and Hugo A. Galletti

    1998   Forest Management in Quintana Roo, Mexico. In: Timber, Tourists, and Temples: Conservation and Development in the Maya Forest of Belize, Guatemala, and Mexico. Richard Primack, David Bray, Hugo A. Galletti, and Ismael Ponciano, eds., pp. 47–60. Washington, DC: Island Press.

Flanagan, Laurence.

    1998   Ancient Ireland. New York: St. Martin's Press.

Flannery, Kent V.

    1969   Origins and Ecological Effects of Domestication in Iran and the Near East. In: The Domestication and Exploitation of Plants and Animals. Peter Ucko and George Dimbleby, eds., pp. 73–100. London: Duckworth.

    1972   The Cultural Evolution of Civilizations. Annual Review of Ecology and Systematics 3:399–426.

Flannery, Kent V. (ed.)

    1982   Maya Subsistence. New York: Academic Press.

Flannery, Kent V., Joyce Marcus, and Robert G. Reynolds
  1989   The Flocks of the Wamani: A Study of Llama Herders on the Punas of Ayacucho,
          Peru. San Diego: Academic Press.

Flannery, Timothy F.
  1995   The Future Eaters : An Ecological History of the Australasian Lands and People.
          New York: George Braziller.

Fletcher, Alice, and Francis La Flesche
  1911   The Omaha Tribe. In: Annual Report of the Bureau of American Ethnology for
          the Years 1905–1906, pp. 17–672. Washington, DC: Government Printing
          Office.

Flood, Josephine
  1980   The Moth Hunters: Aboriginal Prehistory of the Australian Alps. Australian
          Institute of Aboriginal Studies New Series No. 14.

Fog, Agner
  1999   Cultural Selection. Dordrecht: Kluwer Academic Publishers.

Foin, Theodore C., and William G. Davis
  1987   Equilibrium and Nonequilibrium Models in Ecological Anthropology: An
          Evaluation of "Stability" in Maring Ecosystems in New Guinea. American
          Anthropologist 89(1):9–30.

Ford, Jesse, and Dennis Martinez (eds.)
  2000   Traditional Ecological Knowledge, Ecosystem Science, and Resource Management.
          Special section, Ecological Applications 10(5):1249–1340.

Ford, Richard I. (ed.)
  1994   The Nature and Status of Ethnobotany. 2nd edition. University of Michigan,
          Museum of Anthropology, Anthropological Papers No. 67.
  2001   Ethnobiology at the Millennium: Past Promise and Future Prospects. University of
          Michigan, Museum of Anthropology, Anthropological Papers No. 91.

Forde, C. Daryll
  1931   Hopi Agriculture and Land Ownership. Journal of the Royal Anthropological
          Institute of Great Britain and Ireland 61:357–405.

Forde, C. Daryll (ed.)
  1934   Habitat, Economy and Society: A Geographical Introduction to Ethnology.
          London: Methuen.

Forman, Richard T. T., and Michel Godron
  1986   Landscape Ecology. New York: John Wiley & Sons.

Foucault, Michel
  1970   The Order of Things. New York: Random House.

Fox, Charles W., Derek A. Roff, and Daphne J. Fairbairn (eds.)
  2001   Evolutionary Ecology: Concepts and Case Studies. Oxford: Oxford University
          Press.

Fox, James J.
  1977   Harvest of the Palm: Ecological Change in Eastern Indonesia. Cambridge, MA:
          Harvard University Press.

Frake, Charles
    1962   Cultural Ecology and Ethnography. American Anthropologist 64(1):53–59.
    1980   Language and Cultural Description. Anwar S. Dil, ed. Stanford, CA: Stanford
            University Press.
Frank, Robert
    1988   Passions within Reason. Cambridge, MA: Harvard University Press.
Fratkin, Elliot
    1998   Ariaal Pastoralists of Kenya: Surviving Drought and Development in Africa's Arid
            Lands. Boston: Allyn & Bacon.
Froment, Alain
    2001   Evolutionary Biology and Health of Hunter-Gatherer Populations. In: Hunter-
            Gatherers: An Interdisciplinary Perspective. Catherine Panter-Brick, Robert H.
            Layton, and Peter Rowley-Conwy, eds., pp. 239–266. Cambridge: Cambridge
            University Press.
Galletti, Hugo A.
    1998   The Maya Forest of Quintana Roo: Thirteen Years of Conservation and
            Community Development. In: Timber, Tourists, and Temples: Conservation and
            Development in the Maya Forest of Belize, Guatemala, and Mexico. Richard
            Primack, David Bray, Hugo A. Galletti, and Ismael Ponciano, eds., pp. 33–46.
            Washington, DC: Island Press.
Galvin, Kathleen A., D. Layne Coppock, and Paul W. Leslie
    1994   Diet, Nutrition, and the Pastoral Strategy. In: African Pastoralist Systems: An
            Integrated Approach. Elliot Fratkin, Kathleen A. Galvin, and Eric Abella Roth, eds.,
            pp. 113–131. Boulder, CO: Lynne Rienner Publishers.
Garber, P. A.
    1987   Foraging Strategies among Living Primates. Annual Review of Anthropology
            16:339–364.
Gardner, Paul S.
    1992   Diet Optimization Models and Prehistoric Subsistence Change in the Eastern
            Woodlands. Ph.D. dissertation, University of North Carolina, Chapel Hill.
Gardner, Robert, and Karl Heider
    1969   Gardens of War. New York: Random House.
Gaukroger, Stephen
    2006   The Emergence of a Scientific Culture: Science and the Shaping of Modernity
            1210–1685. Oxford: Oxford University Press.
Geertz, Clifford
    1963   Agricultural Involution. Berkeley: University of California Press.
    1984   Anti-Anti-Relativism. American Anthropologist 86(2):263–278.
Ghai, Dharam, Azizur Rahman Khan, Eddy Lee, and Simir Radwan (eds.)
    1979   Agrarian Systems and Rural Development. New York: Holmes and Meier.
Giampietro, Mario, Sandra G. F. Bukkens, and David Pimentel
    1993   Labor Productivity: A Biophysical Definition and Assessment. Human Ecology
            21(3):229–260.

Giddens, Anthony
    1984   The Constitution of Society. Berkeley: University of California Press.
Gidwitz, Tom
    2002   Pioneers of the Bajo. Archaeology 55(1):28–35.
Gill, Richardson
    2000   The Great Maya Droughts. Albuquerque: University of New Mexico Press.
Gillis, Anna Maria
    1991   Should Cows Chew Cheatgrass on Commonlands? BioScience 41(10):668–675.
Gladwin, Christina
    1989   Ethnographic Decision Tree Modeling. Newbury Park, CA: Sage.
Gladwin, Christina, and Kathleen Truman (eds.)
    1989   Food and Farm. Washington: Society for Economic Anthropology.
Glassow, Michael A.
    1978   The Concept of Carrying Capacity in the Study of Culture Process. In: Advances
            in Archaeological Method and Theory, Vol. 1. Michael B. Schiffer, ed., pp. 31–48.
            New York: Academic Press.
Gleick, Peter
    1998   The World's Water. Washington, DC: Island Press.
    2008   The World's Water 2008–2009: The Biennial Report on Fresh Water Resources.
            Washington, DC: Island Press.
Gluckman, Max
    1941   Economy of the Central Barotse Plain. Livingstone: The Rhodes-Livingstone
            Papers No. 7.
    1951   The Lozi of Barotseland in North-Western Rhodesia. In: Seven Tribes of Central
            Africa. Elizabeth Colson and Max Gluckman, eds., pp. 1–93. Manchester, England:
            University of Manchester Press.
Goldschmidt, Walter
    1969   Kambuya's Cattle. Berkeley: University of California Press.
    1979   A General Model for Pastoral Social Systems. In: Pastoral Production and Society:
            Proceedings of the International Meeting on Nomadic Pastoralism. C. Lefebure,
            ed., pp. 15–27. Cambridge: Cambridge University Press.
    2004   The Bridge to Humanity: How Affect Hunger Trumps the Selfish Gene. New York:
            Oxford University Press.
Goldstein, Melvyn C., and Cynthia M. Beall
    1990   Nomads of Western Tibet: The Survival of a Way of Life. Berkeley: University of
            California Press.
Golley, Frank B.
    1993   A History of the Ecosystems Concept in Ecology. New Haven, CT: Yale University
            Press.
Gonzalez, Roberto
    2001   Zapotec Science: Farming and Food in the Northern Sierra of Oaxaca. Austin:
            University of Texas Press.
Goodall, Jane
    1986   The Chimpanzees of Gombe. Cambridge, MA: Harvard University Press.

Goodenough, Ward
    1953   Native Astronomy in the Central Carolines. Philadelphia: University Museum,
            University of Pennsylvania.
Goodenough, Ward (ed.)
    1964   Explorations in Cultural Anthropology. New York: McGraw-Hill.
Goodland, R.
    1975   History of "Ecology." Science 188(4186):313.
Goodman, Alan H., Darna L. Dufour, and Gretel H. Pelto (eds.)
    2000   Nutritional Anthropology: Biocultural Perspectives on Food and Nutrition.
            Mountain View, CA: Mayfield Publishing.
Goodstein, Eban S.
    1999   The Trade-Off Myth: Fact and Fiction about Jobs and the Environment.
            Washington, DC: Island Press.
Goody, Jack
    1982   Cooking, Cuisine and Class. Cambridge: Cambridge University Press.
Goudie, Andrew
    1994   The Human Impact on the Natural Environment. 4th edition. Cambridge:
            Massachusetts Institute of Technology Press.
Gould, Richard A.
    1969   Yiwara: Foragers of the Australian Desert. New York: Scribner's.
    1982   To Have and Not to Have: The Ecology of Sharing among Hunter-Gatherers.
            In: Resource Managers: North American and Australian Hunter-Gatherers.
            Nancy M. Williams and Eugene S. Hunn, eds., pp. 69–91. Boulder, CO:
            Westview Press.
Grady, Denise
    1993   Death at the Corners. Discover 14(12):82–91.
Gragson, Ted L., and Ben G. Blount (eds.)
    1999   Ethnoecology: Knowledge, Resources, and Rights. Athens: University of Georgia
            Press.
Grant, Campbell, James W. Baird, and J. Kenneth Pringle
    1968   Rock Drawings of the Coso Range, Inyo County, California. Ridgecrest: Maturango
            Museum Publication 4.
Grayson, Donald K.
    2001   The Archaeological Record of Human Impacts on Animal Populations. Journal of
            World Prehistory 15(1):1–68.
Green, Donald, and Ian Shapiro
    1994   Pathologies of Rational Choice Theory. New Haven, CT: Yale University Press.
Greenberg, James B., and Thomas K. Park
    1994   Political Ecology. Journal of Political Ecology 1:1–12.
Gregg, Susan Alling
    1988   Forager and Farmers: Population Interaction and Agricultural Expansion in
            Prehistoric Europe. Chicago: University of Chicago Press.
Griaule, Marcel
    1965   Conversations with Ogotemmeli. Oxford: Oxford University Press.

Griffin, Keith
    1974   The Political Economy of Agrarian Change. London: Macmillan.
Griffin, Keith (ed.)
    1984   Institutional Reform and Economic Development in the Chinese Countryside.
            Boulder, CO: M. E. Sharpe.
Grim, John A. (ed.)
    2001   Indigenous Traditions and Ecology: The Interbeing of Cosmology and
            Community. Cambridge, MA: Harvard Center for the Study of World Religions.
Grove, A. T., and Oliver Rackham
    2001   The Nature of Mediterranean Europe. New Haven, CT: Yale University Press.
Guha, R. (ed.)
    1994   Social Ecology. Delhi: Oxford University Press.
Guillet, David
    1987   Terracing and Irrigation in the Peruvian Highlands. Current Anthropology
            28(4):409–430.
Gunda, Bela
    1984   The Fishing Culture of the World (2 vols.). Budapest: Akademiai Kiado.
Hack, John T.
    1942   The Changing Physical Environment of the Hopi Indians of Arizona. Papers of the
            Peabody Museum of American Archaeology and Ethnology 35(1).
Haenn, Nora, and Richard Wilk (eds.)
    2006   The Environment in Anthropology: A Reader in Ecology, Culture and Sustainable
            Living. New York: New York University Press.
Halperin, Rhoda, and James Dow (eds.)
    1977   Peasant Livelihood: Studies in Economic Anthropology and Cultural Ecology. New
            York: St. Martin's Press.
Hames, Raymond
    2007   The Ecologically Noble Savage Debate. Annual Review of Anthropology
            36:177–190.
Hamilton, William J. III
    1987   Omnivorous Primate Diets and Human Overconsumption of Meat. In: Food and
            Evolution: Toward a Theory of Human Food Habits. Marvin Harris and Eric B.
            Ross, eds., pp. 117–132. Philadelphia: Temple University Press.
Hammett, Julia E.
    1997   Interregional Patterns of Land Use and Plant Management in Native North
            America. In: People, Plants, and Landscapes: Studies in Paleoethnobotany. Kristen
            J. Gremillion, ed., pp. 195–216. Tuscaloosa: University of Alabama Press.
Hammond, Kenneth R., John Rohrbaugh, Jeryl Mumpower, and Leonard Adelman
    1977   Social Judgment Theory: Applications in Policy Formation. In: Human Judgment
            and Decision Processes in Applied Settings. Martin Kaplan and Steven Schwartz,
            eds., pp. 1–27. New York: Academic Press.
Handlin Smith, Joanna
    1987   Benevolent Societies: The Reshaping of Charity during the Late Ming and Early
            Ch'ing. Journal of Asian Studies 46(2):309–337.

Hardesty, Donald L.

    1975   The Niche Concept: Suggestions for Its Use in Studies of Human Ecology. Human Ecology 3(2):71–85.

    1977   Ecological Anthropology. New York: John Wiley & Sons.

    1997   The Archaeology of the Donner Party. Reno: University of Nevada Press.

Hardin, Garrett

    1968   The Tragedy of the Commons. Science 162:1243–1248.

    1991   The Tragedy of the *Unmanaged* Commons. In: Commons without Tragedy. Robert V. Andelson, ed., pp. 162–185. Savage, MD: Barnes and Noble.

Harding, Robert S. O.

    1981   An Order of Omnivores: Nonhuman Primate Diets in the Wild. In: Omnivorous Primates: Gathering and Hunting in Human Evolution. Robert S. O. Harding and Geza Teleki, eds., pp. 191–214. New York: Columbia University Press.

Harding, Thomas G., David Kaplan, Marshall D. Sahlins, and Elman R. Service

    1960   Evolution and Culture. Ann Arbor: University of Michigan Press.

Harlan, Jack R.

    1992   Crops and Man. Madison, WI: American Society of Agronomy and Crop Science Society of America.

Harner, Michael

    1977   The Ecological Basis for Aztec Sacrifice. American Ethnologist 4(1):117–135.

Harper, Janice

    2002   Endangered Species. Durham, NC: Carolina Academic Press.

Harris, David, and Gordon Hillman (eds.)

    1989   Foraging and Farming: The Evolution of Plant Exploitation. Cambridge: Cambridge University Press.

Harris, Marvin

    1966   The Cultural Ecology of India's Sacred Cattle. Current Anthropology 7(1):51–66.

    1968   The Rise of Anthropological Theory. New York: Crowell.

    1974   Cows, Pigs, Wars and Witches. New York: Random House.

    1977   Cannibals and Kings. New York: Random House.

    1979   Cultural Materialism: The Struggle for a Science of Culture. New York: Random House.

    1981   America Now. New York: Simon & Schuster.

    1984   A Cultural Materialist Theory of Band and Village Warfare: The Yanomamo Test. In: Warfare, Culture, and Environment. R. Brian Ferguson, ed., pp. 111–140. New York: Academic Press.

    1985   Good to Eat: Riddles of Food and Culture. New York: Simon and Schuster.

Harrison, P. D., and B. L. Turner

    1978   Pre-Hispanic Maya Agriculture. Albuquerque: University of New Mexico Press.

Hart, Terese B., and John A. Hart

    1986   The Ecological Basis of Hunter-Gatherer Subsistence in African Rain Forests: The Mbuti of Eastern Zaire. Human Ecology 14(1):29–55.

Hassan, Fekri A.

    1980   The Growth and Regulation of Human Population in Prehistoric Times. In: Biosocial Mechanisms of Population Regulation. Mark N. Cohen, Roy S. Malpass, and Harold G. Klein, eds., pp. 305–319. New Haven: Yale University Press.

Hatley, Tom, and John Kappelman

    1980   Bears, Pigs, and Plio-Pleistocene Hominids: A Case for the Exploitation of Belowground Resources. Human Ecology 8(4):371–387.

Hawkes, Kristen

    1993   Why Hunter-Gatherers Work. Current Anthropology 34(4):341–361.

Hawkes, Kristen, Kim Hill, and James F. O'Connell

    1982   Why Hunters Gather: Optimal Foraging and the Aché of Eastern Paraguay. American Ethnologist 9(2):379–398.

Hawkes, Kristen, and James F. O'Connell

    1985   Optimal Foraging Models and the Case of the !Kung. American Anthropologist 87(2):401–405.

Hayami, Yujiro, and Masao Kikuchi

    1981   Asian Village Economy at the Crossroads. Tokyo: University of Tokyo and Johns Hopkins University.

Hayami, Yujiro, and Vernon Ruttan

    1985   Agricultural Development. 2nd edition. Baltimore: Johns Hopkins University Press.

Hayden, Brian

    1981   Research and Development in the Stone Age: Technological Traditions among Hunter-Gatherers. Current Anthropology 22(5):519–548.

    1995   A New Overview of Domestication. In: Last Hunters—First Farmers: New Perspectives on the Prehistoric Transition to Agriculture. T. Douglas Price and Anne Birgitte Gebauer, eds., pp. 273–299. Santa Fe, NM: School of American Research Press.

He Bochuan

    1991   China on the Edge: The Crisis of Ecology and Development. San Francisco: China Books and Periodicals.

Headland, Thomas, and Lawrence A. Reid

    1989   Hunter-Gatherers and Their Neighbors from Prehistory to the Present. Current Anthropology 30(1):43–66.

Headley, Lee

    1982   Suicide in Asia and the Near East. Berkeley: University of California Press.

Heather, Peter

    2006   The Fall of the Roman Empire: A New History of Rome and the Barbarians. London: Oxford University Press.

Hedrick, Kimberly

    2007   Our Way of Life: Identity, Landscape, and Conflict. Ph.D. dissertation, University of California, Riverside.

Heider, Karl

    1970   The Dugum Dani. Viking Fund Publications in Anthropology No. 49.

    1979   Grand Valley Dani: Peaceful Warriors. New York: Holt, Rinehart and Winston.

Heiser, Charles, Jr.
    1985   Of Plants and People. Norman: University of Oklahoma Press.
Helm, June
    1965   Bilaterality in the Socio-Territorial Organization of the Arctic Drainage Dene.
             Ethnology 4(4):361–385.
Helvarg, David
    1994   The War against the Greens. Washington: Sierra Club.
Henderson, Junius, and John P. Harrington
    1914   Ethnozoology of the Tewa Indians. Bureau of American Ethnology Bulletin 56.
Henrich, Joseph, Robert Boyd, Samuel Bowles, Colin Camerer, Ernst Fehr, and Herbert Gintis (eds.)
    2004   Foundations of Human Sociality: Economic Experiments and Ethnographic
             Evidence from Fifteen Small-Scale Societies. New York: Oxford University Press.
Henry, Donald O.
    1995   Prehistoric Cultural Ecology and Evolution: Insights from Southern Jordan. New
             York: Plenum Press.
Herman, Arthur
    2001   How the Scots Invented the Modern World. New York: Three Rivers Press.
Herskovits, M. J.
    1926   The Cattle Complex in East Africa. American Anthropologist 28:230–272, 361–388,
             494–528, 633–664.
Higham, Charles
    1995   The Transition to Rice Cultivation in Southeast Asia. In: Last Hunters—First
             Farmers: New Perspectives on the Prehistoric Transition to Agriculture. T. Douglas
             Price and Anne Birgitte Gebauer, eds., pp. 127–155. Santa Fe, NM: School of
             American Research Press.
Hill, Kim, and Kristen Hawkes
    1983   Neotropical Hunting among the Aché of Eastern Paraguay. In: Adaptive Responses of
             Native Amazonians. Raymond B. Hames and William T. Vickers, eds., pp. 139–188.
             New York: Academic Press.
Hill, Kim, and A. Magdalena Hurtado
    1996   Aché Life History: The Ecology and Demography of a Foraging People. New York:
             Aldine.
Ho, Ping-ti
    1975   The Cradle of the East. Hong Kong and Chicago: Chinese University of Hong Kong
             and University of Chicago Press.
    1988   The Origins of Chinese Agriculture. Paper presented at the Fifth International
             Conference on the History of Science in China, San Diego, CA.
Hogg, Gary
    1966   Cannibalism and Human Sacrifice. New York: Citadel Press.
Hooi, Alexis John
    2002   Congo's Civil War Imperils Ituri Livelihood. Cultural Survival Voices 1(4):1, 8.
Hopkins, Raymond F., Donald J. Puchala, Ross B. Talbot
    1979   Food, Politics and Agricultural Development: Case Studies in the Public Policy of
             Rural Modernization. Boulder, CO: Westview Press.

Hrdy, Sarah
    1999   Mother Nature. New York: Pantheon.
Huang, H. T.
    2002   Hypolactasia and the Chinese Diet. Current Anthropology 43(5):809–820.
Huang, Philip
    1990   The Peasant Family and Rural Development in the Yangzi Delta, 1350–1988.
             Stanford, CA: Stanford University Press.
Hunn, Eugene S.
    1977   Tzeltal Folk Zoology. New York: Academic Press.
    1979   The Abominations of Leviticus Revisited: A Commentary on Anomaly in
             Symbolic Anthropology. In: Classifications in the Social Context. Roy Ellen and
             David Reason, eds., pp. 103–116. New York: Academic Press.
    1981   On the Relative Contribution of Men and Women to Subsistence among
             Hunter-Gatherers of the Columbia Plateau: A Comparison with Ethnographic
             Atlas Summaries. Journal of Ethnobiology 1(1):124–134.
    1991   Nch'i Wana, the Big River. Seattle: University of Washington Press.
Hunt, Robert C.
    1988   Size and Structure of Authority in Canal Irrigation Systems. Journal of
             Anthropological Research 44(4):335–355.
Hunt, Terry L.
    2007   Rethinking Easter Island's Ecological Catastrophe. Journal of Archaeological
             Science 34(3):485–502.
Huntington, Ellsworth
    1945   Mainsprings of Civilization. New York: John Wiley & Sons.
Hurtado, Ana Magdalena, Kristen Hawkes, Kim Hill, and Hillard Kaplan
    1985   Female Subsistence Strategies among Aché Hunter-Gatherers of Eastern
             Paraguay. Human Ecology 13(1):1–28.
Ingold, Tim
    1980   Hunters, Pastoralists, and Ranchers. Cambridge Studies in Social Anthropology
             No. 28.
    1987   The Appropriation of Nature: Essays on Human Ecology and Social Relations.
             Iowa City: University of Iowa Press.
Irons, William, and Lee Cronk
    2000   Two Decades of a New Paradigm. In: Adaptation and Human Behavior: An
             Anthropological Perspective. Lee Cronk, Napoleon Chagnon, and William
             Irons, eds., pp. 3–26. New York: Aldine.
Isaac, Glynn
    1978a   Food Sharing and Human Evolution: Archaeological Evidence from the
             Plio-Pleistocene of East Africa. Journal of Anthropological Research
             34(3):311–325.
    1978b   The Food-Sharing Behavior of Protohuman Hominids. Scientific American
             238:90–108.
Iverson, Peter
    1990   The Navajos. New York: Chelsea House Publishers.

Jacobs, Lynn
    1991   Waste of the West: Public Lands Ranching. Tucson: Author.

Janzen, Daniel
    1998   Gardenification of Wildland Nature and the Human Footprint. Science
              279:1312–1313.

Jenike, Mark R.
    2001   Nutritional Ecology: Diet, Physical Activity and Body Size. In: Hunter-Gatherers:
              An Interdisciplinary Perspective. Catherine Panter-Brick, Robert H. Layton, and
              Peter Rowley-Conwy, eds., pp. 205–238. Cambridge: Cambridge University Press.

Jilek, Wolfgang
    1982   Indian Healing. Surrey, British Columbia: Hancock House.

Jochim, Michael A.
    1976   Hunter-Gatherer Subsistence and Settlement: A Predictive Model. New York:
              Academic Press.

    1981   Strategies for Survival: Cultural Behavior in an Ecological Context. New York:
              Academic Press.

    1983   Optimization Models in Context. In: Archaeological Hammers and Theories.
              James A. Moore and Authur S. Keene, eds., pp. 157–172. New York: Academic
              Press.

    1998   A Hunter-Gatherer Landscape: Southwest Germany in the Late Paleolithic and
              Mesolithic. New York: Plenum Press.

Johannes, R. E.
    1981   Words of the Lagoon. Berkeley: University of California Press.

Johns, Timothy
    1990   The Origins of Human Diet and Medicine: Chemical Ecology. Tucson: University
              of Arizona Press.

Johnson, Allen W., and Timothy Earle
    2000   The Evolution of Human Societies. 2nd edition. Stanford, CA: Stanford University
              Press.

Johnston, Francis E. (ed.)
    1987   Nutritional Anthropology. New York: Alan R. Liss.

Jonaitis, Aldona
    1986   Art of the Northern Tlingit. Seattle: University of Washington Press.

Jones, Kevin T., and David B. Madsen
    1989   Calculating the Cost of Resource Transportation: A Great Basin Example. Current
              Anthropology 30(4):529–534.

Kammer, Jerry
    1980   The Second Long Walk: The Navajo-Hopi Land Dispute. Albuquerque: University
              of New Mexico Press.

Kant, Immanuel
    1978[1798]   Anthropology from a Pragmatic Point of View. Victor Lyle Dowdell,
              trans. Carbondale: Southern Illinois University Press.

    2007[1781, 1787]   Critique of Pure Reason. Max Müller and Marcus Weigelt, trans.
              New York: Penguin.

Kaus, Andrea
    1992   Common Ground: Ranchers and Researchers in the Mapimi Biosphere Reserve.
            Ph.D. dissertation, University of California, Riverside.
Kay, Charles E., and Randy T. Simmons (eds.)
    2002   Wilderness and Political Ecology: Aboriginal Influences and the Original State
            of Nature. Salt Lake City: University of Utah Press.
Kay, Richard F.
    1981   The Nut-Crackers—A New Theory of the Adaptations of the Ramapithecinae.
            American Journal of Physical Anthropology 55(2):141–151.
Kay, Richard F., and Wendy Sue Sheine
    1979   On the Relationship between Chitin Particle Size and Digestibility in the
            Primate *Galago senegalensis*. American Journal of Physical Anthropology
            50(3):301–308.
Kearney, Michael
    1984   World View. Novato, CA: Chandler and Sharp.
    1986   From the Invisible Hand to Visible Feet: Anthropological Studies of Migration
            and Development. Annual Reviews in Anthropology 15:331–361.
Keegan, William F.
    1986   The Optimal Foraging Analysis of Horticultural Production. American
            Anthropologist 88(1):92–107.
Keene, Authur S.
    1979   Economic Optimization Models and the Study of Hunter-Gatherer Subsistence
            Settlement Systems. In: Transformations: Mathematical Approaches to Culture
            Change. Colin Renfrew and Kenneth L. Cooke, eds., pp. 369–404. New York:
            Academic Press.
    1981   Prehistoric Foraging in a Temperate Forest: A Linear Programming Model. New
            York: Academic Press.
    1983   Biology, Behavior, and Borrowing: A Critical Examination of Optimal Foraging
            Theory in Archaeology. In: Archaeological Hammers and Theories. James A.
            Moore and Authur S. Keene, eds., pp. 137–155. New York: Academic Press.
    1985a   Constraints on Linear Programming Applications in Archaeology. In: For
            Concordance in Archaeological Analysis: Bridging Data Structure, Quantitative
            Technique, and Theory. Christopher Carr, ed., pp. 239–273. Prospect Heights,
            IL: Waveland Press.
    1985b   Nutrition and Economy: Models for the Study of Prehistoric Diet. In: The
            Analysis of Prehistoric Diets. Robert I. Gilbert, Jr., and James H. Mielke, eds.,
            pp. 155–190. New York: Academic Press.
Keirsey, D., and Marilyn Bates
    1978   Please Understand Me. Del Mar, CA: Prometheus Nemesis.
Kelly, Robert L.
    1995   The Foraging Spectrum: Diversity in Hunter-Gatherer Lifeways. Washington,
            DC: Smithsonian Institution.
Kempton, Willett
    1981   The Folk Classification of Ceramics. New York: Academic Press.

Kennard, Edward A.

1979   Hopi Economy and Subsistence. In: Handbook of North American Indians, vol. 9: Southwest. Alfonso Ortiz, ed., pp. 554–563. Washington: Smithsonian Institution Press.

Keyes, Charles (ed.)

1983   Peasant Strategies in Asian Societies: Moral and Rational Economic Approaches— A Symposium. Journal of Asian Studies 42(4):753–867.

Khazanov, A. M.

1984   Nomads and the Outside World. Cambridge: Cambridge University Press.

Kiernan, Michael J., and Curtis H. Freese

1997   Mexico's Plan Piloto Forestal: The Search for Balance between Socioeconomic and Ecological Sustainability. In: Harvesting Wild Species: Implications for Biodiversity Conservation. Curtis H. Freese, ed., pp 93–131. Baltimore: Johns Hopkins University Press.

King, F. H.

1911   Farmers of Forty Centuries. New York: Mrs. F. H. King.

Kinsley, David

1995   Ecology and Religion: Ecological Spirituality in Cross-Cultural Perspective. Englewood Cliffs, NJ: Prentice-Hall.

Kintz, Ellen

1990   Life under the Tropical Canopy: Tradition and Change among the Yucatec Maya. New York: Holt, Rinehart and Winston.

Kirch, Patrick V.

1980   The Archaeological Study of Adaptation: Theoretical and Methodological Issues. In: Advances in Archaeological Method and Theory, vol. 3. Michael B. Schiffer, ed., pp. 101–156. New York: Academic Press.

1994   The Wet and the Dry: Irrigation and Agricultural Intensification in Polynesia. Chicago: University of Chicago Press.

1997   Microcosmic Histories: Island Perspectives on 'Global' Change. American Anthropologist 99(1):30–42.

Kirk, Ruth

1986   Wisdom of the Elders. Victoria, British Columbia, Canada: British Columbia Provincial Museum.

Kirsch, Stuart

2006   Reverse Anthropology: Indigenous Analysis of Social and Environmental Relations in New Guinea. Stanford, CA: Stanford University Press.

Kitcher, Philip

1993   The Advancement of Science. New York: Oxford University Press.

Klee, Gary (ed.)

1980   World Systems of Traditional Resource Management. New York: V. H. Winston and Sons.

Köhler-Rollefson, Ilse

1988   The Aftermath of the Levantine Neolithic Revolution in the Light of Ecological and Ethnographic Evidence. Paleoriént 14:87–93.

Kohn, Alfie
    1990   The Brighter Side of Human Nature. New York: Basic Books.
Kohn, Eduardo
    2007   How Dogs Dream: Amazonian Natures and the Politics of Transspecies
            Engagement. American Ethnologist 34(1):3–24.
Kormondy, Edward J.
    1996   Concepts of Ecology. 4th edition. Upper Saddle River, NJ: Prentice Hall.
Kormondy, Edward J., and Daniel E. Brown
    1998   Fundamentals of Human Ecology. Upper Saddle River, NJ: Prentice Hall.
Kortlandt, Adriaan
    1978   The Ecosystems in Which the Incipient Hominids Could Have Evolved. Recent
            Advances in Primatology 3:503–506.
Kottak, Conrad P.
    1999   The New Ecological Anthropology. American Anthropologist 101(1):23–35.
    2008   Anthropology: The Exploration of Human Diversity. 12th edition. New York:
            McGraw-Hill.
Koyama, Shuzo, and David Hurst Thomas (eds.)
    1981   Affluent Foragers: Pacific Coasts East and West. Osaka: Senri Ethnological Studies
            No. 9.
Krader, Lawrence
    1959   The Ecology of Nomadic Pastoralism. International Social Science Journal
            XI(4):499–510.
Krech, Shepard III
    1999   The Ecological Indian: Myth and History. New York: W. W. Norton & Company.
Kroeber, Alfred L.
    1939   Cultural and Natural Areas of Native North America. University of California
            Publications in American Archaeology and Ethnology 38.
    1944   Configurations of Culture Growth. Berkeley: University of California Press.
    1953   Cultural and Natural Areas of Native North America. Berkeley: University of
            California Press.
Kroeber, Alfred L., and Clyde Kluckhohn
    1952   Culture: A Critical Review of Concepts and Definitions. Cambridge, MA: Peabody
            Museum Papers, XLVII:1.
Kronenfeld, David B.
    1979   Innate Language? Language Science 1(2):209–239.
Kronenfeld, David B., James Armstrong, and Stan Wilmoth
    1985   Exploring the Internal Structure of Linguistic Categories: An Extensionist
            Semantic View. In: Directions in Cognitive Anthropology. Janet Dougherty, ed.,
            pp. 91–109. Urbana: University of Illinois Press.
Kropotkin, Peter
    1904   Mutual Aid, a Factor in Evolution. London: Wm. Heinemann.
Kuhn, Thomas
    1962   The Structure of Scientific Revolutions. Chicago: University of Chicago Press.

Kurland, Jeffrey, and Stephen Beckerman

    1985   Optimal Foraging and Hominid Evolution: Labor and Reciprocity. American Anthropologist 87(1):73–93.

Kurz, Richard B., Jr.

    1987   Contributions of Women to Subsistence in Tribal Societies. In: Research in Economic Anthropology, vol. 8. Barry L. Isaac, ed., pp. 31–59. Greenwich, CT: JAI Press.

Lacerenza, Deborah

    1988   An Historical Overview of the Navajo Relocation. Cultural Survival Quarterly 12(3):3–6.

Laird, Carobeth

    1976   The Chemehuevis. Banning, CA: Malki Museum Press.

    1984   Mirror and Pattern. Banning, CA: Malki Museum Press.

Laird, Sarah A. (ed.)

    2002   Biodiversity and Traditional Knowledge: Equitable Partnerships in Practice. London: Earthscan.

Lakoff, George

    1987   Women, Fire and Dangerous Things. Chicago: University of Chicago Press.

Lamb, H. H.

    1995   Climate, History and the Modern World. 2nd edition. London: Routledge.

Lamberg-Karlovsky, Martha (ed.)

    2000   The Breakout: The Origins of Civilization. Peabody Museum Monographs No. 9.

Lando, Richard

    1983   The Spirits Aren't So Powerful Any More: Spirit Belief and Irrigation Organization in Northern Thailand. Journal of the Siam Society 71(1/2):121–148.

Lang, George

    1982   The Cuisine of Hungary. New York: Atheneum.

Lang, Susan

    1989   The World's Healthiest Diet. American Health, Sept. 1989:105–112.

Langer, Ellen

    1983   The Psychology of Control. Beverly Hills: Sage.

Langness, L. L.

    1987   The Study of Culture. 2nd edition. Novato: Chandler and Sharp.

Lanner, E.

    1981   The Pinyon Pine. Reno: University of Nevada Press.

    1996   Made for Each Other. New York: Oxford University Press.

Lansing, J. Stephen

    1987   Balinese "Water Temples" and the Management of Irrigation. American Anthropologist 89(2):326–341.

    1991   Priests and Programmers: Technologies of Power in the Engineered Landscape of Bali. Princeton, NJ: Princeton University Press.

Lansing, J. Stephen, and James N. Kremer

    1993   Emergent Properties of Balinese Water Temple Networks: Coadaptation on a Rugged Fitness Landscape. American Anthropologist 95(1):97–114.

Latour, Bruno
    2004   Politics of Nature: How to Bring the Sciences into Democracy. Catherine Porter, trans. Cambridge, MA: Harvard University Press.

Laughlin, William S.
    1968   Hunting: An Integrated Biobehavior System and Its Evolutionary Importance. In: Man the Hunter. Richard B. Lee and Irven DeVore, eds., pp. 304–320. Chicago: Aldine.

Lawton, Harry W., Philip J. Wilke, Mary DeDecker, and William M. Mason
    1976   Agriculture among the Paiute of Owens Valley. The Journal of California Anthropology 3(1):13–51.

Layton, Robert H.
    2001   Hunter-Gatherers, Their Neighbors and the Nation State. In: Hunter-Gatherers: An Interdisciplinary Perspective. Catherine Panter-Brick, Robert H. Layton, and Peter Rowley-Conwy, eds., pp. 292–321. Cambridge: Cambridge University Press.

Leach, E. R.
    1964   Animal Categories of Verbal Abuse. In: New Directions in the Study of Language. Eric Lenneberg, ed., pp. 23–64. Cambridge, MA: Massachusetts Institute of Technology Press.

Leacock, Eleanor
    1978   Women's Status in Egalitarian Society: Implications for Social Evolution. Current Anthropology 19(2):247–275.

LeBlanc, Stephen, and Katherine E. Register
    2002   Constant Battles: The Myth of the Peaceful, Noble Savage. New York: St. Martin's Griffin.

Lee, Richard B.
    1965   Subsistence Ecology of !Kung Bushmen. Ph.D. dissertation, University of California, Berkeley.
    1968   What Hunters Do for a Living, or, How to Make Out on Scarce Resources. In: Man the Hunter. Richard B. Lee and Irven DeVore, eds., pp. 30–48. Chicago: Aldine.
    1972   The !Kung Bushmen of Botswana. In: Hunters and Gatherers Today. M. G. Bicchieri, ed., pp. 327–368. New York: Holt, Rinehart and Winston.
    1982   Lactation, Ovulation, Infanticide, and Women's Work: A Study of Hunter-Gatherer Population Regulation. In: Biosocial Mechanisms of Population Regulation. Mark N. Cohen, Roy S. Malpass, and Harold G. Klein, eds., pp. 321–348. New Haven, CT: Yale University Press.
    1984   The Dobe !Kung. New York: Holt, Rinehart and Winston.

Lee, Richard B., and Richard Daly (eds.)
    1999   The Cambridge Encyclopedia of Hunters and Gatherers. Cambridge: Cambridge University Press.

Lee, Richard B., and Irven DeVore (eds.)
    1968   Man the Hunter. Chicago: Aldine.

Lee, Robert G.
    1987   Community Fragmentation: Implications for Future Wild Fire Management. In: Proceedings of the Symposium on Wildland Fire 2000, pp. 5–14. Berkeley: U.S. Forest Service, Pacific Southwest Forest and Range Experiment Station.

Lees, Susan H., and Daniel G. Bates
    1974   The Origins of Specialized Nomadic Pastoralism: A Systematic Model. American Antiquity 39(2):187–193.

Lehr, Jay H. (ed.)
    1992   Rational Readings on Environmental Concerns. New York: Van Nostrand Reinhold.

Lentz, David (ed.)
    2000   Imperfect Balance. New York: Columbia University Press.

Lerner, M.
    1980   The Belief in a Just World: A Fundamental Delusion. New York: Plenum Press.

Le Roy Ladurie, Emmanuel
    1971   Times of Feast, Times of Famine. Barbara Bray, trans. New York: Doubleday.

Leslie, Paul W., James R. Bindon, and Paul T. Baker
    1984   Caloric Requirements of Human Populations: A Model. Human Ecology 12(2):137–162.

Levi-Strauss, Claude
    1962   La Pensee Sauvage. Paris: Plon.
    1963[1958]   Structural Anthropology. New York: Basic Books.
    1964–1971   Mythologiques. Paris: Plon.

Lewis, Henry T.
    1973   Patterns of Indian Burning in California: Ecology and Ethnohistory. Ballena Press Anthropological Papers No. 1.
    1982   Fire Technology and Resource Management in Aboriginal North America and Australia. In: Resource Managers: North American and Australian Hunter-Gatherers. Nancy M. Williams and Eugene S. Hunn, eds., pp. 45–67. Boulder, CO: Westview Press.

Lewis, Martin
    1992   Green Delusions. Durham, NC: Duke University Press.

Lewis, Walter, and Elvin-Lewis, Memory
    1977   Medical Botany. New York: John Wiley & Sons.

Li, Tania Murray
    2007   The Will to Improve: Governmentality, Development, and the Practice of Politics. Durham: Duke University Press.

Libecap, Gary
    1989   Contracting for Property Rights. Cambridge: Cambridge University Press.

Linden, Eugene
    1991   Lost Tribes, Lost Knowledge. Time, September 23: 46–55.

Linton, Sally
    1971   Woman the Gatherer: Male Bias in Anthropology. In: Women in Cross-Cultural Perspective: A Source Book. Sue-Ellen Jacobs, ed., pp. 9–21. Urbana: University of Illinois, Department of Urban & Regional Planning.

Liu, Li

    2004   The Chinese Neolithic. Cambridge: Cambridge University Press.

Lizot, Jacques

    1977   Population, Resources and Warfare among the Yanomami. Man 12(3/4):497–517.

Locke, John

    1975[1685]   An Essay Concerning Human Understanding. Oxford: Oxford
              University Press.

Loewe, Michael, and Edward L. Shaughnessy

    1999   The Cambridge History of Ancient China. Cambridge: Cambridge University
              Press.

Lopez, Kevin Lee

    1992   Returning to Fields. American Indian Culture and Research Journal 16:165–174.

Lovejoy, C. Owen

    1981   The Origin of Man. Science 211:341–350.

    1984   The Natural Detective. Natural History 10:24–28.

Low, Bobbi S.

    1993   Behavioral Ecology of Conservation in Traditional Societies. Paper presented at the
              annual meetings of the American Anthropological Association, Washington, DC.

Lowie, Robert

    1937   History of Ethnological Theory. New York: Rinehart & Co.

MacArthur, Robert

    1972   Geographical Ecology. New York: Harper & Row.

Mace, Ruth

    1993   Transitions between Cultivation and Pastoralism in Sub-Saharan Africa. Current
              Anthropology 34(4):363–382.

MacLean, William C.

    1984   Nutrition in Infancy. In: Nutrition Reviews' Present Knowledge in Nutrition, pp.
              619–635. Washington, DC: Nutrition Foundation.

MacNeill, J.

    1992   The Mountains of the Mediterranean World. Oxford: Oxford University Press.

MacNeish, Richard

    1992   The Origins of Agriculture and Settled Life. Norman: University of Oklahoma Press.

Madsen, David B.

    1982   Get It Where the Gettin's Good: A Variable Model of Great Basin Subsistence and
              Settlement Based on Data from the Eastern Great Basin. In: Man and
              Environment in the Great Basin. David B. Madsen and James F. O'Connell, eds.,
              pp. 207–226. Society for American Archaeology Papers No. 2.

    1986   Leap and Grab: Energetic Efficiency Tests of Cricket Use. Paper presented at the
              Great Basin Anthropological Conference, Las Vegas.

Madsen, David B., and James E. Kirkman

    1988   Hunting Hoppers. American Antiquity 53(3):593–604.

Madsen, David B., and Dave N. Schmitt

    1998   Mass Collecting and the Diet Breadth Model: A Great Basin Example. Journal of
              Archaeological Science 25(5):445–455.

Malinowski, Bronislaw

 1922 Argonauts of the Western Pacific. New York: Dutton.

 1935 Coral Gardens and Their Magic. Chicago: American Book Co.

 1944 A Scientific Theory of Culture. Chapel Hill: University of North Carolina Press.

Mallory, J. P

 1989 In Search of the Indo-Europeans. London: Thames and Hudson.

Malthus, Thomas

 1960[1798] On Population. New York: Random House.

Mamdani, Mahmood

 1972 The Myth of Population Control. New York: Monthly Review Press.

Mann, Alan E.

 1981 Diet and Human Evolution. In: Omnivorous Primates. Robert S. Harding and Geza Teleki, eds., pp. 10–36. New York: Columbia University Press.

Marcus, Joyce, and Gary M. Feinman

 1998 Introduction. In: Archaic States. Gary M. Feinman and Joyce Marcus, eds., pp. 3–13. Santa Fe, NM: School of American Research Press.

Marsh, George Perkins

 2003 Man and Nature. Ed. D. Lowenthal. Orig. 1864. Seattle: University of Washington Press.

Marshall, Fiona

 1990 Origins of Specialized Pastoral Production in East Africa. American Anthropologist 92(4):873–894.

Marten, Gerald G. (ed.)

 1986 Traditional Agriculture in Southeast Asia. Honolulu: East-West Center.

Martin, Calvin

 1978 Keepers of the Game. Berkeley: University of California Press.

Martin, Gary

 1995 Ethnobotany. London: Chapman and Hall.

Martin, Laura

 1986 "Eskimo Words for Snow": A Case Study in the Genesis and Decay of an Anthropological Example. American Anthropologist 88(2):418–442.

Martin, Paul S., and Christine R. Szuter

 1999 War Zones and Game Sinks in Lewis and Clark's West. Conservation Biology 13(1):36–45.

Marzluff, John, and Tony Angel

 2005 In the Company of Crows and Ravens. New Haven, CT: Yale University Press.

Mason, Otis

 1894 Technogeography, or the Relation of the Earth to the Industries of Mankind. American Anthropologist 7(2):137–161.

Matson, P. A., W. J. Parton, A. G. Power, and M. J. Swift

 1997 Agricultural Intensification and Ecosystem Properties. Science 227:504–509.

Matthiessen, Peter

 1962 Under the Mountain Wall: A Chronicle of Two Seasons in the Stone Age. New York: Viking.

McCabe, J. Terrence, Scott Perkin, and Claire Schofield
  1992   Can Conservation and Development Be Coupled among Pastoral People? An
          Examination of the Maasai of the Ngorongoro Conservation Area, Tanzania.
          Human Organization 51(4):353–366.
McCay, Bonnie
  1998   Oyster Wars and the Public Trust: Property Law, and Ecology in New Jersey
          History. Tucson: University of Arizona Press.
McCay, Bonnie, and James Acheson (eds.)
  1987   The Question of the Commons. Tucson: University of Arizona Press.
McCorriston, Joy
  1992   The Early Development of Agriculture in the Ancient Near East: An Ecological
          and Evolutionary Study. Ph.D. dissertation, Yale University.
McCorriston, Joy, and Frank Hole
  1991   The Ecology of Seasonal Stress and the Origins of Agriculture in the Near East.
          American Anthropologist 93(1):46–69.
McCreedy, Marion
  1994   The Arms of the Dibouka. In: Key Issues in Hunter-Gatherer Research.
          Ernest S. Burch, Jr. and Linda J. Ellanna, eds., pp. 15–34. Oxford: Berg
          Publishers.
McFeat, Tom (ed.)
  1966   Indians of the North Pacific Coast. Seattle: University of Washington Press.
McGovern, Thomas H., Gerald F. Bigelow, Thomas Amorosi, and Daniel Russell
  1988   Northern Islands, Human Error, and Environmental Degradation. Human
          Ecology 16(3):225–270.
McGrew, W. C.
  1979   Evolutionary Implications of Sex Differences in Chimpanzee Predation and Tool
          Use. In: The Great Apes. D. A. Hamburg and E. R. McCown, eds, pp. 440–463.
          Menlo Park, CA: Benjamin/Cummings.
  1981   The Female Chimpanzee as a Human Evolutionary Prototype. In: Woman the
          Gatherer. Frances Dahlberg, ed., pp. 35–73. New Haven, CT: Yale University
          Press.
McIntosh, Roderick J., Joseph A. Tainter, and Susan Keech McIntosh (eds.)
  2000   The Way the Wind Blows: Climate, History, and Human Action. New York:
          Columbia University Press.
Medin, Douglas L., and Scott Atran (eds.)
  1999   Folkbiology. Cambridge, MA: Massachusetts Institute of Technology Press.
Meggers, Betty J.
  1954   Environmental Limitation on the Development of Culture. American
          Anthropologist 56(5):801–824.
Meggitt, Mervyn
  1977   Blood Is Their Argument. Palo Alto, CA: Hayfield.
Meillassoux, Claude
  1981   Maidens, Meal and Money. Cambridge: Cambridge University Press.

Meilleur, Brien A.
    1996   Forests and Polynesian Adaptations. In: Tropical Deforestation: The Human
              Dimension. Leslie E. Sponsel, Thomas N. Headland, and Robert C. Bailey, eds.,
              pp.76–94. New York: Columbia University Press.
Mencius
    1979   Mencius. D. Lau, trans. Harmondsworth, England: Penguin.
Merleau-Ponty, Maurice
    1962   The Phenomenology of Perception. London: Routledge, Kegan Paul.
    1963   The Structure of Behavior. Boston: Beacon Press.
    1964   Signs. Evanston: Northwestern University Press.
    1968   The Visible and the Invisible. Chicago: Northwestern University Press.
Merry, Sally
    2003   Human Rights Law and the Demonization of Culture. Anthropology News
              44(3):4–5.
Metcalfe, Duncan, and K. Renee Barlow
    1992   A Model for Exploring the Optimal Trade-off between Field Processing and
              Transport. American Anthropologist 94(2):340–356.
Meyer, William B.
    1996   Human Impact on the Earth. Cambridge: Cambridge University Press.
Mills, C. Wright
    1959   The Sociological Imagination. Oxford: Oxford University Press.
Minnich, Richard
    1983   Fire Mosaics in Southern California and Northern Baja California. Science
              219:1287–1294.
Minnis, Paul E. (ed.)
    2000   Ethnobotany: A Reader. Norman: University of Oklahoma Press.
Mintz, Sidney
    1985   Sweetness and Power. New York: Viking.
Mischel, Walter
    1984   On the Predictability of Behavior and the Structure of Personality.
              In: Personality and the Prediction of Behavior. Robert A. Zucker,
              Joel Aronoff, and A. I. Rabin, eds., pp. 269–305. New York: Academic
              Press.
Mithen, Steven J.
    1990   Thoughtful Foragers: A Study of Prehistoric Decision Making. Cambridge:
              Cambridge University Press.
Moerman, Daniel E.
    1986   Medicinal Plants of Native America (2 vols.). University of Michigan Museum
              of Anthropology Technical Reports No. 19.
Moldenke, Harold N., and Alma L. Moldenke
    1952   Plants of the Bible. Waltham, MA: Chronica Botanica.
Molles, Manuel C., Jr.
    1999   Ecology: Concepts and Applications. Boston: McGraw-Hill.

Molnar, Stephen, and Iva M. Molnar
    2000   Environmental Change and Human Survival: Some Dimensions of Human
           Ecology. Upper Saddle River, NJ: Prentice Hall.
Montaigne, Michel de.
    1943   The Complete Essays of Montaigne (translated and edited by Donald M.
           Frame). Stanford, CA: Stanford University Press.
Montesquieu, Charles, Baron
    1949[1748]   The Spirit of the Laws. New York: Hafner.
Moore, James A.
    1981   The Effects of Information Networks in Hunter-Gatherer Societies. In: Hunter-
           Gatherer Foraging Strategies: Ethnographic and Archaeological Analyses. Bruce
           Winterhalder and Eric Alden Smith, eds., pp. 194–217. Chicago: University of
           Chicago Press.
    1983   The Trouble with Know-It-Alls: Information as a Social and Ecological Resource.
           In: Archaeological Hammers and Theories. James A. Moore and Authur S. Keene,
           eds., pp. 173–191. New York: Academic Press.
Moore, Omar Khayyam
    1957   Divination—A New Perspective. American Anthropologist 59(1):69–74.
Moran, Emilio F.
    1993a   Deforestation and Land Use in the Brazilian Amazon. Human Ecology 21(1):1–21.
    1993b   Through Amazonian Eyes: The Human Ecology of Amazonian Populations. Iowa
           City: University of Iowa Press.
    1996   Deforestation in the Brazilian Amazon. In: Tropical Deforestation: The Human
           Dimension. Leslie E. Sponsel, Thomas N. Headland, and Robert C. Bailey, eds.,
           pp.149–164. New York: Columbia University Press.
    2006   People and Nature: An Introduction to Human Ecological Relations. Malden, MA:
           Blackwell.
    2008   Human Adaptability: An Introduction to Ecological Anthropology, 3d ed. Boulder,
           CO: Westview Press.
Moran, Emilio F. (ed.)
    1990   The Ecosystem Approach in Anthropology. Ann Arbor: University of Michigan
           Press.
Morgan, Lewis Henry
    1851   League of the Ho-dé-no-sau-nee, Iroquois. Rochester, NY: Sage & Brother.
    1871   Systems of Consanguinity and Affinity of the Human Family. Smithsonian
           Institution, Contributions to Knowledge 17(2).
    1877   Ancient Society. New York: Henry Holt.
    1882   Houses and House-Life of the American Aborigines. Washington: Government
           Printing Office.
Morrell, Mike
    1985   The Gitksan and Wet'suwet'en Fishery in the Skeena River System. Hazelton, B.C.,
           Canada: Gitksan-Wet'suwet'en Tribal Council.
Morton, A.
    1981   History of Botanical Science. New York: Academic Press.

Moseley, Michael
    1975   The Maritime Origins of Andean Civilization. Menlo Park, CA: Cummings.
Murdock, George P.
    1968   The Current Status of the World's Hunting and Gathering Peoples. In: Man the
            Hunter. Richard B. Lee and Irven DeVore, eds., pp. 13–20. Chicago: Aldine.
    1969   Ethnographic Atlas: A Summary. Ethnology 6(2):109–236.
Murphy, Earl
    1967   Governing Nature. Chicago: Quadrangle Books.
Myers, Isabel Briggs, and Peter B. Myers
    1980   Gifts Differing. Palo Alto: Consulting Psychologists Press.
Nabhan, Gary
    1985   Gathering the Desert. Tucson: University of Arizona Press.
    1989   Enduring Seeds. San Francisco: North Point Press.
Nabhan, Gary, Amadeo Rea, Karen Reichhardt, Eric Mellink, and Charles F. Hutchinson
    1982   Papago Influences on Habitat and Biotic Diversity: Quitovac Oasis Ethnoecology.
            Journal of Ethnobiology 2(2):124–143.
Nadasdy, Paul
    2004   Hunters and Bureaucrats: Power, Knowledge, and Aboriginal-State Relations in the
            Southwest Yukon. Vancouver: University of British Columbia Press.
Nagengast, Carole, and Terence Turner
    1997   Introduction: Universal Human Rights versus Cultural Relativity. Journal of
            Anthropological Research 53(3):269–272.
Nash, Roderick
    1973   Wilderness and the American Mind. New Haven: Yale University Press.
National Research Council
    1989   Lost Crops of the Incas. Washington, DC: National Academy Press.
Nazarea, Virginia D.
    1998   Cultural Memory and Biodiversity. Tucson: University of Arizona Press.
Nazarea, Virginia D. (ed.)
    1999   Ethnoecology: Situated Knowledge/Located Lives. Tucson: University of Arizona Press.
Neihardt, John
    1932   Black Elk Speaks. New York: William Morrow.
Nelson, Richard K.
    1983   Make Prayers to the Raven. Chicago: University of Chicago Press.
Nerlove, Sara B.
    1974   Woman's Workload and Infant Feeding Practices: A Relationship with
            Demographic Implications. Ethnology 13(2):207–214.
Netting, Robert
    1974   Agrarian Ecology. Annual Review of Anthropology 3:21–56.
    1981   Balancing on an Alp. Cambridge: Cambridge University Press.
    1986   Cultural Ecology. 2nd edition. Prospect Heights, IL: Waveland Press.
Nichols, Deborah
    1987   Risk and Agricultural Intensification during the Formative Period in the Northern
            Basin of Mexico. American Anthropologist 89(3):596–616.

Nietschmann, Bernard
  1973   Between Land and Water. New York: Seminar Press.
Nisbett, Richard, Eugene Borgida, Harvey Reed, and Rick Crandall
  1976   Popular Induction: Information Is Not Necessarily Informative. In: Cognition and
          Social Behavior. John S. Carroll and John W. Payne, eds., pp. 113–133. New York:
          Academic Press.
Nisbett, Richard, and Lee Ross
  1980   Human Inference: Strategies and Shortcomings of Social Judgment. Englewood
          Cliffs, NJ: Prentice-Hall.
Nishida, Toshisada
  1973   The Ant-Gathering Behavior by the Use of Tools among Wild Chimpanzees of the
          Mahale Mountains. Journal of Human Evolution 2:357–370.
  1987   Local Traditions and Cultural Transmission. In: Primate Societies. Barbara B.
          Smuts, Dorothy L. Cheney, Robert M. Seyfarth, Richard W. Wrangham, and
          Thomas T. Stuhsaker, eds., pp. 462–474. Chicago: University of Chicago Press.
Nishida, Toshisada, and Mariko Hiraiwa-Hasegawa
  1987   Chimpanzees and Bonobos: Cooperative Relationships among Males. In: Primate
          Societies. Barbara B. Smuts, Dorothy L. Cheney, Robert M. Seyfarth, Richard W.
          Wrangham, and Thomas T. Stuhsaker, eds., pp. 165–177. Chicago: University of
          Chicago Press.
Noss, Andrew J.
  1997   The Economic Importance of Communal Net Hunting among the BaAka of the
          Central African Republic. Human Ecology 25(1):71–89.
O'Connell, James F., and Kristen Hawkes
  1984   Food Choice and Foraging Strategies among the Alyawara. Journal of
          Anthropological Research 40(4):504–535.
Odum, Eugene P.
  1953   Fundamentals of Ecology. Philadelphia: W. B. Saunders.
  1975   Ecology. New York: Holt, Rinehart and Winston.
  1993   Ecology and Our Endangered Life-Support Systems. 2nd edition. Sunderland, MA:
          Sinauer Associates, Inc.
Oldfield, Margery, and Janis Alcorn
  1987   Conservation of Traditional Agroecoystems. BioScience 37:199–208.
Olol-Dapash, Meitamei
  2002   Mau Forest Destruction: Human and Ecological Disaster in the Making. Cultural
          Survival Voices 1(3):1, 9.
Orans, Martin
  1975   Domesticating the Functional Dragon: An Analysis of Piddocke's Potlatch.
          American Anthropologist 77(2):312–328.
Orians, Gordon H., and Nolan E. Pearson
  1979   On the Theory of Central Place Foraging. In: Analysis of Ecological Systems.
          David J. Horn, Gordon R. Stairs, and Roger D. Mitchell, eds., pp. 155–177.
          Columbus: Ohio State University.

Orlove, Benjamin S., and Stephen B. Brush
    1996   Anthropology and the Conservation of Biodiversity. Annual Review of
            Anthropology 25:329–352.

Ortiz, Alfonso (ed.)
    1983   Handbook of North American Indians, vol. 10: Southwest. Washington, DC:
            Smithsonian Institution Press.

Ortiz de Montellano, Bernard R.
    1978   Aztec Cannibalism: An Ecological Necessity? Science 200:611–617.

Ostrom, Elinor
    1990   Governing the Commons: The Evolution of Institutions for Collective Action.
            New York: Cambridge University Press.

Ott, Sandra
    1993   The Circle of Mountains: A Basque Sheepherding Community. Reno: University of
            Nevada Press.

Overal, William Leslie
    1990   Introduction to Ethnozoology: What It Is or Could Be. In: Proceedings of the First
            International Congress of Ethnobiology. Darrell A. Posey, William Leslie Overal, Charles
            R. Clement, Mark J. Plotkin, Elaine Elisabetsky, Clarice Novaes de Mota, and José Flàvio
            Pessôa de Barros, eds., pp. 127–129. Belém, Brazil: Museu Paraense Emílio Goeldi.

Painter, Michael, and William Durham (eds.)
    1995   The Social Causes of Environmental Destruction in Latin America. Ann Arbor:
            University of Michigan Press.

Panter-Brick, Catherine, Robert H. Layton, and Peter Rowley-Conwy
    2001a   Lines of Inquiry. In: Hunter-Gatherers: An Interdisciplinary Perspective. Catherine
            Panter-Brick, Robert H. Layton, and Peter Rowley-Conwy, eds., pp. 1–11.
            Cambridge: Cambridge University Press.

Panter-Brick, Catherine, Robert H. Layton, and Peter Rowley-Conwy (eds.)
    2001b   Hunter-Gatherers: An Interdisciplinary Perspective. Cambridge: Cambridge
            University Press.

Parezo, Nancy J.
    1996   The Diné (Navajos): Sheep Is Life. In: Paths of Life: American Indians of the
            Southwest and Northern Mexico. Thomas E. Sheridan and Nancy J. Parezo, eds.,
            pp. 3–33. Tucson: University of Arizona Press.

Park, Robert Ezra
    1936   Human Ecology. American Journal of Sociology 42:1–15.

Parker, R., and H. Toots
    1980   Trace Elements in Bones as Paleobiological Indicators. In: Fossils in the Making. A. K.
            Behrensmeyer and A. P. Hill, eds., pp. 197–207. Chicago: University of Chicago Press.

Parlowe, Anita
    1988   Cry, Sacred Ground. Washington, DC: Christic Institute.

Paulson, Susan, and Lisa Gezon (eds.)
    2005   Political Ecology across Spaces, Scales, and Social Groups. New Brunswick, NJ:
            Rutgers University Press.

Pemberton, Robert W.
    1988   The Use of the Thai Giant Waterbug, *Lethocereus indicus* (Hemiptera:
            Belostomatidae), as Human Food in China. Pan-Pacific Entomologist 64:81–82.
Perrings, Charles
    1987   Economy and Environment. Cambridge: Cambridge University Press.
Peters, David Urlin
    1960   Land Use in Barotseland. Rhodes-Livingstone Institute Communication No. 19.
Peterson, Christopher, Steven Maier, and Martin E. P. Seligman
    1993   Learned Helplessness. New York: Oxford University Press.
Peterson, Larry C., and Gerlad H. Haug
    2005   Climate and the Collapse of Maya Civilization. American Scientist 93(4):322–329.
Piatelli-Palmarini, Massimo
    1994   Inevitable Illusions: How Mistakes of Reason Rule Our Minds. NY: John Wiley &
            Sons.
Piddocke, Stuart
    1965   The Potlatch System of the Southern Kwakiutl: A New Perspective. Southwestern
            Journal of Anthropology 21(3):244–264.
Pimentel, David, S. Christ, L. Spritz, L. Fitton, R. Safouer, R. Blair, C. Harvey,
P. Resosudarmo, K. Sinclair, D. Kurtz, and M. McNair
    1995   Environmental and Economic Costs of Soil Erosion and Conservation Benefits.
            Science 267:1117–1122.
Pimentel, David, M. Herdendorf, S. Eisenfeld, L. Olander, M. Carroquino, C. Corson,
J. McDade, Y. Chung, W. Cannon, J. Roberts, L. Bluman, and J. Gregg
    1994   Achieving a Secure Energy Future: Environmental and Economic Issues.
            Ecological Economics 9(3):201–219.
Pimentel, David, Michael McNair, Louise Buck, Marcia Pimentel, and Jeremy Kamıl
    1997   The Value of Forests to World Food Security. Human Ecology 25(1):91–120.
Pinker, Stephen
    1994   The Language Instinct. New York: HarperPerennial.
    2003   The Blank Slate. New York: Penguin.
Pinkerton, Evelyn (ed.)
    1989   Cooperative Management of Local Fisheries: New Directions for Improved
            Management and Community Development. Vancouver: University of British
            Columbia.
Pinkerton, Evelyn, and Martyn Weinstein
    1995   Fisheries That Work: Sustainability through Community-Based Management.
            Vancouver: David Suzuki Foundation.
Piperno, Dolores, and Deborah Pearsall
    1998   The Origins of Agriculture in the Neotropics. New York: Academic Press.
Plotkin, Mark J.
    2000   Medicine Quest: In Search of Nature's Healing Secrets. New York: Viking.
Plotkin, Mark J., and Lisa Famolare (eds.)
    1992   Sustainable Harvest and Marketing of Rain Forest Products. Washington, DC:
            Island Press.

Ponting, Clive
    1991   A Green History of the World. New York: Penguin.
Popkin, Samuel
    1979   The Rational Peasant. Berkeley: University of California Press.
Porter, Claire, and Frank W. Marlowe
    2007   How Marginal Are Forager Habitats? Journal of Archaeological Science 34(1):59–68.
Posey, Darrell Addison
    2001   Intellectual Property Rights and the Sacred Balance: Some Spiritual Consequences
            from the Commercialization of Traditional Resources. In: Indigenous Traditions and
            Ecology: The Interbeing of Cosmology and Community. John A. Grom, ed., pp.
            3–23. Cambridge, MA: Harvard University Press.
Postel, Sandra
    1994   Carrying Capacity: Earth's Bottom Line. In: State of the World 1994. Lester R. Brown,
            ed., pp. 3–21. New York: Norton.
Pottier, Johan
    1999   Anthropology of Food: The Social Dynamics of Food Security. Cambridge: Polity
            Press.
Pottier, Johan, Alan Bicker, and Paul Sillitoe (eds.)
    2003   Negotiating Local Knowledge: Power and Identity in Development. London: Pluto
            Press.
Potts, Richard
    1988   On an Early Hominid Scavenging Niche. Current Anthropology 29(1):153–155.
Preston, William L.
    1997   Large Game in Colonial California: Precolumbian Mirror or Mirage? Paper presented
            at the annual meeting of the Association of American Geographers, Fort Worth, TX.
Price, David
    1995   Energy and Human Evolution. Population and Environment 16(4):301–319.
Price, David H.
    1994   Wittfogel's Neglected Hydraulic/Hydroagricultural Distinction. Journal of
            Anthropological Research 50(2):187–204.
Price, T. Douglas, and James A. Brown (eds.)
    1985   Prehistoric Hunter-Gatherers: The Emergence of Cultural Complexity. Orlando:
            Academic Press.
Price, T. Douglas, and Anne Birgitte Gebauer
    1995a   New Perspectives on the Transition to Agriculture. In: Last Hunters—First Farmers:
            New Perspectives on the Prehistoric Transition to Agriculture. T. Douglas Price and
            Anne Birgitte Gebauer, eds., pp. 3–19. Santa Fe, NM: School of American Research
            Press.
Price, T. Douglas, and Anne Birgitte Gebauer (eds.)
    1995b   Last Hunters—First Farmers: New Perspectives on the Prehistoric Transition to
            Agriculture. Santa Fe, NM: School of American Research Press.
Prucha, Francis Paul
    1984   The Great Father: The United States Government and the American Indians (2
            vols.). Lincoln: University of Nebraska Press.

Pulliam, H. Ronald
    1981   On Predicting Human Diets. Journal of Ethnobiology 1(1):61–68.
Purseglove, J.
    1972   Tropical Crops (2 vols.). London: Longmans.
Pyke, G. H., H. R. Pulliam, and E. L. Charnov
    1977   Optimal Foraging: A Selective Review of Theory and Tests. The Quarterly Review of
            Biology 52(2):137–154.
Pyne, Stephen J.
    1995   World Fire: The Culture of Fire on Earth. New York: Henry Holt.
    1998   Forged in Fire: History, Land, and Anthropogenic Fire. In: Advances in Historical
            Ecology. William Balée, ed., pp. 64–103. New York: Columbia University Press.
Quinn, Naomi
    1975   Decision Models of Social Structure. American Ethnologist 2(1):19–45.
    1978   Do Mfantse Fish Sellers Estimate Probabilities in Their Heads? American Ethnologist
            5(2):206–226.
Radcliffe-Brown, A. R.
    1957   A Natural Science of Society. New York: Free Press.
Randall, Robert
    1977   Change and Variation in Samal Fishing: Making Plans to Make a Living in the
            Southern Philippines. Ph.D. dissertation, University of California, Berkeley.
Rappaport, Roy A.
    1967   Pigs for the Ancestors: Ritual in the Ecology of a New Guinea People. New Haven,
            CT: Yale University Press.
    1971   The Sacred in Human Evolution. Annual Review of Ecology and Systematics 2:23–44.
    1984   Pigs for the Ancestors: Ritual in the Ecology of a New Guinea People. 2nd edition.
            New Haven, CT: Yale University Press.
    1999   Ritual and Religion in the Making of Humanity. New Haven, CT: Yale University
            Press.
Read, Piers Paul
    1974   Alive: The Story of the Andes Survivors. Philadelphia: J. B. Lippincott.
Redding, Richard W.
    1988   A General Explanation of Subsistence Change: From Hunting and Gathering to Food
            Production. Journal of Anthropological Archaeology 7(1):56–97.
Redfield, Robert, and Alfonso Villa Rojas
    1934   Chan Kom, A Maya Village. Washington, DC: Carnegie Institute of Washington.
Redford, Kent H.
    1990   The Ecologically Noble Savage. Orion Nature Quarterly 9:25–29.
Redford, Kent H., and Jane A. Mansour (eds.)
    1996   Traditional Peoples and Biodiversity Conservation in Large Tropical Landscapes.
            Arlington, VA: Nature Conservancy.
Redman, Charles L.
    1999   Human Impact on Ancient Environments. Tucson: University of Arizona Press.
Reed, Charles (ed.)
    1977   Origins of Agriculture. Hague: Mouton.

Reichel-Dolmatoff, G.
    1971   Amazonian Cosmos. Chicago: University of Chicago Press.
    1976   Cosmology and Ecological Analysis: A View from the Rain Forest. Man 11:307–316.
Reidhead, Van A.
    1979   Linear Programming Models in Archaeology. Annual Review of Anthropology
            8:543–578.
Repetto, Robert
    1992   Accounting for Environmental Assets. Scientific American 266:94–100.
Richards, Audrey
    1939   Land, Labour and Diet in Northern Rhodesia: An Economic Study of the Bemba
            Tribe. Oxford: Oxford University Press.
    1948[1932]   Hunger and Work in a Savage Tribe. London: Routledge, Kegan Paul.
Richards, John F., and Richard Tucker (eds.)
    1988   World Deforestation in the 20th Century. Durham: Duke University Press.
Richerson, Peter, and Robert Boyd
    2005   Not by Genes Alone: How Culture Transformed Human Evolution. Chicago:
            University of Chicago Press.
Richerson, Peter J.
    1977   Ecology and Human Ecology: A Comparison of Theories in the Biological and
            Social Sciences. American Ethnologist 4(1):1–26.
Richerson, Peter J., and Robert Boyd
    1992   Cultural Inheritance and Evolutionary Ecology. In: Evolutionary Ecology and
            Human Behavior. Eric Alden Smith and Bruce Winterhalder, eds., pp. 61–92. New
            York: Aldine.
Richerson, Peter J., Robert Boyd, and Robert L. Bettinger
    2001   Was Agriculture Impossible during the Pleistocene but Mandatory during the
            Holocene?: A Climate Change Hypothesis. American Antiquity 66(3):387–411.
Ridington, Robin
    1981   Technology, World View, and Adaptive Strategy in a Northern Hunting Society.
            Canadian Review of Sociology and Anthropology 19(4):469–481.
Rifkin, Jeremy
    1992   Beyond Beef. New York: Dutton.
Rindos, David
    1984   The Origins of Agriculture: An Evolutionary Perspective. Orlando: Academic Press.
Robarchek, Clayton A.
    1989a   Hobbesian and Rousseauan Images of Man: Autonomy and Individualism in a
            Peaceful Society. In: Societies at Peace. Signe Howell and Roy Willis, eds., pp.
            31–44. New York: Routledge.
    1989b   Primitive Warfare and the Ratomorphic Image of Mankind. American
            Anthropologist 91(4):903–920.
Robarchek, Clayton A., and Carole Robarchek
    1998   Waorani: The Contexts of Violence and War. Fort Worth, TX: Harcourt Brace.
Robbins, Paul
    2004   Political Ecology. Oxford: Blackwell.

Robbins, Wilfred William, John Peabody Harrington, and Barbara Freire-Marreco
    1916   Ethnobotany of the Tewa Indians. Bureau of American Ethnology Bulletin 55.

Roberts, Paul
    2008   The End of Food. New York: Houghton Mifflin.

Robinson, John G., and Elizabeth L. Bennett (eds.)
    2000   Hunting for Sustainability in Tropical Forests. New York: Columbia University
                Press.

Robson, John R. K., and D. E. Yen
    1976   Some Nutritional Aspects of the Philippine Tasaday Diet. Ecology of Food and
                Nutrition 5:83–89.

Roemer, John
    1982   A General Theory of Exploitation and Class. Cambridge, MA: Harvard University
                Press.
    1988   Free to Lose: An Introduction to Marxist Economic Philosophy. Cambridge, MA:
                Harvard University Press.

Roemer, John (ed.)
    1986   Analytical Marxism. Cambridge: Cambridge University Press.

Rogers, Carl
    1961   On Becoming a Person. Boston: Houghton Mifflin.

Rogers, Peter
    2008   Facing the Freshwater Crisis. Scientific American 299:46–53.

Roosevelt, A. C.
    1992   Secrets of the Forest. The Sciences 32(6):22–28.

Rose, Lisa, and Fiona Marshall
    1996   Meat Eating, Hominid Sociality, and Home Bases Revisited. Current Anthropology
                37(2):307–338.

Ruddle, Kenneth, and T. Akimichi (eds.)
    1984   Maritime Institutions in the Western Pacific. Osaka: National Museum of
                Ethnology, Seri Ethnological Studies, 17.

Ruddle, Kenneth, and Ray Chesterfield
    1977   Education for Traditional Food Procurement in the Orinoco Delta. Berkeley:
                University of California Press.

Ruddle, Kenneth, and Gongfu Zhong
    1988   Integrated Agriculture-Aquaculture in South China: The Dike-Pond System of the
                Zhujiang Delta. Cambridge: Cambridge University Press.

Rudel, Thomas
    2005   Tropical Forests: Regional Paths of Destruction and Regeneration in the Late
                Twentieth Century. New York: Columbia University Press.

Sadr, Karim
    1991   The Development of Nomadism in Ancient Northeast Africa. Philadelphia:
                University of Pennsylvania Press.

Sahlins, Marshall
    1972   Stone Age Economics. Chicago: Aldine.
    1976   Culture and Practical Reason. Chicago: University of Chicago Press.

Sahlins, Marshall, and Elman Service
  1960   Evolution and Culture. Ann Arbor: University of Michigan Press.
Saitoti, Tepilit Ole, and Carol Beckwith
  1980   Maasai. New York: Harry N. Abrams.
Saladin d'Anglure, Bernard
  1984   Inuit of Quebec. In: Handbook of North American Indians, vol. 5: Arctic.
          David Damas, ed., pp. 476–507. Washington, DC: Smithsonian Institution
          Press.
Salaman, Redcliffe
  1949   The History and Social Influence of the Potato. Cambridge: Cambridge
          University Press.
Salisbury, Richard
  1986   A Homeland for the Cree. Kingston, Ontario, Canada: McGill-Queens
          University Press.
Salzman, Philip Carl (ed.)
  1980   When Nomads Settle: Processes of Sedentarization as Adaptation and Response.
          New York: Praeger.
Sanday, Peggy R.
  1986   Divine Hunger: Cannibalism as a Cultural System. Cambridge: Cambridge
          University Press.
Sanderson, Stephen
  1999   Social Transformations: A General Theory of Historical Development. Lanham,
          MD: Rowman & Littlefield.
Sargent, Frederick, II (ed.)
  1974   Human Ecology. Amsterdam: North-Holland Publishing Company.
Sarma, Akkaraju
  1977   Approaches to Paleoecology. Dubuque, IA: Wm. C. Brown Company.
Satir, Virginia
  1983   Conjoint Family Therapy. Palo Alto: Science and Behavior Books.
Sauer, Carl
  1925   The Morphology of Landscape. University of California Publications in
          Geography 2:19–54.
  1952   Agricultural Origins and Dispersals. New York: American Geographic Society.
Schalk, Randall F.
  1981   Land Use and Organizational Complexity among Foragers in Northwestern
          North America. In: Affluent Foragers: Pacific Coasts East and West. Shuzo
          Koyama and David Hurst Thomas, eds., pp. 53–75. Osaka: Senri Ethnological
          Studies No. 9.
Schmitt, Jean-Claude
  1983[1979]   The Holy Greyhound. Cambridge: Cambridge University Press.
Schueller, Gretel H.
  2001   Eat Locally: Think Globally. Discover 22(5):70–77.
Schultz, Theodore
  1964   Transforming Traditional Agriculture. New Haven, CT: Yale University Press.

Schulz, Richard
    1976   Some Life and Death Consequences of Perceived Control. In: Cognition and Social
            Behavior. John S. Carroll and John W. Payne, eds., pp. 135–153. New York:
            Academic Press.
Schwarz, Maureen Trudelle
    1995   The Explanatory and Predictive Power of History: Coping with the "Mystery
            Illness," 1993. Ethnohistory 42(3):375–401.
    1997   Unraveling the Anchoring Cord: Navajo Relocation, 1974 to 1996. American
            Anthropologist 99(1):43–55.
Scott, James
    1976   The Moral Economy of the Peasant. New Haven, CT: Yale University Press.
    1985   Weapons of the Weak. New Haven, CT: Yale University Press.
Scudder, Thayer
    2005   The Future of Large Dams: Dealing with Social, Environmental, Institutional and
            Political Costs. London: Earthscan.
Sen, Amartya
    1984   Resources, Values and Development. Oxford: Oxford University Press.
    1999   Development as Freedom. New York: Knopf.
Serpell, James (ed.)
    1995   The Domestic Dog. Cambridge: Cambridge University Press.
Service, Elman R.
    1962   Primitive Social Organization: An Evolutionary Perspective. New York: Random
            House.
Shapiro, Roy D.
    1984   Optimization Models for Planning and Allocation: Text and Cases in
            Mathematical Programming. New York: John Wiley & Sons.
Shapiro, Warren
    1991   Claude Levi-Strauss Meets Alexander Goldenweiser: Boasian Anthropology and
            the Study of Totemism. American Anthropologist 93(3):599–610.
Sharer, Robert J., and Loa Traxler
    2005   The Ancient Maya. 6th edition. Stanford, CA: Stanford University Press.
Shepardson, Mary
    1982   The Status of Navajo Women. American Indian Quarterly 6(1–2):149–169.
Sheridan, Thomas E.
    1988   Where the Dove Calls: The Political Ecology of a Peasant Corporate Community.
            Tucson: University of Arizona Press.
Shils, Maurice, Moshe Shike, A. Catharine Ross, Benjamin Caballero, and Robert J. Cousins (eds.)
    2006   Modern Nutrition in Health and Disease. 10th edition. Philadelphia: Lippincott
            Williams & Wilkins.
Shipek, Florence
    1989   An Example of Intensive Plant Husbandry: The Kumeyaay of Southern
            California. In: Foraging and Farming: The Evolution of Plant Exploitation. D.
            R. Harris and G. C. Hillman, eds., pp. 159–170. Cambridge: Cambridge
            University Press.

Shipman, Pat

  1986   Scavenging or Hunting in Early Hominids: Theoretical Framework and Tests. American Anthropologist 88(1):27–43.

Shnirelman, Victor A.

  1994   *Cherchez le Chien*: Perspectives on the Economy of the Traditional Fishing-Oriented People of Kamchatka. In: Key Issues in Hunter-Gatherer Research. Ernest S. Burch, Jr., and Linda J. Ellanna, eds., pp. 169–188. Oxford: Berg Publishers.

Shrader-Frechette, K.

  1991   Risk and Rationality. Berkeley: University of California Press.

Silberbauer, George B.

  1972   The G/wi Bushmen. In: Hunters and Gatherers Today. M. G. Bicchieri, ed., pp. 271–326. New York: Holt, Rinehart and Winston.

Simmonds, N. W. (ed.)

  1976   Evolution of Crop Plants. London: Longmans.

Simmons, I. G.

  1969   Evidence for Vegetation Changes Associated with Mesolithic Man in Britain. In: The Domestication and Exploitation of Plants and Animals. Peter J. Ucko and G. W. Dimbleby, eds., pp. 111–119. Chicago: Aldine.

Simms, Steven R.

  1984   Aboriginal Great Basin Foraging Strategies: An Evolutionary Analysis. Ph.D. dissertation, University of Utah.

Simon, Herbert A.

  1960   The New Science of Management Decision. New York: Harper.

  1992   Wilderness as a Human Landscape. In: Wilderness Tapestry: An Eclectic Approach to Preservation, Samuel I. Zeveloff, L. Mikel Vause, and William H. McVaugh, eds., pp. 183–201. Reno: University of Nevada Press.

Simoons, Frederick J.

  1967   Eat Not This Flesh. Madison: University of Wisconsin Press.

  1979   Questions in the Sacred Cow Controversy. Current Anthropology 20(3):467–493.

Smil, Vaclav

  2000   Feeding the World. Cambridge, MA: Massachusetts Institute of Technology Press.

  2004   China's Past, China's Future: Energy, Food, Environment. New York: Routledge.

Smith, Adam

  1920[1776]   The Wealth of Nations. New York: Dutton.

Smith, Andrew B.

  1992   Origins and Spread of Pastoralism in Africa. Annual Review of Anthropology 21:125–141.

Smith, Bruce D.

  1995   Seed Plant Domestication in Eastern North America. In: Last Hunters—First Farmers: New Perspectives on the Prehistoric Transition to Agriculture. T. Douglas Price and Anne Birgitte Gebauer, eds., pp. 193–213. Santa Fe, NM: School of American Research Press.

Smith, Carol A. (ed.)

  1976   Regional Analysis. New York: Academic Press.

Smith, Eric Alden
    1983   Anthropological Applications of Optimal Foraging Theory: A Critical Review. Current Anthropology 24(5):625–651.
    1991   Inujjuamiut Foraging Strategies. Seattle: University of Washington Press.
    2000   Three Styles in the Evolutionary Analysis of Human Behavior. In: Adaptation and Human Behavior: An Anthropological Perspective. Lee Cronk, Napoleon Chagnon, and William Irons, eds., pp. 27–46. New York: Aldine.

Smith, Eric Alden, and Bruce Winterhalder
    1992   Natural Selection and Decision-Making: Some Fundamental Principles. In: Evolutionary Ecology and Human Behavior. Eric Alden Smith and Bruce Winterhalder, eds., pp. 25–60. New York: Aldine.

Smith, J. Russell
    1950   Tree Crops: A Permanent Agriculture. New York: Devin Adair.

Smith, Michael E., and T. Jeffrey Price
    1994   Aztec-Period Agricultural Terraces in Morelos, Mexico: Evidence for Household-level Agricultural Intensification. Journal of Field Archaeology 21(2):169–179.

Smith, Thomas
    1977   Nakahara: Family Farming and Population in a Japanese Village, 1717–1830. Stanford, CA: Stanford University Press.

Snyder, Gary
    1969   Earth House Hold. New York: New Directions.

Spear, Thomas, and Richard Waller (eds.)
    1993   Being Maasai: Ethnicity and Identity in East Africa. London: James Curry.

Spencer, Arthur
    1978   The Lapps. New York: Crane, Russak & Company.

Spencer, J. E.
    1966   Shifting Cultivation in Southeast Asia. Berkeley: University of California Press.

Spencer, Paul
    1988   The Maasai of Matapato: A Study of Rituals or Rebellion. Bloomington: Indiana University Press.

Speth, John D.
    2002   Were Our Ancestors Hunters or Scavengers? In: Archaeology: Original Readings in Method and Practice. Peter N. Peregrine, Carol R. Ember, and Melvin Ember, eds., pp. 151–166. Upper Saddle River, NJ: Prentice Hall.

Speth, John D., and Katherine A. Spielmann
    1983   Energy Source, Protein Metabolism, and Hunter-Gatherer Subsistence Strategies. Journal of Anthropological Archaeology 2(1):1–31.

Spielmann, Katherine A., and James F. Eder
    1994   Hunters and Farmers: Then and Now. Annual Review of Anthropology 23:303–323.

Sponsel, Leslie E.
    2001   Do Anthropologists Need Religion, and Vice Versa? Adventures and Dangers in Spiritual Ecology. In: New Directions in Anthropology and Environment. Carole Crumley, ed., pp. 177–202. Walnut Creek, CA: AltaMira Press.

Sponsel, Leslie E., Robert C. Bailey, and Thomas N. Headland

    1996a   Anthropological Perspectives on the Causes, Consequences, and Solutions of Deforestation. In: Tropical Deforestation: The Human Dimension. Leslie E. Sponsel, Thomas N. Headland, and Robert C. Bailey, eds., pp.3–52. New York: Columbia University Press.

Sponsel, Leslie E., Thomas N. Headland, and Robert C. Bailey (eds.)

    1996b   Tropical Deforestation: The Human Dimension. New York: Columbia University Press.

Spooner, Brian

    1973   The Cultural Ecology of Pastoral Nomads. In: Current Topics in Anthropology, vol. 8: Theory, Methods, and Content. Addison-Wesley Module in Anthropology No. 45. Reading, MA: Addison-Wesley.

Sproat, Gilbert M.

    1868   Scenes and Studies of Savage Life. London: Smith, Elder.

Squire, Larry R.

    1987   Memory and Brain. Oxford: Oxford University Press.

Stagner, Ross

    1989   A History of Psychological Theories. New York: Macmillan.

Stahl, Ann B.

    1984   Hominid Dietary Selection Before Fire. Current Anthropology 25(2):151–168.

Stanford, Craig B., and Henry T. Bunn (eds.)

    2001   Meat-eating and Human Evolution. Oxford: Oxford University Press.

Sternberg, Robert J.

    1985   Human Intelligence: The Model Is the Message. Science 230:1111–1118.

Steward, Julian H.

    1936   The Economic and Social Basis of Primitive Bands. In: Essays in Honor of Alfred Lewis Kroeber. Robert H. Lowie, ed., pp. 331–350. Berkeley: University of California Press.

    1938   Basin-Plateau Aboriginal Sociopolitical Groups. Bureau of American Ethnology Bulletin 120.

    1955   Theory of Culture Change. Urbana: University of Illinois Press.

Stinson, Sara

    1992   Nutritional Adaptation. Annual Review of Anthropology 21:143–170.

Stonich, Susan

    1993   I Am Destroying the Land!: The Political Ecology of Poverty and Environmental Destruction in Honduras. Boulder, CO: Westview Press.

Stonich, Susan, and Billie R. DeWalt

    1996   The Political Ecology of Deforestation in Honduras. In: Tropical Deforestation: The Human Dimension. Leslie E. Sponsel, Thomas N. Headland, and Robert C. Bailey, eds., pp.187–215. New York: Columbia University Press.

Stott, Philip, and Sian Sullivan (eds.)

    2001   Political Ecology: Science, Myth and Power. London: Edward Arnold.

Stroup, Richard, and Jane Shaw

    1992   The Free Market and the Environment. In: Rational Readings on Environmental Concerns. Jay H. Lehr, ed., pp. 267–277. New York: Van Nostrand Reinhold.

Struever, Stuart (ed.)
    1972   Prehistoric Agriculture. New York: Doubleday/American Museum of Natural
           History.

Stuart, James W.
    1978   Subsistence Ecology of the Isthmus Nahuat Indians of Southern Veracruz, Mexico.
           Ph.D. dissertation, University of California, Riverside.

Suttles, Wayne
    1987   Coast Salish Essays. Seattle: University of Washington Press.

Sutton, Mark Q.
    1984   The Productivity of *Pinus monophylla* and the Modeling of Great Basin
           Subsistence Strategies. Journal of California and Great Basin Anthropology
           6(2):240–246.
    1988   Insects as Food: Aboriginal Entomophagy in the Great Basin. Ballena Press
           Anthropological Paper No. 33.
    2000   Strategy and Tactic in the Analysis of Archaeological Hunter-Gatherer Systems.
           North American Archaeologist 21(3):217–231.

Suzuki, Akira
    1966   On the Insect-eating Habits among Wild Chimpanzees Living in the Savanna
           Woodland of Western Tanzania. Primates 7(4):481–487.

Swezey, Sean L., and Robert F. Heizer
    1977   Ritual Management of Salmonid Fish Resources in California. The Journal of
           California Anthropology 4(1):6–29.

Tanaka, Jiro
    1976   Subsistence Ecology of the Central Kalahari San. In: Kalahari Hunter-Gatherers.
           Richard B. Lee and Irven DeVore, eds., pp. 98–119. Cambridge, MA: Harvard
           University Press.

Tannenbaum, Nicola
    1984   The Misuse of Chayanov: "Chayanov's Rule" and Empiricist Bias in Anthropology.
           American Anthropologist 86(4):927–942.

Tanner, Adrian
    1979   Bringing Home Animals. New York: St. Martin's Press.

Tanner, Nancy
    1981   On Becoming Human. Cambridge: Cambridge University Press.

Tanner, Nancy, and Adrienne Zihlman
    1976   Women in Evolution, Part I: Innovation and Selection in Human Origins. Signs
           1(3, part 1):585–608.

Taylor, Michael
    2006   Rationality and the Ideology of Disconnection. New York: Cambridge University
           Press.

Taylor, Ronald L.
    1975   Butterflies in My Stomach. Santa Barbara: Woodbridge Press.

Teleki, Geza
    1973   The Omnivorous Chimpanzee. Scientific American 228:32–42.
    1974   Chimpanzee Subsistence Technology: Materials and Skills. Journal of Human
           Evolution 3:575–594.

1981   The Omnivorous Diet and Eclectic Feeding Habits of Chimpanzees in Gombe National Park, Tanzania. In: Omnivorous Primates: Gathering and Hunting in Human Evolution. Robert S. O. Harding and Geza Teleki, eds., pp. 303–343. New York: Columbia University Press.

Tennesen, Michael

2007   Black Gold of the Amazon. Discover 28(4):46–52.

Terborgh, John

1989   Where Have All the Birds Gone? Princeton, NJ: Princeton University Press.

Testart, Alain

1982   The Significance of Food Storage among Hunter-Gatherers: Residence Patterns, Population Densities, and Social Inequalities. Current Anthropology 23(5):523–537.

1988   Some Major Problems in the Social Anthropology of Hunter-Gatherers. Current Anthropology 29(1):1–31.

Thomas, David Hurst

1981   Complexity among Great Basin Shoshoneans: The World's Least Affluent Hunter-Gatherers? In: Affluent Foragers: Pacific Coasts East and West. Shuzo Koyama and David Hurst Thomas, eds., pp. 19–52. Osaka: Senri Ethnological Studies No. 9.

1983   On Steward's Models of Shoshonean Sociopolitical Organization: A Great Bias in the Basin? In: The Development of Political Organization in Native North America. Elizabeth Tooker, ed., pp. 59–68. Washington, DC: The American Ethnological Society.

1986   Contemporary Hunter-Gatherer Archaeology in America. In: American Archaeology: Past and Future. David J. Meltzer, Don D. Fowler, and Jeremy A. Sabloff, eds., pp. 237–276. Washington, DC: Smithsonian Institution Press.

Thomson, A. K., R. E. Hytten, and W. Z. Billewicz

1970   The Energy Cost of Human Lactation. British Journal of Nutrition 24:565–572.

Tiedje, Kristina, and Jeffrey G. Snodgrass

2008   Indigenous Religions and Environments: Intersections of Animism and Nature Conservation. Journal for the Study of Religion, Nature and Culture, special issue, 2(1).

Timbrook, Jan, John R. Johnson, and David D. Earle

1982   Vegetation Burning by the Chumash. Journal of California and Great Basin Anthropology 4(2):163–186.

Tindale, Norman B.

1972   The Pitjandjara. In: Hunters and Gatherers Today. M. G. Bicchieri, ed., pp. 217–268. New York: Holt, Rinehart and Winston.

Tobey, Ronald C.

1981   Saving the Prairies. Berkeley: University of California Press.

Toledo, Victor M.

1992   What is Ethnobiology? Origins, Scope and Implications of a Rising Discipline. Ethnoecológica 1(1):5–21.

Townsend, Patricia K.

2000   Environmental Anthropology: From Pigs to Policies. Prospect Heights, IL: Waveland Press.

Tsing, Anna Lowenhaupt
    2005   Friction: An Ethnography of Global Connection. Princeton, NJ: Princeton
            University Press.

Tucker, Richard P.
    2000   Insatiable Appetite: The United States and the Ecological Degradation of the
            Tropical World. Berkeley: University of California Press.

Turchin, Peter
    2003   Historical Dynamics: Why States Rise and Fall. Princeton, NJ: Princeton University
            Press.
    2006   War and Peace and War: The Life Cycles of Imperial Nations. New York: Pi Press.

Turnbull, Colin M.
    1961   The Forest People: A Study of the Pygmies of the Congo. New York: Simon and
            Schuster.
    1983   The Mbuti Pygmies: Change and Adaptation. New York: Holt, Rinehart and
            Winston.

Turner, B. L., and Peter D. Harrison
    1983   Pulltrouser Swamp: Ancient Maya Habitat, Agriculture, and Settlement in
            Northern Belize. Austin: University of Texas Press.

Turner, Christy G., II, and Jacqueline A. Turner
    1999   Man Corn: Cannibalism and Violence in the Prehistoric American Southwest. Salt
            Lake City: University of Utah Press.

Turner, Jonathan, and Alexandra Maryanski
    1979   Functionalism. Menlo Park, CA: Benjamin/Cummings.

Turner, Nancy J.
    1985   "The Importance of a Rose": Evaluating the Cultural Significance of Plants in
            Thompson and Lillooet Interior Salish. American Anthropologist 90(2):272–290.

Turner, Nancy J., and Barbara S. Efrat
    1982   Ethnobotany of the Hesquiat People of the West Coast of British Columbia.
            Victoria: British Columbia Provincial Museum, Cultural Recovery Papers 2.

Turner, Nancy J., Laurence C. Thompson, M. Terry Thompson, and Annie Z. York
    1990   Thompson Ethnobotany. Victoria, British Columbia, Canada: Royal British
            Columbia Museum.

Turner, Victor W.
    1952   The Lozi Peoples of North-Western Rhodesia. London: International African
            Institute.
    1967   The Forest of Symbols. Ithaca, NY: Cornell University Press.

Tversky, Amos, and Kahnemaqn, Daniel
    1981   The Framing of Decisions and the Psychology of Choice. Science 211:453–458.

Tyler, Stephen (ed.)
    1968   Cognitive Anthropology. New York: Holt, Rinehart and Winston.

Ucko, Peter, and George Dimbleby (eds.)
    1969   The Domestication and Exploitation of Plants and Animals. Chicago: Aldine.

Ugan, Andrew, Jason Bright, and Alan Rogers
    2003   When Is Technology Worth the Trouble? Journal of Archaeological Science 30(6).

Underhill, Anne P.
    1997   Current Issues in Chinese Neolithic Archaeology. Journal of World Prehistory
            11(2):103–160.

United States Department of Agriculture
    1963   Composition of Foods. Agriculture Handbook No. 8. Washington, DC: USDA.

Vale, Thomas R.
    1982   Plants and People: Vegetation Change in North America. Washington, DC:
            Association of American Geographers.

Vayda, Andrew, and Bradley Walters
    1999   Against Political Ecology. Human Ecology 27(1):167–179.

Vayda, Andrew P.
    1986   Holism and Individualism in Ecological Anthropology. Reviews in Anthropology
            13:295–313.
    1989   Explaining Why Marings Fought. Journal of Anthropological Research
            45(2):160–177.
    1993   Ecosystems and Human Actions. In: Humans as Components of Ecosystems. Mark J.
            McDonnell and Steward T. A. Pickett, eds., pp. 61–71. New York: Springer-Verlag.
    1995   Failures of Explanation in Darwinian Ecological Anthropology. Philosophy of the
            Social Sciences 25:219–249, 360–375.
    1996   Methods and Explanations in the Study of Human Actions and Their
            Environmental Effects. Jakarta, Indonesia: Center for International Forestry
            Research-World Wildlife Fund.

Vayda, Andrew P. (ed.)
    1969   Environment and Cultural Behavior. Garden City, NY: Doubleday.

Vayda, Andrew P., and Bonnie J. McCay
    1975   New Directions in Ecology and Ecological Anthropology. Annual Review of
            Anthropology 4:293–306.

Vayda, Andrew P., and Roy A. Rappaport
    1968   Ecology, Cultural and Noncultural. In: Introduction to Cultural Anthropology:
            Essays in the Scope and Methods of the Science of Man. James A. Clifton, ed., pp.
            477–497. Boston: Houghton Mifflin.

Vecsey, Christopher, and Robert Venables (eds.)
    1980   American Indian Environments. Syracuse, NY: Syracuse University Press.

Vietmeyer, Noel D.
    1986   Lesser-known Plants of Potential Use in Agriculture and Forestry. Science
            232:1379–1384.

Vitousek, Peter M., Harold A. Mooney, Jane Lubchenco, and Jerry M. Melillo
    1997   Human Domination of Earth's Ecosystem. Science 277:494–499.

Volhard, Ewald
    1939   Kannibalismus. Stuttgart: Strecker and Strecker Verlag.

Walens, Stanley
    1981   Feasting with Cannibals. Princeton, NJ: Princeton University Press.

Wallace, A. F. C.
    1970   Culture and Personality. New York: Random House.

Waller, Richard, and Neal W. Sobania
    1994   Pastoralism in Historical Perspective. In: African Pastoralist Systems: An
            Integrated Approach. Elliot Fratkin, Kathleen A. Galvin, and Eric Abella Roth, eds.,
            pp. 45–68. Boulder, CO: Lynne Rienner Publishers.
Wallerstein, Immanuel
    1976   The Modern World-System. New York: Academic Press.
Wardwell, Allen
    1996   Tangible Visions. New York: Monacelli Press.
Watson, Patty Jo
    1995   Explaining the Transition to Agriculture. In: Last Hunters—First Farmers: New
            Perspectives on the Prehistoric Transition to Agriculture. T. Douglas Price and
            Anne Birgitte Gebauer, eds., pp. 21–37. Santa Fe, NM: School of American
            Research Press.
Weatherford, Jack
    1988   Indian Givers: How the Indians of the Americas Transformed the World. New
            York: Crown Publishers.
    1991   Native Roots: How the Indians Enriched America. New York: Fawcett
            Columbine.
Webster, David
    2002   The Fall of the Ancient Maya. New York: Thames and Hudson.
Weins, John A.
    1976   Population Responses to Patchy Environments. Annual Review of Ecology and
            Systematics 7:81–120.
Weiss, Mark L., and Alan E. Mann
    1990   Human Biology and Behavior. Glenview, IL: Scott, Foresman/Little Brown.
Wen Duzhong, and David Piementel
    1986a   Seventeenth Century Organic Agriculture in China, Part I: Cropping Systems in
            Jiaxing Region. Human Ecology 14(1):1–14.
    1986b   Seventeenth Century Organic Agriculture in China, Part II: Energy Flows Through
            an Agrosystem in Jiaxing Region. Human Ecology 14(1):15–28.
Werner, Emmy, and Ruth Smith
    1982   Vulnerable but Invincible: A Longitudinal Study of Resilient Children and Youth.
            New York: McGraw-Hill.
Werner, Louis
    1992   Cultivating the Secrets of Aztec Gardens. Americas 44(6):6–15.
West, Paige
    2006   Conservation Is Our Government Now: The Politics of Ecology in Papua New
            Guinea. Durham, NC: Duke University Press.
West, Paige, James Igoe, and Dan Brockington
    2006   Parks and Peoples: The Social Impact of Protected Areas. Annual Review of
            Anthropology 35:251–277.
Western David, and R. Michael Wright (eds.)
    1994   Natural Connections: Perspectives in Community-Based Conservation.
            Washington D.C.: Island Press.

White, Benjamin
 1983 "Agricultural Involution" and Its Critics: Twenty Years After. Bulletin of Concerned Asian Scholars 15(3):18–31.
White, Leslie
 1949 The Science of Culture. New York: Grove Press.
White, Lynn, Jr.
 1967 The Historical Roots of Our Ecologic Crisis. Science 155:1203–1207.
White, Richard
 1997 Indian People and the Natural World: Asking the Right Questions. In: Rethinking American Indian History. Donald L. Fixico, ed., pp. 87–100. Albuquerque: University of New Mexico Press.
White, Tim D.
 1992 Prehistoric Cannibalism at Mancos 5MTUMR-2346. Princeton, NJ: Princeton University Press.
Whiteford, Linda M., and Robert T. Trotter II
 2008 Ethics for Anthropological Research and Practice. Long Grove, IL: Waveland Press.
Whitmore, Thomas, and B. L. Turner
 2001 Cultivated Landscapes of Middle America on the Eve of Conquest. New York: Oxford University Press.
Whitney, Eleanor Noss, and Sharon Rady Rolfes
 1996 Understanding Nutrition. 7th edition. Minneapolis/St. Paul: West Publishing.
Whittle, Alasdair
 1996 Europe in the Neolithic: The Creation of New Worlds. Cambridge: Cambridge University Press. 2nd ed.
Wilk, Richard R.
 1991 Household Ecology: Economic Change and Domestic Life among the Kekchi Maya of Belize. Tucson: University of Arizona Press.
Wilke, Philip J.
 1988 Bow Staves Harvested from Juniper Trees by Indians of Nevada. Journal of California and Great Basin Anthropology 10(1):3–31.
Wilke, Philip J., Robert L. Bettinger, Thomas F. King, and James F. O'Connell
 1972 Harvest Selection and Domestication in Seed Plants. Antiquity 46(183):203–208.
Wilken, Gene
 1987 Good Farmers. Berkeley: University of California Press.
Will, Pierre-Etienne
 1990 Bureaucracy and Famine in Eighteenth-Century China. Stanford, CA: Stanford University Press.
Will, Pierre-Etienne, and Bin Wong
 1991 Nourish the People: The State Civilian Granary System in China, 1650–1850. Ann Arbor: University of Michigan Press.
Williams, Dee Mack
 1996 Grassland Enclosures: Catalyst of Land Degradation in Inner Mongolia. Human Organization 55(3):307–313.

Williams, Michael
　　2003　　Deforesting the Earth: From Prehistory to Global Crisis. Chicago: University of
　　　　　　Chicago Press.
Winkelman, Michael
　　1998　　Aztec Human Sacrifice: Cross-Cultural Assessments of the Ecological Hypothesis.
　　　　　　Ethnology 37(3):285–298.
Winterhalder, Bruce
　　1981　　Optimal Foraging Strategies and Hunter-Gatherer Research in Anthropology:
　　　　　　Theory and Models. In: Hunter-Gatherer Foraging Strategies: Ethnographic and
　　　　　　Archaeological Analyses. Bruce Winterhalder and Eric Alden Smith, eds., pp.
　　　　　　13–35. Chicago: University of Chicago Press.
　　1986　　Optimal Foraging: Simulation Studies of Diet Choice in a Stochastic
　　　　　　Environment. Journal of Ethnobiology 6(1):205–223.
　　2001　　The Behavioural Ecology of Hunter-Gatherers. In: Hunter-Gatherers: An
　　　　　　Interdisciplinary Perspective. Catherine Panter-Brick, Robert H. Layton, and Peter
　　　　　　Rowley-Conwy, eds., pp. 12–38. Cambridge: Cambridge University Press.
Winterhalder, Bruce, and Carol Goland
　　1997　　An Evolutionary Ecology Perspective on Diet Choice, Risk, and Plant
　　　　　　Domestication. In: People, Plants, and Landscapes: Studies in Paleoethnobotany.
　　　　　　Kristen J. Gremillion, ed., pp. 123–160. Tuscaloosa: University of Alabama Press.
Winterhalder, Bruce, Flora Lu, and Bram Tucker
　　1999　　Risk-Sensitive Adaptive Tactics: Models and Evidence from Subsistence Studies in
　　　　　　Biology and Anthropology. Journal of Archaeological Research 7(4):301–348.
Winterhalder, Bruce, and Eric Alden Smith
　　1992　　Evolutionary Ecology and the Social Sciences. In: Evolutionary Ecology and
　　　　　　Human Behavior. Eric Alden Smith and Bruce Winterhalder, eds., pp. 3–23. New
　　　　　　York: Aldine.
Winterhalder, Bruce, and Eric Alden Smith (eds.)
　　1981　　Hunter-Gatherer Foraging Strategies: Ethnographic and Archeological Analyses.
　　　　　　Chicago: University of Chicago Press.
Winthrop, Kathryn
　　2001　　Historical Ecology: Landscapes of Change in the Pacific Northwest. In: New
　　　　　　Directions in Anthropology and Environment. Carole Crumley, ed., pp. 203–222.
　　　　　　Walnut Creek, CA: AltaMira Press.
Wishart, David J.
　　1979　　The Dispossession of the Pawnee. Annals of the Association of American
　　　　　　Geographers 69(3):382–401.
Wissler, Clark
　　1926　　The Relation of Nature to Man in Aboriginal America. Oxford: Oxford University
　　　　　　Press.
Witherspoon, Gary
　　1983　　Navajo Social Organization. In: Handbook of North American Indians, vol. 10:
　　　　　　Southwest. Alfonso Ortiz, ed., pp. 524–535. Washington: Smithsonian Institution
　　　　　　Press.

Wittfogel, Karl
    1957   Oriental Despotism. New Haven, CT: Yale University Press.

Wittwer, Sylvan, Yu Youtai, Sun Han, and Wang Lianzheng
    1987   Feeding a Billion: Frontiers of Chinese Agriculture. East Lansing: Michigan State University Press.

Wolf, Eric
    1972   Ownership and Political Ecology. Anthropological Quarterly 45(3):201–205.
    1982   Europe and the People without History. Berkeley: University of California Press.

Wolpoff, Milford H.
    1999   Paleoanthropology. 2nd edition. Boston: McGraw-Hill.

Wood, John J.
    1985   Navajo Livestock Reduction. Nomadic Peoples 9:21-31.

Wyman, Leland C., and Flora L. Bailey
    1964   Navaho Indian Ethnoentomology. University of New Mexico Publications in Anthropology No. 12.

Yamamoto, Norio
    1985   The Ecological Complementarity of Agro-Pastoralism: Some Comments. In: Andean Ecology and Civilization: An Interdisciplinary Perspective on Andean Ecological Complementarity. Shozo Masuda, Izumi Shimada, and Craig Morris, eds., pp. 85–99. Tokyo: University of Tokyo Press.

Young, James Clay, and Linda Garro
    1994   Medical Choice in a Mexican Village. Boulder, CO: Westview Press.

Zigas, Vincent
    1990   Laughing Death: The Untold Story of Kuru. Clifton, NJ: Humana Press.

Zihlman, Adrienne L.
    1981   Women as Shapers of the Human Adaptation. In: Woman the Gatherer. Francis Dahlberg, ed., pp. 75–120. New Haven, CT: Yale University Press.

Zohary, Daniel
    1982   Plants of the Bible. Cambridge: Cambridge University Press.

Zohary, Daniel, and Maria Hopf
    1988   Domestication of Plants in the Old World. Oxford: Oxford University Press.

Index

abiotic (component of the environment), 35, 36, 40, 97, 99, 109–111, 120, 153, 164, 207, 223, 277
abortion, 65, 66, 143
Aché of Paraguay, 87, 127, 135, 139
adaptation, 12
affluent society, original, 142
Afghanistan, drug production in, 109
African Americans, as victims of toxic waste, 27
agricultural involution, 308–309; in Indonesia, 308–309; in Mexico, 309
agriculture, 180; among the ancient Maya, 295–297; among the Bila, 173; among the Chinese, 278–294; among the Grand Valley Dani, 211–213; impact of, 189–193, 190 table 6.3; among the Lozi, 219–223; among the Maasai, 246; among the Navajo, 252; origins of, 183–188, 184 table 6.1; types of, 188–189, 188 table 6.2; among the Yucatec Maya, 299–303
agroforestry, 296
Agta of the Philippines, 139
alcohol, 62, 64
Alive (film), 80
Allen's Rule, 63
Anasazi (or Ancestral Puebloans), 80

anatomical adaptations, 61 table 3.1, 62–63; to altitude, 62; to cold, 62–63; to heat, 62
Ancestral Puebloans (or Anasazi), 80
animal husbandry. *See* pastoralism
anthropogenic, 117
anthropological linguistics, 7
anthropology, 5
Apache of the American Southwest, 21, 154
Arcadian tradition in human ecology, 13
archaeoastronomy, 111
archaeology, 7, 7–8, 31, 73, 75, 87, 98, 100, 105, 107, 152, 179, 207, 295
Ariaal of northern Kenya, 248
Aswan Dam (Egypt), 121, 192, 273
Ayers Rock (Uluru) in Australia, 110, 120
Aztec. *See* Mexica

Bali, traditional water management in, 276
band, 20, 138, 139, 140, 168, 250, 314
Bantu (in Africa), 139, 165, 166, 167, 175, 286
Basque of France and Spain, 227, 228
Bergmann's Rule, 62

About the Authors

Mark Q. Sutton began his career in anthropology in 1968, doing archaeology with the local community college while still in high school. He went on to earn a BA (1972), an MA (1977), and a PhD (1987) in anthropology. He has worked as an archaeologist for the U.S. Air Force, the U.S. Bureau of Land Management, and various private consulting firms, and taught at a number of community colleges and universities. He taught at California State University, Bakersfield from 1987 to 2007, where he retired as emeritus professor of anthropology. He now works for Statistical Research, Inc., in San Diego. Dr. Sutton works on understanding hunter-gatherer adaptations to arid environments but has also investigated entomophagy, prehistoric diet and technology, and optimal foraging theory. Dr. Sutton has published more than 150 books, monographs, and papers on archaeology and anthropology, including textbooks in archaeology, Native American studies, paleonutrition, and cultural ecology.

E. N. Anderson is professor of anthropology emeritus at the University of California, Riverside. He has done field work in Hong Kong, Malaysia, south Mexico, and elsewhere, and is the author of several books, including *The Food of China* (1988), *Ecologies of the Heart* (1996), *Everyone Eats* (2005), and *Political Ecology of a Yucatec Maya Community* (2005).